Learning and Talent Development

Jim Stewart and Clare Rigg

Jim Stewart is Running Stream Professor of HRD at Leeds Business School.

Clare Rigg lectures at the Institute of Technology, Tralee, Ireland.

The Chartered Institute of Personnel and Development is the leading
publisher of books and reports for personnel and training professionals,
students, and all those concerned with the effective management and
development of people at work. For details of all our titles, please contact
the publishing department:
tel: 020 8612 6204
email: publish@cipd.co.uk
The catalogue of all CIPD titles can be viewed on the CIPD website:
www.cipd.co.uk/bookstore

Learning and Talent Development

Jim Stewart and Clare Rigg

Chartered Institute of Personnel and Development

Published by the Chartered Institute of Personnel and Development,
151, The Broadway, London, SW19 1JQ

This edition first published 2011

Typeset by Fakenham Photosetting Ltd, Norfolk

Printed in Malta by Gutenberg Press Ltd

British Library Cataloguing in Publication Data
A catalogue of this publication is available from the British Library

ISBN 978 1 84398 250 0

Chartered Institute of Personnel and Development, CIPD House,
151 The Broadway, London, SW19 1JQ

Tel: 020 8612 6200
Email: cipd@cipd.co.uk
Website: www.cipd.co.uk
Incorporated by Royal Charter
Registered Charity No. 1079797

Contents

List of Figures

List of Tables

Learning and Talent Development

The content of this CIPD module is covered as follows:

Learning and Talent Development learning outcomes	Learning and Talent Development chapters
1. Critically analyse and evaluate the formulation and implementation of processes of learning and talent development strategies for defining and achieving current and future effectiveness at national, organisational, group and individual levels.	4, 6
2. Critically evaluate the potential and appropriateness of a range of learning and talent development strategies, policies and methods with reference to relevant contextual factors.	2, 3, 4
3. Lead the initiation, development and implementation of learning and talent development strategies, interventions and activities.	8, 9
4. Work effectively and collaboratively with key internal and external partners and stakeholders to diagnose and manage learning and talent development response to problems and issues and ensure clarity of role and contribution to agreed responses.	7, 10
5. Critically assess the role and influence and the politics of learning and talent development policy and practice in a range of contexts.	3, 4, 5
6. Act ethically and professionally with a demonstrated commitment to equality of opportunity and diversity in learning and talent development and to continuous personal and professional development.	1, 11, 12

Part 1

CHAPTER 1

Introduction

OVERVIEW

Learning and talent development is the name of one of the modules in the new CIPD advanced-level qualifications. The new qualifications are one element in a revised approach to professional membership of the CIPD. The new learning and talent development module provides one reason for writing this book. Thus this book is intended to support those studying the subject and that module. A second reason is that both authors have been researching and writing on the topic of human resource development (HRD) for many years, both separately and together. The book provides an opportunity to share and disseminate our joint thinking and our current and shared view of the subject based on that research. It is fair to say that the content of the book is the result of our thinking as much as it is of empirical research, although the latter clearly informs the former. An additional reason for the book is that both authors share a commitment to influencing and, as far as we can, shaping professional practice. We hold a common commitment to promoting a more critical approach to that practice and a shared belief that education is a significant and effective means of developing critical practice. Hence, within the confines of 'textbook', we seek to show the nature and benefits of a critical understanding of and approach to the professional practice of learning and talent development.

We should perhaps say a brief word at this point about the terms 'learning and talent development' and 'HRD'. Most of our previous joint and separate writing has been within the framework of HRD rather than learning and talent development. Later chapters will examine the meaning of each in more detail. For now we will say that 'HRD' is a term more commonly used by academics than by practitioners, while 'learning and talent development' is a term associated with the recent rise in interest in the notion of talent and so may suggest a specific focus for HRD. As a general rule of thumb the terms can be seen as synonymous, but there can be significant nuances of meaning attached to each that make a case for having both to represent different concepts. We do, though, use them interchangeably in this first chapter.

FOLLOW UP

See Chapter 2 for an initial discussion of key terms.

PURPOSE, AIMS AND OBJECTIVES

We have opened the book by declaring our reasons for writing it. These give some indication of the purpose of the book. However, it is useful to devote particular and direct attention to aims and objectives. Doing so reflects what is considered good practice in learning and development and, therefore, declaring a purpose in specific detail will illustrate that practice. In addition, it will provide some means for readers to judge both the relevance and success of the book. The overall aims of the book are as follows:

- to introduce and explore concepts associated with and relevant to the syllabus of the CIPD Learning and Talent Development module
- to provide a practical and accessible exposition of key theories informing the professional practice of HRD/learning and talent development
- to provide a useful and useable resource to support the teaching and learning of HRD/learning and talent development as an academic subject
- to facilitate and support a critically informed examination of the theory and practice of HRD/learning and talent development.

It will be worth expanding on these aims. They suggest a clear connection with the CIPD syllabus, and this is deliberate. The book is intended to cover the ground indicated in the CIPD learning and talent development module descriptor. However, this does not mean that the syllabus has determined the content or that we have provided either *all* the information or *only* information relevant to that syllabus. The book has an openly declared purpose of preparing students for assessment against the CIPD syllabus. This purpose is achieved, however, by our interpretation of the syllabus in terms of which are the *key* or *critical* concepts, and in terms of the understanding required to utilise and apply those concepts in professional practice.

This raises a second important point about the aims of the book. While the final aim explicitly assumes a separation between theory and practice, we do not believe such a separation is either valid or useful. We share the CIPD philosophy that professional certification must mean the ability to practise in the profession. Therefore a key purpose of the book is to help equip individuals to meet the expectations placed upon those performing specialist roles in developing others. This 'practice' orientation and purpose is reflected in the title of the book.

A final point on the CIPD connection is to recognise that the book is intended to have relevance to and application in the study of HRD as a subject. This means that its content is not restricted to the CIPD module but is intended to have value in the full range of learning and development-related modules in the CIPD advanced qualifications. Particular chapters will, of course, have greater or lesser relevance to particular modules. However, as indicated above, the book is intended to support the teaching and learning of learning and talent development as a subject rather than being restricted to one specific syllabus.

Two more points are worth articulating. First, we have attempted to create a resource which will be valuable both to those teaching and to those learning HRD. Although the book is written primarily for those learning to practise learning and talent development, we believe and hope that the content will include some insights and perspectives which will give pause for thought on the part of experienced teachers of the subject. We will not achieve our grand purpose of influencing development of the subject unless this is the case. So our intention is that the book will provide a resource of interest and value to both teachers and learners in their joint examination and exploration of the subject.

The final point to make about the aims of the book is that we wish to encourage alternative paradigms and perspectives to be applied to support critical thinking about the subject. We have sought to achieve a similar aim in previous joint work but do not believe we can go further in a book with an overt aim of supporting entry to professional practice through meeting the syllabus and requirements of a professional body. However, we have deliberately introduced concepts and theories from outside mainstream treatments of learning and talent development, and equally deliberately encourage their use in evaluating the validity and utility of mainstream treatments.

This statement and discussion of the aims of the book allows us to articulate some clear objectives. Again reflecting what is considered good practice in HRD and indeed in teaching and learning practices in higher education, these are expressed in terms of what readers can expect to have achieved through using the book:

- to explain and analyse the national and organisational context of learning and talent development
- to describe, compare and critically evaluate a range of theories and concepts related to individual and organisational learning
- to describe, compare and critically evaluate a range of approaches to and methods of applying learning and talent development in practice
- to identify, explain and critically evaluate the assumed functions and activities associated with managing learning and talent development in the context of professional practice.

READERSHIP

It will be clear by now that a primary readership for the book will be anyone studying HRD/learning and talent development as part of their CIPD qualification programme. This will include those studying in universities that provide their own postgraduate diploma or Masters degree courses accredited by the CIPD, as well as those studying for CIPD qualifications in approved centres. However, the book has not been written exclusively for this audience and other readers are envisaged and expected. In fact, all those who 'study' HRD, including academics, constitute the intended readership. It is, however, possible to identify some specific audiences.

It seems to be an increasing trend to include HRD in undergraduate studies. We have in mind potential readers at undergraduate level, although we have assumed they will be final-year students who have either recent or current exposure to and experience of employment and/or management practices in work organisations. As already stated, the book is concerned with application. Therefore its value to undergraduate studies will be limited to the extent that students can relate personal experience of work organisations to the content. This experience does not have to be in practitioner roles. However, the book has not been written to consider the subject at a purely or exclusively conceptual level, and achievement of its aims and objectives assumes and requires regular interaction between reader and text based on personal experience. The book is relevant then only to the extent that such interaction can be achieved.

There are a number of other postgraduate programmes where the book will be relevant. Perhaps the most obvious of these will be Diploma in Management Studies and MBA programmes which include human resource and/or learning and talent development content, either as mandatory or elective modules. The book assumes no prior specialist knowledge or experience and therefore will be appropriate for and relevant to non-specialist readers. In addition, many universities offer well-established Masters degrees in the professional areas of human resource management and human resource development. Some of these specialist programmes may require CIPD membership at the point of entry, and the book is aimed primarily at those studying for such membership. However, the book will be valuable for specialist and post-CIPD Masters programmes, for two reasons. First, some students on such programmes will not be specialist development practitioners and may not have studied the subject at CIPD level. Second, even those who are specialists are likely to have been exposed to traditional or mainstream treatments. The inclusion of alternative perspectives and encouragement of critical evaluation will provide a fresh look at the subject, and one which may lead to a questioning of established beliefs and practices. Therefore, the book will have value in advanced studies of the subject.

A final group of intended and expected readers is that of professional practitioners not involved in a course of formal study. The points made in the previous paragraph on a fresh look at the subject, and the practice orientation of the book already emphasised, provide sound reasons for the book's relevance to practitioners. It is not assumed that all readers will be students, and the content and design of the book does not require that to be the case. It can be read and used by practitioners who are not also, formally at least, students, and we hope the book reaches such a readership.

STRUCTURE AND CONTENT

There are two levels of structure to be aware of: the overall organisation of the content and the common structure of each of the substantive chapters. Each will be dealt with in turn.

The book is organised into three parts. This reflects our personal view of how the subject can be usefully categorised. The categorisation also reflects a personal view on how the various elements of the CIPD syllabus relate to each other. The categorisation is purely arbitrary and other possibilities are recognised and acknowledged. However, the categorisation does have a logic which, from experience, seems to work. The three parts to the book are as follows:

- Part One – The nature, purpose and context of learning and talent development
- Part Two – The process of learning and talent development
- Part Three – The management of learning and talent development.

Part One is concerned with factors, issues, concepts and theories which *affect* the professional practice of learning and talent development. The book is premised on a view that learning and talent development is subject to many influences and is always contextual and contextualised, whether it is viewed as an academic subject or as an area of professional practice.

Chapter 2 sets the subject in the context of organising and managing, and provides some working definitions. Governments have policies related to vocational education and training (VET) which can and do influence professional practice. Similarly, while organisations provide unique contexts, there are common factors associated with processes of organising and managing which create potentials and limit the possibilities of and for learning and talent development. Each of these contexts – the nature of organising and managing, government policies and initiatives, and varying and various organisational conditions – has an impact upon and influences the roles adopted by professional practitioners. A chapter is devoted to each of these influencing factors, and Part One closes with a chapter examining the critically important factor of the politics of learning and talent development. We use the word 'critically' here in all potential meanings.

Part Two is concerned with the 'what' and 'how' of learning and talent development. It is therefore concerned with the *processes* of professional practice. A sound understanding of learning lies at the heart of professional practice, and so Part Two begins with an examination of learning theories in Chapter 6. Chapters 7 and 8 form the rest of Part Two. Chapter 7 is concerned with establishing needs and solutions for talent development, while Chapter 8 examines some commonly used development strategies.

Part Three focuses on those activities that can be associated with managing employee development. Thus, design and evaluation of development strategies are explored in Chapter 9. The two critical activities of formulating policy and resourcing the function form the subjects of Chapter 10. Chapter 11 includes an examination of 'ethics' and how that concept relates to the notion of professionalism. The final substantive chapter is Chapter 12, which provides advice and guidance on conducting research projects. Informed practice requires the ability to access, generate and evaluate 'evidence' and to critically assess claims to truth. So we are grateful to our colleague Victoria Harte for agreeing to draw on her experience as a full-time researcher and teacher of research methods to write this chapter. The book's concluding chapter, as well as attempting to draw together some threads, speculates about future directions for the subject and the profession.

Each substantive chapter (that is, all except this one and the conclusion) follows a common structure. This includes the following features:

- Overview
- Intended learning outcomes
- Main content
- In-text activities
- Case histories and illustrations
- Summary
- Application activities
- Discussion questions
- Extended case study
- Suggested reading.

The introduction sets the scene for the chapter and outlines its main purpose. This is then translated into a set of specific learning outcomes. Readers are encouraged to check and assess whether these are achieved as they work through the chapters. The main content of each chapter is interspersed with 'activities'. These are designed and intended to encourage exploration and application of the concepts discussed in the main content. They are also, in some cases, sequential and cumulative; that is, in any given chapter, the third activity, for example, will assume that the first and/or second activities have been completed. However, they are not sequential and cumulative in terms of the book, although the main content is intended to have that feature.

Completing the activities within each chapter is essential if the chapter outcomes are to be achieved. It is possible to read the main content and ignore the activities. However, this will not serve or help to meet any of the purposes of the book. Many activities refer to 'your organisation'. This can be taken to mean any organisation with which you are familiar. Most also refer to 'a colleague', sometimes with an instruction that this means a work colleague. In the absence of this instruction, 'a colleague' is meant to indicate someone with whom you are studying and who also carries out the activity. If either of these presents a problem (that is, you are not a student and/or you do not have work colleagues) then any other person can and will serve a valuable purpose. The important and critical requirement is that you *discuss* your responses to activities with some other person who will have views on the topic.

Each chapter closes with a summary of the main arguments, a range of application activities, some discussion questions and an applied case study. All case studies are based on recent or current research and therefore present actual scenarios experienced by professional practitioners. The intention is to encourage identification with the problems and issues encountered in professional practice. The purpose of the case studies is to facilitate discussion at least of applying the concepts examined in the chapter. They also serve the purpose of illustrating the practical implications of theoretical concepts.

Given the points made about activities and case studies, it will be clear that they are an essential and integral component of the book. They are certainly important in achieving the objectives of the book and those of individual chapters. The book as a whole has a logical structure and sequence. Our expectation and advice, therefore, is that the book should be read and worked through from start to finish. However, it is recognised that alternative categorisations are possible and so a different order might be chosen. In addition, particular parts and/or combinations of chapters may have specific relevance for particular modules or courses of study or issues being faced in practice.

This book is concerned with the professional practice of HRD/learning and talent development and definitions are addressed in Chapter 2. It addresses a wide and eclectic conceptualisation of HRD/learning and talent development.

As part of this eclecticism, Chapter 2 examines potential and possible meanings of the concepts of *organising* and *managing*, as well as of terms associated with learning and talent development. In doing so, it introduces a variety of paradigms which lead to differing perspectives on the meaning of the concepts and therefore plays an important role in setting the scene for the rest of the book.

Organising and Managing Learning and Talent Development

OVERVIEW

The purpose of learning and talent development in work organisations is always related to achieving some combination of individual and organisational desired results. However, these often vary enormously depending on the organisation's setting. Whilst some features of learning and talent development might be shared in common, the specific context of an organisation, particularly its size, ownership, core activity, technology and sector, has a number of key implications for how learning and talent development are used and organised. The aim of this chapter is to illustrate these varying organisation contexts and, through these examples, to define and critically examine basic terms such as 'HRD', strategic HRD', 'critical HRD', 'learning', 'talent' and 'talent management'.

LEARNING OUTCOMES

After reading this chapter and completing the activities, the intention is that you will be able to:

- demonstrate understanding of how learning and talent development is employed in diverse organisation contexts

- differentiate between different ways of organising and managing learning and talent development

- identify options for organising and managing learning and talent development

- critically appraise the meanings attached to key terms in the field of learning and talent management, in particular the notions of HRD, strategic HRD and critical HRD and their connections with learning and talent development

- evaluate the multiple purposes of learning and talent development for different stakeholders and identify potential tensions and contradictions.

The chapter begins with a series of case studies to establish the way choices and arrangements for learning and talent development can vary across large companies and small enterprises in the private sector; in public sector bodies such as local authorities, health, police and fire services; and in voluntary and community organisations of the not-for-profit or third sector.

The following points should become clear through these case studies:

- diverse contexts
- options for who leads, organises and provides learning and talent development
- diversity of intended outcomes
- variety of method
- the significance of language used to describe the array of activity we call learning and talent development.

The chapter goes on to discuss each of these in more depth after the case studies.

CASE STUDIES

1. PUBLIC SECTOR – LOCAL GOVERNMENT

 UNLOCKING INTERNAL LEADERSHIP POTENTIAL – SOUTH TYNESIDE COUNCIL

CASE STUDY

Faced with problems of low staff morale, a need to provide clearer leadership direction, and a difficulty in recruiting external top-calibre staff, South Tyneside Council sought to grow their internal leadership and management skills by establishing its own leadership academy, to develop leadership skills at senior managerial levels, but also among the politicians – the locally elected councillors.

Launched in October 2006, led by an assistant chief executive working closely with the council's organisational development team, the leadership academy is being run jointly between the local authority and Sunderland University. The aim is to help develop the 'leaders of the future'. The focus has been on improving management and leadership skills, not just for middle and senior managers, but also among those who are not in management positions, the hidden talent, who 'may be doing amazing things outside work, but because they are not properly engaged at work their potential is not realised' (Keith Harcus, Assistant Chief Executive).

Source: www.idea.gov.uk/idk/core/page. do?pageId=7117372, accessed 29 September 2009.

South Tyneside Council Leadership Academy illustrates an approach to talent development within the public sector that is wide in scope, encompassing both existing managers and councillors, as well as others described as 'hidden talent' in the workforce. Internally driven and organised with a clear strategic purpose of raising organisation performance, the development is provided in partnership with an external provider, the local university. As a public sector organisation the purpose of developing employees is ultimately to benefit the citizen or service user, through better or more efficiently provided services such as housing, adult social services, children and young people's referral services, waste collection, local libraries and arts and leisure facilities.

2. VOLUNTARY AND COMMUNITY SECTOR

CASE STUDY

SEWA, INDIA'S SELF-EMPLOYED WOMEN'S ASSOCIATION

SEWA is an organisation of thousands of poor, self-employed women workers across most states of India. These are women who earn a living through their own labour or small businesses, for example, street trading, domestic work, agriculture. Constituting 94 per cent of India's labour force, these are unprotected workers of the unorganised sector who do not obtain regular salaried employment with welfare benefits like workers in the organised sectors. SEWA puts emphasis on promoting individual and district economic sustainability. Core to achieving this is a Managers' School begun in 2005 with the twin goals of facilitating economic self-sustainability through developing the capacity of members as grassroots managers. Management capacity-building addresses the needs of team leaders and coordinators, who in turn use the acquired knowledge to more effectively manage member-run organisations like district associations.

Training conducted by the Managers' School falls under the following categories:

1 General capacity building: primarily with introductory training for new members to SEWA, empowerment training and leadership skill development

2 Management capacity building: financial and management-related training topics to build the organisational capacity of member-run institutions

3 Technical training: skill training in technical areas with the goal of developing new member livelihood activities and improving efficiency and effectiveness of already existing activities.

The Managers' School is developing a mini-MBA project in collaboration with India's Infrastructure Leasing and Financial Services Ltd (IL&FS). This project will train and equip rural SEWA members with the skills they need to successfully develop small businesses.

Source: www.SEWA.org, accessed 13 October 2009.

SEWA is an example of learning and talent development organised in the voluntary/community or third sector through a network. Neither public sector nor a commercial company, this non-state organisation focuses capacity development on a specific, very large group. Investment in individual development is designed to achieve wider family, as well as regional, economic and social benefits. In Britain, employing around half a million staff, with at least a further 7 million volunteers, the third sector includes substantial employers, encompassing voluntary organisations of all kinds, from large national bodies such as the Royal National Institute of Blind People, Scope or Royal National Lifeboat Institution, to community groups working at a local level.

3. GRADUATE PROGRAMME IN INTERNATIONAL CORPORATION

Kerry Group, the international food ingredients company, has a long-established graduate programme that provides an example from the private sector of a focus on high-flyers, who could, given the company's size and scope, conceivably develop their entire career within the company, as in fact has the current CEO, who joined the graduate recruitment programme in 1976 (www.kerrygroup. com/page.asp?pid=257). With headquarters in County Kerry, Ireland, the Group employs over 20,000 people across Europe, North and South America, Australia, New Zealand and Asia, with manufacturing facilities in 23 different countries and international sales offices in 20 other countries. The Group is a world leader in food ingredients and flavours, serving the food and beverage industry, supplying over 15,000 foods, food ingredients and flavour products to customers in more than 140 countries worldwide.

 KERRY GROUP GRADUATE PROGRAMME

CASE STUDY

Kerry Group offers two distinct types of graduate programme that recruit in Ireland, the UK, Asia Pacific and other regions, including the USA and Canada, Europe more widely and Asia:

1 geared towards undergraduates and taught Masters students across the disciplines of finance, operations, production, engineering, new product development, sales, quality assurance and information technology

2 a PhD programme, aimed at people possessing a PhD or Research Masters in Food Science or in other science-related disciplines, who want to demonstrate commercial ability in an international business environment.

Source: www.kerrygroup.com/page.asp?pid=191, accessed 22 October 2009.

Ireland's graduate programme

The Ireland Kerry Group, throughout the 2000s, has run a graduate management development programme in partnership with the Irish Management Institute (IMI), with the aim of assisting the transition from college to building solid foundations for a long-term career in the company. Graduates join a well-structured training and development programme, embracing both offsite and onsite training, designed by management teams through discussion with each graduate. Participants receive assistance and support in fulfilling their individual training requirements, and the Group also actively encourages the attainment of further relevant professional qualifications. The graduate programme consists of a Transition to Work programme and a Management Development programme, run and accredited by the IMI and aimed at complementing the on-the-job development, accelerating graduates' overall development and progression within the Group.

Source: www.kerrygroup.com/page.asp?pid=192, accessed 22 October 2009

Transition to Work programme The 9-month-long Transition to Work programme involves graduates learning technical skills and developing management competency through practical experience. Core elements include time management, self management, presentation skills, communications and team building. This programme helps graduates to enhance and strengthen their own personal skills and build strong relationships across the organisation.

Management Development programme

The Management Development programme leads to a Diploma in Management Practice accredited by the IMI, and involves the application of skills and responsibilities relevant to the respective management or technical discipline. It runs over 12 months and heightens graduates' exposure to the different aspects of the business. Core elements include people management, negotiation skills, strategy, project management, presentation skills, marketing and independent one-on-one personal and career coaching, in addition to exposure to various Kerry leaders.

After the Graduate Programme

Ongoing development of employees is offered through a number of leadership development initiatives, educational assistance, functional and technical courses and online training. In addition, Kerry has an excellent global online learning management system which offers employees the flexibility to learn at a time and location that suits them.

Source: www.kerrygroup.com/page.asp?pid=194, accessed 22 October 2009.

4. SMALL BUSINESSES — COMBINING FORMAL AND INFORMAL LEARNING

 METAL TUBES

CASE STUDY

Metal Tubes is a small company of 10, founded in the early 1990s by two directors, friends who used to work together for a large company before setting up on their own. Their business project manages the design and installation of air-conditioning systems across Britain. Company members' engagement in formal HRD consists of:

- Fifty per cent of staff have engineering degrees.

- Both directors have a postgraduate Diploma in Management Studies (DMS) and MSc undertaken as they were starting the business.

- One has begun a Doctorate in Business Administration.

- Two project staff have DMS.

- One trainee is sponsored on a part-time degree.

- Two modern apprentices are employed and sponsored in training.

In Metal Tubes there is a strong ethos that improvement comes from learning, whether that be formal courses or from reviewing everyday events. Much of this is done collectively among the staff, socially interacting through reviews that enable reflection and questioning of experience. Mistakes are used as a parable for learning, and successes are also systematically reviewed. Individuals use external expertise (books, journals, courses) as a source of ideas (eg quality management, risk management and project management) and prepare presentations to share with all staff. Formal, course-based learning is not seen just to benefit an individual's knowledge and qualification. Rather any individual who attends a course is encouraged to share their learning with other organisation members.

As a project management company, a project review stage is built into the project management steps applied to every piece of work. A monthly meeting, termed the 'communication forum', is attended by all staff, except the apprentices. At this each project manager reviews their progress, problems and achievements, whilst others question them on what they have done and why. This is the forum where members exchange what they have learnt from courses, present ideas they have investigated and review critical incidents from their work that might offer learning more widely. It is also a space for 'bringing issues with other people to the table', for giving and receiving feedback. A standard item on the communications forum agenda is 'training and development', when each person's current or future training and development is discussed.

The two directors used the action learning and action research approaches of their DMS and MSc to trial ways of establishing the business in its early days. The resultant practice of investigate, experiment and review has become an established ethos for the entire company.

Small and medium enterprises (SMEs) are defined according to their staff headcount and turnover or annual balance-sheet total. An SME in general is defined as an enterprise which employs fewer than 250 persons and whose annual turnover does not exceed 50 million euros or whose annual balance-sheet total does not exceed 43 million euros (European Commission 2005). A small enterprise is defined as an enterprise which employs fewer than 50 persons and whose annual turnover and/or annual balance sheet total does not exceed 10 million euros. A micro-enterprise is defined as an enterprise which employs fewer than 10 persons and whose annual turnover and/or annual balance sheet total does not exceed 2 million euros (European Commission 2005).

By current estimates 59.4 per cent of the UK workforce work for SMEs. Most recent figures from 2008 showed there are approximately 4.8 million SMEs in the UK which together account for 99.9 per cent of all enterprises and employ an estimated 13.7 million people (Department for Business Innovation and Skills 2009). Across the entire European Union of 25 countries, some 23 million SMEs provide around 75 million jobs and represent 99 per cent of all enterprises (European Commission 2005).

These figures show the significance of the SME sector, yet the learning and development issues are often not as well known as larger corporations and public sector bodies. In reality the vast majority of SMEs in society are actually micro-business with fewer than 10 employees, and in this sense the case study of Metal Tubes demonstrates many of the characteristics of SMEs, and indeed other small organisations, in their learning and talent development. Small organisations do not have the resources to set up their own leadership academies. They do not have an HR function, full-time trainers or even, usually, any one individual whose sole role is to lead these functions. In well-organised companies one of the managers will wear the hat of leading on learning and development, but it will be one among several other roles they have to fulfil.

Metal Tubes illustrates the combination of formal and informal approaches used by SMEs to advance learning and talent development. They may buy in formal learning and development through requiring, funding or allowing time off to staff for participation in external accredited courses, conferences and short courses. It should be noted that Metal Tubes is not typical of most SMEs in the extent of putting all its employees through extended accredited courses. They do this as an engineering company dependent on a high level of technical skill in all organisation members, but this would not be typical of companies in lower-technology industries. The CIPD 2009 Learning and Development survey found small organisations were particularly unlikely to provide financial support for employees studying for undergraduate or postgraduate degrees with business content (CIPD 2009, p12).

SMEs commonly place strong emphasis on informal learning for developing employees, and here Metal Tubes illustrates how opportunistic, informal workplace learning can be maximised through systematic review steps and dedicated meeting time, what they term the communications forum.

 ILLUSTRATION

Informal learning – definition

Learning that takes place outside formal education and training settings. Informal and incidental learning are based on learning from experience, through activity in an organisational context, enhanced by critical reflection (Watkins and Marsick 1992; Beckett and Hager 2002).

 YEP – YOUNG ENTREPRENEUR PROGRAMME

CASE STUDY

The YEP, developed by the Institute of Technology, Tralee, Shannon Development and Jerry Kennelly (winner Ernst & Young Entrepreneur of the Year, and former CEO of Stockbyte), is in its third year and has become a staple on the curriculum of secondary schools and for third-level students in the region. In 2009 the programme expanded to take in Limerick Secondary Schools and the University of Limerick.

Organised through a collaboration between the Institute of Technology, Tralee (a higher education/third-level institution) and Shannon Development (a government-owned regional development company), YEP is financed through both government funding and private sector sponsorship.

YEP's mission is stated as:

to help identify, inform, recognise and celebrate Kerry's next generation of business leaders – and their educators... They may develop to become local or global entrepreneurs in business or alternatively bring entrepreneurial thinking to their place of work, to Government or to education itself (YEP 2009).

What makes the YEP different from other youth entrepreneurship-focused programmes is the connections it creates between business, teachers and students.

Students get to learn from the best. Starting with Blue Sky Day, they hear from some of Ireland's top entrepreneurs. They learn interactively how to put their business idea to paper, how to craft a unique business model, and how to pitch their business idea, as well as to fine-tune the financials at the Business Plan Workshop

In 2009–10, 600 students from over 21 schools, along with students from the Institute of Technology, Tralee, and University of Limerick will also be mentored by top business people from the region, adding the critical reality check to the different business ideas as well as support to the educators. Teachers, lecturers and mentors, supported by the Institute

of Technology, Tralee, and Shannon Development are given the best possible induction to their roles on the programme. For example, as part of educator-training, teachers themselves have had the opportunity to work on taking their own business idea from concept to business plan.

The idea and business plan from the previous year's winner became a reality, with the finished product going to market for Christmas 2009.

Source: www.youngentrepreneur.ie, accessed 22 November 2009.

5. STIMULATING A REGION THROUGH YOUNG ENTERPRISE

The Young Entrepreneurship Programme (YEP) is a not-for-profit organisation in South-West Ireland dedicated to demonstrating the validity of entrepreneurship as a career choice to secondary school and third-level (higher education) students. In a region with limited job opportunities, YEP's underlying purpose is to ignite young people's entrepreneurial talent with the aim that they might go on to create their own employment, through which sustainability of the local economy can be supported.

The case studies above provide insights into three key aspects of learning and talent development, which will now be discussed further:

- how learning and development is organised, managed and provided
- the variety of interventions that are used to stimulate learning and development
- the language used to talk about activities that in this book we are labelling under learning and talent development.

FOLLOW UP

The comparative agendas for learning and development across organisation contexts within different sectors, private, public, voluntary and community, which have been raised here, will be examined in more depth in Chapter 4.

ORGANISING AND MANAGING LEARNING AND TALENT DEVELOPMENT

In each of the case studies above we can see diversity in how learning and talent development is organised and managed. Comparison can be made by asking the simple questions:

- Who is it for?
- Who set it up?
- How is it funded?
- Who manages it?
- Who delivers?

Table 2.1 summarises the data from each of the five case studies. They reveal different ways in which learning and talent development can be organised and managed. Larger organisations across all sectors will tend to have at least an individual, if not a team or department, who leads on learning and talent development. Small organisations do not. If they have anyone formally nominated to lead, this will be a role they combine with other responsibilities.

Delivery of learning and development interventions is again achieved in a variety of ways. Complete internal provision may be feasible within a larger organisation, such as Kerry Group. Small organisations, such as Metal Tubes, will completely buy in what they need from external providers, whether these be colleges, universities, commercial training companies or freelance providers. The middle ground is some form of partnership between the organisation and providers, as illustrated by SEWA Managers' School collaboration with IL&FS and the YEP partnership between entrepreneur Jerry Kennelly, Shannon Development Agency and third-level education, Institute of Technology, Tralee. Common strategies and approaches for providing learning and talent development are further discussed in Chapter 9.

 ACTIVITY

Find out who has the lead role for organising and leading on learning and development within your organisation. What is their official title?

Compare notes with others in your group.

Table 2.1 Organising and managing learning and talent development

Illustration of context	South Tyneside Council	Self-Employed Women's Association (SEWA)	Kerry Group	Metal Tubes	Young Entrepreneur Programme (YEP)
Example of learning and talent development	Leadership Academy	Managers' School	Graduate Trainee Programme	Training courses and structured reflection	Enterprise training programme
Who is it for – target participants	Internal managers, politicians and hidden talent	Self-employed women across India	High-flying graduate recruits	All organisation members	Young entrepreneurs
Who is it for – wider objectives	Local citizens + service users	Their families and districts	Future talent Succession planning Shareholder value	Company owners – company survival	Regional economy
Who set it up?	Local authority	Voluntary sector organisation	International commercial company	SME	Entrepreneur, third-level education body and development agency
How is it funded?	Internal budget	Independent	Internal budget	Internal budget, government schemes Individual self-funding	Government scheme funds
Who manages it?	Assistant chief executive and organisation development team	Managers' School	Graduate training manager reporting to HR director	Owner manager +any other members	Enterprise champion at Institute of Technology reporting to a partnership board
Who delivers?	Local university	Internal and external partners	On the job assignments, structured assignments and accredited training providers	Accredited training providers and organisation members	Institute of Technology, Tralee mentors

LEARNING AND DEVELOPMENT INTERVENTIONS

An 'intervention' can be defined as any event that is deliberately undertaken to support, provoke, stimulate or assist learning to take place, with individuals, groups or across organisations.

 ACTIVITY

Read through the case studies again and list as many different kinds of learning and talent development intervention as you can find. Share your list with others in your group.

Now add to this list with any additional kinds of intervention you are familiar with from your own experience.

As we saw in the case studies, the field of learning and talent development is made up of a wide variety of intervention activities. Your list is likely to include formal education and training, accredited courses, conferences, mentoring, coaching, master classes, shadowing, special projects, work assignments, structured review and reflection to capture informal learning, action learning, management and leadership development, and graduate training programmes.

FOLLOW UP

Strategies and approaches to learning and development for different contexts, purposes and groups are examined in further depth in Chapter 8, as well as being covered with numerous examples throughout the book. For detail on particular interventions, see the Index.

THE LANGUAGE OF LEARNING AND TALENT DEVELOPMENT

Although this book emphasises the term 'learning and talent development', in practice many organisations use other terms instead of, or as well as these, to mean much the same. This can be confusing, so in this section we will clarify some of the terms which can be said to be part of the broad family of 'learning and talent development'.

Diverse use of language was evident in the case studies above. As we saw in the example of South Tyneside, it was organisation development professionals who took a key role. In SEWA, the language of capacity building is repeatedly used. In Kerry Group the term 'development' is used several times, as in 'graduate development' and 'career development', but the term 'talent management' is not present. 'Learning' was the dominant term in the SME Metal Tubes, whilst the account of the YEP uses all the terms: 'learning', 'training' and 'development'.

Table 2.2 Terminology in job titles

Head – Talent Management & Succession Planning Company: Quest on the Frontier Location: China – Hong Kong An exciting and wide-scoped opportunity with a leading insurance organisation to be at the helm of their talent management and succession planning initiatives for 14 countries across Asia. http://jobs.efinancialcareers.com/job-4000000000579863.htm, 29/11/09	**New Health Leadership Centre targets effective capacity building for NHS chiefs,** 9 June 2008 The future of leadership in the NHS is the focus of a new centre at Lancaster University Management School (LUMS). Launching the Health Leadership Centre, Director Professor Iain Densten said the centre would work with NHS Trusts in the North West initially to 'increase the capability and capacity of managers'. It will research and evaluate best practice leadership development for the health sector, run a series of leadership development workshops for senior managers, and act as a broker of leadership development advice and development. http://onrec.com/newstories/21927.asp, 29/11/09	**Senior Manager, Learning & Development** Job Role: Change Consultant Location: London A professional services organisation based in London, seeking to recruit a learning and development manager on a permanent basis, with the intention of starting as soon as possible. This role requires a candidate to be responsible for the design of global development programmes, predominantly focusing on fee earners. Working closely with the training events team to ensure the smooth set up and running of programs. The role reports into the head of learning and development, and has an officer and personal assistant for support. http://www.personneltoday.com/jobs/job/senior-manager-learning-development-london-city-200650655.htm, 29/11/09
		Transformation Manager Job Role: HR Consultant, Change Consultant, Change Manager Location: London A 9-month interim contract within a large public sector organisation based in South East London. You will be required to support the Head of Procurement and the existing HR Function in the organisational changes and restructuring anticipated over the next 9 months – there will be anticipated redundancies which the transformation manager will need to lead on and discuss the strategic impact on company and deal with the daily operational requirements as well as being a point of contact for the workforce and HR Function. http://www.personneltoday.com/jobs/job/transformation-manager-south-east-london-200647930.htm, 29/11/09
	Talent Manager – technology/defence – London An international defence company is looking for an experienced Talent Manger with a background in Learning and Development in the technology industry to work in their offices in the South West on a permanent basis. Typical responsibilities will include, but not be limited to: • Sitting with the senior management team to set the strategic direction, reporting into the Head of Learning and Director of HR • End to end management of the project cycle, from inception to delivery including ongoing review of agenda • Working closely with relevant managers to encourage active participation in talent management initiatives such as internal recruitment, rotation and transfer programmes, talent mapping, succession planning etc	

Group Human Resource Development Manager	Citigroup names McKinnon Head of Talent Management	Asia Leap Pte Ltd
Group Human Resource Development Manager Almarai Company Saudi Arabia To facilitate performance and preparedness for organisational change through development of individual and collective competence, by instituting international standards in HRD policy and practice and by addressing human resource development and organisational change needs, in conjunction with the HR Executive Team http://www.gulfTalent.com/home/Group-Human-Resource-Development-Manager-jobs-in-Saudi-Arabia-35444.html, 29/11/09	**Citigroup names McKinnon Head of Talent Management** Citigroup Inc, the largest US bank, named Paul McKinnon head of talent management, responsible for all aspects of senior-level executive development. McKinnon joins Citigroup from computer maker Dell Inc where he was senior vice president of human resources. In the memo, Pandit said 'attracting, developing and retaining people at the most senior levels of our company is one of my top priorities and requires constant attention.' http://uk.reuters.com/article/idUKWEN33732008O114, 28/10/09	**Asia Leap Pte Ltd** We are an integrated HR consulting company specialising in customised solutions for organisations, including recruitment and locating talents. We offer professional career guidance services of top quality and look forward to networking with top talents as we facilitate your career success in Asia. Organisation Development Specialist: Taiwan We are currently working with a group of clients and seek highly qualified candidates for the posts of Human Resource – Organisation Development Specialist Key scope of responsibilities would include: • Develop organizational development plans and interventions to support organisation-wide strategic approaches to changes • Support the organisation's overall effectiveness. You will analyze and address key areas such as leadership development, work culture, structure, processes, employee engagement and mission statement • Responsible for the organisation's talent management programs to ensure seamless succession arrangements • Maximize employee performance, provision of strategy, processes, systems and line support for performance assessment and development • Manage organisation change http://www.jobsdb.com/TW/EN/Job.asp?R=JDBTW01817461S, 29/11/09

Organisations do not necessarily advertise jobs for a director of learning or a talent manager, although the latter is becoming more widespread. A trawl of job advertisements across a number of countries in November 2009 produced the range of job titles captured in Table 2.2. They include: Group Human Resource Development Manager, Head – Talent Management & Succession Planning, Transformation Manager, Training Manager, Change Manager, Senior Manager Learning and Development, and Organisation Development Specialist. From this it is very clear that a variety of terms are used to describe overlapping activity. It is therefore important to be flexible when thinking about learning and talent development, and open to the fact that similar practices might be discussed in different ways across different organisations and different parts of the world.

ACTIVITY

Language in your organisation

What are the main terms used in your own organisation to describe policy and practice for learning and talent development?

Conduct an interview with (i) your line manager and (ii) your organisation's learning and talent development lead (whatever they are officially called) to ask what they mean when they use the terms you have found.

We have established that the term 'learning and talent development' might better be understood as a broad family of related terminology. Nevertheless, it is useful to make working definitions of the key terms or at least to be aware of the debates that surround the meaning of core terms.

ILLUSTRATION

Human Resource Development (HRD)

The integrated use of training and development, organisation development, and career development to improve individual, group, and organisational effectiveness (McLagan 1989).

a process of developing and/or unleashing human expertise through organisation development and personnel training and development for the purpose of improving performance (Swanson and Toracco 1995).

One useful source of perspectives on HRD comes from each of the main HRD journals in existence (see Explore Further, at the end of the chapter). According to these HRD is:

all aspects of practice and research that explore issues of individual, group and organisational learning and performance, wherever they might be located (*Human Resource Development International, HRDI,* www.tandf.co.uk/journals/titles/13678868.asp, accessed 20 November 2009);

the realms of performance, learning, and integrity within an organisational context

(*Advances in Developing Human Resources*, www.sagepub.com/journalsProdDesc.nav?prodId=Journal201475&, 20 November 2009);

an interdisciplinary field ... informed by research from related fields, such as economics, education, management, sociology, and psychology (*Human Resource Development Quarterly*, www.ahrd.org/associations/10425/files/HRDQinfo.pdf, 20 November 2009).

 ILLUSTRATION

Organisation development

Organisation development (OD) originated with Kurt Lewin's (1958) work on groups and systems theory as an ongoing, planned and systematic approach to achieving organisation change, particularly through more effective and collaborative problem-solving management, with the catalyst of a change agent. Such cycles of planning–action–review were developed into organisation improvement through *action research*.

The CIPD definition of organisation development is a '*planned and systematic approach to enabling sustained organisation performance through the involvement of its people*'.

Source: www.cipd.co.uk/subjects/corpstrtgy/orgdevelmt/orgdev.htm, accessed 22 October 2009

 ILLUSTRATION

Capacity building

This term is used most frequently in voluntary and community organisations and public service bodies, but rarely in commercial organisations.

In the contexts of both the Western third sector and developing countries, internationally capacity development is associated with empowering individuals, communities and underdeveloped regions or states. For example, the UNCED Agenda 21 definition is '*capacity building encompasses the country's human, scientific, technological, organisational, institutional and resource capabilities* (www.gdrc.org/uem/capacity-define.html, accessed 29 November 2009).

Here capacity building is viewed as much more than training to include the following:

- Human resource development: the process of equipping individuals with the understanding, skills and access to information, knowledge and training that enables them to perform effectively

- Organisational development: the elaboration of management structures, processes and procedures, not only within organisations, but also the management of relationships between the different organisations and sectors (public, private and community)

- Institutional and legal framework development: making legal and regulatory changes to enable organisations, institutions and agencies at all levels and in all sectors to enhance their capacities.

In Britain, capacity building has become an oft-used term in public service organisations, one example being the NHS North West Leadership Academy 'Building Leadership Capacity Programmes', which aims to provide opportunity, experience and personalised learning that will enable participants to break through career barriers.

Source: www.nwacademy.nhs.uk/buildingleadershipprogs/bme/regionalbt.html, accessed 15 November 2009

Learning

ILLUSTRATION

What is learning? *Is it new knowledge, a change in behaviour or understanding? Is it a process?*

Learning is one of those concepts used frequently as if its meaning was self-evident. Much literature on learning and development rarely gives an explicit discussion of what it means to say someone is learning or has learnt. There is much focus on how we might learn, but a definition of learning is usually implicit. Arguably this might reflect how little is really understood about learning processes, in terms of neurology, emotion and consciousness, rather than the cognitive and developmental psychology which dominates discussion of learning.

For example, for David Casey, learning is about 'doing things differently' (1983, p39). Sheila Harri-Augsten and Laurie Thomas suggest:

> learning is better thought of as a change within the person. It appears as a new or improved way of thinking or feeling about something or of perceiving it or doing it (1991, p47).

Their definition seems to collapse several categories together, as does Reg Revans' thesis that:

> true learning consists mainly in the reorganisation, or reinterpretation, of what is already known – does call for the learners to understand what may be preventing them from using more fruitfully that to which they already might have access, if only they knew also how to secure that access (1980, p289).

Virginia Griffin's questions to learners produced an interesting list of 40 learning processes, which they named, including: making meaning; creating knowledge; expanding alertness releasing creativity; creating energy; being aware of self as a learner; validating oneself; unlearning; questioning assumptions and ideas; reframing with new assumptions; changing the past (Griffin 1987, p216).

Some writers try to distinguish between different learning processes to present a dichotomy of learning, differentiating between an external view of learning, where a person adds on new knowledge, or an internal view, where a person is deeply changed (Carl Rogers 1983; Paulo Freire 1972; Argyris and Schön 1996). What these share is a view that there are different levels of learning, one at which the self is untouched, another at which it is affected, producing changes in values or perspectives. Other writers conceive of levels of learning, but along a spectrum, rather than as a dichotomy. For example, Gregory Bateson (1973) outlined four levels of learning: Level 0, where there is no learning, responses are habitual, without regard to context, and response to feedback is poor; level I at which there is error correction, through trial and error responses to new contexts; level II, where there is an ability to recognise and inhabit different contexts, to be able to take different perspectives, but still to hold one world view; level III, at which a person has an ability to step outside their previous world view, has an awareness of their own subjectivity, has gained control over habitual ways and can take responsibility for making changes.

This perspective on learning connects with what people think they are doing when they are learning, almost what they will allow themselves to learn. Writing on women's learning, Belenky *et al* (1986) encapsulate this idea when they talk of five stages of development (or learning) they can move through:

1. Silence: they experience themselves as having no voice and being subject to external authority;

2. Received knowledge: they believe that they are capable of receiving and reproducing knowledge, but not creating it;

3. Subjective knowledge: knowledge is seen as personal, private and subjectively known;

4. Procedural knowledge: application of objective procedures for obtaining and communicating;

5. Constructed knowledge: where the learner comes to view knowledge as contextual and themselves as potential creators of knowledge, through both subjective and objective strategies.

What this suggests is that an individual's learning is connected to their relationship with themselves and their world, in particular their sense of control over and contribution to it. It also implies an interplay between cognition and emotions in learning (Vince, 2001).

In contrast the CIPD definition limits itself to work, categorising learning as: 'a self-directed, work-based process leading to increased adaptive capacity' (www.cipd.co.uk/subjects/lrnanddev/general/lrndevoverview.htm, accessed 11 October 2009).

You might ask yourself whether this last view of learning is sufficiently far-reaching to capture the range of influences on people's learning and development. It certainly seems to exclude many of the sources (sport, home, spirituality, survival experiences, key life moments) that people frequently name as key stimulants of learning.

The practical significance of our understanding of learning relates to how learning and talent development interventions are designed, what level of learning they aim to stimulate and whether the design is appropriate to deliver on the intended objectives.

FOLLOW UP

See Chapter 6 for further in-depth discussion on individual learning.

Talent

The terms 'talent' and 'talent management' came into use after the American consultancy firm McKinsey referred in 1997 to the 'war for talent' as being a key driver for corporate performance, referring to recruitment of an organisation's most valuable employees.

Although the word 'talent' is an everyday term that we might think we all understand, its use in learning and development is varied, and this can cause confusion. Some commentators see talent as the gifted, young high-flying individuals. Others see talent as a collective characteristic of an organisation, the sum of its members, processes and practice. Here are some definitions to illustrate the variety:

> Talent consists of those individuals who can make a difference to organisational performance, whether through their immediate contribution or in the longer term by demonstrating the highest levels of potential (Tansley *et al* 2007, pxi).

Talent describes a well-rounded manager with

> a sharp strategic mind, leadership ability, emotional maturity, communication skills, the ability to attract and inspire other talented people, entrepreneurial instincts, financial skills and the ability to deliver results (Michaels *et al* 2001, px).

Talent refers to

> highly talented individuals with the potential to create disproportionate amounts of value from the resources that the organisation makes available to them (Goffee and Jones 2009, p57).

Talent is

> inherent in each individual, one person at a time (Rothwell 1994, p6).

Talent means:

> everyone at all levels [working] at the top of their potential (Redford 2005, p20).

So we can see here that when people talk of 'talent' they can have quite different meanings, ranging from the sum of all organisation members to just some individuals perceived as exceptional. Even these Brittain (2007) separates into two groups: first the high performers identified as the future leaders (HIPOs), representing between 2 and 10 per cent of people in organisations; second a further 5–10 per cent of employees with essential technical skills, knowledge or know-how, such as commercial contacts. This variation then affects what is mean by talent management and by the options taken for talent development, as the next two sections discuss.

TALENT MANAGEMENT — WHAT IS IT AND WHAT IS ITS PURPOSE?

Approaches to talent management depend on how an organisation conceives of talent and what their purpose is for managing talent. Below we offer some contrasting approaches to the kinds of interventions required to manage talent.

Some see talent management as the nurturing, development and career advancement of those identified as having unique and special skills:

> talent management is the systematic attraction, identification, development, engagement/retention and deployment of those individuals with high potential who are of particular value to an organisation (Tansley *et al* 2007, pxi).

Others see talent management as an ongoing capacity issue for all organisation members: 'enhancing of an employee's ability to cope with changing work demands' (Garavan *et al* 2009, p267).

Yet other perspectives look at talent management from an organisation's perspective, to ensure succession management:

> a set of organisational processes designed to ensure an effective flow of human resources, including leadership resources (Garavan *et al* 2009, p 266).

Garavan *et al* suggest talent management has replaced the notion of succession planning because it is concerned not only with leadership and management development, but more broadly with recruitment and retention of top-class talent.

Table 2.3 Perspectives on talent and talent management

Individual focus			
Talent as scarce resource	Stars High-flyers Organisation processes to attract, nurture and keep exceptionally talented people for future top positions	L&D and HR processes to maximise everyone's potential Ensure right person in right job	**Talent as plentiful**
	Succession planning – integrated organisation processes to nurture supply of future managers/leaders for key positions Configuration of organisation resources to enable talented people to achieve full potential	Interventions to develop talent pool across the workforce Developing collective organisation capacity	
Organisation focus			

As Table 2.3 on p28 shows, these different perspectives on talent and talent management can be differentiated, on the one hand, between those that focus on individual capability and those that focus on organisation-wide capacity, and on the other hand, between those that see talent as exceptional or rare, and those who see talent as potentially broad.

TALENT DEVELOPMENT

Following the explanations above of contrasting ways in which the purpose of talent and talent management is approached in organisations, we can see that the practices or interventions designed to develop talent will vary across organisations. When talent is used to refer to the exceptional few, interventions tend to focus on the attraction, retention and development of the best employees through such steps as leadership development, work–life balance, employer branding and corporate social responsibility. In the case study of the Kerry Group graduate development programme above, this was clearly focused on an exceptional few, designed to support succession planning of future company leaders.

Taking the more general view that talent management is about maximising everyone's potential, developing capabilities and competency more extensively, interventions include a broader range of learning and development interventions at all levels, from training to management and leadership programmes to international assignments, coaching and mentoring. However, they are also open to existing employees at many levels, not only to specific recruits.

The purpose of learning and talent development

Going back to the case studies above, a further contrast between them lies in the purpose which learning and talent development interventions were designed to achieve. Look back at Table 2.1 'Organising and managing learning and talent development' to remind yourself of this. One way to think of this is to map the intended beneficiaries on the spectrum in Figure 2.1 below.

Figure 2.1 Spectrum of outcomes: the purpose of learning and talent development

Individual performance	Organisation performance	Social group benefit	Wider society benefit

Learning and development interventions will always have individual participants so at one level a purpose could always be said to enhance individual performance. However, the interesting question is, who are the wider, or secondary, intended beneficiaries? In South Tyneside Council, the local government example at the start of the chapter, it was intended that enhanced leadership skills would lead to improved public services for local citizens. The anticipated outcome for SEWA of self-employed women's learning is that they would have increased earning power to benefit their families as well as sustain local economies. This wider society benefit is similar for the Young Entrepreneur Programme in South West Ireland, where it is hoped that the regional economy will benefit from the creation of future wealth-generating enterprises that are stimulated by young people's learning. In the international company, Kerry Group, the purpose of investment in the Graduate Development Programme is to grow future talent, support succession planning and in the shorter term deliver a return on investment through contributing to shareholder value. For the SME, Metal Tubes, the purpose of learning and talent development is more short-term, to have the skills required to undertake the projects the company wins contracts to do, and so to keep the company surviving.

Another way to think about these issues is to consider how learning and talent development is being used to support organisation strategy, or in other words to look for Strategic HRD. Each organisation has its own strategy– a core purpose, an intended direction, strategic objectives and identified resource needs, which learning and talent development, if strategically planned, will be designed to support. When learning and talent development assures employees are competent to implement an organisation's current strategies successfully (as with Metal Tubes above), it is playing a Strategic HRD role contributing to the organisation's competitive advantage or its performance standards.

However, as Garavan *et al* (2009) argue, echoed by Swanson *et al* 2009), Strategic HRD is not only about implementing strategy, but also about 'shaping future strategy and enabling organisations to take full advantage of emergent business strategies' (Swanson and Toracco 1995, p11). This more proactive view of the potential purpose of learning and talent development flows from recognising the competitive and performance advantage that can come from investing in people to develop human capital (knowledge, skills and abilities), social capital (relationships in social networks) and intellectual capital (ways of knowing and knowledge within social groupings, such as tacit knowledge and procedural knowledge).

 ILLUSTRATION

Strategic human resource development (Strategic HRD)

Linking learning and development interventions to organisation strategy, so as to implement current plans effectively, to be prepared take advantage of emergent opportunities or to influence and inform future strategy-making.

Critical HRD: Revisiting the purpose – who and what is left out?

Within learning and talent development there are a number of tensions and questions that lead some commentators to a more critical perspective. Perhaps most obviously, when talking of talent development, is the question of who is not seen as talented. According to Brittain's (2007) categorisation above, does that mean the remaining 80–93 per cent of employees are untalented? Is this a useful way to prioritise investment in development or a dismissive waste of potential? And, what of attempts to manage increasingly diverse workforces fairly and equitably while at the same time defining some as talented and some as not? (See Stewart and Harte 2010.)

O'Donnell *et al* (2007, p413) critique the 'managerialist appropriation of social capital in pursuit of largely economic ends'. They argue that 'social well-being is as relevant to HRD practice as economic well-being' (p413). Others point out that it is rare in learning and talent development to question for what business purposes people are being developed (Rigg *et al* 2007). Not for the first time, the recent global financial crisis resulting from unbridled profit-seeking behaviour has raised the question of whether the world can sustain organisational practices that do not incorporate wider societal responsibilities. Likewise when public service organisations, despite investments in management and leadership development, fail to meet basic standards or obviously waste public money, it is relevant to ask what is the value of learning and talent development, and where is its evidence-base?

There is a growing body of concern among learning and development practitioners over the wider consequences of their work. Whilst learning interventions are often described in benign terms such as enabling, developing potential, empowerment and such like, there is a failure to scrutinise the bigger picture, to question if learning and talent development might in some contexts have the consequence of refining individual skills and developing organisational capabilities to perpetuate ways of running organisations that have serious detrimental human and environmental consequences.

There has been very little consideration of the role talent development might play in either preventing or sustaining such corporate behaviour as the scandals such as the well-known case of Enron exemplifies. There is rarely consideration of the non-financial costs across a value chain in mainstream learning and talent development programmes. In contrast, a **Critical HRD** approach is cognisant of the significant power work organisations wield in the world, how the size and resources of major international corporations surpass the GDP of many small developing nations, and how the activity of organisations touches the wealth, social divisions and natural environment of the wider world, for good or ill. Critical HRD asks questions of the appropriateness of marketing strategies that create new 'needs' for consumer products in a world of diminishing natural resources. Critical HRD helps practitioners explore questions of management as a social and political as well as an economic practice.

> **FOLLOW UP**
>
> See Chapter 5 for more on the politics of learning and talent development.

A recent response in the USA is a movement for business and management students to voluntarily pledge to create value responsibly and ethically (see Figure 2.1).

> **Business Graduates Pledge to Raise Their Game**
>
> 'As a manager, my purpose is to serve the greater good by bringing people and resources together to create value that no single individual can build alone. Therefore I will seek a course that enhances the value my enterprise can create for society over the long term.' This is the oath being signed by increasing numbers of MBA students internationally. Inspired by two Harvard business school professors, Rakesh and Nitin Nohria, they are making a voluntary pledge to create value responsibly and ethically. *Management Today*, September 2009, p.41.

Figure 2.2 Business graduates pledge to raise their game

SUMMARY

This chapter has introduced examples of various organisation contexts: international corporate, SME, public sector, voluntary and community, and explored how these affect the organisation, management, delivery and purpose of learning and talent development in work organisations. It has introduced a variety of types of learning intervention which will be further examined in later chapters. In addition, some of the language and terminology of learning and talent development and related practices have been compared.

The following key terms have been scrutinised and defined:

- HRD
- strategic HRD
- organisation development
- critical HRD
- learning
- informal learning
- talent
- talent management
- talent development.

From reading this chapter, its extended case study and completing the activities, you should be able to:

- demonstrate an understanding of how learning and talent development is employed in diverse organisation contexts
- differentiate between different ways of organising and managing learning and talent development
- identify options for organising and managing learning and talent development
- critically appraise the meanings attached to key terms in the field of learning and talent management, in particular the notions of HRD, strategic HRD and critical HRD and their connections with learning and talent development
- evaluate the multiple purposes of learning and talent development for different stakeholders and identify potential tensions and contradictions.

 REVIEW ACTIVITIES

1. Summarise five key things you have learnt from this chapter.

   a. Write down two or three new questions the chapter has raised for you or things that you are unclear about.

   b. Select 1 of these questions that you will enquire into further.

   c. Write down what action you can take next in pursuit of your question (for example: read one of the references in this chapter, talk to someone more experienced at work, look on CIPD website, take time to reflect on your own experience).

2. Construct a rationale for your personal understanding of the purpose of learning and talent development in organisations.

   a. Examine your rationale in the light of the arguments presented in this chapter. Explain how the arguments either support or challenge your rationale.

   b. Discuss the results with colleagues and compare the similarities and differences of your rationales.

3. Select and describe one major or significant learning/talent development initiative you are currently involved with or affected by. Map out the following:

   a. who it is designed to benefit

   b. who 'owns' it – who commissioned it or is it the client?

   c. how it is delivered

   d. any other stakeholders

   e. In the light of the discussion in the chapter, identify any changes you would recommend.

   f. Share the results with colleagues and examine how they compare. Discuss whether any differences can be explained by the different kinds of organisations you work for.

4. Look back at the five organisation case studies at the start of the chapter. Make a case for which could be described as showing evidence of strategic HRD in the way they used learning and talent development.

5. Create a statement for each of the following terms that summarises your understanding of each in your own words:

   a. HRD

   b. critical HRD

   c. strategic HRD

   d. learning

   e. informal learning

   f. talent

   g. talent management.

EXTENDED CASE STUDY + DISCUSSION QUESTIONS

 Garvey group

CASE STUDY

Company ownership, sector and size

The Garvey Group is a family-owned retail and hotel company in Ireland, primarily Munster-based (covering Counties Kerry, Cork and Waterford in the South of Ireland). It has 10 stores across this region plus two hotels and a sports and leisure shop in Dingle, Co. Kerry.

There are 850 employees, rising to around 1000 in the summer months. Most staff are department sales assistants working in the retail shops on the meat or fish counter, for example, or on the tills. In the hotels, most would be employed in the bar or restaurant. Each store and hotel has a manager and assistant manager, as well as at least one and sometimes two training managers. Strategic leadership is provided by a small board of directors, comprising five people: the founder and chairman, one other family member and three non-family members.

Making learning and talent development strategic

Until the early 2000s, when the company was smaller, with just three stores and one hotel, training and development in the company was fairly ad hoc. In 2001 Garvey Group brought in an Operations & HR Director to the board, who came from an Irish-based multinational company where she had been responsible for leading achievement of Excellence through People (Ireland's national standard for human resource management, comparable with the British 'Investors in People' kitemark).

The Operations & HR Director saw Excellence through People as a positive way of structuring HR systems and practices, and of linking learning and development within the overall business strategy. So she led its implementation in the Garvey Group. The result by the mid-2000s was a very structured approach to training, driven now by the business strategy. A corporate training plan is prepared annually, costed and evaluated through deliverables such as sales and profitability. A modified balanced scorecard (Kaplan and Norton 1996) provides a framework for the strategy, starting with the core belief that 'if you had your people trained, your operations would be right, if this was right, in turn your customers would be happy; in turn your business would be right. So the starting building block was always the people' (Operations & HR Director).

The independent audits provided by Excellence through People were welcomed as a useful source of feedback and suggestion, that helped the company become more systematic. Prior to that training was more ad hoc, and not systematically aligned with business strategy. In the days when the Garvey Group had just three stores and one hotel all within the same areas, this relative informality was perhaps manageable, but as the Group grew throughout the decade Excellence through People was used as a framework to help grow the group, to facilitate acquisition of other business and integrate them in a seamless manner.

From business strategy to training needs analysis

Each year a training plan is prepared for each location. Considerable time is spent identifying employees' training needs, using the appraisal system to provide opportunity to identify training needed and based on a needs analysis for their job. Some training needs are technical, for example, specific to those who work in the fish department or meat section of the stores. The company uses a competence-based approach, with much emphasis put on behavioural competences applicable to all jobs, such as customer care, working as a team and 'subtle selling'. These skills underpin the business strategy. For sales assistants in particular, great emphasis is placed on customer service training, being ambassadors for the company and selling skills – telling customers in a friendly way about promotions, so customers might not even notice, 'subtle selling' as the company call it. Customer service is seen as so central to the achievement of business strategy that there could be training three times a year, to reinforce and deepen the learning. In general if people cannot complete training in their own store they generally get to attend in another area.

Training providers – external and internal

The main provider of training for Garvey Group is the Musgrave Group (the Irish group that owns many household grocery brands across Ireland, the United Kingdom and Spain and provides sales, marketing, IT, finance and logistical expertise to retail companies such as Garvey Group. www.musgravegroup.com/en/about/what_we_do.php, accessed 25 November 2009). Garveys use Musgrave Group's training department for specialist retail training, for example, in flowers or fish, whilst for specialist hotel training, such as bar and restaurant skills, the Irish Hotels Federation (IHF) is used. For other generic skills, such as customer service or team building, great emphasis has been placed on developing internal training expertise. Each store has at least one and often two trained trainers, even occasionally three. The HR person from each store is one of the trainers; whilst the second one is typically one of the checkout supervisors because of their experience of having many people report to them. Trainers typically originate on the shop floor, starting on the checkout tills. They regularly meet with the company's Operations & HR Director and are appraised by her. They receive training themselves twice a year training on for, example, evaluation, transfer to work, making training relevant.

This emphasis on investing in people's skills, competences and behaviours, driven by a clear strategic plan is at the forefront of practice in the retailing sector, to the extent that Garvey Group trainers are often called on to run training for other retailers.

External trainers are used only very

selectively. The Musgrave group have a retail diploma accredited by Dublin Institute of Technology and also operate a list of approved trainers across the country, people with retail experience who can deliver practical, hands-on and experiential training directly informed by real scenarios, rather than being generic.

Planning and evaluating

Every course has objectives, and the Kirkpatrick model is used to identify these and to systematically ask what individuals expect to get from any training event. So rather than being sent on a fish course, for instance, a person will know why they are going and what are the objectives. After the training, they will be asked what they learned, whether it matched the objectives, what they will do now. Also added in is the question of what they will share. Employees are very much encouraged to summarise key learning from any course in their next week's meeting at work. Even with on-the-job, 'sit by Nelly' training, for example in using the tills, there are training objectives set and a review afterwards, to ensure there are no remaining gaps. The focus is constantly on trying to make the training relevant to the job and relevant to the longer-term business objectives.

Training managers feed back the evaluations to the Operations & HR Director, who communicates back to providers, whether these be internal or external from Musgraves and the IHF.

At a corporate level the ROI (return on investment) measures used for evaluation were primarily sales and profit figures. For example, comparison would be made of fish sales and margins before and two months after a fish course. Generally there was an improvement evident, an uplift in sales figures following training and this data was used to justify training investment to retail managers and the board.

Employee expectations

When the company's focus on training began, initially there was a degree of apprehension from the workforce. Whilst some of these were young college and school students, many were 40 and older. Fears were voiced of 'Is there a test?' 'I'll never be able for it'. So the initial hurdle was to get people's buy-in, and encourage them to attend at least the first course. As it happened, once they went on one course, they were generally delighted to be able to go again. Part of this was achieved through getting their input, for example, asking for their ideas on what is the best way to give customer service. The company culture is open, with an emphasis on personal development and improvement. The team of HR and trainers across the whole group regularly meet together around twice a year to explore how they can we make training better. Participation in training is celebrated and annually people get a printout of their training record. The company deliberately 'hero' their staff, for example, publicising pictures across the stores of a Master Butcher, Master Baker or star of the Baby department, to give people a sense of pride in their job and to acknowledge them as an expert. All this contributes to a culture where people are positive towards training, feel a sense of achievement and are proud of their training records.

Managing the managers

Initially the Operations & HR Director had to work hard to persuade the middle managers (store managers, hotel managers) of the value of releasing people for training, because it is an industry where the wage bill is high and they have very specific operational targets regarding rostered hours. To release an employee for 8 hours' training means not only do they have to pay the person for these hours although they are not on the shop floor, but they also have to buy in a replacement for the 8 hours to cover the shift. So initially there was a huge debate. However, the managers also had other performance measures, such as mystery shoppers, and they could see that if they did not put investment into the training, they were not getting the same recognition for customer service. Often, if there was a poor mystery shopper result, the excuse was 'well, she never went on the training course'. In time managers recognised a direct result between the training of their employees and achievement on the job.

Induction was another point of potential tension between the training strategy and managers. Newcomers had two days invested in their induction, covering the basics such as company culture and the emphasis on customer service, even before they began to learn such skills as how to use a till. There was a tension when a retail manager could be crying out to have them on the till immediately and trainers saying, wait, you want them with the right attitudes and behaviours, they'll add so much more value.

Persuading the board of the value of investing in training was not so difficult, because the Operations and HR Director was a member of the board and was explicitly hired into the company with this brief. Nevertheless, it was important to highlight deliverables and to continuously provide evidence to link the training to profitability or sales, for example, demonstrating improvements that followed training.

Employer branding

Garvey Group are very proud of their training record and their recognition with Excellence through People. They were the second Irish retailer to achieve gold and are the first retailer and (by early 2009) one of only 18 Irish companies to achieve platinum. These achievements are seen as a major contributor to their employer branding, and the logos are proudly and widely displayed. The retail sector does not pay high wages, the work is tough, including regular evening and weekend working, dealing with customers, so to make employment attractive, an employer has to be able to highlight how they are distinctive, For Garvey Group this is the

experience and development offered to employees. Being known to treat employees well and train well has meant the group recruited some excellent employees. Once Excellence through People was achieved it gave the company a huge competitive edge; there was a noticeable increase in the quality of applications and a rise in graduate applicants. Candidates were clearly aware of the Excellence through People recognition and would mention it as one of their reasons for wanting to work with the company, because it signalled they were serious about training and learning and were a company that could offer career opportunities. Excellence through People put them in a different league.

Talent management

Garvey Group have a segment in their balanced scorecard termed 'talent management', which was introduced because, in previous years of relatively full employment there had been a real difficulty in recruiting talent. For the retail sector this is a challenge because a career in the sector is not seen as offering great potential. Having found it difficult to attract supervisors and good trainee managers they made the decision to home-grow their own. The Garvey understanding of 'talent' is people 'having capacity to be more than they currently are'. There is also a recognition that talent in this sector is very much related to personality and whether a person can relate to the customers or has people management skills, regardless of the degree they have on paper.

To grow their own, investment was made in spotting and developing talent. Managers had, once a month, to identify someone who had the potential to progress. Often they were someone working on the till for a few hours after school or in their college breaks. Talent development consisted of an 18-month trainee manager structured fast track development. Trainee managers can also be recruited directly to the programme, which involves on-the-job training to learn all aspects of the job as well as external training, devised with Musgraves, to be retail specific. During the 18 months they would be met bi-monthly to agree training objectives and there were monthly milestones. Their line manager was accountable for making sure they progressed and were adding value to the store.

Each 'talent' is assigned a mentor, with regular review meetings held. Mentoring, however, has proved something of a challenge, because in most cases the mentor has been the trainee's direct line manager, with the result that meetings became more performance reviews than true mentoring sessions. It has proved difficult with the size of the company to give people a different mentor.

Mentoring has been more successfully used with the store managers, who each have been mentored by one of the Board members who is not their line manager.

Another unresolved aspect of the company's talent management is that the system only developed towards the position of trainee manager. There was no similar system for development towards supervisor although until the recent economic downturn there was a need. With the recession, there is now a flood of external supervisors to choose from so growing internal talent is no longer essential.

Top management development

The company to date has not had a systematic or strategic approach to developing Board members. Individuals have pursued development opportunities at their own discretion.

The language of learning, training and talent

Until recent years Garvey Group spoke of training and development in all their strategy documents. However, one night, triggered by an Excellence through People audit recommendation, they rewrote all the policy documents, substituting the word 'learning' for 'training'. The employee reaction was quite unexpected. Staff questioned how learning could be the subject of strategy or be documented and recorded because it was what they did anyway. Training, by contrast, was seen as involving courses, something special and important, that could be documented and signed off. For senior managers this highlighted the evolution the company had been through, coming from having no formal HR to developing good systems to having Excellence through People to achieving Gold then Platinum. Employees needed more time to adjust to talking of 'learning' as being part of what they did each day.

The language of 'talent' posed a second source of challenge, with some asking 'are you just singling out special people?' The answer was, unfortunately yes, because of the need to develop the internal management team.

Into the future?

Overall the company has no doubt that investment in people's learning and talent development produces results to the bottom line. Also, that strategically managing training and learning is essential to get the best out of people. But what of the future challenges in the face of the current economic downturn? It is tougher to keep the focus on investing and the risk is that training will be less, not only because of the cost of training, but also the operational impacts of covering people taken out for training. In the medium term the company believe that, because staff turnover is low, there is some cushioning from past investment in development, although that could become more of an issue in time. There are strengths in being closely tied to the Musgrave group and accessing highly relevant, industry-specific training. They also have a degree of internal sustainability through having a well-developed network of trained internal trainers as well as the established framework derived from Excellence through People of using training plans, setting objectives and review. Maintaining this will be the challenge.

This case was created with the assistance of Caroline McEnery, Operations and HR Director, Garvey Group.

For more information see:

Garvey group website: www.garveygroup. ie/

Excellence through people: www. excellencethroughpeople.ie/

Investors in People: www.investorsinpeople. co.uk/Pages/Home.aspx

Discussion questions

1. What are some of the specific challenges for learning and talent development in the retail sector?

2. What are the advantages and disadvantages of having a specific talent strategy?

3. What do you think is the implication of having the lead HR person on the company Board?

4. The case study illustrates at least two significant tensions within the Garvey Group's learning and talent development approach. What are these?

5. Applying the matrix in Table 2.3, Perspectives on talent and talent management, where would you position Garvey Group's approach to talent management?

6. To what extent do you consider Garvey Group's approach to learning and talent development can be described as Strategic HRD?

EXPLORE FURTHER

Books
Essential

Garavan, T.N., Hogan, C. and Cahir-O'Donnell, A. (2009) *Developing Managers and Leaders*. Dublin: Gill and Macmillan. Chapter 7, 'Managing talent and succession in organisations'.

Gold, J. *et al* (eds). (2009) *HRD Theory and Practice*. Basingstoke: Palgrave.

Rigg, C., Stewart, J. and Trehan, K. (eds). (2007) *Critical HRD: Beyond Orthodoxy*. London: FT Prentice Hall.

Tansley, C. *et al* (2007) *Talent: Strategy, Management and Measurement*. London: CIPD.

Recommended

Brown, P. and Hesketh, A. (2004) *The Mismanagement of Talent: Employability and jobs in the knowledge economy*. Oxford: Oxford University Press.

Gibb, S. (2007) *Human Resource Development: Processes, practices and perspectives*. 2nd ed. Basingstoke: Palgrave.

Grugulis, I. (2007) *Skills, Training and Human Resource Development: A critical text*. Basingstoke: Palgrave.

Hill, R. and Stewart, J. (eds). (2007) *Management Development: Perspectives from Research and Practice*. London: Routledge.

Sambrook, S. and Stewart, J. (eds). (2007) *Human Resource Development in the Public Sector: The case of health and social care*. London: Routledge.

Smith, P.J. and Sadler-Smith, E. (2006) *Learning in Organizations: Complexities and diversities*. London: Routledge.

Journals

Human Resource Development International

Journal of European Industrial Training

International Journal of Training and Development

Human Resource Development Quarterly

Advances in Human Resource Development

Human Resource Development Review

Useful websites

www.cipd.co.uk

www.cipd.co.uk/subjects/lrnanddev/general/lrndevoverview.htm

www.ufhrd.co.uk

www.ahrd.org

www.ukces.org.uk

www.lsc.gov.uk

www.idea.gov.uk

Podcasts

CIPD: 'Strategies for attracting and retaining talent' – podcast episode 24

Philippa Lamb discusses the issues with: Emily Lawson, partner in the London office of McKinsey & Company and the global leader of McKinsey's talent management and HR service line; Claire McCartney, CIPD Adviser, Organisation and Resourcing; Scott Hobbs, Head of Talent at the support services organisation Amey; Matthew Guthridge, Expert Associate Principal in the London office of McKinsey & Company and a leader in McKinsey's talent management initiative and European organisational behaviour service line; and Richard Roberts, head of the People Team at Virgin Mobile.

www.cipd.co.uk/podcasts/_articles/_strategiesforattractingandretainingtalent.htm?link=title

CHAPTER 3

International and National Contexts

OVERVIEW

This introduction sets out what the title of this chapter means to us, writer and reader, in the context of this book. The chapter is simply about the wider and external context within which learning and talent development carried out in work organisations operates. We recognise and acknowledge that this is something many professionals find less interesting and exciting than aspects of what they perceive to be actually about 'doing the job'; you may be one such professional. But we believe this view is mistaken. The external context directly influences and indirectly affects doing the job because it has impact on the organisations where the job is done. It does not matter whether learning and talent development is being practised in the private, public or voluntary sector; in a large, medium or small organisation; at strategic or operational level; in a stable or changing internal context; for executive, professional or operative-level employees. In all of these cases the possibilities and limitations of professional practice are influenced directly by public policy and indirectly by social and economic trends affecting organisations. And those same trends affecting organisations are also affecting public policy and so have a direct line of influence to practice through their influence on public policy relevant to the practice of learning and talent development. All of this being the case, learning and talent development professionals cannot really claim to be doing the job without knowledge and understanding of the external context as explained in this chapter. Or, if the claim is made without that knowledge and understanding, then it is likely to be true that the job is not being done as well as it could or should be. So, read on.

LEARNING OUTCOMES

After reading this chapter and completing the activities, the intention is that you will be able to:

- identify and examine key trends in the external environment that affect learning and talent development practice

- define and apply the notion of globalisation as a way of understanding those trends

- evaluate the influence of EC policies in relation to VET and learning and talent development

- evaluate the influence of UK public policy in relation to NHRD, VET and learning and talent development

- critically assess and evaluate the implications for employing organisations and learning and talent development practice

- provide informed advice and guidance on how to take account of the external context in learning and talent development practice.

DEFINITIONS AND SCOPE

It may be worth explaining some of the terms used in the objectives, and so three important definitions are provided in the box below. It is also worth delineating the limits of the content of the chapter since the objectives suggest a large and ambitious undertaking. The next section does this by explaining the scope of the chapter.

 ILLUSTRATION

Definitions

VET – This abbreviation stands for Vocational Education and Training. It refers primarily to public policy aimed at improving international, national, organisational and individual skills as a means of improving economic performance at those same levels. In our context, international refers to policies of the European Union Commission (EC) and national refers to those of the UK and devolved governments.

NHRD – This abbreviation stands for National Human Resource Development. It is a recent innovation in the lexicon of learning and talent development and so is subject to some debate as to meaning. In general terms, though, it has a similar meaning to VET and so applies to policy adopted by governments and state agencies to stimulate economic and social progress through education, training and wider HRD activities.

Employing/Work Organisations – These terms are used interchangeably and both refer to organisations where a formal and legal employment relationship exists. This is the main but not exclusive context of L&D practice. It is recognised and accepted that L&D does occur in other contexts, such as voluntary organisations where all work is done on a voluntary basis. The focus here may apply to voluntary organisations but does not include all contexts of practice.

Scope

The chapter has six sections including one examining implications and conclusions. The first main section looks at economic and social trends across the world, in Europe and in the UK. This will not be comprehensive since it would take a book at least to achieve such coverage. Trends examined under each heading will therefore be selective and will be those of most relevance to learning and talent development practice. The same criteria will be used in the following section examining globalisation. There are many books on this subject, demonstrating again that the content will necessarily have to be selective. The following two sections examine public policy in the EU and in the UK respectively. There is less need for selectivity here but even so there are myriad policies emerging from each set of institutions and so not all can be covered. The criteria of most relevance are again applied. The following section provides a brief overview of some international comparators, and the final substantive section attempts to identify the implications of the previous sections for learning and talent development practice in work organisations and to provide some advice and guidance. This will not be definitive since by definition professional practice calls for professional judgement. If simple and universal prescriptions were possible and available then professionals would not be needed. So, the advice and guidance will be just that and not 'how to' recipes. The final section also offers some overall conclusions.

The objectives above will be more easily achieved, and the advice and guidance will be of more value if an overall framework is provided to help analyse and make sense of the content. The final part of this introduction suggests and explains such a framework.

ILLUSTRATION

An analytical framework

Social	Technological	Economic	Political
Demographics	New raw or synthetic materials	Macro level such as exchange rates and international and national labour markets	International and national law
Consumer tastes	New equipment and machinery (eg hardware)		Policy of international institutions
Social norms			
Social and geographic mobility	New processes and systems (eg software)	Micro level such as costs of production and local labour markets	Policy of national Government
	Inventions		Activities of political parties and pressure groups

G L O B A L I S A T I O N

ANALYTICAL FRAMEWORK

The box above contains a framework which both reflects the organisation of some of the content of the chapter and provides a means of analysing the content. It can be applied to specific contexts as well as to the content so as to identify and assess the significance of each section of the chapter to those specific contexts. You will be able to use the framework therefore in your own separate and unique contexts to apply the chapter to your own circumstances. The chapter ends with a case study, and you are encouraged to try out the framework on that case.

The basic framework is that of a STEP analysis, which is commonly used to identify and analyse factors in the external environment that are of strategic importance to work organisations. 'Strategic' in this context simply means factors which will have a positive or negative impact on the medium- to long-term future viability and success of an organisation. Factors of significance are organised according to the acronym STEP for convenience and clarity. This does not mean that they are or act independent of each other. For example, the policy of the UK is directly affected by that of the EU, which in turn is directly influenced by global social and economic trends and on occasions is facilitated and supported by developments in technology. An example of this is the growth in attention to and investment in 'e-government' in the UK, which reflects increasing home ownership of access to the Internet and a EU policy of creating a knowledge-based society and economy. So, e-government as a policy direction is based on social, economic and technological trends. The addition to the STEP model is that of globalisation. We will examine this in more detail later in the chapter. It is included in the framework because the word refers to the argument that trends encapsulated in STEP are now common across the world and because it is also identified as a separate phenomenon which affects all of our lives and therefore the organisations in which we work.

WORLD AND UK TRENDS

This section takes a brief look at some general trends across the world and identifies which are also affecting and happening in the UK, with some particular trends in our context also being examined. The analytical framework described in the previous section will be used here but not in a direct or formal fashion since, as indicated, the factors are interconnected and interrelated.

POPULATION AND DEMOGRAPHICS

A significant world trend illustrates the last point. In the recent past a concern was with a rising global population. For example, a recent report from a UN agency expressed concern about satisfying the needs of nearly 500 million new jobseekers worldwide entering the labour market for the first time between 2002 and 2012. However, while the population is still rising globally it is doing so at lower rates than in the past and at a declining rate of increase. The rate of increase has in fact halved since 1960, and the total world population is predicted to begin to fall sometime in the next 50 years. A specific example is the USA, where the rate of growth has declined from 13 per cent to 5 per cent in less than 15 years. More significantly, the distribution is changing and many countries are now concerned about a declining rather than rising population. An example is Russia where cash incentives were introduced a few years ago to encourage families to have two or more children. A similar declining birth rate is being experienced in the European Union, where it currently stands at 1.5 children per woman, a similar rate as that in Russia.

There are, though, a number of factors that affect the size of populations in particular countries of which the birth rate is only one. Two others are mortality rates and related life expectancy, and the difference between emigration and immigration. Life expectancy for men in Russia, for example, is 59 while in the USA and UK it is over 75 years. The average in the EU is also 75. This is one reason why a low but similar birth rate has different consequences for Russia than countries in the EU, for example. Replacement or 'natural' population change is a function of number of deaths compared to number of births. Both of these are affected by social, economic and technological factors. To take the latter, advances in medical science develop new treatments and technologies which increase life expectancy and reduce annual death rates. In Russia, a relatively high death rate is attributed in part to preventable diseases such as alcoholism. But, that is also associated with social and cultural norms related to alcohol consumption. That in turn, though, is also related to economic conditions which make alcohol an attractive alleviator of harsh living conditions. And economic factors also contribute more directly to a lower birth rate in Russia, since women are not certain of being able to afford to raise more children because of poverty levels and low incomes. A lower birth rate because of economic conditions combines with a higher death rate related in part to those same conditions to produce a declining population. Technological solutions in the form of medical treatments are available to arrest some of the death rate if social norms allow their application.

The second factor of migration is of significance in the UK. Higher rates of immigration compared to emigration produce net immigration. Net immigration is now a more significant factor in UK population growth than natural change in the population. The contribution of natural change to a rise in population size compared to the contribution of net immigration has been falling for over 10 years. Both produce net contributions but of different proportional size. Much of the net immigration is due to world economic factors, with the majority of immigrants being what are termed 'economic migrants'. They can and do have significant positive effects on the UK economy in supplying labour and new businesses. Net immigration, though, is a significant social factor and changes the ethnic and cultural composition and norms of the national population and of local communities.

An additional significant factor arising from population change is age distribution. In the UK there is the well-known phenomenon of an ageing population. This results mainly from a declining death rate and increasing life expectancy, which in turn are related to improved health from living conditions, associated with economic factors, and medical and health care, connected with new technologies such as drug regimes. Another effect is that the rising numbers of older people are also older; eg the proportion of people over the age of 85 has increased from 7 per cent to 12 per cent in 20 years. The lower birth rate also means fewer young people at a time of increasing numbers of old people. Over the last 30 years or so the absolute number in the population under the age of 16 has declined by a greater amount than the absolute number of people over the age of 65. Thus the distribution of age in the population is changing at both ends of the distribution curve.

ACTIVITY

How is the population changing in your locality? Research how you might answer this question and then attempt to do so.

TRADE AND EMPLOYMENT

There are a number of factors related to trade which have an effect on employment and these will be considered together. First, there is a global shift in the distribution of trade which has impact on jobs and employment. Manufacturing has been moving from Western industrialised countries for many years to lower-cost economies, perhaps best illustrated by the fact that exports from developing countries have on average shown higher annual increases for the last 10 years compared to those from developed countries. In addition and at the same time, there have been significant annual increases in direct capital flows to developing countries. Over the last 25 years or so different countries such as South Korea have progressed to be major players, and more recently China and India have become significant exporters of manufactured goods.

This shift has been behind the second factor, which is the trend to a greater role for service and knowledge-based industries in Western countries. However, that can be an oversimplification as India in now well established in higher technology industries such as software design and in customer service products such as contact centres. 'Offshoring' of the latter to countries such as India is now common among companies in the USA, Europe and the UK. It is also common in 'back office' work such as data processing. This situation arises in part because of technologies which make work independent of location. Telephonic and computer and internet-based work can be provided anywhere in the world to anywhere else in the world. That said, those companies who are leading exponents of offshoring themselves tend to operate in the service sector of the economy and so the general trend of that shift is still clearly apparent.

Taking a closer look at Europe supports both of these trends. On a broad scale, employment in the agriculture and industrial sectors has continued to fall over the last 10 years while the service sector has not only met those falls, but also been the source of net growth in employment in the EU. Within the industrial sector, while manufacturing has continued to fall as a source of employment, construction saw increases between 2002 and 2007. The increase is probably related to property and renting, together with general business services, within the services sector enjoying the largest increase in employment. In addition to that sector of the EU economy, health and social work, and education, have provided most of the increase in employment. There have been some changes in these trends at the time of writing because of the banking crisis and worldwide recession. However, the general direction of shift to services is not expected to change.

One of the consequences of these two trends is a third trend of changing demand for labour. Work in the services sector on average requires different skills and has a greater proportion of roles demanding professional qualifications. This is in part associated with new technologies but such skills are also increasingly required in lower-level jobs as well. Another influencing factor is the growth of what is referred to as 'knowledge work' which demands 'knowledge workers'. It is these latter which tend to be well educated and highly qualified professionals, but again this is not a simple relationship; providing excellent quality customer service in a contact centre, for example, can be defined as knowledge work but does not require high-level qualifications. Such work also, though, does not require well-developed technical and physical skill, which is the case in low and craft-level manufacturing jobs. The work is of a different kind of labour; what is termed 'emotional labour'. This requires the ability to display and engender desired emotions and is associated with customer and personal service industries and jobs. The overall trend therefore is demand away from physical to intellectual and social skills in the world labour market. That being the case, it is also a feature of EU and UK labour markets.

SOCIAL AND CULTURAL

One interesting social and cultural change being experienced worldwide follows from the factor of net immigration effects on national populations. This is simply that national and local communities are populated by many different ethnic, national and cultural groups. The USA used to be described as a 'melting pot' of different ethnic and national groups. That description can now apply to many other countries. Three examples, two based on everyday experience and one based on 'hard data', will illustrate this point. First, it is possible to visit for example a Chinese, Indian, Japanese, Greek or Moroccan restaurant in any major city in the world and in most large towns in the majority of countries. And these restaurants commonly have authentic cuisine because they are owned and staffed by people of that ethnic origin. Second, during the 2006 World Cup the Independent newspaper printed a front page with photographs of UK resident supporters of over 30 different countries. Third, the majority of EU member states have experienced a rise in the proportion of non-national citizens in their labour markets over the last 10 years. So, a significant social change is direct experience of a wide range of nationalities and cultures without having to travel outside of a home town, let alone home country. This factor also suggests increasing global movement of people and so an increasingly diverse labour market in all countries and localities. However, a recent OECD report has highlighted that education for the children of immigrant families lags seriously behind that of national citizens in many developed countries. This fact does and will have significant consequences for both the children themselves and future potential employers.

The 'melting pot' factor can be contrasted to an extent to one which seems slightly contradictory and that is increasing nationalism. This is not meant to imply nationalism in a negative sense. It merely acknowledges the fact that the number of national entities such as countries applying for membership of the United Nations has increased significantly in the last 20 years or so. One major cause was the break-up of the former Soviet Union, which had direct effects in its own borders and indirect effects in its sphere of influence in Central and Eastern Europe. But there are many other parts of the world, in Africa and Asia for example, where new nations are either being established or nationalist armed struggles are being fought. There are too examples in Europe with the Catalan and Basque regions of Spain and devolution of government to Scotland and Wales in the UK. So, despite a rise in the 'melting pots' of the world there remain deep attachments to national and ethnic identities, a point perhaps illustrated again by support for teams in the 2006 World Cup. These attachments will have implications for organisations operating their business globally and as employers in achieving integration of diverse groups of employees into corporate cultures. And a business does not have to operate globally to experience the same challenge; recruiting from a local labour market means for many attracting applicants from a diverse range of national, ethnic and cultural origins.

Turning to a more specific look at social and cultural patterns in the UK, two reports from the Social Issues Research Centre provide an interesting insight into changing attitudes and behaviour. From one of these reports it is clear that a significant shift is occurring. The average age when people marry has increased by an average of 8 years in the last 20 years or so and, again on average, the age of becoming a parent for the first time has increased by even more. Twenty years ago people could and would expect to experience two jobs by the age of 25; today it is four jobs. These behaviours have been characterised by the term YEPPIE: Young Experimenting Perfection Seekers; or by the term Peter Pan generation. The latter suggest delaying maturity and hanging on to youth as long as possible, a phenomenon also characterised by the phrase 'yoyo children' who keep returning to the parental home rather than settling down to career and family. The former term, though, is more accurate in describing attitudes. People in their 20s and 30s are now less willing to accept compromise in their choices. They expect and demand more satisfaction in both work and personal relationships, and are willing to wait, experiment and search for what will meet their expectations. In terms of work and career, personal fulfilment is much more important than material rewards. People in the 'noughties' generations seek to add purpose to their lives and to achieve their potential through work and employment. These attitudes and motivations are associated with a counter-argument to that suggested by the description 'Peter Pan'. The counter-argument is that these generations are in many ways more mature at a younger age than previous generations.

This willingness to experiment and delay firm career choices may help to explain another empirical observation. Contact centre work and jobs are largely seen as available to and suitable for individuals with a reasonably successful secondary education. However, in the UK over 35 per cent of such jobs are held by university graduates. A PhD research project undertaken at Nottingham Business School clearly showed that the motivation of most graduates in contact centre jobs was related to financing a desired lifestyle while serious life and career decisions are explored and investigated.

The global and UK changes briefly examined here are associated with what is termed 'globalisation', and that is the subject of the next section.

 ACTIVITY

Discuss with student or work colleagues the implications for learning and talent development arising from changing attitudes and values of recent generations and how organisations need to respond.

GLOBALISATION

Globalisation is a subject of much debate which concerns first its very existence as a phenomenon, second (and assuming it does exist) what exactly it is, and third whether it is a force for good or evil. The first and third of these debates will not form part of this section. We will assume that something is going on in the world which is usefully described by the term globalisation and so we accept its existence. We will also leave debate as to the desirability and value of its effects to other times and places. The major focus therefore will be on defining and explaining what is meant by the term and illustrating that with examples. The discussion in this section will draw heavily on previous work, especially Stewart (1999) and CIPD (2002). Those works and especially the references they in turn draw on provide rich sources for those who have an interest in engaging in the other debates.

A useful starting point is to give a definition. One that is very straightforward and helpful is that of Giddens (1989), who suggests that globalisation is simply the increasing interdependence of world society. This definition indicates that the phenomenon at the heart of globalisation, that of interdependence, is not new. What is new is the fact and rate of *increasing* interdependence. The definition also indicates the location of that interdependence, which is 'world society'. This is not meant to imply the existence of a world state in the same sense as the UK is a state. It does, though, usefully signal the role of international, or 'world', institutions, which we will examine further later in this section. The definition also implies that 'interdependence' will influence those that are dependent. This includes nation states such as the UK, their citizens such as you and me and the organisations in which we work. So, globalisation has implications for us as private individuals, as citizens and as employees. The latter point is emphasised by Dicken (2004), who argues that globalisation has changed and is changing the very conditions that give rise to work organisations and so it inevitably also changes their nature and form, which, in turn, has implications for those employed in those organisations.

Despite the fact that globalisation is not a new phenomenon, the word itself is relatively recent as a way of naming and describing the process. What is of interest is the extent to which different parts of the world, and the different facets of human society and experience – which we label here social, technological, economic and political – are becoming similar or remain different. In earlier analyses this question was framed as the 'convergence thesis' (Kerr 1983). In other words, to what extent are social arrangements such as societies, communities and work organisations becoming *similar* irrespective of the influence of national and local culture, and to what extent is the world becoming *unified?* Those were the central questions addressed by the convergence thesis and they are the same addressed in the debate on globalisation. Those who argue that globalisation is a real phenomenon with significant effects are saying that *similarity* and the degree of *unification* are on the increase. There are others who argue that this is not the case and point to, for example, the rise in the number of nation states which are members of the United Nations over recent years mentioned in the last section as evidence of this. These debates, though, are set in the context of globalisation, and that concept is now established and accepted as the best way of framing the phenomenon. Interestingly, it is possible that increasing numbers of nation states can support an argument for globalisation in the sense that the nation state as a social arrangement of large collections of individuals has spread across the world through globalisation and so is an example of rather than an argument against globalisation.

Returning now to our earlier definition of globalisation, it is clear from the literature (Dicken 2004, for example) that much of the focus on globalisation from a business perspective emphasises economic factors and relationships in the argued increasing interdependence. However, social, political and cultural factors are also of interest and importance, and so relevant from an organisation perspective. For example, the social trend we noted earlier of declining birth rates and population size has implications for both labour and product markets. In the latter case spending power shifts to different demographic groups with different wants, needs, motives and aspirations. A simple example is in relation to leisure pursuits and associated products and services which are not the same for people in their 60s and 70s as those in their 20s and 30s. In the case of labour markets, a reducing and ageing population has implications for all aspects of personnel and development, for example recruitment methods, training methods and reward and compensation. So, while it is important to focus on economic factors, these examples show that frameworks such as STEP are useful in identifying other significant factors. The examples also show, though, that the labels and categories in frameworks such as STEP are not in fact separate and independent. They are useful as analytical devices but the reality is that they are all interconnected and interdependent; social factors have economic consequences and vice versa. They also have political consequences as the make-up of electoral constituencies changes and politicians shift their policy priorities in response.

Explanations of globalisation do, though, tend to differ according to whether the analysis is from an economic or sociological perspective. One definition that perhaps hints at both is given in the box below.

ILLUSTRATION

Definition of globalisation

The compression of the world as a whole and the intensification of consciousness of the world as whole ... both concrete global interdependence and consciousness of the global whole (Robertson 1992, p8).

The first of the conditions in the definition, that of 'compression of the world as a whole', refers to the reordering of time and distance in the everyday lives of the majority of the world's population. To illustrate what this means, think about the typical life experience of someone born in the UK early in the last century; perhaps one of your own great-grandparents. For the majority of such people life would have consisted of being born, raised and dying in the same town or village without direct contact or even a visit to many if any other parts of the UK, let alone other countries. In addition, they would have little awareness or interest in places and events elsewhere. The exceptions to this, of course, are the two World Wars and other conflicts, but outside of such significant experiences life was largely focused on the immediate locality. Now contrast that experience with your own. Communication of information about events across the world including visual images is commonplace through the Internet and satellite television. So too is international travel for both business and pleasure, especially because of low-budget airlines. We have now, then, both interest in and direct experience of societies and cultures outside of the UK as well as most if not all parts of our own country as a normal part of the lives of most people. In fact, and as we will see shortly, we do not even have to leave our own towns and cities, let alone our country, to directly experience elements at least of other cultures. These examples of information and communications and international travel show again the interconnectedness of the factors in the STEP framework since both are enabled by developments in technology and both have economic and social consequences. Taking information and communication technology (ICT) for example, we can now join global social communities through the Internet, and services for customers in the UK can be delivered by employees or sub-contractors in India.

The second condition in the definition follows in significant part from developments in ICT. 'Consciousness of the global whole' is related to awareness; knowledge and understanding of places and events outside of our own direct experience. I know, for example, that Disneyworld is a fantastic place to holiday although I have never been there. On a more serious note, I also know that war is horrible through the 'embedded' reporting of TV journalists of conflicts such as those in Iraq but I have never had personal experience. This condition is equally important as the first in globalisation. We now know that what we take for granted in the UK as 'normal' ways of behaving and doing things is not the only way and that there are alternative possibilities. In fact, we probably take that understanding for granted. But, that would not have been the case only a few generations ago. And that condition is not exclusive to those of us in the UK or even in the 'advanced and industrialised' countries. It is a condition shared with the majority of the world's population in all countries, which makes it part of the phenomenon of globalisation.

There are three additional factors which are argued to be significant in the process of globalisation:

- **The role of global institutions**
  These can be of two different types. The first is known as 'non-state actors' and includes organisations such as the United Nations and the International Monetary Fund. The second type is known as 'trading networks' and includes, for example, the European Union and the Organisation of Petroleum Exporting Countries. Some might argue now that the EU is much more than a trading network, but it is clearly not fully international and so does not meet the criterion of the first type. A significant feature, though, of all global institutions is that they are not and cannot be controlled or bound by any one single participating country or their government.

- **Global issues**
  This factor refers to those issues confronting the world as a whole and which have impact or implications for all countries but which cannot be totally solved or resolved by the independent action of any single country. The most obvious of current examples is global warming and all the other environmental concerns facing the planet. Independent action is needed but so too is collective and collaborative action to deal with 'green' issues. Another example here is natural disasters and famine. There are, of course, sound humanitarian and ethical reasons for collective action. Often though, as with the tsunami disaster in 2004, more than one country is affected. In addition, there are often social and cultural connections between countries, such as those in the Commonwealth, which make a case for collective action in response to natural disasters. Political and economic ties can also be major factors, for example, there may be considerable trade and investment links between a country experiencing a disaster and other countries.

- **Cultural influences**
  This factor reflects the growth and spread of cultural styles, tastes and influences across the globe. Examples abound in our everyday lives to such an extent that we are unaware of them most of the time, but things like clothing, food, music, film and literature are now part of our common experience across the world. This element of globalisation is perhaps the one where its emergence from the 'convergence thesis' is most apparent. For example, the ubiquitous availability and popularity of fast food through burger and pizza chains in all parts of the world. ICT plays a significant role in spreading cultural influences through the compression of time and space, and availability of music from

anywhere and to anywhere in the world through the Internet is probably the best example of the enabling role of technology.

ACTIVITY

Locate two articles in academic journals on international HRD or HRM. Compare and contrast their content in relation to how, if at all, they are informed and influenced by the concept of globalisation.

Discuss your findings with student or work colleagues.

These defining characteristics of globalisation suggest support for the view that the world is becoming more similar and unified. However, it is important to recognise that there is competing evidence and arguments. In relation to managing work organisations, for example, the well-known research of Hofstede (1991) suggests important cultural differences in organisational cultures and related efficacy of managerial approaches, which in turn are related to significant differences in national cultures. Work such as this may be more accurately located in the convergence thesis rather than globalisation. One piece of work by the American sociologist George Ritzer (2004) crosses this conceptual divide and makes a strong case for the convergence effects of globalisation. He does this through his idea of 'McDonaldisation'. This refers to Ritzer's argument that the eponymous fast food chain represents the paradigm case of what he sees as a wider process, which is producing similarities and commonalities in all aspects of life, and which he argues transcends national borders and boundaries. Ritzer's work therefore supports a view of globalisation producing convergence in, among other things, approaches to organising and managing. The critical characteristics of what Ritzer labels McDonaldisation are described in the case study below.

THE FEATURES OF MCDONALDISATION

CASE STUDY

Efficiency

This refers to a concern with and value attached to reducing the time and effort required to satisfy a need or want. Needs and wants can be material such as hunger, which McDonalds and other fast food companies meet most efficiently, but they can also be cultural or social. Examples here might be downloading music from the Internet and the rise in popularity of ideas such as 'speed dating' or, in business, 'speed networking'. The efficient satisfaction of all types of needs and wants

is, though, an economic activity and factor which concerns work organisations whether commercial or public service. An example of the latter is the fixation on waiting lists for hospital treatment.

Calculability

Hospital waiting lists is also an example of a focus on and value attached to only that which is measurable in a standardised way. The effect of this is to associate quality with quantity, or indeed to measure quality by quantity. Examples of this process include ratings for television programmes, box office takings for films and bestseller lists for books. All of these quantitative measures are taken as indicators of quality. In public services such as health, education and local government league tables fulfil a similar function. Again, calculability is central to economic activity and economic actors; consumers are likely to be swayed in their choices by such measures, for example. But, providers of economic goods also want to calculate and measure their performance. This often means also calculating and measuring the performance of their employees as well.

Predictability

The concern here is with reducing uncertainty through standardising products and services. This is again well illustrated by McDonalds, who take pride in their claim that consumers anywhere in the world receive exactly the same product and service. So, a burger in the USA has the same ingredients and is grilled for exactly the same number of minutes/ seconds each side as one in the UK or in China. McDonalds is not, though, the only example; think for a minute of boarding an aeroplane of a well-known airline or staying in a branch of a well-known hotel chain anywhere in the world and you know what to expect in terms of the product and experience. Consumers are reassured and comforted by the claim made by McDonalds and having their expectations met by them and other companies. Achieving predictability and the desired reassurance it gives consumers has clear and obvious implications for employees of those companies and especially in relation to emotional labour.

Control

The previous sentence is related to this last feature of McDonaldisation. Bureaucracy and technology are used to control the decisions and behaviour of employees in order to achieve predictability. However, control is not limited to employees. Ritzer argues that the same process affects us as consumers and as citizens to such an extent that the 'sovereign consumer' is or even has been replaced by docile conformists who comply with the demands of the producers and suppliers of goods and services. An example here might be that we accept the transport costs associated with out-of-town supermarkets and now increasingly also provide our labour free of charge by not only pushing a trolley up and down aisles, but also carry out the pricing and charging process as well. Another example is provided by parcel companies who now have customers complete forms on-line, which become the address label and bill of lading and so remove part of the work previously done by employees.

The basic argument of this section is that globalisation is a significant and important feature of the external environment and that it has direct connections with each element of the STEP analytical framework. Globalisation is also both an input and an output to work organisations. It is an output in the sense that it is the result of decisions made by social and economic actors, and work organisations are major examples of those. But, it is also an input in the sense that work organisations have to take account of the influences, implications and effects of globalisation in making strategic and operational decisions. Both product and labour markets are now global and so it is irrelevant if a company operates only in a limited and local geographic area; it will have competitors in both the product and labour markets who operate globally, including in the local and limited geographic area, and the local population who form both the product and labour markets are influenced by global trends in social norms and cultural preferences. So, even the smallest and most specialised companies need to take some account of globalisation.

ACTIVITY

Identify between three and five global trends that have an impact on an organisation you know well and analyse the implications and possible responses to those impacts.

Discuss your findings with student or work colleagues.

IMPACT AND INFLUENCE OF EU POLICIES

Policy in the EU is obviously influenced by the impact of global change and globalisation in particular. The EC has set an overall objective of developing a knowledge-based society and economy in response to global changes such as the shift in manufacturing capacity. It is seeking to build comparative advantage in high-technology and high-skills industries and associated secure, high-wage and long-term jobs. This sets the overall context for its employment strategy, which is intended to contribute to full employment, quality and productivity at work and the goal of social cohesion within and across member states. The main elements of the European Employment Strategy (EES) as they are intended to inform and guide member states as well as EC policy are set out below:

- achieve full employment, quality and productivity and strengthen social and territorial cohesion

- promote a life cycle approach to work

- ensure inclusive labour markets

- improve matching of labour market needs

- promote flexibility combined with employment security and reduce labour market segmentation

- ensure employment-friendly labour cost development and wage-setting mechanisms

- expand and improve investment in human capital

- adapt education and training systems in response to new competence requirements.

The last two of these are most directly relevant to VET at the European level as well as in member states. It is, though, worth noting that a key element of the strategy is integration both within the EES and with other strategies related to economic and social development. For example, the EC Social Agenda for 2005–10 had two priority areas within which are a number of themes as detailed below:

1. moving towards full employment, making work a real option for all

   achieving full employment

   a new dynamic for industrial relations

   towards a European labour market

2. a more cohesive society; equal opportunities for all

   modernising social protection

   combating poverty and promoting social inclusion

   promoting diversity and non-discrimination.

Three elements of concern to and within the EU are reflected in these complementary strategies. First is gender inequality in the labour market, which is still widespread in terms of participation, segmentation, salary and career opportunities. This is also of wider international concern as shown in a recent UN report titled 'The World Commission on the Social Dimension of Globalisation'. Second is age distribution and participation in the labour market of both the young and the old. Measures are being and will be taken to increase participation opportunities for both groups. Paying for pensions, for example, is not the only reason to encourage longer working lives. Supply of labour is another reason. A higher level of youth unemployment is a related concern at that end of the age spectrum. The third concern is migrant labour. This refers to both migration within and across EU member states and from outside of the EU. The focus of the former is free movement of labour within the EU, and one measure, for example, is the European Passport and the new European Employment Services network jobs portal. This is an online service currently detailing over 1.5 million job opportunities across the EU. You may wish to find and access the portal and consider the potential benefits to employers and individual citizens.

The EES and especially the last two elements are most relevant to VET. The element relating to human capital has the following detailed requirements:

- inclusive education and training policies and action to facilitate access to secondary, initial vocational and higher education, including apprenticeships and entrepreneurship training
- reducing the numbers of early school leavers
- efficient lifelong learning strategies open to all in schools, businesses, public authorities and households to enhance participation in continuous and work-place training throughout the life cycle and especially for lower-skilled and older workers.

The element related to education and training systems and new competence requirements has the following detailed requirements:

- raising and ensuring the quality and attractiveness of education and training
- broadening the supply of education and training opportunities, ensuring flexible pathways and enlarging the possibilities for mobility for students and trainees

- enabling and diversifying access for all to education and training and to knowledge

- responding to new occupational needs, key competencies and future skill requirements by improving the definition and transparency of qualifications, their effective recognition and the validation of non-formal and informal learning.

Applying these requirements is a matter for both the EC in relation to EU programmes and also for individual governments in member states. For example, there are major cross-national projects related to recognition and accreditation of informal learning currently funded by the EC.

Much of the above is derived from and connected to the EU Social Agenda 2005–2010. This policy was reviewed in 2008, and a new set of policies known as the Renewed Social Agenda was agreed and adopted in that year. Part of the rationale for change was the need to adopt an approach that was more 'cross cutting'; ie one that integrated policy and programmes across all areas of EU activity. This is an example of the interrelated nature of factors in STEP analysis. Another part of the rationale for change was the continuing impact of globalisation, and what we might argue is one manifestation of that in the enlargement project of the EU itself. The Renewed Social Agenda seeks to support achievement of three equally important goals:

- Creating opportunities – This focuses on promoting more and better jobs and labour mobility while reducing overt and direct discrimination.

- Providing access – This promotes equal access to high-quality education, social protection, health care and other services. It also includes specific focus on youth education and training, skills development and life-long learning.

- Demonstrating solidarity – This focuses on measures to help and support disadvantaged sections of the EU population, promoting social inclusion, combating poverty and helping those experiencing temporary and transitional problems associated with globalisation and technological change; the last of these also has a particular emphasis n the labour market.

These overarching goals are translated into specific programmes and actions under seven priority areas as follows:

- children and youth

- investing in people, more and better jobs, new skills

- mobility

- longer and healthier lives

- combating poverty and social exclusion

- fighting discrimination

- opportunities, access and solidarity on the global scene.

These priorities are implemented through a mixture of the established EU instruments; eg the various levels of legislation, social dialogue and EU funding. There are three main funding programmes:

- European Social Fund – This has a main focus on employment, education and skills.

- PROGRESS – This funding mechanism supports policy development in employment, social inclusion and protection, working conditions, non-discrimination and gender equality.

- European Globalisation Adjustment Fund – This is a fund to support active employment measures to help individuals experiencing redundancy due to structural changes in world trade.

There are too many specific programmes emanating from the EU to detail and examine here. Policy and action in the UK both takes advantage of the funding programmes and is influenced by EU policy and, in some areas, directly by EU legislation. We will examine what is happening in the UK in relation to VET in the next section, and it will be instructive to bear these EU priorities and strategies in mind to look for links and connections between these and UK policies.

IMPACT AND INFLUENCE OF UK GOVERNMENT POLICIES

INTRODUCTION AND A BRIEF HISTORY

It is interesting and instructive to begin an examination of UK public policy on VET by providing a brief historical overview. A useful starting point in this is to consider the observation in the box below and to attempt to estimate the year when the report referred to was published. The answer will be given later in the section. Write down your estimate to compare with the correct answer.

 ILLUSTRATION

The UK economy and VET

A Royal Commission concluded that UK VET compared unfavourably with major continental competitors such as France and Germany. What year was the Commission's report published?

The comment in the above box makes clear the conventional wisdom and accepted view that there is a relationship between skills levels and economic performance at national level, and also between provision of and for VET and skills levels. It is also widely accepted that the same is true at the micro level of individual employers; skills available within and deployed by employees will impact on productivity, and other measures of economic and financial performance and skills levels will reflect levels of investment in VET. So there is a widely shared belief in a straight causal relationship between investment in VET, skills levels and economic performance of firms and countries. We will leave aside the question of the validity of that belief and pose another big question: Who pays for the investment in skills development? There are three main possibilities: the individual, the employer and the government. Of course, the latter in reality means both of the other two since government resources are mainly sourced from taxation of individuals and organisations, but the significant difference is that when financed through taxation the choice is taken out of the hands of taxpayers.

One problem with funding education and training is that skills have some of the characteristics of a 'public good'. This means that once developed they are generally available. So, if an employer funds your education and training and thus improves your skills you can take them to a new employer whenever you wish. This can and does act as a disincentive to employers paying for VET.

Another significant question is what role government should play in VET irrespective of its direct involvement in funding. Answers to this question will vary because of ideological differences but, that said, VET has never been a major political issue on which political parties have sought to differentiate themselves in elections. The sentiments expressed in the quote above have enjoyed and do enjoy a high degree of political consensus and cross-party support for a variety of approaches to improve VET as a means of raising both macro- and micro-level economic performance. This is evident in the history of VET in the UK. The main focus of difference has been between an interventionist and voluntarist position adopted by government. The former supports state control and regulation over VET, while the latter assumes the market, in this case individual employers and employees interacting with VET suppliers, is best placed to make decisions and the role of government is to create supporting frameworks. The UK has tried both positions (see the illustration 'A brief history of UK VET policy'), although neither in pure form as most governments have and do vary the degree of emphasis on interventionist or voluntarist policies rather than totally rejecting one in favour of the other. An additional complicating factor is the impact of related issues such as unemployment, which can lead a government such as that of the Conservatives in the 1980s to abandon a strong belief in the market and to adopt a high degree of intervention. VET in that case was used as a policy instrument to alleviate both the number of unemployed and the effects of unemployment.

So what has this meant in practice? The illustration below summarises arbitrary periods of the last century and up to the present time, and details the major VET-focused policies and initiatives in each. It also classifies each as being a primarily voluntarist or interventionist period. The following sub-section outlines current challenges facing VET and current government responses.

ACTIVITY

Discuss with student or work colleagues the pros and cons of government intervention in VET. Identify some practical differences a high level of state intervention might make to individuals and to organisations. Then discuss to what extent these differences are positive or negative from the perspective of individuals and employers, and identify if there may be reasons for individuals to support and employers to oppose state intervention or vice versa.

ILLUSTRATION

A brief history of UK VET policy

A brief digression: The answer to the question 'What year was the Commission's report published?' is '1884'.

The Royal Commission report was titled 'Report on technical instruction in Great Britain'. What is interesting is that many other official reports since then have reached the same conclusion, and the same failings identified then are still being addressed in current policy in the twenty-first century. Or at least the same rationale of having to improve VET to match that of our national competitors, including near neighbours, in order to compete as a nation with them and others is used to inform and explain current policy. It seems, though, hardly credible that public policy has failed for well over 100 years to make enough of a difference. But that is presented as the rationale and seems to be the case.

Pre-1945

Before the Second World War the approach to VET was almost exclusively voluntarist, with very little intervention by the government. There were some isolated and very specific examples of measures following the First World War such as provision of training for the unemployed and people with disabilities, but there was no overall strategy or active role for the state.

1945 to 1960s

The immediate post-Second World War period was a boom time for industry. That said, the Employment and Training Act of 1948 made additional and new provision for training the unemployed and those in temporary or intermittent employment. The main form of VET was through apprenticeships in the craft trades. These were supported by the 1944 Education Act, which made statutory provision for entitlement to day release for 15- to 18-year-olds. A previous report in 1943 had recommended the introduction of a tripartite system of secondary education: grammar, secondary modern and technical schools; but only the first two were adopted and the day release provision was the response for technical education and training. By the time of the mid-1950s, though, there was growing concern with vocational training, and the Carr Commission was set up to investigate. This produced a report in 1959 which mirrored the conclusions reached in the report of 1884. The then Conservative government produced a White Paper in 1962, partly in response to the 1959 report. The White Paper was enacted as the 1964 Industrial Training Act by the then new Labour Government. This is an example of the political consensus on VET. The 1964 Act created Industrial Training Boards (ITBs), which adopted what is known as a 'corporatist' approach, with membership from employers, trades unions and education. ITBs focused on their own economic sector or industry – for example, construction, engineering and retail – and raised levies from employers and provided grants to those employers who met education and training standards set by the relevant ITB. Levies, though, also funded ITB operating costs and so there was little direct investment from government. This lack of direct investment and control by government are two key characteristics of the voluntary approach consistently adopted in the UK.

1970s to 1980s

The early 1970s saw the return of a Conservative government, which reviewed the operation of ITBs. The major conclusions were that VET was fragmented, no major impact had been made by ITBs on skill levels and that the levy grant system was providing insufficient incentive to employers to invest in workforce training. The response in 1973 was to create the Manpower Services Commission (MSC). The MSC provided a cross-sector coordinating role and channelled government funds into schemes and programmes designed to help the less skilled and unemployed. While increasing the level of direct government investment through, for example, taking on the operating costs of ITBs, the MSC still reflected a voluntarist and corporatist approach to VET. The operating costs of the MSC, which were substantial, were met by the government, and membership of the commission itself reflected the same stakeholders as ITBs. Interestingly, the MSC was an agency in the then Department of Employment, and at about the same time the then Department for Education set up the Further Education Unit, a move which some interpreted as a competitive response. Having different agencies with different agendas and different ministerial masters with different accountabilities has perhaps been one of the continuing weaknesses in UK VET. Successor Labour governments in the 1970s did little to change this situation, which continued until the 1980s.

The election of the Conservative government in 1979 saw a change of emphasis. The role of the MSC had by now been influenced by the results of the 1970s' oil crisis and it had focused mostly on the unemployed, with schemes such as the Training Opportunities Programme (TOPS) and the Youth Unemployment Programme (YOPS), each of which required significant government funding. The MSC itself had also grown to be a major employer and had done little to reform the operation of ITBs, apart from setting limits to levies that individual ITBs could set and introducing the operation of levy abatement and exemption, which replaced direct grants for employers meeting their ITB standards. This, though, had the effect of reducing employer incentive to train employees. The 1979 Conservative government reviewed the situation and set a new direction in a White Paper published in 1981. This led to most (19 of 24) of the ITBs being abolished and replaced by (200+) voluntary Industry Training Organisations. This change reflected that government's emphasis on voluntarism and the working of the market. However, even greater unemployment in the period called for an increase in state intervention and investment through, for example, the Youth Training Scheme (YTS). Much of this investment was based on and directed by the UK's rebate from the EC: the rebate could only be spent on EC-approved programmes, which had to be designed to alleviate and overcome unemployment. A further emphasis of the government was to move away from corporatism and to give more power and influence to employers rather than have them share that with trades unions and educationalists. This factor was reflected in many of the initiatives of the 1980s, including the creation of Training and Enterprise Councils (TECs), which arose from a 1988 White Paper. TECS were geographically rather than sector- or industry-based bodies, which were dominated in membership by employers and tasked with identifying and meeting local educational and training needs. A direct quote on what needed to be done from the 1988 White Paper shows a clear link with 1884 and the same problems being tackled:

a training and enterprise framework that will meet Britain's key employment needs and increase its international competitiveness.

The main difference is dropping the word 'Great' from before the word 'Britain' and perhaps with good reason! By now the MSC had been abolished and replaced with two successive but short-lived new agencies. The only significant factor from their existence was a clear signal that VET in future would be more concerned with raising the skills of the employed rather than responding to unemployment.

A significant development in the 1980s was a review of vocational qualifications. The UK had, and probably continues to suffer from, a status divide between academic and vocational education and associated qualifications. A report published in 1986 led to the National Council for Vocational Qualifications (NCVQ) being established and what are now known as NVQs being introduced. The formal aims of the NCVQ were to rationalise the qualification system, provide a means of comparability of qualifications in different subjects and industries and provided by different awarding bodies, and to apply employer-led and determined 'outcome'-based standards to vocational qualifications. A further priority set in the 1980s, linked also to the focus on employed rather than unemployed, was adult education and training to increase skills levels in the UK, and this led to initiatives such as the Open Tech Programme and later the Open College. The idea behind these initiatives was to apply the idea of the Open University to vocational as opposed to academic education and training, and to utilise emerging technologies to increase access to such opportunities. It might be argued that a 'latent' purpose of both NCVQ and these latter initiatives was to raise the status of VET compared with academic education.

The period of the 1970s to 1980s by and large continued a voluntarist approach; even though there was an increase in state investment and control that was largely targeted at dealing with unemployment. However, corporatism was replaced by a greater role for employers and there was less but still some political consensus. What was and is still less clear is the degree of beneficial impact, if any, of VET on the economy and the problems identified in 1884. This, though, has much to do with actually applying the assumed causal chain between VET, skills and national economic performance.

1990s to 2009

The policy priorities and mechanisms summarised above continued to dominate VET in the 1990s. The election of the Labour government in 1997 brought some changes. As is now hopefully clear, new governments commission reviews and reports which, lead to White Papers and a shift in emphasis, together with new policy instruments. In the case of the 1997 Labour Government and those since, there have been a number of White and Green papers up to and including the latest at the time of writing: the 2009 Apprenticeships, Skills, Children and Learning Act. Key outcomes over the last 10 years or so include:

- the creation of a national Learning and Skills Council (LSC), which now funds colleges of FE and other providers as well as managing other government programmes such as apprenticeships (the LSC will be abolished in 2010 under the 2009 Act)

- the introduction of two-year-long foundation degrees with a large element of work-based learning

- Introduction of fees for HE, paid by students

- the creation of a Sector Skills Development Agency (now replaced by the UK Council for Employment and Skills in response to the Leitch report)

- creation of Sector Skills Councils (SSCs) which provide a national focus on skills and education/training needs in economic and industry sectors

- the creation of Learndirect, which provides both advice and training using ICT; the creation of the Qualification and Curriculum Authority, which combines the work of a number of previous agencies including the former NCVQ and those with responsibility for the curriculum and qualifications in compulsory education (from 2010 this becomes the Qualifications and Curriculum Development Agency created by the 2009 Act)

- the creation of a number of more specific and targeted programmes for both the employed and unemployed.

The stance taken in relation to VET since 1997 is somewhere in the middle ground between voluntarism and interventionist, and so continues a trend in that direction begun by a Conservative government in the 1970s; but it has reversed the trend away from corporatism, with more influence and involvement of trades unions in the national skills strategy. One example of this is the introduction of Union Learning Representatives. The other trend is an attempt to reduce Whitehall rivalry and competition and increase integration of policy and policy measures, with combined new and variously titled government departments holding responsibility for both post-compulsory education and skills, and through a national skills strategy. Looking for continuities in policy, we might say that the national LSC had some similarity to the old MSC, local LSCs some similarities to the old TECS, SSCs to the old ITBs and Learndirect to the Open College. However, none of this would be strictly true as the remits, responsibilities and accountabilities do not map directly or neatly. That said, though, it might at least suggest that there are limits to policy possibilities, both in terms of actual measures and goals to be achieved, as perhaps illustrated by a quote by the then responsible government minister:

> Our ability to compete in an increasingly global marketplace depends on our ability to equip people with the skills employers need now and in the future.

The same policy goals if not policy measures are being pursued and with the same faith in the causal chain that was evident in 1884.

CURRENT UK VET POLICY AND INITIATIVES

The historical overview in the box above demonstrates the continuing focus and purpose of VET public policy and a degree of similarity in government attempts to achieve those purposes. So, while things change they also remain very similar. What the illustration also demonstrates is the continuous change in structures, agencies and policy and associated instruments; governments, even the same government, are always and endlessly trying to 'get it right'. A lesson that might be learned by some from this is that 'right' is not possible. You might want to think about your own position on that question. The various changes in emphasis in policy are in the majority of cases argued to be responses to particular circumstances facing governments at particular times, as well as to their own priorities. But, circumstances and priorities change constantly, and one consequence is that it is impossible to write a chapter such as this without it being out of date before it is published! It is, though, safe to say that there are a number of issues facing the UK VET system arising from the particular circumstances of the twenty-first century. These include the following:

- **Growth of ICT**
  Continuous developments in ICT provide new possibilities for delivery of VET and some of these are being exploited, for example by Learndirect. However, it also demands responses in equipping people to work in the new jobs and industries.

- **World markets**
  As was seen in the earlier section on globalisation, the UK economy is interconnected with other national economies and the 'world economy'. As we also saw in an earlier section, this has implications for industries, jobs, employers and therefore skills.

- **Shift from manufacturing to services**
  One element of the above examined in an earlier section is the shift in the UK economy from manufacturing to services. This changes the kinds of skills that are needed, but providers of education and training do not necessarily have the ability to respond to this change. The infrastructure of qualifications, awarding bodies and providers has to keep pace with changing demand in the economy.

- **Flexible labour markets**
  Patterns of employment are changing. The profile of those in employment is changing. Both of these features of labour markets, and the demand for more flexibility from both employers and individuals, have implications for VET.

While not unique in history, current policy and strategy is probably the most serious attempt to achieve an integrated approach across government. The major tool for achieving is formulation of a national skills strategy; the latest at the time of writing was launched in 2009. Current policy is also now influenced to a more significant degree by the EC than it was in the days of the 'Thatcher rebate' and associated YTS programme, and so some initiatives are in response to EC directives. The attempt at integration also reflects the EU 'cross-cutting approach'; an approach which mirrors the concept of 'joined up government' in the UK. In simple terms, it is an approach which seeks to ensure that policy, programmes and initiatives from different departments all support achievement of the same policy goals. Another example of EU influence is the work previously and currently done by the QCA. A future project there is to develop a Framework for Achievement which will link in with the EC 'European Passport', which is a means of facilitating movement of labour across national boundaries through making comparison of experience and qualifications easier. Some of the other main elements of current VET policy which are likely to continue for some time are described below:

- **Apprenticeships**
  This programme is built on what was previously known as Modern Apprenticeships. Financial support is provided for the costs of training. Apprenticeships are available to both new and existing employees and for both young and mature learners. They normally last 12 months and lead to a level 2 NVQ. A variant is Advanced Apprenticeships, which last for two years and lead to a level 3 NVQ. The 2009 Act will create a statutory framework for apprenticeships and also a statutory right to an apprenticeship place for all suitably qualified 16- to 18-year-olds.

- **Foundation degrees**
  Foundation degrees are designed in conjunction with employers but validated and delivered in partnership with a university. They are part of the strategy to develop intermediate and higher-level skills and again are available to new

or existing employees, and indeed non-employed individuals, and learners of any age. They have now largely replaced HND and HNC qualifications. A key characteristic of foundation degrees is that they must develop a range of skills including vocational, key and generic (sometimes known as transferable) as well as academic knowledge and skills. There must be engagement with employers to provide experience of application in work. Their purpose, though, is also linked to achieving a government target of 50 per cent of young people entering higher education. They also facilitate links into honours degrees, as did the 'old' HNDs and HNCs.

Train to Gain

This scheme has grown out of what was previously known as Employer Training Programmes and Employer Training Pilots. The scheme initially provided advice, guidance and a brokerage service to only small firms but has been available to all employers from August 2006. The service aims to help organisations accurately assess their needs and to match with appropriate providers and to facilitate access to government-subsidised programmes and qualifications, including some that are free to employers.

Qualifications framework

One role of the QCA (QCDA from 2010 under the 2009 Act) is to produce and operate a qualifications framework. This has actually been in existence since the days of the NCVQ but has been amended and updated by the QCA. There are in fact three different and separate frameworks currently in existence in the UK: the National Qualifications Framework (NQF) is the main one and has nine levels, from entry level to level 8, which covers specialist awards. While the QCA approves and regulates many qualifications and awarding bodies, it does not cover awards made by universities. These are covered, but not directly regulated, since universities are independent bodies, by the Quality Assurance Agency (QAA). The framework of higher education awards, though, is consistent with the QCA National Framework and the latter shows how university awards compare in terms of level with vocational and professional qualifications. As an example, the CIPD professional qualification sits in the QCA framework at the same level as a university masters degree. The QCDA is developing the third framework, which is known as the Qualifications and Credit Framework (QCF). The work of the QCDA and especially its qualifications framework could be said to contribute to lessening the status problem of vocational versus academic qualifications. The same might be said of foundation degrees.

Skills accounts

A major policy aim for a number of years has been to create 'a demand led' VET system. There is debate and argument about what that means, but one prevalent view is that employers and individual citizens are those who 'demand' VET and so should have a greater say in what is 'supplied'. Skills accounts, which are currently being piloted, are aimed at achieving a greater say for individuals through giving them control over some funding to meet personal needs and aspirations. There is also a link here with a statutory right to 'time to train' in the

2009 Act. However, as designed and operated in the pilot programme, the actual control individual citizens who qualify for an account will have over resources, ie money, is very limited. This is probably related to the controversy over and failure of an earlier similar scheme known as Individual Learning Accounts.

The various organisations and agencies mentioned in the illustration above, and the new bodies being created by the 2009 Act, also of course constitute part of the current skills strategy and VET system. Their role is primarily about delivery of policy and targets. There is, though, a long way to go in solving the problems identified in 1884. For example, a recent report for HM Treasury by Lord Leitch has indicated among other things that:

- More than one-third of adults of working age do not have basic school-leaving qualifications.

- Five million adults have no qualifications at all.

- Nearly 20 per cent of adults lack the literacy skills expected of an 11-year-old.

- Half of all adults do not have equivalent levels of functional numeracy.

- The UK skills levels still compare badly with international competitor nation: the UK is ranked 24th out of 29 nations on the proportion of young people staying in education after 16.

Additional research by the government found that the majority of UK employers believed skills shortages are a greater threat to business performance than falling consumer demand. Over a third of employers, though, also reported that they are not involved in any form of vocational training for their workforce and so perhaps illustrating a continuing problem in UK VET, based again, perhaps, on the 'public good' problem. A National Employer Skills Survey by the LSC gave similar cause for concern. It found that 16 per cent of employers had staff believed to be less than fully proficient for their jobs. Put in a different way, 1.3 million workers, or 6 per cent of the national workforce, are not skilled enough for their jobs. However, the same survey also found better news. The proportion of employers reporting skills shortages fell for the second year in succession, as did the proportion reporting 'hard to fill' vacancies. Research and surveys such as these, though, are not entirely reliable. For example, the LSC survey shows that the total expenditure on training by employers is £33.3 billion, which gives an average spend per employee of £1550. The CIPD Learning and Development Survey of the same year found an average spend of £488. This is a significant difference, which illustrates the difficulty of obtaining accurate and reliable data. However, the LSC survey does suggest some progress in raising the quality of VET and raising skills in the UK.

This examination of UK VET nearly brings the chapter to a close. The next section will provide a brief account of practice in some other countries and the final section will try to identify the main conclusions and implications for learning and talent development practice and practitioners.

ACTIVITY

Establish to what extent if any learning and talent development practice in your organisation is influenced by government policy and programmes. Identify whether there are opportunities presented by government programmes that are open to your organisation that are currently being ignored.

SOME INTERNATIONAL COMPARISONS

As illustrated in the quote at the start and others elsewhere in this chapter, the UK VET system and approach to NHRD is often compared with policy and practice in other countries. These comparisons are often unfavourable, which might be one reason why the details of initiatives, institutions and programmes change on a regular basis. A research project conducted in 2007/2008 for the LSC, called World Class Comparisons, is an example of the UK attempting to improve NHRD through learning lessons from other countries. However, the project reached two conclusions among others which question the conventional wisdom that the UK approach needs to adopt lessons from elsewhere in the world. The first was that all NHRD is context-specific and reflects national and cultural traditions and histories. That being the case, it is difficult and probably of limited value to attempt to transfer policy and practice from one setting to another. The second conclusion was that stability and continuity in policy and practice can be a key part of the explanation of why a particular approach to NHRD is successful. A good example of both of these points is the German 'dual system'. This is based on a shared responsibility for and provision of preparation for qualifications in technical and vocational occupations. Trainees attend what are termed vocational schools while they are also placed with employers, where they receive training and supervised practice. They spend about 50 per cent of their time in class and about 50 per cent with the employer for periods of between two and four years, depending on the qualification and occupation they are working towards. However, Germany has a long and settled history of a state-sponsored and directed corporate approach to VET, and so the dual system reflects and is successful in part because of that tradition.

Germany continues to operate the dual system, which was formalised in federal law in 1969 but which has its roots in the nineteenth century. While not revising the dual system Germany has more recently turned attention to three other matters in response to European-level developments. These are: increased emphasis on vocational and career guidance, development of a national qualification framework, and improving the responsiveness of providers, courses and qualifications to changing demands in the labour market. The illustration below summarises a number of other examples of approaches to NHRD/VET in three other countries.

ILLUSTRATION

Some international comparisons

Czech Republic

As a post-Communist country and relatively new member of the EU, NHRD here is heavily influenced by policy and practice in the longer-established members of the EU. One interesting feature of the Czech Republic is one of the highest rates in the EU of youth participation in post-compulsory education and training. This reflects a cultural and long-established value placed on education. The VET system is being reformed currently, with many elements being modelled on practice in the UK and EU guidance. These include: a national qualifications framework, a centrally determined curriculum with high employer involvement, regional and sector agencies being established, separation of teaching/training and assessment/accreditation of qualifications, and agencies established to provide career information and advice.

California

States in the USA have a high degree of autonomy in relation to VET, and policy and practice vary. California is the most populous state and is widely seen as one of the most successful in adapting to new industries and changing demands for VET. Reflecting the general approach in the USA, California adopts an approach of voluntarism, with individuals and employers being major funders of VET, and so the system can also be characterised as demand led. However, part of the success of the system in recent years is due to more intervention by the state government and its agencies. These include a Post Secondary Education Commission and a Master Plan for Education, both of which have operated since 1974. A state Workforce Investment Board was established along with 50 local Boards in 1998, with the remit to analyse local labour markets, identify VET providers and monitor the effectiveness of VET. An Employment Training Panel funded by an 'employment training tax' was introduced in 1983 to provide work-based customised training to new and established employees facing risks because of high competition in product markets. California also benefits from one of the largest networks of community colleges in the USA; these are education institutions with some similarities to FE colleges in the UK.

Australia

Australia experienced high youth unemployment in the early 1990s, associated in part with a decline in the apprenticeship system. The response has some commonality with that of the EU in aiming to develop a high-skills economy based on knowledge-intensive industries. To accommodate both young people and adults there has been a re-emphasis on apprenticeships, opened up to adults, and a new emphasis on recognition of prior learning. This latter is also a feature of EU and UK policy. A new approach to NHRD has been developed based on Training Packages (TP) which define competence standards, assurance of these by the Australian Quality Training Framework, delivery of courses by approved Registered Training Organisations and finally a single system of qualifications embodied in the Australian Qualifications Framework. The number of apprentices and trainees is now four times the number in the early 1990s. Apprenticeships are coordinated by Australian Apprenticeship Centres, who work closely with employers to market and promote apprenticeship places.

ACTIVITY

Compare and contrast the approaches in the international examples with that of the UK. What are the differences and similarities? What elements from elsewhere do you think the UK could adopt and why?

Discuss your answers with student or work colleagues. Identify areas of agreement and disagreement and the reasons for these. See if you can reach consensus on one change to the UK approach and system.

IMPLICATIONS

One implication of the content of this chapter not yet mentioned is the changing form of organisations. An important example is that of multinational corporations (MNCs), which are primarily attributed as being both a cause and an effect of globalisation. In many cases MNCs have greater influence and impact than national governments on the lives and experience of individuals. This is related to size as well as international and global reach. As an illustration, Wal-Mart, the American retailer, employs 1.25 million people worldwide and has a business turnover of US $275 billion. This is larger in population than some countries and larger money size than the gross domestic product of many countries. It is the power and influence of MNCs and their role in globalisation that provided part of the impetus for the World Commission mentioned earlier. But they are not the only new form. Strategic alliances are also now more common. The One World and Star Alliances in the air transport industry are a good illustration of this and so too are the many alliances in, for example, car manufacturing. Indeed, a variant of strategic alliances which likens organisations to battle fleets, with a large 'aircraft carrier' surrounded by and in mutually dependent relationship with a flotilla of many smaller 'vessels', is argued by some to be the future of work organisations. The implication here is that work teams could have many different employers even though they have shared objectives and tasks.

A second implication is change management. This chapter has demonstrated that product and labour markets are experiencing significant change and this will affect all organisations irrespective of size or form. Significant change is argued to now be continuous and so managing change is a full-time part of the job for all managers. But, since the major changes are to do with the size, composition, location, attitudes and aspirations of global, national and local populations, then HR professionals have to manage change in learning and talent development policy and practice. Populations provide, indeed constitute, both product and labour markets. Learning and talent development professionals therefore have a significant contribution to make to managing business and organisation change, since understanding from one perspective and for one purpose can be applied in others. Since learning and talent development has to understand the nature and changing dynamics of labour markets for learning and talent development purposes, they can benefit other business managers with that understanding. There are, though, two more specific learning and talent development contributions. Change implies learning and successful change management always requires learning. Learning and talent development specialists therefore have much to contribute to change management. Second, the significant shift in trade and the associated ambitions of the EU, for example, imply growth in knowledge-intensive work in Western countries, including the UK. There is an established and accepted connection between knowledge creation, sharing and exploitation and learning. This provides additional opportunities for contributions from learning and talent development specialists.

A third implication arises from some of these dynamic changes. Populations are becoming more diverse and so, therefore, are labour markets. Workforces in organisations already reflect this and will do so more and more in the future. Diversity will manifest itself in more diverse and probably new ways as well. Free movement of labour, for example, will bring more citizens of members of the EU to work in the UK and that membership itself is also increasing. While the UK and work organisations in it have long experience of dealing with migrant labour, this has in the past been primarily from Commonwealth countries which had some connection with the UK. Different locations and countries will provide a growing proportion of migrant labour in the future, and their connection and relationship with the UK is very different; so too will be their expectations.

A final implication is the rise and spread of ICT. This does and will have implications for the design of work and the form of employment contracts, both legal and psychological. The rise of 'virtual teams', for example, is already well established as a form of work organisation, and how these function and need to be managed is subject to much research interest. Many employers have direct experience of outsourcing and offshoring, but this is not the same as virtual working and virtual teams. Learning and talent development will have significant contributions to make to maximising the opportunities presented by ICT in developing managers and teams working in these new and virtual environments. Additional opportunities are presented by ICT as a delivery mechanism through e-learning and blended learning. The EU is spending significant amounts on researching, supporting and facilitating the use of e-learning as part of the EES and is a good source of advice and guidance.

The advice to close this chapter is to return to the start and the relevance of the content of the chapter. The external environment is the source of many implications for HR practice and for learning and talent development. These present many opportunities and threats. An effective professional has good knowledge and understanding of these. The advice, therefore, is to utilise the analytical framework used in this chapter on a regular basis to focus on the specific threats and opportunities facing the particular context and organisation where you work.

SUMMARY

This chapter has described and explained a range of external factors that affect the practice of learning and talent development in all organisations. These factors are a mix of general trends and specific responses by supra-national and national institutions. The specific responses of most relevance to learning and talent development are those focused on NHRD and VET policy. While policy can and does vary over time and from government to government, or even by the same government over a limited time scale, policy does tend to pursue the same purpose and objective, and many of the policy initiatives, interventions and institutions created to achieve the policy purpose are markedly similar. This seems to be irrespective of political differences between governments and suggests a high degree of consensus on both ends and means.

The chapter has illustrated how the notions of globalisation and of McDonaldisation are useful in analysing and understanding global trends, and how the analytical tool of STEP analysis is also useful in identifying, getting to grips with and sorting out the complex range of factors that all organisations have to contend with if they are to survive and prosper in both product and labour markets. An important point made is that such tools are simply devices and abstractions and so do not represent reality. This is important because none of the factors identified or highlighted by the concepts and tools act independently. For example, the chapter introduced globalisation as a contested concept; some argue it exists and some that it doesn't. We would argue that it doesn't exist in one important sense: it is a term and idea invented by humans to help explain and understand phenomena, and so 'globalisation' as such has no existence independent of the idea and term invented by humans.

There are a number of implications for work organisations and so for learning and talent development practice and practitioners that arise from the international and national context. In addition to limitations and opportunities presented by national VET policy, these implications include:

- changing organisation forms
- change management
- increasingly diverse populations
- ubiquity and role of ICT.

Effective learning and talent development professionals need to understand and respond to these and other implications.

REVIEW ACTIVITIES

1. Summarise five key things you have learnt from this chapter.

   a. Write down two or three new questions the chapter has raised for you or things that you are unclear about.

   b. Select one of these questions that you will enquire into further.

   c. Write down what action you can take next in pursuit of your question. (For example: read one of the references in this chapter, talk to someone more experienced at work, look on the CIPD website, take time to reflect on your own experience.)

2. List five characteristics that arise from global trends which might apply to any local labour market.

   a. Discuss the results with colleagues and compare the similarities and differences of your lists.

   b. Discuss the implications for learning and talent development practice.

3. Research current government initiatives and programmes and identify one your organisation is not currently engaged with.

   a. Discuss with a senior learning and talent development professional why not.

   b. Analyse the pros and cons of becoming engaged.

   c. Hold another discussion with the same person.

4. Visit the suggested websites and decide which you will check regularly.

EXTENDED CASE STUDY + DISCUSSION QUESTIONS

SMITHERS AND JONES

CASE STUDY

Smithers and Jones is a long-established and family-owned chain of department stores. The company owns and operates six stores in city centre locations across East Anglia and the South East of England. Products are aimed at middle- to high-income families and include a broad range of household goods, including furniture, 'white' and 'brown' goods, haberdashery and kitchenware. Other departments provide clothing for all members of the family, as well as mother and baby products, health and beauty, and sports and leisure goods. Some departments, for example, fashion and beauty, include concessions where space is rented to manufacturers who are responsible for their own merchandising and employees. The company stands or falls on its reputation for high-quality merchandise, fair prices and excellent customer service. While there

have been periods of challenge in the 75 years since the first store was established, recent history suggest that these qualities are still valued by customers. Despite the intensification of competition illustrated by the growth of 'out of town' retailing, of specialist retailers, of giant shopping centres and of Internet shopping, Smithers and Jones continues to prosper. The previous five years have seen steady increases in sales turnover and in profits, and the current year is set to continue that trend.

There is a head office with the usual functions located in the original and still largest store. Each store, though, still has a relatively high degree of independence but operates a common structure. This comprises a general manager at the top, with a series of department and functional heads managing operations. Functional heads include a store personnel manager who reports to the general manager but with a 'dotted line' relationship with the services director on the main board. This director is located within head office and has responsibilities additional to personnel. Each store also has a training and development officer who reports to the store personnel manager but who also has a 'dotted line' relationship with a group management development manager at head office, who reports to the services director.

This apparently confusing structure is perfectly clear to Clare Hill. Clare has worked at Smithers and Jones since leaving school 15 years ago, initially as a management trainee, which means that Clare has experience of most of the stores' operations. Her career has included six years as a department manager in three different departments at two different stores before her current appointment as store training and development officer four years ago to achieve her ambition of working in personnel rather than store management. Having recently completed her CIPD qualification, Clare expects another promotion soon to a generalist personnel role, either in a store or at head office. She has no real desire to leave Smithers and Jones as long as her career ambitions can be satisfied.

Clare's current concern is with rising labour turnover and absence among sales staff in her store. This is particularly marked among younger and junior staff across all departments. Apart from these figures Clare has also been receiving increasing numbers of complaints from senior sales staff, supervisors and department managers about the behaviour and performance of junior staff. Clare provides induction and initial training of new staff following the recruitment by department managers who are supported in that task by the store personnel manager. The training provided by Clare consists of four half-day formal sessions for induction in the first

two weeks of employment, followed by a structured series of five one-day courses and on-the-job modules delivered by Clare and supervisors over the first six months of employment. With more than 800 staff and the traditional high labour turnover in retail, this training forms a substantial part of Clare's job. Clare has made what she considers to be improvements in this training and had previously seen some improvements in labour turnover. However, Clare has also thought for some time that a radical rethink and redesign is required and, while she is not yet sure of the cause of the recent problems with junior staff, Clare senses an opportunity to persuade others of her view.

Clare is aware from her CIPD studies of various government-supported initiatives such as apprenticeships and Train to Gain, and recently met and talked with someone from Business Link at a CIPD branch event. This has set her thinking about the potential value of NVQs at levels 2 and 3 in retailing and 3 and 4 in management for store employees. The former would be relevant to initial training and levels 3 and 4 for career development. The CIPD event was about new developments in IIP accreditation, and that too seems to Clare to present potential opportunities and benefits. Use of NVQs in retailing would be in the store's remit to decide, although Clare would need the support of her personnel manager and agreement from the general manager. Use of management NVQs would have to be approved for company-wide use by the head of management development and the services director.

Discussion Questions

1. In what ways is Smithers and Jones as a business being influenced by the external environment?

2. How useful and in what ways will STEP analysis be to the business and to Clare Hill?

3. What advice would you give to Clare to help her investigations of the potential of NVQs?

4. What relevance, if any, will NVQs have to the current problems with younger and junior employees?

5. What relevance and value, if any, will NVQs in management have to the company?

EXPLORE FURTHER

This topic is ever changing and so it is difficult to provide definitive suggestions. The references below provide some guidance on texts dealing with general issues such as globalisation and some have regular new editions – Dicken's book, for example, which should be accessed rather than the edition cited here. Of most relevance, though, are research reports published by research organisations and by governments and other agencies. So the websites listed below need to be regularly checked for the latest data, information and policy statements.

Books

CIPD (2002) *Training in the Knowledge Economy*. London: CIPD.

Dicken, P. (2004) *Global Shift: Reshaping the Global Economic Map in the 21st Century*. London: Sage Publications.

Giddens, A. (1989) *Sociology*. Cambridge: Polity Press.

Hofstede, G. (1991) *Cultures and Organisations*. London: HarperCollins.

International Labour Office (2005) *World Employment Report 2004–2005: Employment, productivity and poverty reduction*. Geneva: International Labour Organisation.

Marsh, P. (2005) *The Noughties Report*. London: Social Issues Research Centre/Egg PLC.

National Statistics Office (2006) *Social Trends No. 36*. London.

Ritzer, G. (2004) *The MacDonaldisation of Society*. London: Sage Publications.

Robertson, R. (1992) *Globalisation*. London: Sage Publications.

Shaw, F. *et al* (2007) *Thomson Future Forum: Holiday 2016*. London: Thomson PLC.

Stewart, J. (1999) *Employee Development Practice*. London: FT Pitman Publishing.

Journals

Winterton, J. (ed). (2009) European approaches to competence. *Journal of European Industrial Training*. Vol. 33, Issue 8/9.

Websites

www.direct.gov.uk.

www.ilo.org/.

http://europa.eu/.

www.sirc.org.

CHAPTER 4

Various and Varying Organisation Contexts

OVERVIEW

This chapter is concerned with the strategic role and contribution of learning and talent development to organisation success. The interactive and iterative relationship between organisation strategy, culture, structure and objectives, and how these emerge, are designed and formulated will be examined. So too will the interplay of learning and talent development with strategic human resource management. The nature, content, purpose and contribution of learning and talent development programmes and processes to organisation strategies will be also reviewed. Core terms for this chapter include:

- deliberate strategy
- emergent strategy
- resource-based strategy
- competitive strategy
- co-operative strategy
- culture
- strategic learning and talent development
- strategic human resource management

LEARNING OUTCOMES

After reading this chapter and completing the activities, the intention is that you will be able to:

- explain how learning and talent development can both contribute to and follow from organisation strategies
- appraise options for learning and talent development interventions depending on different corporate strategies

- identify connections between learning and talent development and strategic HRM
- develop a practical understanding of the interactive, dynamic and iterative relationships between organisation strategy, structure, culture and learning and talent development
- explain the meaning of strategic HRD (sHRD) and strategic learning and talent development.

PERSPECTIVES ON STRATEGY-MAKING

All work organisations exist for the purpose of organising people, materials, investments and other resources in ways that produce outputs such as products and services, and achieve outcomes such as return on investment or quality of life (Watson 2006). Strategy is concerned with the purpose, direction and performance of an organisation. Deliberate strategy is the intended direction, as planned by controlling organisation members (such as owners, chief executive, senior management team or board of directors). Deliberate, intended or planned strategy is typically laid out under the staged headings shown in Figure 4.1.

Figure 4.1 Stages of deliberate strategic planning

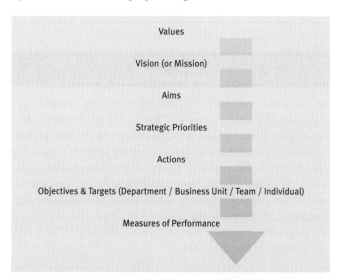

Values

Vision (or Mission)

Aims

Strategic Priorities

Actions

Objectives & Targets (Department / Business Unit / Team / Individual)

Measures of Performance

ACTIVITY

Get hold of the strategic plan for a company. This could be where you work or one you can access through the Internet. Observe how their intended strategy is laid out.

Compare notes with others in your class.

Many organisations adopt the stages shown in Figure 4.1 for their own strategic planning. However, many people argue (eg Mintzberg *et al* 2003; Watson 2006) that in reality strategy is better understood as emergent – as an evolving direction, when planned strategies are thrown off course by interference inflicted by factors in an organisation's environment, such as rising costs, declining markets, volcanic ash clouds, competition or unavailability of skills. Watson (2006) argues that all organisational strategies are better understood as emergent, combining at least some planning with incrementalism and experimentation.

DELIBERATE AND EMERGENT STRATEGY

CASE STUDY

In March 2008 AOL paid $850 million to acquire Bebo, the first social networking site popular with young people. As the first such site, Bebo had an advantage over its competitors. Strategically the acquisition bought AOL learning about social networking technologies and practices and gave entry into the youth market. This could be described as its planned, or deliberate strategy.

However, within a year Facebook had entered the market and established itself as a popular, entertaining, innovative social networking site. Bebo's popularity has dropped to a third in Britain over 2008–10 and in 2009 it made a loss. Far from achieving its intended strategic objectives, the strategy that has emerged for AOL in 2010 is one of exit – sell at almost any price to cut its losses.

Source: *Management Today*, May 2010, p15

STRATEGY, RESOURCES AND RESOURCEFULNESS – THE STRATEGIC ROLE OF HUMAN RESOURCING

Decisions and practices involved in attracting, recruiting, rewarding, engaging and developing, even departing from, employees are fundamental to an organisation's success. These are the activities affecting the employment relationship that are characterised as HRM (human resource management). They affect the extent to which the resourcefulness of employees is brought out to the full. They contribute to an organisation's capacity to grow, compete and adapt and they are central to the employer brand. When HRM activities are aligned with organisation strategy, so 'enabling the utilising of employee efforts and capabilities to bring about long-term organisational survival' (Watson 2006, p407), this is understood as strategic HRM (sHRM).

A common question within organisations is 'whose responsibility is HRM?' In practice this varies, particularly with the size of organisations. The breadth of roles is typically shared, with line managers leading on some of the attracting, recruiting and development decisions, and some roles are often outsourced, for example payroll, training and aspects of employee welfare. Perhaps the greatest source of variation between organisations is the role played by HR professionals and the extent to which HR is explicitly recognised as playing a strategic role. Ulrich's model of potential HR roles (Ulrich 1997) provides a useful framework for thinking about the extent to which HR is focused strategically or operationally and the balance of focus on people and business processes.

The underlying logic of HRM is to obtain a return from the employment of labour (Watson 2006). Ulrich's model offers a way of conceptualising the role that HR specialists can play in organisations so that HR practices are both aligned to customer needs and focused on building organisational capabilities:

a. Employee champion – employee advocate + human resource developer

b. Strategic partner – business partner

c. Administrative expert – incremental improvements, shared services

d. Change agent – transformational role.

To be strategic HR activities are not only internally aligned with each other, but are also externally aligned with the organisation's strategic direction.

Where the role of HR, in Ulrich's terms, is strategic partner or change agent, HR interventions may well be driving strategy. Ways in which learning and talent development can contribute strategically will be explored in the following discussion.

 ACTIVITY

Alignment of HR activities with corporate strategy

For an organisation with which you are familiar, talk to either the lead HR person or a line manager and use Ulrich's model to identify which role HR specialists play in the organisation.

Having introduced some generic ideas about strategy-making, the structure of the remainder of this chapter will follow the framework shown in Figure 4.2. The issues will be examined through three perspectives on strategy – competitive, co-operative and process-relational – each of which will be explained and linked to questions of structure and culture, with illustrations across the private, public and third sectors. This will be followed by consideration of how learning and talent development can contribute differently to different strategic approaches as well as the integration with other human resourcing interventions such as recruitment, reward, performance, engagement and redundancy, that together might be termed 'strategic human resource management' (sHRM).

Figure 4.2 Framework for the chapter

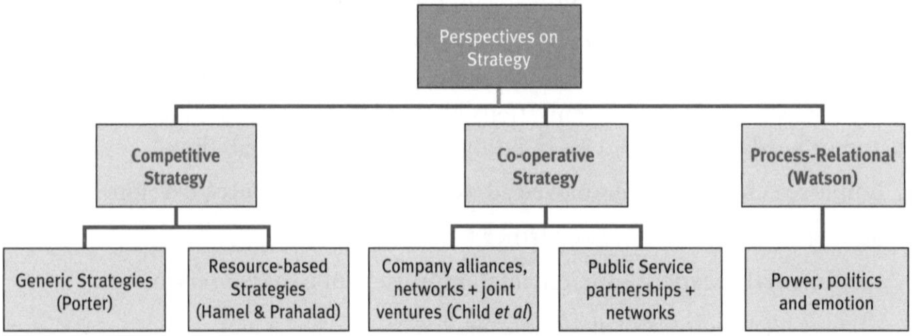

COMMERCIAL STRATEGY

Child *et al* (2005) distinguish between competitive strategy and co-operative strategy, when talking of commercial companies.

COMPETITIVE STRATEGY

This is the question of how a company acts to gain advantage over a competitor, for example, to win market share, to secure major customers, to position themselves to be first to enter emerging international markets. Competitive strategy has two main traditions of thought. The first is the positioning view, attributed to Michael Porter (1980, 1985), who has been particularly influential in focusing attention on the generic competitive strategies a company could pursue to position itself and its products within its particular industry. His argument is that companies must choose whether to compete through leading on cost, differentiation or focus on a specific niche. Porter's approach to strategy formulation is concerned with the relative position of a firm in a specific industry. That is, it starts by analysis of a company or a particular product's external market environment, in terms of the five forces of competitors, suppliers, power of buyers, ease of entry into the market and intensity of competition. From this analysis of the opportunities and threats within a market, the approach is to assess what generic strategy is optimal to maximise the company or product's competitive positioning and therefore its performance. It is not that company resources are ignored in the positioning approach, rather that they are seen as secondary to environmental analysis.

Learning and talent development would be expected to trickle down from the positioning strategy decided upon. This would be consistent with a manpower or workforce planning approach, as in the example below.

CASE STUDY

CASE STUDY OF COMPETITIVE POSITIONING

Learning and talent development to support a cost reduction strategy

In a company with a low skilled workforce, where employer branding is not considered significant because the company does not have to compete for talent, training is typically seen as a cost not an investment.

A corporate strategy of cost reduction will commonly result in a learning and talent development strategy that cuts investment in training to a minimum and focuses on absolute priorities such as health and safety training to ensure the company remains legally compliant.

A second tradition of competitive strategy is the *resource-based* view, associated with Penrose 1959, Kay 1993, and Hamel and Prahalad 1994. Here the starting point is consideration of a company's internal resources, with the argument that competitive strategy is advanced by development of strong, distinctive internal resources such as technology, intellectual property, capital, supply chain management, employee skills and capabilities, including knowledge management. Formulation of strategy is driven by assessment of internal capabilities and how these can be used to innovate, compete and outperform rivals. The argument made by Hamel and Prahalad (1994) is that competitive strategy comes from providing solutions for customers through developing products or services they might not have anticipated. This means constantly pushing at the boundaries of technology, design and international borders. This requires an enduring requirement for talent renewal and a permanent state of learning and development, what might be termed an *innovation culture*, as will be explained further later in the chapter.

It should be clear that learning and talent development are central to a resource-based view in that a company's internal resources, in addition to physical and financial resources, include both employees' individual resourcefulness, such as their specialist skills and tacit knowledge, as well as collective aspects, such as organisation routines, culture and reputation. Individual and collective attributes can work interactively, so for example, highly skilled employees in an IT company such as Google or Intel, with a culture of high innovation, also contribute to a high rate of intellectual property products such as patents or copyrights, on which the company's ongoing success will depend. A distinctive capability (or what Prahalad and Hamel, 1990, term 'core competency') becomes a strategic capability when it is a feature that competitors cannot readily imitate. For Kay (1993) these difficult-to-copy capabilities derive from stakeholder relationships, what he categorises as architecture, reputation and innovation. Examples of external architecture include customer trust and knowledge, whilst internal architecture would include the collective cultural abilities to handle complexity and work with diversity, for example with suppliers and a workforce straddling across multiple countries and time zones. Reputation describes the relationship with customers, suppliers, shareholders, investors, and prospective employees. Reputation guides customer choices; a reputation for solving problems and sustained customer care may attract a premium price; trust will buy leeway with investors in hard financial times; a strong employer brand will attract the best talent. An innovative culture is another example of internal architecture. And innovation, through continuous creation of new products as well as product or process modification is the source of competitive advantage for many Silicon Valley firms, such as Facebook, Apple, Cisco and Google.

From a resource-based view of competitive strategy, the contribution of learning and talent development is central, because it is not only fundamental to developing individual skills, but also to influencing organisation routines and behaviours, from induction through to performance appraisal.

 ACTIVITY

For an organisation with which you are familiar, collect data on the following:

- What capabilities does the organisation have that are difficult for competitors to copy?
- Which of these distinctive capabilities are connected to employees' skills or knowledge?
- Which of these distinctive capabilities are connected to employees' relationships with each others customers, suppliers or other stakeholders?
- Share your findings with others in the group.

CO-OPERATIVE STRATEGY

Co-operative strategy is a second approach commercial companies might adopt, although, as we will discuss a little later in the chapter, co-operation is also central to public service strategies. Child *et al* (2005, p3) suggest that co-operative strategy is not really an alternative to competitive strategy, rather it is another 'domain of policy options' concerned with 'the configuration and constitution of actual and potential alliances'.

 ILLUSTRATION

Definition

Co-operative strategy: '*the achievement of an agreement and a plan to work together*' (Child et al 2005, p7).

Collaboration between commercial companies will often combine co-operation alongside competition, in varying combinations, so-called *co-ompetition*. Also the balance of co-operation–competition is commonly dynamic and varying over time (see Airline Industry case study). Co-operative arrangements can be adopted for varying reasons, which are explored in the next section, and can take various forms:

- joint venture

- consortium
- network
- outsourced organisation
- partnership
- franchise.

However, whatever the form or rationale, skill, knowledge and learning are central to all, which means learning and talent development practitioners can play a significant, strategic role in maximising such learning and knowledge exchange both through specific learning interventions, and also more broadly though stimulating institutional conditions that are fertile for such exchange.

> ### FOLLOW UP
>
> Discussion of forms of co-operative arrangements relates to the question of organisation structure. See section on strategy, structure, culture later in this chapter.

WHY COMPANIES CO-OPERATE

Companies co-operate in the range of forms of strategic alliance for a number of reasons, which can include the following:

- to enter new markets that they could not enter alone. For example, in India legislation requires that an international company entering many sectors, such as retail, can only do so by co-operating with one or more Indian companies, in a form in which the domestic company (or companies) is the majority partner;
- to enter markets that are unfamiliar, where a local partner can be learned from;
- to acquire skills and technology;
- to acquire capabilities, for example, an existing supply chain or IP (intellectual property);
- for mutual learning, for example, sharing R&D;
- to spread risk;
- to eliminate competition and help shape the market;
- to achieve economies of scale.

CHANGING COMBINATIONS OF COMPETITION AND COLLABORATION IN THE AIRLINES INDUSTRY

United Airlines was for many years a competitor of Continental Airlines, as well as co-operating as members of the Star Alliance, a network of airlines that allowed the sharing of routes and enabled a degree of risk-sharing.

In April 2010, the two airlines announced a complete merger.

STRATEGY IN THE PUBLIC AND THIRD SECTORS

ACTIVITY

Look up the websites of two different public and third sector organisations and find their strategic plans such as mission values, strategic priorities, and goals or objectives (use framework from the first activity in this chapter).

In what ways are these similar and in what ways different compared to the intended strategy of the commercial company that you looked into for the first activity of the chapter?

Chapter 2 explored some of the range of kinds and activities of public and third sector organisations. Primarily they exist for the purpose of improving the quality of people's lives, usually through providing or commissioning services. Few services are entirely free and clearly citizens pay for public services through national and local taxes. Often there is also direct payment exchanged for services, for example, when we use public swimming baths, go to a theatre, rent social housing, live in a public residential home or pick up medical prescriptions. Certain services provided by public services, for example, housing, residential care, education and medical care, are also provided by private companies to some sections of the public. For example, most people who can afford to buy their own home will. Many people who can afford to do so take out private medical insurance in the hope that it will buy them, if not better medical care, at least faster attention in more hotel-like facilities. Publicly provided services are often not charged at their commercial cost, on the grounds that they would not then be widely afforded so could not be made available to the entire public on a commercial basis and it is deemed in the public interest that they be publicly funded from taxes. Public services may also be provided by commercial companies. For example, many British local authorities procure the services of private companies to run the weekly waste collection for residents, or to clean civic buildings. Increasingly local authorities do not directly run their own residential homes, but commission the service from private or third sector providers.

All this is presented to illustrate how strategy-making in public services can be both complex, and in many ways similar to that in the private sector. So whilst competition between local authorities or between, say, the police and army, is not advocated in the same way as between private companies, competitive strategy, as discussed earlier in the chapter, certainly comes into public services as private and third sector organisations compete for contracts with public bodies. And more so than competitive strategy, co-operative strategy is fundamental to public sector and third sector organisations, as assessed in the next section.

CO-OPERATIVE STRATEGY IN PUBLIC SERVICES

Collaboration in public services has many similarities to co-operation for commercial ends, though there are some important distinctions. Of the various forms of collaborative discussed above in the private sector, those in public services are most commonly partnerships or networks and contractual outsourcing.

 ILLUSTRATION

Forms of public service co-operation

Public service co-operative arrangements exhibit a variety of forms and sizes, most commonly:

- Partnerships – two or more autonomous organisations agree to work together to achieve shared objectives, accepting that in order to do so they have to concede some power and influence over decisions (Sullivan and Skelcher 2002).
- Networks are organised on a non-hierarchical basis on common issues, and usually continue to operate only while participants perceive a need to exist (Taket and White 2000).
- Contractual outsourcing – formal, specific and legally binding agreements where one organisation delivers a service on behalf of another organisation, such as the delivery of residential care for adults by a private or not-for-profit contractor.

WHY PUBLIC SERVICE BODIES CO-OPERATE

Badrach (1998) has joked that collaboration between government agencies is an unnatural act committed by non-consenting adults.

Certainly one key distinction for the rationale behind co-operative strategy in the public sector compared with commercial collaborations is it is often driven by central government through making funding contingent on some kind of multi-agency co-operation. However, even alongside such coercion, many working within public bodies recognise that society is riven with a host of complex problems and issues, such as poverty and social exclusion, urban decay, drug use, obesity, teenage pregnancy, an ageing population with multiple needs and community safety, which cut across organisational boundaries and defy the expertise, resources or efforts of any one organisation to resolve them working alone. These are the so-called 'wicked' issues (Conklin 2005) or 'messes' (Trist 1983) that require the efforts of a collaborative process.

So, often public service organisations adopt a co-operative strategy because their leaders recognise this will produce a better result for the clients/customers or citizens. Chris Huxham (1996) describes this as the 'collaborative advantage' that can be achieved when an objective is met which would not be met if an agency worked on its own, and when each agency is able, through collaboration, to achieve its objectives better than it would alone.

Whilst collaborative strategy may at times be financially motivated, co-operation can also occur for efficiency reasons to avoid duplication and deliver services more efficiently (see the Shropshire County case study).

As with commercial co-operation, others again emphasise the learning benefits of inter-organisational networking:

> including being at the leading edge of information, having access to new ideas, gossip and happenings in other sectors, professions and organisations, and being able to seek support from and influence people in other organisations (Williams 2002, p118).

The extent of engagement between partners can also vary, from simply being information exchange, through to adjustment of members' activities, to resource sharing to full synergistic enhanced capacity (Rourke 2007) (see Figure 4.3 below).

Figure 4.3 Spectrum of inter-organisation collaboration in public service delivery

	Extent of collaboration			
	Networking	Co-ordinating	Co-operating	Collaborating
Activities				
Exchanging information for mutual benefit	X	X	X	X
Altering activities to achieve a common purpose		X	X	X
Sharing resources			X	X
Enhancing the capacity of partner(s) to achieve a common purpose				X

Source: Adapted from Rourke (2007)

Sullivan and Skelcher (2002) found that realistically organisations collaborate for a combination of strategic objectives, both political and economic. Companies judge the benefits of collaboration in terms of 'value creation', as we saw above. In public services an alternative concept is public value (Benington 2007), the notion that activity can contribute value to the public sphere in terms of three areas:

● **Economic value** – through generation of economic activity and employment

- **Social value** – through contributing to social capital, social cohesion and social relationships
- **Political value** – by stimulating and supporting democratic dialogue and active participation.

 CASE STUDY OF PUBLIC SERVICES STRATEGY-MAKING

CASE STUDY

Shropshire County

On 1 April 2009 a new local authority, Shropshire County, was formed from a merger of the previous Shropshire County Council and five district authorities. In brief the rationale was (i) to reduce costs overall, through streamlining back office costs and cutting down on tiers of management, and (ii) to improve the customer interface with integration of finance and IT systems.

The purpose of the new unitary council is expressed in its vision and statement of top priorities.

Vision:

To improve significantly the quality of life for Shropshire people by working together (Shropshire Corporate Plan 2009–13, p5).

Top priorities:

Our top priorities show how important it is to us that we support the most vulnerable people in our society, that we deliver our services in ways which Shropshire people tell us best meet their needs and that we respect and care for Shropshire's environment (Shropshire Corporate Plan 2009–13, p6).

Three of the five district councils initially opposed the merger and supported a legal challenge (judicial review) to the merger plan. Ultimately this legal case was unsuccessful, after which a number of the district council chief executives began to leave. Regardless of their performance historically, all existing senior managers had to reapply for the new senior management team positions. As people took up posts in the new

structure, considerable emphasis was put on developing a single strong culture, with shared values and behaviours as a key element of creating and maintaining robust performance, through developing a statement of values and running an organisation development programme with top managers. The arrangement of elected councillors also changed, with the numbers overall reducing from over 300 to around 70. In May 2009, the newly elected Council contained many new, relatively inexperienced councillors and an unfamiliar range of functions, so new member training was also a priority.

Business case for unitary authority

The business case sets out the vision for the unitary council and highlights desired benefits to the people of Shropshire. These can be summarised as follows:

- strong visible strategic leadership
- strong voice for Shropshire
- local voice for Shropshire
- improved service delivery
- better customer access
- improved procurement
- financial savings.

Role of learning and talent development

During the merger period, the six Shropshire authorities committed to explore how joint working could be developed during the interim, including joint delivery of training, such as management programmes and design of induction programmes for the new unitary authority. Shropshire County Council opened up its existing Corporate Training Programme to all district council staff. New member training was designed for induction to Shropshire Council. A new management development programme was commissioned from an external provider to support the one-culture policy.

Source: www.shropshire.gov.uk, accessed 9 May 2010.

THE ROLE OF LEARNING AND TALENT DEVELOPMENT IN SUPPORTING COLLABORATIVE CAPACITY

The discussion so far has examined how in both commercial and public service collaborative alliances the motivations for co-operation can be understood in different ways. On the one hand they can be seen as a form of transaction, an exchange or sharing of resources that enables partners to match their own weaknesses with another's strengths or to buy access to resources, whether capital, technology, markets or other contacts. However, other motives concern the expectation that co-operation increases the potential for innovation and learning. Talking of inter-firm co-operation, Powell identifies that:

> sources of innovation do not reside exclusively inside firms; instead they are commonly found in the interstices between firms, universities, research laboratories, suppliers and customers (Powell *et al* 1996, p118).

The motive for companies to collaborate, even with competitors, lies in the recognition that it will be through such interactions that new learning will be produced and new ideas generated. The drivers for public service organisations are often similar. As such the drive to co-operate has particular relevance for learning and talent development.

Successful collaboration depends on how the alliance begins and how the collaborative partners are brought together (Sullivan and Skelcher 2002). Formation of collaborative relationships or alliances will always pass through certain stages (Child *et al* 2005), with a number of points that relate directly to learning and talent development as well as to wider HRM practices (see Figure 4.4).

Figure 4.4 Stages of co-operation

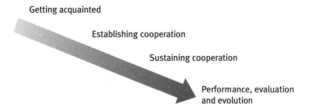

Getting acquainted

Establishing cooperation

Sustaining cooperation

Performance, evaluation and evolution

Time spent on the initial set-up is vital to the process (Pedler *et al* 2004). Trust, communication and understanding are central to forming and sustaining successful collaboration (Child *et al* 2005), which means that learning and talent development can make an impact in a number of ways:

1. Cultural audit – assessing the cultural match and variation between prospective partners

2. Skill audit – assessing the potential for a prospective collaborator to provide complementary or substitute skills; assessing the potential for learning and skills transfer

3. Expectations match – this entails a degree of similarity between partners' motives and intentions

4. Cross-cultural communication – identifying interventions to advance cross-cultural understanding and communication

5. Facilitating learning – with, from and between partners

6. Developing international managers

7. Management development of alliance managers

8. Supporting collaborative teams

9. Facilitating virtual teamwork.

The assumptions underlying such interventions relate back to underlying theories of organisation, as introduced in Chapter 2. When organisational thinking goes beyond seeing organisations simply as structures, there is recognition that interventions are required to promote collaborative processes and facilitate relationship-building.

Management development

So far in this chapter we have explored some of the main approaches to making strategy, and distinctions between competitive and co-operative strategy as they relate to the private, public and third sectors. Mention has been made of ways in which learning and talent development can impact strategically and how their role and contribution will vary depending on whether a company is emphasising a competitive compared to a co-operative approach to strategy.

Here we want to consider further the implications for management development of co-operative strategy. Research (Child 2005; Kanter 1994; Simonin 2002) indicates that collaborative working requires some distinctive management competences and that these are particularly heightened when co-operation crosses international entities and creates teams working virtually across time, organisational and geographical zones. Simonin (2002) terms this 'collaborative know-how'.

ILLUSTRATION

Management competences for co-operative working

In addition to general management capabilities:

Cultural sensitivity, both to diverse corporate cultures and national cultural differences (Kanter 1988).

Negotiation across social and cultural boundaries:

- ability to relate and align own views and preferences to others (sense-making)
- ability to reach shared understanding
- ability to commit – reaching acceptance and informal contract (Child *et al* 2005, p203).

Ability to maintain active co-operative relationships.

Dispute resolution with cultural awareness.

Adoption of a 'learning philosophy' (Child *et al* 2005, p211).

Facilitating learning in collaborative working

De Gues (1988) has suggested that the only competitive advantage a company will have is the managers' capacity to learn faster than those of its rivals. And this is even more so in a knowledge economy. Three levels of organisational learning are described by Child *et al* (2005, p273) and Argyris and Schön (1996): strategic (deutero), involving changes in mindsets; systemic (double loop), involving changes in organisation frameworks or systems, and technical (single loop), involving learning new techniques without changes to systems of mindsets. As with inter-professional learning (Ni Mhaolrúnaigh 2009), learning from co-operation can involve learning with, about and from partners.

STRATEGY AS PROCESS – RELATIONAL

So far in this chapter we have explored some of the main approaches to making strategy, and made distinctions between competitive and co-operative strategy as they relate to the private, public and third sectors. You will recall that competitive strategy can be positioning in response to the competitive environment or building competitive competence through cultivation of distinctive talent resources. Co-operative strategy was seen to be driven by a number of factors, including need to share resources and opportunities for learning. You will also recall at the beginning of the chapter we identified how strategy is best thought of as an emergent, experimental process, rather than an exercise in predictable planning for a certain environment.

Some observers suggest that strategy is best understood as the dynamic outcome of processes of interaction between stakeholders as organisations struggle for survival, what Watson (2006) calls 'process–relational' or Mintzberg (2003) characterises as 'pattern in a stream of actions'. Watson contrasts this with what he calls the traditional 'systems-control' view of strategy making, which assumes strategies are rational plans that can be drawn up by senior managers as a blueprint for implementation by others who are not seen as strategic. He argues this is not helpful for understanding how people throughout an organisation, as well as outside, exert agency and influence its strategic direction. He suggests it is more helpful to see an organisation as 'a pattern of activities and understandings involving a range of human constituencies, all of which have their own interests and strategic priorities' (Watson 2006, p213). Managers, suppliers and other staff all bring their identities, personal values and emotions into their work orientation. Any work organisation also has a history and context which will also affect the evolution of its strategy. This is not to deny that planning occurs and is valuable, rather to see that strategic direction is also the product of many other influences than rational planning and formal information. In other words, strategy can follow on from culture and structure.

STRATEGY, STRUCTURE, CULTURE

Structure–organisational forms for implementing strategy

The rise in prevalence and importance of co-operative strategy can be related to trends in the use of markets and networks as organisation forms from the mid-twentieth century and into the twenty-first century, replacing the vertically integrated, internally hierarchical corporate model that prevailed as the ideal form for three-quarters of the twentieth century. Chapter 2 explored various organisation contexts for learning and talent development and introduced organisational forms. Figure 4.5 summarises the uses of hierarchies, markets and networks as means of co-ordinating work organisations.

CULTURE AS STRATEGY

The discussion on strategy-making above showed how for many organisations an early stage of planning is to articulate a number of values that are seen as defining the purpose of the organisation. From values flow behaviours that employees are expected to demonstrate in order to embody these values. Once we are talking of values and behaviours we are in the realm of culture, and indeed for an increasing number of companies, as well as third sector and public organisations, organisation culture has become central to the pursuit of strategic objectives. Culture is understood in broad terms as the 'way things are done round here', the shared values and meanings attached to an organisation. More complex definitions of organisation culture are offered by such models as Johnson and Scholes' culture web, as illustrated in Figure 4.6.

Figure 4.5 Markets, hierarchies and networks

As mentioned in the opening to this chapter, all activity involves the coordination of disparate inputs, resources and people in order to produce intended products or services. Three dominant approaches to coordination are familiar: hierarchy, markets and networks.

In a **Hierarchy** all employed are classified in specific roles and ordered in ascending ranks of seniority, co-ordinated through a pyramid. An archetypal hierarchy is the army, but most very large companies co-ordinate through hierarchy. Co-ordination in a hierarchy is through the authority of position.

A **Market** is any structure that enables buyers and sellers to exchange any type of product, service or information. Any outsourcing contract which involves the exchange of a service for money is a market. Freelance programmers selling their skills to a core employer constitute a market. Co-ordination in a market is achieved through competition.

Networks as a way of organising involve continuous patterns of interaction and information flow between individuals and groups, interconnected through nodes – the individuals or organisations through which communications flow. Co-ordination is through interdependence, shared values, loyalty and use-value.

In reality these different coordination mechanisms will often coexist next to each other. For example, the hierarchical local authority participating as an equal member in a Community Safety forum (Network) alongside a not-for-profit refuge group and a housing organisation that itself contracts to provide social housing (Market).

Hierarchy

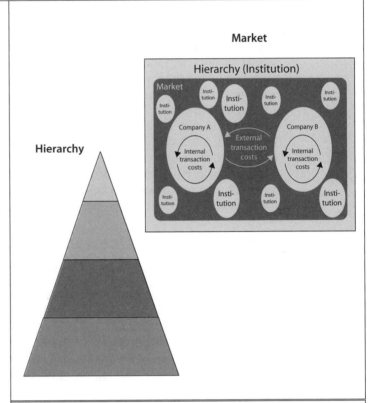

Network

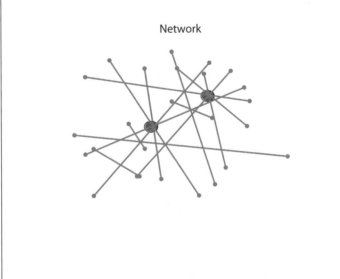

In one sense every organisation has its own culture, and even different building societies, hospitals or IT companies will have their own distinctive cultures despite engaging in the same work. In terms of strategic cultures, we suggest it is useful to distinguish between the following broadly distinct recognisable types:

- high-performance culture
- cost-reduction culture
- innovation culture
- customer-focus culture.

Table 4.1 outlines ways in which learning and talent development interventions can be aligned to the particular strategic focus and to sustain particular organisational cultures, as well as being internally aligned with other HR interventions such as recruitment and selection, engagement, diversity management, performance management and reward. It also shows the strategic role (in terms of Ulrich's model at the start of the chapter) learning and talent development specialists might play.

Figure 4.6 Culture web

Source: Adapted from Johnson and Scholes 2008

Table 4.1 Learning and talent development interventions for different strategic cultures

Strategic culture	Strategic HR/learning and talent development interventions	Role of learning + talent development professionals (in terms of Ulrich's model)
High-performance culture	Induction, coaching and mentoring, high-performance team training Leadership development Action learning Continuous development Regular peer or 360° review Tight integration with sHRM interventions Close integration with performance management framework	Strategic partner Employee champion
Cost-reduction culture	Induction Training to meet immediate priorities, for example, to ensure legal requirements for training in health and safety are covered Learning at work	Administrative expert
Innovation culture	Stimulation of experiential learning and learning through work Learning through networking Cross-disciplinary learning at interface of customers and design Engagement with R&D Collaborative learning groups across a supply chain to identify improvements Talent management focused on enhancing employees' ability to cope with complexity and changing demands Diversity management approach that sees diversity as source of learning about complexity in context of mixed teams, virtual organisations, international suppliers and customers Value on all learning	Change agent Strategic partner
Customer-focus culture	Learning from customer feedback Capturing formal and informal feedback from customers Consultation or co-production Virtual and/or international action learning sets to stimulate new product development	Strategic partner Administrative expert

SUMMARY

This chapter has been concerned with the strategic role and contribution of learning and talent development to organisation success. The interactive and iterative relationship between organisation strategy, culture, structure and objectives, and how these emerge, are designed and formulated, has been critically examined. The interplay of learning and talent development with strategic human resource management has been considered, and the contribution of learning and talent development programmes and processes to organisation strategy has been reviewed. The extended case study on Google, at the end of this chapter, provides further in-depth illustration of this interplay.

The following key terms have been scrutinised and defined:

- deliberate strategy
- emergent strategy
- resource-based strategy
- competitive strategy
- co-operative strategy
- culture
- strategic learning and talent development
- strategic human resource management.

Through reading this chapter and completing the assorted activities, you should be able to:

- explain how learning and talent development can both contribute to and follow from organisation strategies
- appraise options for learning and talent development interventions depending on different corporate strategies
- identify connections between learning and talent development and strategic HRM
- develop a practical understanding of the interactive, dynamic and iterative relationships between organisation strategy, structure, culture and learning and talent development
- explain the meaning of strategic HRD (sHRD) and strategic learning and talent development.

 REVIEW ACTIVITIES

1. Summarise five key things you have learnt from this chapter.

   a. Write down two or three new questions the chapter has raised for you or things that you are unclear about.

   b. Select one of these questions that you will enquire into further.

c. Write down what action you can take next in pursuit of your question. (For example, read one of the references in this chapter, talk to someone more experienced at work, take time to reflect on your own experience.)

2. Make a business case for investing in learning and talent development in an organisation with which you are familiar.

3. In what ways do the competences of a manager of a collaborative or co-operative venture vary compared to those of a manager generally? Draw up a person specification for the former.

EXTENDED CASE STUDY + DISCUSSION QUESTIONS

CASE STUDY

 GOOGLE

Company origins

Now (May 2010) Google is a global enterprise, with more than 10,000 employees worldwide and offices in multiple countries. Google has grown phenomenally since its founding in a California garage in 1998 by Stanford University students Larry Page and Sergey Brin (www.googlelabs.com). Whilst remaining centrally involved, in 2001 the two founders brought in an experienced CEO, Eric Schmidt, previously with Novell and Microsystems, who has steered Google's growth from Silicon Valley start-up to international brand, processing over one billion search requests daily round the world. Under his leadership, Google has escalated its operations and expanded its product portfolio. Whilst doing this, a core objective has been to sustain the original start-up culture of strong innovation.

Sources: http://politicalticker.blogs.cnn.com/2009/12/18/google-unveils-top-political-searches-of-2009/, accessed 8 May 2010; Company Timeline www.google.com/corporate/history.html.

Strategy and culture of innovation

In early May 2010 Google Labs, the on-line 'playground' where the 'more adventurous users can play around with prototypes of some of our wild and crazy ideas and offer feedback directly to the engineers who developed them' listed 40 alpha (early) stage ideas currently being experimented with by Google engineers and researchers. Ultimately these embryonic products may or may not make it to become fully developed applications, to join the growing portfolio of cloud computing and Internet search technologies, such as Google Maps, Google Apps and Google Search.

Often developed speculatively by individual engineers in their 'spare time' (usually called 'innovation time off'), outside their core role, such creativity is encouraged as the source of a stream of new products. As a motivation technique, all Google engineers are encouraged to spend 20 per cent of their work time on projects that interest them. It is claimed that 50 per cent of Google's new products evolved from this 20 per cent time, including familiar products such as Gmail and AdSense (ETL Seminar Series/Stanford University. 17 May 2006).

The company mission is 'to facilitate access to information for the entire world and in every language'. To this end Google has offices in many countries around the world and operates Google search in over 100 languages. The financial model is that revenue is generated by selling search technology to companies and from the sale of advertising displayed on both the Google site as well as other websites.

Explicit values

'Google is not a conventional company. We do not intend to become one' (Larry Page and Sergey Brin, Google founders).

'At Google, our world is flat. When everyone in the company is reaching out, not up, good ideas can go a lot farther.

The breadth of our team's cultural, professional and geographical histories greatly enriches us, and we continue to embrace diversity in our applicants' backgrounds.' www.google.com, accessed 8 May 2010

Google culture: 'Ten things' Google philosophy

1. Focus on the user and all else will follow.
2. It's best to do one thing really, really well.
3. Fast is better than slow.
4. Democracy on the web works.
5. You don't need to be at your desk to need an answer.
6. You can make money without doing evil.
7. There's always more information out there.
8. The need for information crosses all borders.
9. You can be serious without a suit.
10. Great just isn't good enough.

Source: www.google.com/corporate/tenthings.html, accessed 8 May 2010.

Workplace environment

Google has evolved around the idea that work should be challenging, and the challenge should be fun. Stretch targets and achievement are expected; high commitment is valued and there is a core belief that the unconventional, the interactive and creative will be a source of future business ideas:

We believe that great, creative things are more likely to happen with the right company culture... There is an emphasis on team achievements and pride in individual accomplishments that contribute to our overall success. We put great stock in our employees – energetic, passionate people from diverse backgrounds with creative approaches to work, play and life. Our atmosphere may be casual, but as new ideas emerge in a cafe line, at a team meeting or at the gym, they are traded, tested and put into practice with dizzying speed – and they may be the launch pad for a new project destined for worldwide use.

The work environment has a reputation for being creative and positive, catering for the food, transport and social needs of employees in multiple ways that free them to commit more time and energy to the company. Regular food docks throughout the workplace make energy snacks permanently available; meals are provided from breakfast through to dinner; a laundry service means employees do not have to be distracted by washing their clothes at home; games rooms, barbecues, social evenings, sports facilities encourage fun and socialising among employees. Most staff work in open plan offices where desks are personalised and 'corporate' is considered a swear word. Bicycles, skateboards and scooters can be found parked by desks ready for efficient travel between meetings. Small meeting rooms are furnished with soft chairs and white boards to promote creative conversations. Local expressions of each location, from a mural in Buenos Aires to ski gondolas in Zurich, showcase each office's region and personality.

'Google is not a conventional company and we don't intend to become one. True, we share attributes with the world's most successful organisations

– a focus on innovation and smart business practices comes to mind – but even as we continue to grow, we're committed to retaining a small-company feel. At Google, we know that every employee has something important to say, and that every employee is integral to our success. We provide individually tailored compensation packages that can be comprised of competitive salary, bonus, and equity components, along with the opportunity to earn further financial bonuses and rewards.'

Source: www.google.com/intl/en/jobs/ lifeatgoogle/, accessed 8 May 2010

HR Interventions to support innovation culture

A challenge for any company growing from entrepreneurial origins is to sustain the strengths of an innovative culture whilst developing the systems and processes required to co-ordinate an expanding infrastructure of new offices in multiple countries. With the aim of sustaining the company's culture and keeping true to the core values on which the company was founded, in 2006 Google assigned a chief culture officer, a role combined with the director of human resources.

Learning and talent development

Learning and talent development is led by the GoogleEDU team, who design and implement learning programmes to support and develop the company's talent across all functions and geographic regions. There are three integrated components of learning:

- GoogleEDU learning programmes, many of which are sales related
- leadership development
- talent management.

Their mission is summed up as combining individual and business objectives: 'We reach to support Googlers' personal and professional development in a way that contributes to their and our success.'

Further illustration of the roles played by learning and talent development specialists is provided by Table 4.2, 'People wanted' (www.google.com/intl/en/jobs/ uslocations/mountain-view/hr/index.html).

Recruiting and rewarding talent

Google places great emphasis on recruiting people with technical talent, but also with passion and energy, ability to think non-traditionally and to fit the culture.

A 'Google-y' is defined as somebody who is fairly flexible, adaptable and not focusing on titles and hierarchy, and just gets stuff done.

The reward package that helps attract recruits and sustain commitment includes the work environment as described above, including the ability for people to bring their dogs to work; but also such perks as stock options, a US $5000 incentive if people buy a hybrid or electric car. In California there is a commuter shuttle service to and from San Francisco, and surrounding areas, and offerings such as an annual Google-wide ski trip.

Recruitment is active, including 'sourcer' jobs: people who are responsible for sourcing candidates from on-line databases as well as through networking, cold calling, Internet searches and research. Sourcers partner with other recruiting team members to align qualified candidates with appropriate positions and work with them through Google's hiring process.

Employee happiness survey

Since employee commitment is so central to the company culture, an annual happiness survey is used to try to find out how happy people are, how committed they are to the company, what's causing that commitment level to be high or low and what will keep them working at the company. Findings on what makes a particular difference

Table 4.2 People Wanted

Learning and Development Manager, Leadership and Management

As a Learning and Development Manager, you will design, manage, deliver and continuously improve exceptional leadership development and people management offerings.

Responsibilities:

- Co-deliver a number of key leadership and people management programs, locally and globally.
- Design (conceive, initiate, develop), manage (facilitate delivery of program, continuously improve) and innovate one or more leadership development or people management programs globally and ensure all learning offerings match Google's culture.
- Collaborate with internal partner groups (eg other Learning and Development groups, HR Business Partners) and clients to assess developmental needs, and design programs that build leadership and people management skills and capabilities.
- Select the appropriate blend of learning modalities that will maximize relevance, impact and understanding and will scale to a global audience.
- Mentor and develop more junior members of the team.

Requirements include:

- Experience facilitating large groups at senior levels of organizations.
- Ability to work effectively with diverse clients at all levels in a large, complex, non-hierarchical organization.
- Willingness to travel globally up to 40% of the time.

Manager/Director, Global Diversity and Talent Inclusion

The value Google places on our employees knows no bounds. We revolutionized search, and now we're redefining human resources in the way we work closely with our management teams to attract, hire, develop and reward talented people. Google's HR team – which we call People Operations – is focused on bringing this discipline to the next level. The people who work with us have a wide variety of talents and experience, including HR, program management, marketing, team management and analytical skills. Our common trait is that we share a commitment to preserving Google's uncommon culture as we continue to grow worldwide.

Responsibilities:

- Develop a deep understanding of the company's workforce diversity, hiring needs, and retention levers, as well as opportunities for Google to broaden participation in the technology industry and education pipeline.
- Drive the creation of Google's annual strategic plan for diversity and inclusion, set quarterly objectives that are consistent with longer-term themes, and iterate often to ensure continued contribution to Google's business priorities.
- Lead a senior, global team that owns the full cycle of project management – including conception, design, implementation, launch and tracking – for programs related to strengthening workforce diversity, career development programs, talent management approaches, an inclusive culture, and other areas.
- Employ a data-driven and culture-nuanced approach, in order to truly build diversity and inclusion into the way Google operates.

People Programs Coordinator, Human Resources	Specialist, Talent Scout and Development
Google's People Programs are geared to anticipate the demands and meet the requirements of the company's rapid expansion throughout the world. Our mission is to spread the word about Google's innovation, impact and culture, and to encourage talented people to explore career opportunities with us. We help Google's recruiting and HR processes work effectively, extol Google's many virtues as an employer, engage in ongoing dialogs with university students and professors, and develop programs to promote and celebrate Google's culture of diversity.	As a Talent Scout and Development Specialist, you will contribute to Google's growth by identifying and building short and long-term strategic relationships with event leads sourced from various Google events, programs and projects. You will work to develop a candidate pipeline of both new grads and experienced professionals. You will be in constant contact with Google's internal departments to determine the most relevant outreach efforts based on the company's short-term and long-term hiring needs.

Source: www.google.com, accessed 8 May 2010

to employees and their managers have emphasised career development and growth, over giving more stock options or increasing salaries ('Meet Google's culture czar'. *ZDNet*. 30 April 2007, accessed 8 May 2010).

Performance management

Google's strategic intent is expressed in its mission. There is a broad road map for the medium and longer term, and more specific targets for the short term, for example, to launch particular products currently in development. Detailed goals are set for each quarter for teams and individually.

Regular reviews are undertaken through individual and team-self-grading and peer grading. Peer review is also used as part of employees' bi-annual appraisal.

Pay is highly performance related, with employees being rewarded for innovation, being strategic and working collaboratively (www.google. ie/intl/en/corporate/culture.html, accessed 8 May 2010).

Employer branding

Pride is expressed that Google has been externally recognised as one of *FORTUNE* Magazine's prestigious '100 best companies to work for'.

'For the third consecutive year, Google has achieved a top-5 ranking. Innovative benefits, flexibility, and the opportunity to pursue ideas that challenge the status quo are just a few of the attributes that have continued to earn us this exciting recognition. As we continue to grow, we strive to preserve the best aspects of our start-up culture. From welcoming our Nooglers (new Googlers) with their very own Google buddies to celebrating team accomplishments at our Friday TGIF company meetings – we work to cultivate employee satisfaction every step of the way.'

Discussion questions

1. In what ways do you think the values and goals of the founders now influence the dominant culture of Google?

2. Explain the interrelationships between strategy, culture, structure and learning and talent development in the company.

3. How are learning and talent development integrated with other HR interventions to sustain Google's culture?

4. Assess what might be any strategic weaknesses of the company's current strategy–culture–structure–learning relationships.

EXPLORE FURTHER

Books
Essential

Garavan, T., Hogan, C. and Cahir-O'Donnell, A. (2009) *Developing Managers and Leaders*. Chapter 4, A strategic approach to management and leadership development. Dublin: Gill & Macmillan.

Ulrich, D. (2009) *HR Transformation: Building human resources from the outside in*, with J. Allen, W. Brockbank, J. Younger and M. Nyman. New York: McGraw-Hill.

Watson, T. (2006) *Organising and Managing Work*. London: FT Prentice Hall.

Recommended

Benington, J. (2007) in Moore and Benington, *In Search of Public Value*. Basingstoke: Macmillan. *Administration Review* May/June Vol. 60. No. 3.

Child, J., Faulkner, D. and Tallman, S. (2005) *Co-operative Strategy: Managing alliances, networks and joint ventures*. Oxford: Oxford University Press.

Mintzberg, H., Lampel, J., Quinn J. B., Ghoshal, S. (2003) *The Strategy Process: Concepts, contexts, cases* (4th ed). Upper Saddle River, NJ: Pearson Prentice Hall.

Pedler, M., Burgoyne, J. and Boydell, T. (2004). *A Manager's Guide to Leadership*. London: McGraw-Hill.

Ulrich, D. (1997). *Human Resource Champions: The next agenda for adding value and delivery results*. Boston, MA: Harvard Business School Press.

Williams, P. (2002). The competent boundary spanner. *Public Administration* Vol. 80. No.1. pp103–124.

Journals

Action Learning: research and practice

Human Resource Development International

Journal of European Industrial Training

International Journal of Training and Development

Human Resource Development Quarterly

Advances in Human Resource Development

Human Resource Development Review

Useful websites

www.cipd.co.uk

www.cipd.co.uk/subjects/lrnanddev/general/lrndevoverview.htm

www.ufhrd.co.uk

www.ahrd.org

Podcasts

World HRD Congress (2010), Dave Ulrich

www.youtube.com/watch?v=W63LPccNCGA&feature=related

Medetronic vidoclip

www.workplacestrategy.ie/discussion/discussion.asp?id=1

www.cipd.co.uk/podcasts?IsSrchRes=1

CHAPTER 5

The Politics of Learning and Talent Development

OVERVIEW

Notions of emotion, power, politics and influence form the content of this chapter. Sources of power and influence in a range of organisation contexts will be examined, as will processes of organisation politics. Related theories and models and their application in practice will be critically evaluated. The relevance of these to organisation decision-making, resource allocation and regulation will be explored. Implications for learning and talent development and professional practitioners will be identified and explored.

Core terms for this chapter include:

- power
- powerlessness
- unitary
- pluralist
- regulation
- discursive act/communicative act
- discursive space
- structure–agency
- strategic exchange
- structuralist
- negotiated order.

LEARNING OUTCOMES

After reading this chapter and completing the activities, the intention is that you will be able to:

- develop a practical understanding of organisational power and politics and the implications for the function of learning and talent development within organisations, as well as for individual professionals

- analyse and explain sources of power and influence in a range of organisation scenarios

- explain how learning and talent development are both subject to influence and able to exert influence within organisation contexts

- identify connections between power and emotion in work organisation

- analyse how organisation power and politics affect decision-making, resource allocation and regulation.

POLITICS, POWER, DIVERSITY AND DIFFERENCE

Power describes the ability to influence outcomes. Such outcomes can include influencing peoples' actions, achieving material or symbolic resources, getting things done, shaping people's understanding of a situation, controlling what goes on and what stays off an agenda. In this chapter we will explore ways in which individuals and groups can exert power, but also we will look at how power can be understood not as a function of individuals, but as residing within the social and organisation structures in which individuals live and work, subjecting them to influences that they may or may not be aware of.

Historically organisation power was understood simply as a product of role and position. In other words, an individual was seen as influential by virtue of having the title Director, for example, and a seat on the senior management board. To an extent this can be true – an HR director with equivalent status to the operations or finance director may be able to get more done and influence more outcomes than an HR manager who lacks equivalent status and is not part of the senior management team. However, as we shall see, this structural way of thinking about organisational power is too simplistic to help us understand all aspects of power and influence. It does not, for instance, explain the variation in influence of different HR directors who all have equivalent formal structural role and status yet vary widely in their ability to influence outcomes.

In this chapter we will argue that organisational politics is inevitable and that it is important for learning and talent development practitioners to be aware of the ways they can influence outcomes, to be conscious of ways in which they are subject to other people's influence, to be insightful into powerlessness where it exists and to become skilled in exerting power without abusing others. We start with the activity below, designed to illustrate how power and politics is inescapable in learning and development.

 ACTIVITY

Power and influence of directors of HR/learning and talent development

Read the job advertisements in Figure 5.1.

a. For any one of the job roles advertised, identify:

- Who or what does the job role have influence over?
- Who or what will be the main influences over the person appointed?
- In the company, what kind of status will the person have in this role?

b. Looking at all the adverts:

- Identify as many words as you can that relate to power and politics in the organisation.
- What does this tell you about the kinds of skills and capabilities required by the job holder?

Compare notes with others in your class.

Figure 5.1 Selected job advertisements for directors of HR, learning and talent development

Global Talent & Resourcing Specialist

This role will work across Talent and Resourcing to support the development and deployment of the Resourcing Lead Talent Strategy in a financial services company.

The candidate:

– Project based skills such as trend analysis and benchmarking will be essential.
– Exposure to leading large-scale projects with a talent content.
– Ability to influence senior stakeholders when delivering fit-for-purpose talent and resourcing initiatives and products.
– Ability to balance conflicting business line priorities and advocating new models.
– Highly efficient with a high level of commercial understanding and execution ability.

HR Director

The business is currently going through a very interesting stage of its 50 years evolution. It invests 10% of its revenue into R&D and is recognised as a true innovator. A recently hired new CEO is leading the business towards achieving world class standards not only in its Manufacturing footprint, but also commercially and throughout its end-to-end supply chain.

This is a stand-alone business, so the HR buck will stop with you. It will be your role to ensure that the strategic needs of the business are translated into the organisational platform required to achieve the short-term and long-term business objectives.

International experience is essential, ideally with a background which includes Manufacturing or Industrial Services. You will have exceptional problem-solving skills as well as strong persuasive influencing skills.

Influencing repertoire – The individual will be able to build deep, trusting relationships and maintain a high degree of integrity. Strong influencing and communications skills, political awareness and high levels of emotional intelligence are key requirements.

Figure 5.1 continued

Human Resources Director, Legal Firm

Human Resources Director to lead the People, Learning and Development (PLD) function within a large legal firm and to contribute to the firm`s strategic and operational goals. The role will serve as a key member of the senior management team working closely with Key Leaders, Directors and Managers within the Business. HR Director will build firm-wide organisational capability and will be responsible for driving best in class employment practices that help the business to continue to differentiate itself as an employer of choice.

The candidate:
– An outstanding HR Leader with exceptional people skills and a detailed
  understanding of HR Strategy/Operations/Policy
– Minimum MCIPD, ideally an MA in Human Resources Strategic Management
– Significant experience of implementing change and cultural transition
  in organisations
– Highly developed coaching skills and experience of working intimately with
  leaders at the highest level
– Adept at handling complex organisational politics and be sophisticated in your
  approach to building relationships and facilitating others
– Appreciation of professional services environments
  and partnerships
– Strong negotiation, mediation and conflict-resolution skills
– Able to demonstrate gravitas and credibility in dealing with senior stakeholders

OD and Change Consultant

An OD & Change consultant to work at both an operational and a strategic level rolling out employee engagement strategy and a Learning and Development strategy for a leading financial services organisation in the EMEA region.

The key responsibilities of the role include the following:
– Work with the EMEA Operations Management Team, country Heads and HR to deploy all Talent
  Frameworks, Succession Planning and Development plans for key management in regions
  across EMEA
– Champion best practice across Learning and Development
– Develop key management reporting and management information (MI) on the
  people/engagement agenda
– Work with finance to deliver financial MI around people agenda
– Initiate support and champion staff engagement activities within EMEA
– Work with HR on talent management programs. Candidates must have a strong people
  background with experience of Organisational Development, Learning and Development;
  internal communications and staff engagement strategies and will have preferably have worked
  within a large, matrix organisation. Financial Services experience is not essential but would be
  beneficial and experience working on senior stakeholder engagement and management plans is
  also desirable.

Figure 5.1 continued

UK HR Director

HR Director within the company's UK commercial business, the largest market in Europe. Reporting to the Regional Vice President UK and ROI with a direct line to European HR Director, the UK HR Director will provide HR direction and leadership to the UK business around organisational development, culture, talent, leadership and change, implementing HR initiatives to address to the needs of the business.

As part of the UK leadership team, you will be responsible for developing capabilities and culture and developing strong business partnerships with the UK leaders and their teams and manage all aspects of talent management and organisational change. You would also be required to coach and advise the senior management team.

Educated to graduate level and CIPD qualified, you will be extremely driven, able to build strong relationships, project a positive attitude, and have exciting leadership skills and the ability to motivate your team. Commercial focus is essential, with previous experience in a business facing role.

HR Director (Health)

Working for a multinational, multi-site business that provides a range of services to a diverse client base, this role will be responsible for the Health Sector of this organisation. You will set the HR strategy and will ensure that it is aligned to commercial objectives. You will work closely with the MD for the Business Unit and with other senior stakeholders and you will sit on the management team.

You will be responsible for cultural change initiatives and embedding the organisational values and behaviours into the business. You will lead organisational design and change activity and build succession plans to support the corporate strategy.

The Candidate:
- have operated at director level in a multi-site, complex business environment
- have experience of working in a unionised environment
- be able to operate at the most senior level
- be commercially driven to achieve business goals
- be an excellent relationship builder, able to make an impact quickly in a fast-paced complex environment

---

Source: www.totaljobs.com, 3 June 2010

ORGANISATION POLITICS – INEVITABLE AND UNAVOIDABLE

Micro-politics refers to the processes by which such influence is exerted by individuals or groups within an organisation.

In the job adverts in Figure 5.1 you will have found reference to language such as: 'influence senior stakeholders', 'balance conflicting business line priorities', 'advocating', 'strong persuasive influencing skills', 'an excellent relationship builder', 'adept at handling complex organisational politics', 'sophisticated in your approach to building relationships', 'stakeholders', 'strong negotiation, mediation and conflict-resolution skills'. These all point to an inevitability of micro-politics within the workplace. But what does that mean people do in practice and how does this arise?

The origins of organisation politics can be attributed to four realities of organisational life:

1. *Individual goals and priorities.* When individuals encounter each other at work they bring diverse and sometimes conflicting goals to the table. Some of these may be professional differences, as when housing officials, social workers and the police come together in a criminal justice partnership, each with differing organisation targets and priorities that often do not overlap. However,

the individuals concerned also carry their own values, personal priorities and habitual ways of behaving into the interactions, as the case study below illustrates.

CASE STUDY

Market ReDesign describes itself on the company compliment slip, as: 'designing the customer brand experience'. The management team consists of:

Rowan Marketing Director, male, mid-40s

Ron Managing Director, male, mid-50s

Sue Account Manager, female, 30ish

Adrian Senior Account Manager, male, late 30s

Catriona Account manager, female, 30ish

Jack Brand Consultant, male, late 30s

Reanne Creative Director, female, late 30s

Nick Operations Manager–Automotive Director, male 40ish

Anna Finance Director, female, mid-30s.

Here, in the words of Jack, is an illustration of each individual:

Ron is very quiet. He's looking to retire in a couple of years. He's pulling back... He's emotionally retired.

Rowan and Reanne like to control.

Nick is political, back room, gets things done without show.

Rowan fights from the front.

Adrian is always fighting to get what he does understood.

Sue is newer, she occasionally speaks.

Anna is new. She's not used to a design environment. The Accounts job in a design environment must be the worst.

Jack, me – I hate the politics.

2. *Competition for resources.* No organisation is so well resourced that there are no negotiations and arguments over resource allocations. This may be at the level of budget allocations to different business units or departments. It would also be true when project leaders fight over talent for their team, for example, to have the best programmer/accountant/designer work on their project. Yet another example is the competition that inevitably exists between more junior staff for the limited number of promotion opportunities higher up the hierarchy. In most organisations not every one who wants promotion to senior positions will achieve it. The result is that just as colleagues might co-operate they may simultaneously be viewing their co-workers as competitors for the opportunities and recognition that offers the path to promotion.

3. *Competing world views and interpretations.*

 SECURITY SERVICES

CASE STUDY

A new Operations Director was recruited into a successful, growing security services company, a move which many existing employees suspected was the founder and Managing Director (MD) laying the ground for a succession plan to replace him when he retired. A hard-nosed operator with a successful background in acquisitions and asset stripping, the new Operations Director put great emphasis on paring back costs and streamlining operations. He soon clashed with the existing Director of HR and Learning, a woman who the founder had also personally headhunted a few years earlier. She had had great success in inspiring people's enthusiasm for learning and for stimulating talent development activity in the company and was passionate in her belief in the link between investment in learning, innovation and business growth. The Operations Director was quickly frustrated with the lack of apparent ROI measurables available to justify the HR department and learning activity. He could not see that HR had any strategic contribution to make and was convinced it was an excessive cost that could be largely delegated to line managers or outsourced. In this view he was supported by the Director of Finance, who, although she had never voiced such doubts before, could now see that this new Operations Director was being primed to take over the MD's shoes, so she thought her own interests would be best served by allying with him now. It suited the Operations Director perfectly to have his questions about ROI backed up the Director of Finance of all people. How could the MD possibly resist their arguments?

The Director of HR and Learning soon began to realise she was being excluded from certain senior management team communications and she no longer felt she had such easy access to the MD. Soon afterwards the Operations Director managed to persuade the MD to scale back the size of the HR department, to outsource several activities and to remove the Director of HR and Learning from the senior management team. A short while later she left the company. There is now no strategic HR role or contribution in the company.

In this case study, how do we explain the growing antagonism between the Operations Director and the Director of HR and Learning? Often within organisations it would be common to hear such a conflict dismissed as a clash of personalities. Such explanation is invariably too simplistic. Alternatively, because the tension is between a man and a woman it might be suggested he has a discriminatory attitude towards women. This may or may not be the case; however, another way of understanding the stand-off is to see it as resulting from competition between the two directors' interpretations of what needs to be done in the company, and in particular a competition over their ability to influence the MD of the accuracy of their views. The Operations Director appears to hold a framework of management that could be characterised as systems-control (Watson 2006), which presumes the organisation can be run and engineered as if it were a machine, in contrast to that of the Director of HR and Learning, whose framework might be described as more process-relational (Watson 2006), in the sense of seeing an organisation as a network of relationships in which success comes from attending to the processes of how things happen. What we are describing as a competition between world views is more than a difference of opinion which could be resolved if only the two sat down and talked it through. These kind of distinct frameworks run right through to an individual's sense of identity, incorporating core values and beliefs they hold about themselves, their purpose, social identity and their ways on interrelating with others. We do not suggest that people have a fixed, essential self-identity, rather that their identity is something actively negotiated, reinforced and open to modification as they interact with others and find themselves in differing circumstances and places over time.

4. *Dependency and interdependency.* In all organisations, perhaps with the exception of sole traders, people are dependent on one another to get their job done as the overall job of the organisation is broken down or differentiated between sections, teams and individual roles. This is described as principal–agent theory, whereby managers (principals) need other people's time and expertise to get work done (the agents). Inevitably this involves influencing, bargaining, negotiating and exchanging, regardless that employees have contracts that define work to be done.

All these examples are illustrations of what is termed a *pluralist* understanding of power. A pluralist view takes as given that organisations are sites of conflict and competition between different groups and individuals, and that the temporary stability that holds is a *negotiated order* – the outcome of particular bargaining and exchanges, as we discuss below.

HOW IS POWER EXERTED?

FORMAL AUTHORITY

A surface understanding of how power operates within an organisations points to the organisation chart, as in Figure 5.2.

Figure 5.2 Generic organisation chart

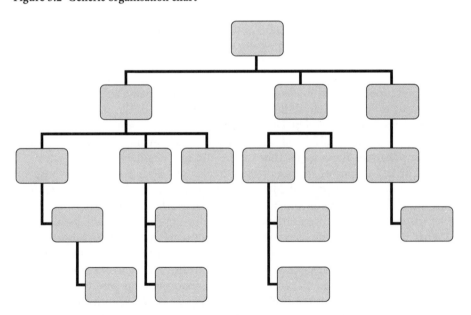

Many organisations have an organisation chart which maps the official roles and reporting relationships between different posts and sections. These are termed 'bureaucratic', not in the pejorative sense in which the word is often used, but in the Weberian ideal type sense of 'rationally organised' and 'technically efficient' (Weber 1978). Looking at such an organisation chart, it might be expected that the managing director or chief executive at the top would be most powerful because of her or his formal authority. S/he might be assumed to be able to lead decision-making and resource allocation between the sections lower down the hierarchy on the basis of information and rational criteria. It is assumed in this kind of model that there is order and regulation of people's behaviours because they have defined job roles and know the extent and limitation of their formal authority. However, much research has shown that this formal, overt picture of power relationships is only a partial account of how organisations function (see, for example, Burns and Stalker's classic study, 1994). Informal, covert power relations also operate, often described by the iceberg metaphor. Above the surface of the water is the visible, official, formal hierarchy of relationships; under the surface is the less easily seen pattern of interconnections, informal alliances, bargaining and exchange that goes on, cutting across the formal authority positions and also strongly influencing how decisions are made, where resources get allocated and how conflict is manifest.

INFORMAL ALLIANCES: COALITIONS, CLIQUES AND CABALS

The security services case study above also illustrates another political tactic – the emergence of a *coalition* between the finance director and operations director, an association from which each can benefit, who together are more influential. Another kind of informal alliance that can exercise influence is *cliques* or *cabals* – exclusive groupings connected through friendship or some other association such as participation in sports, business network or club membership (Burns 1955).

 ACTIVITY

Think about your own organisation or another that you are familiar with – for example sports club, school, college:

What is the formal organisation chart?

What informal influential alliances exist – cliques, cabals or coalitions?

TRADING AND EXCHANGE

Watson (2006, p113) uses the term 'strategic exchange' to capture the way people bargain and trade material and symbolic resources with each other not only within their employing organisations, but also with others outside, including customers, suppliers, friends and family. Through a constant process of dialogue, individuals exchange mental and physical effort, emotional labour, risk of injury, time and energy in exchange for monetary reward and other symbolic rewards such as status, stimulation or career enhancement. Deals are done and negotiations made as they trade favours, compliments, promises, money and skills to build up relationships and goodwill, to secure space on agendas and introductions to useful contacts and to procure resources to enable them to get work done.

In the field of learning and talent development, senior managers see bartering and dialogue as central to the processes of aligning human resource development to the long-term priorities or their organisation, according to the findings of a recent British study conducted by Anderson (2009). As one HRD executive from a private company put it: 'I have to be influencing the CEO, influencing the other [executive committee]members, confronting any negativity I hear – I am straight there, you know ... and persuading (Anderson 2009, p270).

Anderson relates four ways in which HRD managers describe their use of dialogue or bartering:

- involvement in business planning and reviews with line managers, looking for areas where results could be related back to their input
- construction of rationales to justify learning and development investment expressed in terms of their impact on strategic priorities
- the deliberate cultivation of good working relations with line managers
- engagement with external business partnering opportunities.

Her conclusions report managers' depiction of alignment 'as an iterative process, involving formal and informal dialogue between HRD and line managers' (Anderson 2009, p275), which she speculates means HRD professionals take any opportunity they can to influence strategic thinking and practice.

The idea that the way work activity gets organised, decisions made and resources allocated emerges from the outcomes of organisation members' dialogue and actions as they barter and exchange over differing interests and resources is captured by the term 'negotiated order'.

INSTITUTIONAL RULES AND NORMS

The social positions within any organisation, like HR director, chief executive, secretary, trainer, customer, are defined by the relations of power in which they are situated. We suggest it is not particularly useful to think about this as if individuals possess power, as if it were some kind of discrete resource, which has been a traditional way of thinking. It is more useful to understand power in work organisations as existing in the relations between organisation members, in ways that are acknowledged and tolerated in the context of tacit rules of the organisation and wider society. For example, within a hierarchical organisation, as most work organisations are, members generally accept the normative assumption that those in the senior roles within the organisation are entitled to issue directions to those in more junior roles. Alongside this, particularly in a unionised organisation, there will also be agreements that some aspects of decision-making cannot be unilaterally decided on by managers, but must be subject to union consultation or negotiation. Similar 'rules' may be followed in a company with strong employee-engagement, whereby employees expect consultation and may resist a new decision made without a level of discussion that has become an accepted norm. This is an example of how normative rules at a collective level influence or, in other words, exert power over the behaviour of individuals. A common concept for describing this kind of institutional power, where the suggestion is that individuals' actions and choices are determined by their context is '*structuralist*'.

STRUCTURE–AGENCY: COMBINED INFLUENCE OF INDIVIDUALS AND SOCIAL STRUCTURES

Pierre Bourdieu (1993) offers one particular model for understanding how power is better understood not simply as the property of individuals, but through the interrelationship between individuals and social structures. He introduces the concepts of 'habitus', 'capital' and 'field'(see Figure 5.3), which can be applied to make sense of the power dynamics of any social situation, including work organisations. Below we explain the concepts before illustrating their application in practice.

Figure 5.3 Bourdieu model of power

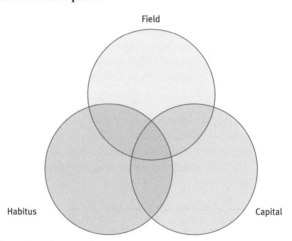

Source: adapted from Bourdieu 1993

'*Habitus*' describes the constellation of inclinations, habits and ways of perceiving, understanding and behaving that an individual brings to social interactions. The confidence with which a person carries themselves physically, their manner of voicing dissent in a management meeting, their style of speaking with colleagues, their innate sense of entitlement to be listened to, are all aspects of habitus, which, in a particular institutional setting, with its particular rules of operation, will contribute to an individual's influence over others. Habitus is informed by a combination of a person's personal and social background as well as their professional training and experience:

> These unconscious schemata are acquired through lasting exposure to particular social conditions and conditionings, via the internalisation of external constraints and possibilities. This means that they are shared by people subjected to similar experiences even as each person has a unique individual variant of the common matrix (Wacquant 2006, p6).

A person's habitus is strongly influenced by the resources or '*capital*' available to them by virtue of their social positions, including their socio-economic family background, geographical location, ethnicity and gender, all of which Bourdieu identifies as sources of capital resources. He describes three forms of capital: social capital (resources acquired through connection with social networks and membership of social groups), cultural capital (symbolic skills, abilities or assets) and economic capital (financial and material assets, such as land and property).

'*Field*' is a sphere of human activity, a context or setting, what Wacquant (2006) describes as 'distinct microcosms endowed with their own rules, regularities, and forms of authority'. 'Field' could describe a particular organisation, but may refer to a specific industrial sector, or the professional field of HR, learning and talent development for example. A field is governed by both explicit and tacit rules of operation, which impress on anyone who enters the field and which define a distinction from other, potentially competing fields. So, for example, an explicit rule of professional HR in Britain is that membership of the CIPD is generally a prerequisite for entry into corporate HR career jobs. The CIPD Code of Conduct sets out standards expected of members. Regulation from this perspective comes largely from internalisation of rules of behaviour by field members. If they break the rules they are liable to be expelled, if not formally, through castigation by other field members.

The extent to which individuals have influence over others in a particular setting, or field, depends on a combination of the resources (economic, social and cultural capital) they can draw on and the choices open to them within the norms and rules of the field. The case study below provides an illustration of these concepts in action.

 BOURDIEUIAN INTERPRETATION OF GROUP DYNAMICS

CASE STUDY

An action learning set

A newly formed action learning set of a management development programme comprised Nirmal, a Sikh man; Wolé, from Nigeria; Dave and Geoff, two white English men; Sally, a white English woman; and Mohamoud, a Somali refugee. The group's facilitator was a white woman.

After 4 four weeks of meeting and just prior to going on a one-week residential, Mohamoud told the other group members he was likely to have to withdraw from the course because he could not afford the course fees, so he would not be attending the residential.

On the residential the group sat talking one afternoon about Mohamoud's absence and probable departure from the group.

Geoff: So that's why Mohamoud's not here. But it's probably just as well because he wasn't a very good communicator. We couldn't understand him very well.

The facilitator challenged, asking whether the group consider cultural differences. There was no answer and an awkward silence filled the room.

Sally: Look, it's almost tea-time, shall we stop for a break now?

This suggestion appeared welcomed by most with relief. However, despite the attempted avoidance of an uncomfortable issue, after the tea-break, the subject was revisited.

Wolé: If I don't say something now I'm not going to be able to work with this group. It's been said that Mohamoud is a poor communicator. You should consider that he speaks six languages and he does not have a communication problem. If people find it difficult to understand him it's because they're not being patient. I'd say it's them who have the communication problem... I've been observing over the weeks the body language people show to Mohamoud, how people cut him out when he talks, the ways people look impatient when he starts talking just because he has a way of expressing something that is different from those who speak English as their first language. I've been thinking how the way people behave towards him would destroy his confidence.

You have no understanding of the structure of Mohamoud's first language which will influence how he speaks English. And I feel you would have been patient if the person was French or German. So I think the behaviour displayed by the listeners was racist.

The other group members looked taken aback.

Wolé: Many small everyday actions and statements can feel racist even though the person might not mean them to be. Take my name for example. You've been finding it hard to say Wolé, so you've just anglicised it to Wally. But my name is very precious to me. I was given it by my parents at birth and it has a real meaning for me. To have another nickname given is like naming a dog, and it's not what I want.

Two weeks after the residential the group have met twice more. Mohamoud has continued on the course. The facilitator described Geoff and Dave as visibly trying hard not to repeat their earlier behaviour towards Mohamoud. She recounted one incident as illustrative:

> The group were planning a presentation based on what they had learnt about team building from the residential. Nirmal had written a skit modelling the group on Black Adder, complete with medieval English.

Geoff: This is great, but we must remember that not everyone in the group has English in their first language so maybe we shouldn't use the Shakespearean English.

Wolé: Yes, although you can't make the assumption that we won't understand. I've read quite a lot of Shakespeare myself.

And on it goes...

Source: adapted from Rigg and Trehan 2004.

This group dialogue illustrates in a number of ways how relations between individual power and status within a social setting directly connects to the social structures of class, ethnicity, gender or sexuality. In this extract, Mahomoud, from Somalia, is initially marginalised in the group of students. The micro-politics within the group, which treated him as low status and 'difficult' to communicate with, can be directly seen to mirror the low status, or poor cultural capital, of minority ethnic groups in British society and the particular low social position accorded to refugees, both economically and legally.

The field here is the management development programme in a UK university setting. This is characterised by certain ritualised practices and norms such as certification, assessment, group work and group grades. In the light of these field characteristics, how can the apparent readiness to lose Mohamoud be understood? He certainly had few sources of capital to draw on: as a refugee without great economic resources, detached from social networks and, in a society that broadly is suspicious of refugees, he brings little cultural capital. His habitus, through his particular way of speaking, was not valued by the native English speakers of the group and, in the context of the field norm of assessments and group grades, one can imagine some group members anxious that this member might lower their average. Yet the conflict is not as simple as black/minority ethnic = powerless, white = powerful. Wolé, a Nigerian man, spoke assertively and was able to influence other group members. His powerfulness in these interactions could be attributed to his eloquence (habitus) and, as a manager on a management programme with a knowledge of Shakespeare, he certainly sounded as if he had cultural and economic capital behind him. In other contexts Wolé's assertion might not have been welcomed, but another feature of this field is that it was also a management development programme that deployed a psychodynamic and open systems approach that promoted the giving and receiving of direct feedback. Arguably it was this norm that enabled Wolé to initiate his critique and enabled the other members to receive it. In other words, he was able to act with influence, as an individual, by structural conditions of the field.

Any social situation can be analysed through the interplay of habitus, capital and field, to identify and understand how power operates in that setting. Bourdieu's model is a useful way of understanding organisational power and politics through the combined interplay of individual actions (agency) and contextual factors (structure). This is much more helpful than trying to understand how decisions get made in organisations only in terms of individuals' choices and behaviours. Such an approach involves asking questions of the field, such as: What shared beliefs and unquestioned assumptions exist? What forms of capital and what actions (habitus) explain the relative power of different professional groups in an organisation? When there is conflict, what interests are being served by particular actions? How are forms of social inequality perpetuated or disrupted within the organisation? What social networks are individuals able to draw on?

DISCOURSE: THE POWER OF LANGUAGE AND COMMUNICATION

Another model for understanding power as embodied in relationships between individuals and groups is offered by Foucault (1969). However, his perspective is that power is exercised through discourse – through the ideas, terminology and practices that comprise a body of knowledge that defines a field. Some discourses dominate and others are marginal, yet this is a dynamic, contested situation as individuals and groups jostle to influence meaning. For example, in the field of what we currently call 'learning and talent development', the language in the 1980s was 'training' and in the 1990s, 'training and development', before 'learning and development' came to prevail in the early 2000s. This is more than simply words, as each term came with definitions and debates, rationales and packages of ideas on practice – an example of changing discourse. Here there is not space to go into why the changes were made, but the significant question is: How did they come about? They resulted from discussion and argument among individuals in various settings, such as CIPD (and its precursors) meetings, in practitioner and academic journals, conferences and boardrooms, as they attempted to exert their own individual or professional definitions on the field and have their own priorities predominate. Those that advocated for talent development as a way of thinking, talking and acting in the field have exerted greater influence than those who argued for the retention of training as the definition.

CONTROLLING THE LANGUAGE – SHAPING KNOWLEDGE

Social constructionists argue that we know and understand things in our social world, including organisational world, through the language, terms and ideas available to us to name and describe what we experience. To communicate with others, we use this language and make sense of our experiences:

> We do not just passively interpret the organisational activities that we observe using some objective or neutral language or analytical scheme. Rather, we actively make sense of or enact that reality, as Weick (1995) so helpfully puts it. We do this by applying meanings, terms and concepts to what we observe and experience, taking these from the languages, stock of knowledge and ongoing interpretations of others to whom we relate. In this way, human beings 'socially construct' their realities: work together to make sense of their existence (Watson 2006, p57).

FOLLOW UP

See Chapter 12 for further explanation of social constructionism.

Key to this thinking is that language does not just describe things, it does things. To speak or communicate in non-verbal ways is in itself a form of action that achieves an effect, both for the speaker as well as those communicated with. Such effect could include inspiration, clarity, confusion, belittlement, a sense of appreciation or exclusion, for instance. In this sense to communicate is in itself an exercise in influence. Such understanding of language as action is captured by the terms 'communicative act' and 'discursive act', which in this chapter we use interchangeably.

As an example, think about the name change over the years of the professional body for HR professionals, which since 2000 has been known as the CIPD,

Chartered Institute of Personnel and Development, but over the years, since its origins in 1913, has had different names as shown below.

Figure 5.4 Evolving naming of the CIPD

Welfare Workers' Association (WWA – 1913)

Institute of Industrial Welfare Workers (IIWW – 1924)

Institute of Labour Management (ILM – 1931)

Institute of Personnel Management (IPM – 1946)

Institute of Personnel and Development (IPD – 1994)

Chartered Institute of Personnel and Development
(CIPD – 2000)

What does this change of language mean in practice? What is different about being a member of the CIPD compared to being an IPM member?

ACTIVITY

Either at work or in your local CIPD branch, find someone to interview who is currently a CIPD member and was also a member of IPD before 2000 (or even of IPM before 1994). Ask them what the name change has meant for them.

Now look up on the CIPD website (www.cipd.co.uk/about/howcipdrun/history.htm?IsSrchRes=1) for an official rationale for the transition. Compare this with your interviewee's perspective.

Certainly the intentions of those leading the creation of the CIPD included the objective of raising the professional status of HR practitioners as well as to signal high-quality practice through the symbolism of a royal charter.

CONTROLLING UNDERSTANDING THROUGH USE OF LANGUAGE

At times we are restricted in our understandings by the limitations of the language available to us. This is most obvious if we try to communicate with others in a language we are not fluent in and they are, when we might struggle to follow a discussion at all and, even if we understand many words and phrases, we typically will miss much of the meaning with which fluent language speakers are using those phrases. A classic example is to compare the average English-speaking European's comprehension of snow with that of Inuit speakers,[1] a language which reportedly contains many different words to describe different kinds of snow, where English just has a few (snow, slush, sleet). Imagine how much narrower an understanding the English speaker has of snow simply because there are few terms with which to think about the phenomenon.

In work organisations communication is often explicitly constructed with deliberately chosen terminology with the aim of exerting influence over others' understandings and meaning. Language use is often a site for competition of hearts and minds within organisations as different individuals or groups compete for influence over employees' understandings. This is perhaps no more obvious than in times of troubled industrial relations when there is overt conflict and strong negotiation between employee representatives, such as trade unions and employer representatives and battles over terminology are often very public. For example, when a bank chooses to reduce the number of small town branches, senior managers might talk of 'rationalisation' and 'efficiency savings' whilst employee representatives might speak of 'redundancy' and 'cuts'. The official language is intended to persuade staff (and customers) into accepting the strategy as rational, perhaps unfortunate, but necessary in the wider interest of the business's survival. In contrast, terms such as 'redundancy' and 'cuts' communicate a sense of loss and are often used with the intention of mobilising support for opposition to the strategy.

CONTROLLING DISCURSIVE SPACES – MEETINGS, SMALL ROOMS AND BOARDROOMS

So far we have discussed how the content of communication can exert influence. Another aspect of understanding power at work is to look at how control over the places in which communication happens can also exert influence over people's behaviours and decision-making. These are the 'discursive spaces' such as board meetings, committee meetings, annual shareholder meetings, team meetings, intranets, company newsheets, corridors and golf courses in which official and unofficial conversations occur as organisation members undertake their work. They are an integral part of organising work, but the important point is to understand how power is exercised through the set-up and control of such spaces, for example, through shaping the agendas, determining who can participate and controlling the outputs. A wonderful example is given in the case below, where one organisation member, in theory an equal peer, was unable to influence a key decision by being excluded from a particular discursive space.

CASE STUDY

Sonja recalled how a decision was made on the market repositioning of a learning and development consultancy she, along with two others, Ahmed and Will, was a partner in:

> We had spent the morning discussing the future of the company and arguing over where we saw the greatest opportunities in the coming two to three years. We really couldn't agree on the kind of clients to prioritise. So the time went into the afternoon, and we decided to break for lunch and pick up the discussions afterwards. As we headed out of the building the guys both went to the bathroom. They came out again a few moments later really animated. 'We've got it,' said Will, 'we've got a decision. We'll bring you up to speed over lunch...'

This case illustrates how exclusion can happen inadvertently; how people can be powerless in particular contexts not because of any conscious decision to exclude them, but because of the ways in which conversations and spaces happen to be structured, as well as how they are deliberately arranged. In this case, we can speculate that the particular manner of reaching the decision was unlikely to have happened if all three partners had been men or women. The case illustrates again how organisational power relations can mirror social inequalities.

MEETINGS

Meetings are invariably a discursive space in which a variety of micro-political practices can be observed. Not uncommonly the formal meeting is merely a ritual for formally recording decisions that have already been made beforehand in informal discussions and lobbying trade-offs. However, a meeting can also be a forum in which people use language and employ a range of communicative (or discursive) acts to attempt to influence others. For example, praise, criticism, interruption, invitation to speak, a smile or glare, are all communicative acts that in the context of a conversation or meeting contribute to the power dynamics between participants and serve to influence the outcome of decision-making. The following activity illustrates this with an extract from a meeting.

 ACTIVITY

Read the following dialogue and consider the questions below.

The context is the communications forum – the regular meeting of all 10 employees at Metal Tubes, a company that project manages the design and installation of industrial heating and ventilation systems.

Sam (the MD) began abruptly, assertively: 'Right, review of projects. Martin, you start.'

Martin (a project engineer) started to report on his first project, but had hardly opened his mouth before Sam butted in again: 'When will you do the cost account? … Is it not something you could write to him? …When are you planning to do it? With all your other jobs, when are you planning to do it? Because I know you've been planning to do this… Can we at least say that you'll have the meeting by the end of June?'

Martin reluctantly agreed that he would try.

Sam concluded: 'For the next communication forum can you do a full report and present some learning points. Because the design was great, we could show that, but the running has caused a lot of problems… And give me the cost of quality.'

Questions

1. Sam is clearly trying to influence Martin to produce certain actions from him. What communicative acts does Sam use?

2. How do you imagine Martin felt?

3. Why do you imagine Sam chose to say what he did in a meeting with others listening rather than privately to Martin alone?

In this illustration Sam was steering Martin very strongly in a particular direction. There was considerable implied criticism of how Martin had been managing his project, although some positive affirmation was also given. Sam presented a clear view of what he wanted Martin to do. His discursive acts included interruption and bombardment with questions, which conveyed a strong meaning that Martin's view on this occasion was not important as well as communicating that Martin was relatively powerless. However, despite the implied criticism of Martin, there was also some praise of his design work. This kind of discursive act is described as an act of emotional energising (Collins 1981 in Hardy *et al* 1998) in the sense of trying to re-engage Martin in the conversation. The practice of airing this issue in the context of the meeting rather than privately is another discursive act, designed by Sam to use Martin's project as a parable of learning for the rest of the team. Without anything being said directly to them they would all have left the meeting in the clear knowledge of what Sam, the MD, would want them to be doing on their own projects.

CONVERSATIONS

Meetings are of course one kind of formalised conversation, but much work gets done through informal conversations, in the corridor, the canteen, whilst people travel between sites, at sports events. As such, these are another discursive space in which people can exert influence and often when we observe the interactions between people within a conversation there is a clear sense of who is exercising power and who is positioned as relatively powerless. Again it is the communicative or discursive acts as well as the language used which achieve such effects as welcoming an individual in, positioning participants as peers or subordinates, giving acknowledgement or excluding a person from full engagement, as the case below illustrates.

 RENDERED POWERLESS

CASE STUDY

Two members of a company's management team, the brand consultant and marketing director, stood chatting in their glass-walled office. The door was open and although they were talking about work it was neither a formal scheduled meeting, nor an urgent issue. A woman member of staff, junior, entered the room, went out, came back, hovered at the door, went and came back. The two men carried on talking. She seemed hesitant to interrupt and they both ignored her, although she was barely two metres away. Eventually, as the marketing director continued talking, the brand consultant asked her which of them she wanted, but she shrugged and indicated she'd leave it – clearly wanting to talk to the former. Although he had said nothing to her or about her, his absence of speech constituted an act of exclusion, which she appeared too fearful to broach. The influence at that moment was to silence her.

SUMMARY – THE POWER OF DISCOURSE

To recap: In this section we have introduced a Foucauldian model of
understanding organisational power, politics and influence (Foucault 1969),
whereby power is exercised through discourse – through the ideas, language,
communicative acts and discursive practices that are employed as people interact
to get things done. Through these acts of communication and the content of
language, agendas get shaped, some things get left off, things get named in ways
that affect how organisation members think about them, conversations and
meetings are conducted in ways and places that sometimes invite contribution
and sometimes structure it out, and all this combines to produce the decisions
that get made. This is a very different way of understanding power from the

Table 5.1 Understanding decision-making and regulation

Perspective on power	Perspective on decision-making	Assumption of the regulation of individuals
Unitary: individual interests aligned with a shared organisation goal	Rational decisions made on the basis of evaluation of information against pre-set decision criteria	Individual behaviours are regulated through the formal authority and roles of the organisation hierarchy
Pluralist: negotiated order	Decisions are affected by the political behaviours of groups and individuals pursuing their own career and status interests, and the extent to which they exploit uncertainty and incomplete information to control agendas and influence the availability of information	Individuals are empowered or constrained by the extent to which they are members of influential groupings such as strategically significant work-groups, cliques or coalitions
Structuralist	Decision-making forums are defined by organisational procedures and norms, which limit the kinds of decisions that can be taken or who can participate	Institutional rules and norms exert a self-regulating influence on individuals
Bourdieu: structure + agency through habitus, capital and field	Individuals' capacity to influence decision-making is the result of the interplay between conditions in the context (field), individuals' predispositions and way of presenting themselves (habitus) and their individual social and economic resources (capital)	Individual action is regulated by a combination of structural constraints in the context (eg rules, procedures, formal authority) and self-regulation by internalised acceptance of norms of behaviour in the context
Discourse: language as power	Influence is exerted on decision-making by the way a problem is defined by dominant individuals or groups, the spaces available for dialogue and the communicative acts that at times open up engagement and at other times constrain participation	The language used to name things and frame problems shapes thought, subconsciously regulating the choices individuals consider available to them for action

classical unitary perspective, which assumes there is a common organisation goal that all members share and a formal machinery for making decisions that operates rationally and transparently.

In Table 5.1, we summarise the different perspectives on power discussed in this chapter and their contrasting views on both how decisions get made and how individual behaviours are regulated.

POWER, POWERLESSNESS AND EMOTION

It should be clear from the range of examples above that power and powerlessness will tend to provoke emotion. This is perhaps easy to see in relation to being subject to other people's influence, experiencing them exerting control and feeling relatively powerless. In work organisations this is an everyday reality, whether through interaction with customers, employers or external regulators, which we somewhat accept in exchange for employment and the rewards it offers. Nevertheless, accepting the exchange does not mean people do not experience associated emotions which at times can be strong. The notion of *emotional labour* acknowledges the effort that goes into maintaining what is deemed an appropriate facade in an interaction, whilst concealing internal feelings of, say, insult, fear or belittlement.

In addition, the very act of living and working in conditions which are uncertain and complex can create a sense of being out of control, in other words of not having power in the situation. For many, perhaps most people, such a sense of powerlessness provokes discomfort, fear and/or anxiety. A psychodynamic approach provides a useful way of understanding this aspect of organisational life, what Vince describes as: 'the inseparability of emotion and politics, ...[where] relationship is at the heart of what it means both to learn and to organise' (Vince 2002, p73).

Strong emotions, however, can also accompany the consequences of being powerful within work relationships, particularly when the actions have negative consequences. as the case below illustrates.

 CREATING REDUNDANCY: THE MANAGING DIRECTOR SPEAKS

CASE STUDY

It's been a horrendous year what with the recession and the rationalisation that followed our acquisition by a new American parent the year before, and it's not over yet. We've spent months on three-day weeks, my management team have all been on three-day pay even though we've continued to work a six-day week. But that hasn't been enough to stop us losing a third of the workforce. Twice in recent months I've thought I've secured the promise of new product lines in this plant which would have kept jobs, then each time, at the last minute, the MD backtracks and the work has gone to our plants in India or Hungary. I don't know why or who has persuaded him. I have my 'mole' at headquarters who keeps me informed, but even she says the MD is very secretive on this. I've done my utmost to try and keep jobs in this town. I've brought the MD down here from America to show him around. I know the metrics show we compare really well with other plants. We're as cheap as other plants, we're quicker, we've shown how well we can solve problems. I could say there are 12 less redundancies than headquarters wanted, that at least I managed to hold out against the full number they wanted. But still there have been more than 50 men losing their jobs – they go at the end of next week. So as you can imagine the atmosphere in the plant is awful. It's very hard. I find it hard – I

don't want to lose most of them at all. And I'm well aware of the impact on all those families out there. But in here, after next week, we have to pick ourselves up and focus on the future.

And the role of learning and development in that? Actually I've been clear for a while about some of the things we need to be doing, and the management team is in agreement with this, that we need to develop ourselves further as a team – to raise our game. We're good, I think I can safely say that, but we need to be excellent. I think we do need development, as a team, and in some cases as individuals. But I have not felt it was politic to be seen to be spending money on training ourselves whilst these redundancies are going through.

A psychodynamic understanding of organisation suggests that anxiety is a fundamental part of being human. In other words, it is normal to feel anxious about many things in life, particularly when we do not feel in control, which in organisational life can be often. The responses people make and the ways they respond to their anxiety translates into ways of organising and trying to gain control.

POWER, POLITICS AND EMOTION – IMPLICATIONS FOR LEARNING AND TALENT DEVELOPMENT

In this section we consider some of the implications for learning and talent development that follow an understanding of the dynamics of power and emotion at work. These can be placed in two categories:

1. implications for the skills and actions of learning and talent development practitioner in an institutional and organisation context.

From a Foucauldian perspective power is inevitable within all relationships and can be used creatively and constructively. This presumably is normally the intention of learning and talent development professionals. So the important elements are:

- to be aware of one's potential power as an individual and in a learning and talent development professional role
- to give consideration to how to exercise power appropriately

- to be aware of ways in which one is subject to influence both from other people as well as structurally

- to be aware of others' disempowerment and one's own role in that.

Awareness of organisational power and politics places an onus on learning and talent development professionals to develop their micro-political skills and to ask questions about power and powerlessness; for example, to be inquisitive about whose interests they serve so that they act with deliberate intent rather than in ignorance; also, to consider how the adage 'knowledge is power' can be applied to address the exclusion of structurally marginalised social groups.

2. implications for the content, design and methods employed for learning and talent development interventions.

The potential of 'classroom as real world' has been demonstrated by Reynolds and Trehan (2001) and Rigg and Trehan (2004) as an opportunity to engage participants in critical learning in a process of making connections between their experiences of power and emotion within their learning and their work experiences, so as to understand and change interpersonal and organisational practices. Process radical methods that challenge traditional power asymmetries in the trainer/learner relationship can themselves provoke insight into power asymmetries within the workplace. Such methods might include, for example, taking an experiential learning approach, using action research and critical reflection, negotiated curricula or engaging trainers and participants as co-learners in a learning community or action learning set. Learning groups very often mirror the socio-dynamics of the organisation and also wider society, so they can easily recreate environments that silence and disempower some participants. However, within the diversity and the power imbalances lies great potential for learning, not only about power and inequity, but also how to be, or in other words, how to become more influential and how to exercise power in acceptable ways.

Emotions are evident as a source of significant learning in two additional ways. Firstly, the dynamics of learning groups – their processes of organising – often provokes emotions. Attending to and making sense of these is a rich source of experiential learning about organisational behaviour. Secondly, the process of critical reflection provides language and concepts which help people acknowledge and make sense of feelings they may have long carried, but ignored; for example, over tensions and contradictions they experience in the ways they think they ought to act as a manager compared with their values. The illustration below is an example of questioning management, where ideas from critical management helped the manager to develop new perspectives on ways of exercising power in relation to others, as well as making her more confident in her identity as a manager.

ILLUSTRATION

Learning about power from critical management learning

Throughout the [management] course I was continually questioning, both in my personal and in my working life. I began to challenge ideas which I had previously accepted. An example of this was when I realised I was uncomfortable with the style of my immediate line manager. His whole ethical and moral standpoint on some issues led me into conflict situations. I recall a time when I had taken a serious staff issue to him to discuss. When I discussed it with him, I informed him that the staff would like him to be present at a meeting to discuss the issue. He said, 'You keep them quiet, it will blow over. They are just looking for extra money.' He told me that if I had any trouble, I should remind them that they were lucky to have jobs. We had what could only be described as an argument over this issue. He exploded and told me to stop being 'an emotional woman' and basically implied that my hormones were amiss.... The situation was exacerbated when one day he told me that I was 'taking the touchy feely stuff [I was] learning too far'. I decided that if I was going to work with this individual I would have to 'toughen up'. I therefore used my manager as a role model.

For a while it seemed to work well. I was promoted by the organisation and my working life was very successful. I did have doubts about some of the ethical issues. We seemed to be ignoring staff morale and well-being in order to look efficient and therefore produced an extremely task-led environment, which appeared very successful. On reflection I did exactly what Steinberg and Shapiro (1982, pp306–310) describe in their research. They argue that female managers may exaggerate the masculine facets of their personality to help them compete more effectively in managerial roles... Alvesson and Wilmott (1996) argue that even when women and ethnic minorities join the ranks of management, a condition of entry and promotion is adherence to established values of white middle-class males.

This is exactly what happened to me. I had been moulded by my manager and organisation. I was being managed, I was being controlled... I tried to find another role model for my career as a manager, one that was closer to what I believed in and I found it very difficult. Deep in thought whilst writing this [coursework] paper, my mother came to mind. She needed all the skills of management and used them to produce the challenging task of bringing up a family of six. She was a member of a large Irish family, she came to England when she was 17, having left school at 14. She taught us the values of sharing, considering other people's feelings, listening and above all, honesty. These are qualities which are still fundamental to my struggle to become a successful manager and qualities which I feel are paramount in any individual, so why should they be compromised as a manager? I have therefore decided that my mother may be one of the most successful managers I know.

...In conclusion ... I now feel confident to trust my instinct and manage in the style which complements my ethical and moral beliefs.

POWER AND THE PROFESSION

It is not possible to talk of organisational power and politics, particularly in relation to learning and talent development, without exploring the issue of professional power in general and influence over the professional field of HR in particular.

Earlier in the chapter, we considered the intentions behind the acquisition of chartered status and the renaming that produced the CIPD in 2000. This was a move that was most certainly intended to raise the professional status of HR practitioners through the symbolism of a royal charter. The discourse of professionalism is one 'which recognises certain occupations as being special by virtue of their control of specialist knowledge and their rules of treating clients with confidentiality and with discretion' (Watson 2006, p104).

The extract in Figure 5.5 illustrates the CIPD's stated aim and mission.

Figure 5.5 Chartered Institute of Personnel and Development (CIPD): extracts from code of conduct

The Chartered Institute of Personnel and Development (CIPD) is Europe's largest HR development professional body. We're a globally recognised brand with over 135,000 members, and pride ourselves on supporting and developing those responsible for the management and development of people within organisations.

Our aim is to drive sustained organisation performance through HR, shaping thinking, leading practice and building capability within the profession.

The mission of the Chartered Institute of Personnel and Development is:

[1.1] to lead in the development and promotion of good practice in the field of the management and development of people, for application both by professional members and by their organisational colleagues
[1.2] to serve the professional interests of members
[1.3] to uphold the highest ideals in the management and development of people.

The objects for which the Institute is established are:

[2.1] The promotion of the art and science of the management and development of people for the public benefit.

CIPD aims to be the 'must belong' professional body for all those involved in the management and development of people. In delivering the information, learning and networking opportunities, qualifications and other services, the Institute is supporting people management and development professionals and their line management colleagues to do their jobs better, at whatever stage they've reached in their careers.

Source: www.cipd.co.uk, accessed 13 June 2010

Professional power – good or bad?

It may be thought as self-evident that to be professional and to be a professional are good things. However, as we shall see, there are voices that are critical of professionalism. Firstly, however, the positive viewpoint.

Optimistic perspectives indicate professionalism is a route to higher standards, consistency and protection of standards for clients. This is evident in the quote below from a CIPD newsletter in May 2010.

 ILLUSTRATION

Extract from CIPD member newsletter May 2010

It's never been a better time to be a CIPD member. The HR industry is changing, with employers' expectations of HR professionals changing too. As a CIPD member, you're in a good position to benefit. Your CIPD membership keeps you in touch with developments in the profession and gives you the recognition you deserve.

Remind yourself of everything that comes from being a CIPD member:

Credibility and recognition in the workplace, plus increased earning potential

Exclusive access to a wide range of member-only resources and services

Exclusive networking, online and at special events.

Unabashedly this extract argues that to be a member of a professional body, elevates professionals' influence, by increasing their social, cultural and financial capital (in Bourdieuian terms).

Elsewhere in the chapter we posed the question of why the custodians of CIPD had advocated for its acquisition of chartered status in 2000. A key driver was an attempt to raise the influence of the profession of HR management and development. Prior to this, in 1994 when the IPD (Institute of Personnel and Development) was formed from a merger of IPM (Institute of Personnel Management) and ITD (Institute of Training and Development), all members of both were automatically transferred to membership of the new IPD, and from that date new members had to either pass IPD exams or gain accreditation for equivalent learning.[2] Up until that point membership of ITD had been very open to anyone describing themselves as engaged in training and development. Here we see an example of the entry criteria tightening as the profession sought to both raise the status of the profession as well to control standards.

Negative viewpoints on professionalism are voiced by some who, talking about professions in general, not the CIPD in particular, suggest the priorities of professions are to maintain their own privileges and to protect status and income-generation potential:

> All trade associations are attempts by those who sell their labour to determine how that work shall be done and by whom. Professions also do this, but they go further: they decide what shall be made, for whom and how their decrees shall be made... Professionals tell you what you need and claim the power to prescribe. They not only recommend what is good, but actually ordain what is right (Illich 1977, reproduced in Clark *et al* 1994, p207).

Professional society is based on human capital created by education and enhanced by closure, that is the exclusion of the unqualified...

...The professions live by persuasion and propaganda, by claiming that their particular service is indispensible to the client or employer and to society and the state. By this means they hope to raise their status and through it their income, authority and psychic rewards (deference and self-respect) (Perkin 1989, reproduced in Clark *et al* 1994, pp204–205).

For our purposes, whether professionalism is a positive or a sinister development is not the real issue here, rather we are interested in how professional power operates and how this applies to learning and talent development. The job adverts at the start of the chapter illustrate the value placed on CIPD qualification for these senior roles. This suggests that the CIPD is seen as providing a gatekeeping function as signifier of standards. The unqualified are excluded (see www.cipd. co.uk for latest categories of and routes to membership). However, learning and talent development is not a profession in the way of law, accountancy or medicine, in the sense that registration with a professional body (whether CIPD, European Foundation for Management Development – EFMD – or other) is not required in order to call yourself a learning and talent development practitioner. And the field of practice is quite diverse, with a very high proportion of practitioners working freelance or for small consultancy companies. So whilst CIPD membership is used as an entry criterion for many corporate jobs, a cursory trawl of tender bids for suppliers of in-company training and development programmes will show that CIPD membership is not a widespread prerequisite for becoming an external supplier.

FOLLOW UP

See Chapter 11 for further exploration of the nature and meaning of professionalism.

SUMMARY

This chapter has been concerned with power, politics, emotion and influence in organisations. Power is defined as the ability to influence outcomes, such as affecting people's actions, achieving material or symbolic resources, getting things done, shaping people's understanding of a situation or controlling decision-making agendas, for example. We have explored ways in which individuals and groups can exert power, but a key argument throughout the discussion has been to understand power not as the property of individuals, but as residing within the social relationships and organisation structures in which they live and work. Contrasting views of power and their applications in practice have been critically evaluated, including unitary, pluralist, structuralist, Bourdieu's structure–agency model and a Foucaudian view of the power of language and discourse.

The relevance of these different ways of analysing and understanding power to organisation decision-making, resource allocation and regulation has been explored and is summarised in Table 5.1. Several of the case studies included throughout the chapter have drawn on situations involving learning and talent development, which should help readers see the implications of thinking about power, politics and emotion for this field of work. Perhaps the key implication for practitioners is demonstrated in the cases and job adverts presented above, which illustrate the many ways in which learning and talent development professionals require both an awareness of power and micro-politics so as to be able to read a situation and also skills to exert influence if they are to get things done and achieve the outcomes of their job.

Having read this chapter and completed the activities below you should be able to:

- explain the core terms addressed in the chapter:
  - power
  - powerlessness
  - unitary
  - pluralist
  - regulation
  - discursive act/communicative act
  - discursive space
  - structure–agency
  - strategic exchange
  - structuralist
  - negotiated order.
- demonstrate a practical understanding of organisational power and politics and the implications for the function of learning and talent development within organisations, as well as for individual professionals
- analyse and explain sources of power and influence in a range of organisation scenarios
- explain how learning and talent development are both subject to influence and able to exert influence within organisation contexts
- identify connections between power and emotion in work organisation
- analyse how organisation power and politics affect decision-making, resource allocation and regulation.

REVIEW ACTIVITIES

1. Summarise five key things you have learnt from this chapter.

   a. Write down two or three new questions the chapter has raised for you or things that you are unclear about.

   b. Select one of these questions that you will enquire into further.

   c. Write down what action you can take next in pursuit of your question. (For example, read one of the references in this chapter, talk to someone more experienced at work, look on CIPD website, take time to reflect on your own experience.)

2. Reflect back on your experience of work or education organisations.

   a. List examples of micro-political behaviours you have witnessed.

   b. Identify any examples of strategic exchanges you observed.

   c. Share the results with colleagues and examine how they compare. Discuss whether any differences can be explained by the different kinds of organisations you work for.

3. It is clear learning and talent development professionals require both awareness of power and micro-politics and political skills to exert influence in order to achieve outcomes at work. With this in mind, design a recruitment process for a learning and talent development manager's job that would enable you to evaluate applicants' knowledge and capability in this area.

4. Look back over the chapter and create a statement for each of the following terms that summarises your understanding of each in your own words:

   - power
   - powerlessness
   - unitary
   - pluralist
   - regulation
   - discursive act/communicative act
   - discursive space
   - structure–agency
   - strategic exchange
   - structuralist
   - negotiated order.

EXTENDED CASE STUDY + DISCUSSION QUESTIONS

Read the case study and answer the following questions:

 MARKET REDESIGN

CASE STUDY

From its origins 10 years ago as a design agency in England, Market ReDesign is a company now offering brand consulting to other organisations, integrating building design and interior design with advice on logos to create a '*customer journey*' that takes the customer through a '*brand journey*'. The company compliment slip describes their business as: 'designing the customer brand experience'. Thirty people are now employed, including 10 graphic designers and interior designers, 5 architects, 5 admin people, 7 people in sales and account management, a marketing director, one brand consultant and Ron, the founder and MD. Ron, a man in his 50s, has expressed a wish to retire in the next two to three years, or as soon as he can sell the company at an acceptable price.

Market ReDesign's building is an old Methodist church, converted in the early 1990s. There's paper everywhere – drawings, boards. Dress code is smart or not-so-smart casual, mainly T-shirts, jeans and chinos. The initial image confronting the visitor is one of openness, artiness, work-as-life, work-as-social life. The coffee jug is constantly on.

At 8.30am promptly the Monday morning sales meeting begins in a top floor meeting room. People sit around a rectangular table, occupying the same seats each week, as illustrated below:

Rowan	Marketing Director, male, mid-40s
Ron	Managing Director, male, mid-50s
Sue	Account Manager, female, 30ish
Adrian	Senior Account Manager, male, late 30s
Catriona	Account Manager, female, 30ish
Jack	Brand Consultant, male, late 30s
Reanne	Creative Director, female, late 30s
Nick	Operations Manager– Automotive Director, male 40ish
Anna	Finance Director, mid-30s

Rowan chairs, though there is no apparent agenda and no one seems to take minutes. However, people have in front of them a balance sheet containing financial figures for projects. Rowan initiates the meeting, addressing Nick first in a sharp tone: 'I won't ask questions about why we haven't got a PO [purchase order] on this.' This sets the tone for the entire meeting. The agenda that unfolds covers the following items:

- review of current projects
- hot proposals
- warm proposals
- any other issues.

8.30 am Monday morning sales meeting

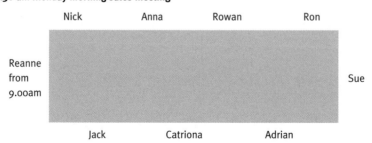

The meeting is finished in 50 minutes. The tone is muted, curt, fast. Rowan is pushy, even bullying, with little respect for any of the others. The tone in which he speaks to others at the meeting treats them as recalcitrant children, with few rights to speak. It was as if he viewed everyone else as deficient and lazy. He was keen to direct the outcome and to produce specific ways of working from them, but the meeting has an air of passive resistance to him.

Ron makes only three comments throughout the sales meeting. All are ignored by the other members. Despite his position as MD, he appears to have little status in the eyes of the others. An example of his marginalisation is shown in the following excerpt:

Rowan was talking about potential contracts they had a strong chance of winning – the so-called hot proposals:

Rowan: 'If we were to convert the Hot proposals it would be very attractive.'

Jack: 'We don't need them all.'

Rowan: 'Well, I think we do… It'll tide us through. Two reasons to do: 1. to get our bonus; 2. September drops. I'm sorry there's no let up. Wouldn't be great to declare a 50k profit ahead if we can do another 50k. So I think it's a mistake to let up because July looks good.'

Then in an afterthought, in a flippant tone, which waited for no answer, he added: 'What do you think of that, Ron?'

Up until then Rowan had not included Ron in the meeting, had ignored comments he had offered and this aside was a belated recognition that such attention to the company income is the MD's domain.

The studio

The Market ReDesign studio occupies the open plan ground floor of the old church, furnished with desks and two old settees, where the graphic designers prepare branding designs and the architects design physical spaces. The design staff are mainly women in their 20s and early 30s; about 15

in total, though not all in. A Bob Marley CD is playing. Paper designs and boards are everywhere. Everyone is in jeans and T-shirts or other casual clothes. The atmosphere within the studio is relaxed and social and work is punctuated with cereal-eating, personal phone calls and chat about films and books. Phone calls are left ringing until the receptionist tannoys for someone to pick up the phone: 'How can I help you mate?… no, that's cool.' It was a stark contrast to the driven sales meeting. But perhaps this was the appropriate environment for the designers to be productive in. Jack's view of the studio was: 'The culture here, a lot of people work long hours, it's their social life, they eat here. If I get up to leave at 6pm, they look at me as if I'm going early.' Rowan, however, was dismissive: 'They're a different company. They don't appreciate the financial/business concerns of ours; they're just designers.'

Changing the business

The MD

Ron, the MD, avoids conflict because he likes to feel the company (which he set up) is a family environment. At this stage of his life he primarily views the company as his pension, so his key objective is to 'fatten' it up to sell at the best price. This is not a priority shared by the other senior managers. For example, Rowan and Jack were plotting a meeting with an agency that had expressed interest in buying Market ReDesign, without telling Ron. As part-owners of the company they are sceptical of the financial benefit to themselves of selling the company at present, so their rationale for meeting was to find out what the agency were offering to help them plan a management buyout.

The Brand Consultant

Jack talked with enthusiasm about his learning from his postgraduate Diploma in Marketing and how he has drawn from this to organise seminars for his colleagues, with the aim of sharing his newly formed ideas on brands and the role of design to try and influence how the other members think about and enact their work:

> I've done presentations internally to the staff and the whole organisation is becoming more commercially focused because of that… I stand back and say, you're designers fundamentally, and there are people out there who are business focused. You also don't talk the same language. The one thing that holds you together is this thing called brands, which is what you're building for and they're building towards. Let me explain some of the core fundamentals of those and then we can build around them. So I do all these presentations, where I just brought them alive.

Catriona, Account Manager

In her view Rowan's approach stifles interaction between members, to the detriment of exchanging experiences of each other's projects. She described the company's style as a macho dictatorship, dictated by Rowan's way of operating; she conveyed a climate of fear and expressed discomfort with his drive to get them to 'farm' clients for yet more money:

> From me personally, I think a different personality would get more from me because I don't think he's particularly, I don't think he's necessarily a good people manager. There's a bit of a personality clash there, for a lot of people, I think. Because he can be a very insensitive person, and so I do feel defensive and will go like this around my work [arches body and arms over protectively to signify secrecy, protection], and create this kind of, me, and I'm defending me, and I'm making sure every things alright for me before I go into the meeting.
>
> …If I was working in combination with somebody, or with a team then it would be very different, you'd have to share, it would be more female. And I think, I can't say for sure, but I think more would be got out of me, I don't know exactly how, but it would be a

more honest interaction. And maybe I would, well I would work differently, I'd work with other people.

> …we never ever sit down together, apart from that Monday morning meeting, we never sit down as a team of people, running accounts, and say 'What's happening on yours?' So I've got no idea what Adrian does, and I don't really know what Louise does. We chat occasionally, but it's not a relaxed atmosphere downstairs either. Because everybody needs to be seen to be working because of that driving person there.

Rowan

Rowan is impatient to see changes in the company and impelled by a sense of urgency. If he could, he said he'd close the company down and restart it, as a way of achieving the changed ways of working he'd like to see. When contemplating organisation development interventions, which are designed to involve people, to generate ideas from them; to work with 'hearts and minds', his response, made without irony, was 'You mean, pretend to ask them what they think?'

Rowan tries to achieve a desired action from others by the words and particularly tone of what he says. The entire discourse of the sales meeting seemed to concern the importance of financial goals, and Rowan's priority that members should define their work in terms of finance first, with other considerations second. To this end he tried to influence the ways cost is monitored, invoiced and accounted for in the course of projects, using the tactic of threatening people's bonuses:

Rowan to Nick 'I won't ask questions about why we haven't got a PO. [purchase order] on this.'

> Nick was blatantly very angry at this apparent critique of his work:
>
> 'We work on a letter of intent from the client. Is that clear … for the umpteenth time.'

Rowan	'It's just to have clarity. Let's look at the PO section. Do all of these now have written confirmation?'
Adrian	'No.'
Rowan	'I'm probably just being thick.'
Adrian	'No. There's a project plan which has...'
Rowan	'Can I be pedantic? Can it go on the proposals list? The reason for this panic ... being tougher on POs is if there's slippage it affects the bottom line and you won't get your bonuses... So that lies hard.'

any means. I don't think it is anyway, 'cause I think there's a lot of lies that go around in that atmosphere as well. Because you have to defend yourself, 'cause you're in a forum, public debate in front of your colleagues. So, if you have to blag it a bit, then you probably will. And I have done in the past. You feel like ... I feel like you need to be delivering. Or be seen to be.

She laughed, communicating a recognition of the acting game she engages in.

Not that avoidance appeared to save people from criticism, as Catriona said: 'If you're not at the meeting you tend to get slagged off... So it becomes, if you're not here you've got to be a bit careful, you've got to watch your back.'

Resistance to change: avoidance and cover-up

In Market ReDesign there was little sense in which mistakes might be something tolerated and to learn from. The tone of the sales meeting suggests that only good news and better were acceptable. Many of the members avoid the meeting if they can produce a good enough reason to justify it, primarily because it felt like an inquisition, particularly if what they had to report on their customer accounts was not what would please Rowan.

If avoidance was not possible, pretence was an alternative – playing the game to keep up appearances of good news. For example, Catriona described her perception of how people conceal their mistakes and become adept at managing appearances within the sales meetings:

> if you can blag it in the meetings, you can get away with it anyway. If you can just say 'Yep, done that. Two grand, no problem.' You could be lying. It's all about attitude, it's not about a reality, it's not about honesty. By

Learning and talent development

In Market ReDesign, learning is not a dominant feature of the company, and neither formal nor informal learning interactions are part of the discursive practices deployed to develop new ways of working. A few individuals have attended formal courses, but they initiate this themselves, and whether their learning affects their practice or not is paid not attention to by the MD or other senior managers. There is no training and development agenda item within regular meetings; there is no developmental appraisal system. Rowan has no postgraduate management education; Catriona is undertaking the same postgraduate Diploma in Marketing that Jack has completed. Jack, as described above, has drawn enthusiastically from his course to remodel how he combines design work with marketing as a brand consultant. However, despite these few examples of new practices developing through the impact of formal courses and from external recruitment, overall, it can be argued that the dominant company practice is one of non-learning.

1. What micro-political behaviours do you see mentioned in this case study?
2. Give an example of trading and strategic exchange in the case study.
3. Catriona explains her and others' difficulty with Rowan as a 'bit of personality

clash'. In the light of the concepts of power, politics and emotion discussed in this chapter, how else could you explain the tense relationships?

4. How does Rowan use language and discursive acts in the sales meeting in his attempt to influence other people's actions?

5. Use Bourdieu's concepts of habitus, capital and field to analyse the marginalisation of Ron, the MD, in the company.

6. How do any of the following four 'realities of organisational life' help explain the micro-politics in the case?

   a. individual goals and priorities

   b. competition for resources

   c. competing world views and interpretations

   d. dependency and interdependency.

7. There is a contradiction between Rowan's espoused desire to see changes in the company and the apparent dominant ethos of non-learning.

What different discursive practices and different language would you recommend Rowan introduce in order to remove this contradiction?

EXPLORE FURTHER

Books
Essential

Anderson, V. (2009) Desperately seeking alignment: reflections of senior line managers and HRD executives. *Human Resource Development International*. pp263–278.

Odih, P. and Knights, D. (2007) Political organizations and decision-making. In Knights, D. and Wilmott, H. *Organisational Behaviour and Management*, Chapter 8. London: Thomson.

Watson, T. (2006) Managing to manage, power, decision-making, ethics and the struggle to cope. In T. Watson, *Organising and Managing Work*, Chapter 6. London: FT Prentice Hall.

Recommended

Buchanan, D. and Badham, R. (1999) *Power, Politics and Organizational Change: Winning the turf wars*. London: Sage.

Clark, H., Chandler, J. and Barry, J. (1994) *Organisations and Identities*. London: Chapman Hall.

Reynolds, M. and Trehan, K. (2001) Classroom as real world: Propositions for a pedagogy of difference. *Gender and Education*. pp357–372.

Rigg, C. and Trehan, K. (2004) Reflections on working with critical action learning. *Action Learning – Research and Practice* Vol. 1, No. 2. pp149–166.

Vince, R. (2002) Organizing Reflection. *Management Learning*. Vol. 33, No. 1. pp63–78.

Wacquant (2006) Pierre Bourdieu. In R. Stones (ed). *Key Contemporary Thinkers*. London and New York: Macmillan.

Part 2

CHAPTER 6

Learning

OVERVIEW

This chapter will identify, explore and evaluate a range of theories and models related to people's learning. The purpose is to examine the basis of designing learning and talent development programmes and interventions, how these connect to specific theories of learning and the practical implications of learning theory for selecting methods and designing programmes. Related to this will be an examination of variation in approaches to learning and talent development for different kinds and levels of intended outcome.

LEARNING OUTCOMES

After reading this chapter and completing the activities, the intention is that you will be able to:

- understand that the term 'learning' refers to a variety of mental and social processes
- differentiate between a range of learning theories and models
- identify how these can be applied to inform the design of learning and talent development programmes and interventions
- connect specific methods of learning and talent development to theories of learning
- critique the misapplication of learning theory
- make evidence-based choices in the design of programme and selection of methods appropriate to intended outcomes.

LEARNING THEORIES AND LEARNING STYLE

Behind every learning and talent development intervention is the assumption that it will result in learning for an individual, group and/or organisation. But what is the evidence for these assumptions? The practical significance of our understanding of learning relates to how learning and talent development interventions are designed, what level of learning they aim to stimulate and whether the design is appropriate to deliver on the intended objectives.

We will look at this question from two angles: firstly, theories of how people learn, and secondly, the debate about learning styles. Following some initial introduction of key terms and two illustrations of learning for work, the chapter is divided into two parts. The first presents four main families of learning theory and explores the application, implications, strengths and limitations of each for learning and talent development in work organisations. The second part discusses current thinking and controversy about the extent to which people have different learning styles.

The chapter starts with an outline of key terminology, followed by two illustrations of interventions, one relating to induction, the other to customer service training.

KEY 'LEARNING' TERMS

In this chapter the key terms you will become familiar with are the following. As you read, you will become aware that most do not have a single, commonly agreed definition, so it is valuable for you to think about how you currently understand each term and be prepared to critically reflect on your own assumptions.

- learning
- learning style
- learning strategy
- information processing
- learning modality
- experiential learning
- action learning

- constructivist
- constructionist
- social learning
- behaviourist
- cognitive dissonance
- mental schema

LEARNING FOR AND AT WORK — TWO ILLUSTRATIONS

 ACTIVITY

Read the two following illustrations and discuss what assumptions are made in each about how people learn.

ILLUSTRATION

Induction at the deep end

Murphy's Icecream is a small company manufacturing and retailing high-quality ice cream, dedicated to providing a unique customer experience through its quirky cafés. Two factors are considered absolutely fundamental to reproducing this experience across all their outlets: first, a consistent product, and second, the café culture and the way staff interact with customers. To ensure a cultural fit of new staff, induction consists of being thrown into the frontline – the first week is spent in one of the cafés serving, observing how it is done by existing staff, dealing with customers, experiencing what the job involves. Only then (assuming the staff member decides to stay) are the formal systems and policies introduced.

ILLUSTRATION

Customer service training course

The aim of the course is to provide the delegates with the knowledge, skills and attitudes necessary to provide excellent standards of service. It covers the three core types of communication along with the main elements of customer service, which are necessary to ensure that the objectives of both the customer and the organisation are met. The course also covers the difference between face-to-face communication and telephone communication.

The course is interactive, fun and full of ideas that can be used in the workplace to enhance performance.

Objectives

By the end of the course delegates will be able to:

- handle telephone calls professionally and effectively
- understand the key principles of the telephone as a communication tool
- use a proven method for achieving quality customer service
- establish the client's needs quickly and effectively
- handle conflict and complaints successfully
- resolve problems by questioning and listening
- communicate clearly and effectively
- understand the three core areas of communication
- know the pitfalls to avoid
- demonstrate empathy
- calm the customer and keep focus
- understand the three basic types of human behaviour
- solve customer problems with a proven method
- deal with difficult situations.

Training methods

Our training methods are based on best practice for the most appropriate transfer of knowledge and learning:

- Trainer presentation
- Training exercises
- Syndicate workshop
- Skill practice/role play
- Group discussion.

LEARNING

 ACTIVITY

What is learning? Look for definitions of 'learning' on the CIPD website, within your own organisation's learning and talent development policy and in one of the references at the end of this chapter. Compare the three.

When you have read this chapter produce your own definition of learning.

The term 'learning' is used with various meanings. Griffin's questions to learners produced an interesting list of 40 learning processes, including: making meaning; creating knowledge; expanding alertness; releasing creativity; creating energy; being aware of self as a learner; validating oneself; unlearning; questioning assumptions and ideas; reframing with new assumptions; changing the past (Griffin 1987, p216).

'Learning' can be a verb that describes a process – the how of learning. Also it is a noun that describes the result of a process – the outcome of learning. It can refer to new knowledge, a change in behaviour or understanding, or even to personal transformation. For example, for Casey learning is about 'doing things differently' (1983, p39). Harri-Augsten and Thomas (1991, p47) suggest:

> Learning is better thought of as a change within the person. It appears as a new or improved way of thinking or feeling about something or of perceiving it or doing it.

This is echoed by others, for example:

Reg Revans:

> True learning consists mainly in the reorganisation, or reinterpretation, of what is already known (1980, p289).

Etienne Wenger:

> Learning – whatever form it takes – changes who we are by changing our ability to participate, to belong, to negotiate meaning (1998, p226).

Some writers try to distinguish between different learning processes to present a dichotomy of learning, differentiating between an external view of learning, where a person adds on new knowledge, or an internal view, where a person is deeply changed (Rogers 1983; Freire 1972; Argyris and Schön 1996). What these share is a view that there are different levels of learning, one at which the self is untouched, another at which it is affected, producing changes in values or perspectives. Other writers conceive of levels of learning, but along a spectrum, rather than as a dichotomy. For example Bateson (1973) outlined four levels of learning: level 0, where there is no learning, responses are habitual, without regard to context, and responses to feedback are poor; level I, at which there is error correction, through trial and error responses to new contexts; level II, where there is an ability to recognise and inhabit different contexts; to be able to take different perspectives, but still to hold one world view; and level III, at which a person has an ability to step outside their previous world view, has an awareness of their own subjectivity, has gained control over habitual ways and can take responsibility for making changes.

It is clear from this discussion, that the term 'learning' has a broad meaning, so when we talk of people learning this can range from acquisition of knowledge and information, a new skill, development of understanding, through to significant personal change. This variation, inevitably, means that how people learn can take different forms.

HOW DO PEOPLE LEARN?

Our understanding of how people learn is informed by the following groups of theories:

- Behaviourist – learning as behaviour change or conditioning
- Cognitivist – learning as understanding
- Constructivist – learning as construction or creation of knowledge
- Social – learning as social practice

Each is a cluster of family of theories, rather than being a single model. In this book we can do no more than introduce them, but further reading and web links are given to enable you to follow up any of them in more detail.

LEARNING AS BEHAVIOUR CHANGE – BEHAVIOURIST LEARNING THEORIES

Behaviourists argue that learning is behaviour change produced as a result of an external stimulus and the consequences of these. The origins of behaviourist learning theory is in Pavlov's work with dogs (Pavlov 1927), from which he developed ideas of stimulus–response conditioning, which were further developed by the work of Skinner (1953).

Key principles of behaviourism are:

1. Observable changed behaviour is the sign that learning has occurred.

2. Learning is triggered by external stimulus from the environment. This could be the prospect of promotion or the threat of redundancy, for example, or can be the form of verbal explanation or the novel interest of a learning event.

3. Repetition: On the grounds that 'practice makes perfect', repeated stimulus is given to produce the desired response.

4. Reinforcement of new behaviours is necessary to establish them as new habits; for example, by positive reinforcers such as performance-related financial reward, a manager's praise, kudos with colleagues, or a personal sense of achievement. Negative reinforcers can also produce a learned response; for example, through personal sense of embarrassment at making a mistake or negative customer feedback.

The assumption of behaviourism is that people can be conditioned or 'trained' to behave in set ways if clear objectives are specified. So a trainer would specify learning outcomes and create a stimulus to bring about the desired response, through, for example, small learning chunks, rote learning of required phrases, repeated practice of desired behaviours. The standardised customer greeting given in certain major supermarkets is an example of such training – reinforcing the set phrases and expressions required by all checkout staff until they become almost instinctive. Similarly, a behaviourist approach is taken to the standardised training received by new employees of McDonald's designed to produce a common sequence of greetings, selling and steps to complete a transaction, across the chain. Much e-learning instructional design has been heavily reliant on a behaviourist approach, for example using chunking of learning materials, a defined sequencing, frequent recall checks and repetition of practice and reinforcement of the intended new behaviours.

IMPLICATIONS OF BEHAVIOURISM FOR LEARNERS, TRAINERS AND DEVELOPERS

One implication of behaviourism is that the learner is completely passive, unthinking and unfeeling. Emotion, motivations, other cognitive or social processes and learning environment would not be considered significant for behaviourists. This means behaviourists would not expect an individual's learning to be affected by their enthusiasm or otherwise for the content of a course or their fear or love for a computer.

A second implication is the assumption that the trainer can control the learning through manipulating the stimuli and reinforcers to produce the desired behaviours successfully. This presumes they are all-knowing about the reactions that can be anticipated in people as a result of particular stimuli.

Behaviourism allows little room for creativity, independent learning or idiosyncratic human responses, and you might ask yourself just how predictable human beings are.

PROS AND CONS OF BEHAVIOURIST LEARNING THEORIES

Behaviourist learning theory guides certain practices that are known to be effective in producing learning, such as the value of repetition, of expressing what is intended through specifying measurable learning outcomes and of careful planning and sequenced delivery of content. These ideas strongly influence current principles of instructional design (analysis needs–design–develop–implement–evaluate) and curriculum planning in post-compulsory education. The whole competency-based approach to development and assessment is also strongly influenced by behaviourism.

Behaviourism is associated with Taylorist scientific management ideas, which, though influential in the early and mid-twentieth century, came to be seen as ineffective in many organisational settings, particularly, for example, in dynamic, uncertain industry environments and when managing knowledge workers. The focus on standard, correct responses to specific situations is unlikely to prepare learners for non-standard situations. If people's jobs are highly predictable and standardised this is not a problem, but if their work contains many diverse daily situations, then habitual responses will not be adequate. For these contexts, other learning theories will be more useful. Likewise, when jobs require development of problem-solving, professional judgement and originality, behaviourist approaches to development are too limited, as has been found, for example, with the attempt to apply competences to management development beyond the supervisory level.

A further critique of behaviourism has been that at worst it fosters the kind of authoritarian manipulation of people found in the Bourne trilogy of books/films: the 'reconditioning' of their agents.

FOLLOW UP

www.learningandteaching.info/learning/behaviour.htm

LEARNING AS UNDERSTANDING – COGNITIVIST LEARNING THEORIES

Cognitive learning theories view learning as the mental processing of new pieces of information into existing knowledge through assimilation and accommodation (Piaget 1971). Assimilation is the integration of new facts, whereas accommodation is the adaptation of mental models to incorporate new information. Learning occurs when individuals reorganise experiences so as to make sense of new external input from the environment. This enables them to extend their knowledge base. Cognitive dissonance is said to arise when individuals cannot explain a new event in terms of their existing mental schema. They are forced to revise these patterns in order to reduce the level of dissonance, or otherwise to reject the new information. Trainers and developers can help catalyse such rethinking through the presentation of alternative conceptual models or helping the learner to look from alternative perspectives.

Cognitive learning theories are concerned with human thought processes, for example, perception, cognition, encoding, memory, and how these are used to acquire, process and retain information. A key interest of cognitivists is people's strategies for thinking and how these might be developed. Cognitivism implies interventions that help learners recognise their mental models, to deconstruct and reconstruct conceptual maps. Familiar cognitivist-inspired ideas in learning and development include 'mind-mapping' (Buzan 2006) and Bloom's taxonomy of learning (Bloom 1956), as well as many models of learning style (see later in this chapter).

IMPLICATIONS OF COGNITIVISM FOR LEARNERS, TRAINERS AND DEVELOPERS

Cognitivism suggests that the trainer/developer's main function is to help the learner process information and transfer-to long-term memory. Attention to the individual's past experiences and current state is required. The following are examples of suggested methods:

- Techniques like concept maps (Hay and Kinchin 2006) and formative assessment help reveal learners' existing schema.
- Vary the presentation method and format.
- Provide an organising framework for the whole material before breaking up into sections for stepped learning. For example, determine the knowledge/skills and attitudes (KSA) objectives.
- Progress from simple to complex tasks.
- Encourage alternative perspective-taking.

PROS AND CONS OF COGNITIVE LEARNING THEORIES

If learning is viewed as the processing and committing of information to memory, the assumption is that the trainer/developer is in full control of what content is required. This may well be so when job roles and competences can be clearly specified, but, as for the critique of behaviourism, in jobs that require the development of know-how, judgement and contingent action, then individuals need more.

The other main criticism levelled at cognitivist perspectives is not so much targeting the learning theories themselves, but the learning style models and instruments that have been spawned.

FOLLOW UP

See the Learning styles section later in this chapter for a critical review of learning styles and cognitive styles.

Cognitivist-inspired assessment can tend to emphasise assessment of memory, which may not be the most accurate reflector of work-based learning, or ability of a person to perform competently in a particular role.

FOLLOW UP

www.learningandteaching.info/learning/cognitive.htm

LEARNING AS INDIVIDUAL CREATION OF KNOWLEDGE – CONSTRUCTIVIST LEARNING THEORIES

Constructivist theories claim that people 'construct' their own personal meaning by integrating new ideas and experiences into their previous knowledge. Knowledge is not something 'out there' waiting to be collected, like pebbles on a beach, as Isaac Newton reputedly said. Instead, individuals are active in creating their own understanding, using 'constructs' to represent the world (Kelly 1955). This means that different individuals can come away from the same experience with different insights, and what they learn from the same training course will differ, for example, influenced by their emotions, prior experience or power in the situation.

In constructivist theories the individual learner is central to the learning, and the role of the trainer or developer is not to see themselves as putting content into an empty vessel, as if depositing money in a bank account, but to design interventions which help learners make sense of new material. People are assumed to want to find meaning in situations, and only when they have does it become useable knowledge. The implication is they learn best through active engagement in problems, analysis, planning and reflection.

 ILLUSTRATION

Experiential learning and reflection

Experiential learning approaches are one example of constructivist learning, with core ideas that people learn from reflecting on experiences, as well as in the midst of action. Building on the ideas of John Dewey (1938) and Kurt Lewin (1951), more recent advocates of experiential learning include Kolb (1984), Boud *et al* (1993) and Vince (2002). For Dewey, the context of learning is shaped by the relationship between the individual, their actions and their social world.

IMPLICATIONS OF CONSTRUCTIVISM FOR LEARNERS, TRAINERS AND DEVELOPERS

● Trainers/developers are encouraged to think of themselves as facilitators of learning, less expert deliverers able to control what each individual learns.

- action enquiry-based methods, such as action learning, appreciative enquiry
- reflective journals
- problem-based learning
- coaching
- mentoring
- other student-directed methods.

PROS AND CONS OF CONSTRUCTIVIST LEARNING THEORIES

Constructivist learning theories provide an explanation for why individuals vary in the ways they engage with the same learning and development interventions and how their learning from the same experiences might vary dramatically, where behaviourist and cognitivist theories cannot. Learning is understood to be dependent on wider factors than simply the glossy handouts, the snazzy PowerPoints or the dynamism of the trainer. Individuals' prior learning, experiences, job position, mental models and even personal values will affect what meaning they construct and hence how they learn. This is more complex and demanding for trainers than behaviourist or cognitive learning theories would suggest.

However, you might also ask yourself whether this level of complexity is always helpful when designing learning interventions. For example, if the objective is for employees to learn how to use a defibrillator, how relevant are their personal values or mental models?

LEARNING AS SOCIAL PRACTICE – SOCIAL LEARNING THEORIES

Social learning theories emphasise the role of social aspects of learning, in two ways. The first is the idea that without interaction and communication between people there can be no thinking. Contrary to the constructivist notion of learning taking place in an individual's head, social learning perspectives suggest that people make sense of new ideas and are able to give them meaning only through dialogue with others. This is termed social constructionism. The idea that social interaction is essential to at least some kinds of learning originated with Vygotsky (1978), who observed that children were able to perform well above their age if given the chance to interact with someone older. He is particularly renowned for the concept 'zone of proximal development' – the notion that we learn best at the edge of familiarity – not too stretched and not too comfortable, and that social interaction helps extend this boundary more effectively than an individual alone.

The second angle on social learning is the role of the social environment or culture for learning. This is the idea that the surrounding cultural values and practices play a key role in fostering and promoting learning or indeed in stifling learning. The idea that learning is a sharing of the surrounding culture (Bruner

1996) focuses on the role within work organisations of context in inducting new members to the institutional norms and ways to be in a 'community of practice' (Wenger 1998).

ILLUSTRATION

Cultures of learning and non-learning

Different organisation, trade and professional cultures have differences in their dominant views on the purposes of learning and development. For example, self-funded continuous professional development (CPD) is accepted as a fundamental part of being a professional by some groups (eg medical professions), whilst others might assume their initial training which qualified them was sufficient.

ACTIVITY

Look back at the Murphy's Icecream illustration at the start of the chapter. How does the idea of 'community of practice' help explain why this approach to induction might be successful?

The suggestion that some people's learning possibilities might be disabled by the learning culture of a particular organisation or learning intervention (James and Biesta 2007) is a useful one, with particular implications for diversity and equality. Recent research into lifelong learners has identified how the socio-cultural context of individual learners can affect their learning. For example, communities and social groups who believe formal learning has not benefited them may be reluctant to engage further as adults (Warren and Webb 2007).

ILLUSTRATION

CASE STUDY

Learning disablement

Erita is a company that project manages the implementation of integrated IT systems in organisations internationally. It has a proud reputation for strong project management, completing projects on time and often under budget. A key element seems to be the strong team ethos throughout the company. Project teams are often away from home all week, staying in hotels near their client organisation. They work long hours and late-evening socialising

is common, often involving alcohol. Discussion of work never stops and much learning happens through these informal social interactions.

This all sounded too good to be true, but, for the programme director Andy, when he recruited a smart, non-drinking young Sikh, he could see that the informal, drink-based culture could well be problematic. Was this new man going to be excluded from the social learning of the team?

IMPLICATIONS OF SOCIAL LEARNING FOR LEARNERS, TRAINERS AND DEVELOPERS

In practice, design of learning and talent development informed by social learning theories might include:

- interventions that promote interaction with others, such as peer review, action learning, coaching, mentoring, buddying
- collaborative action enquiry-based methods that encourage experimentation and reflection, such as action learning, appreciative enquiry
- team working
- cross-organisational project work
- post-project reviews
- learning and talent development professionals model collaborative learning in the ways they interact with employees
- use of problem-based learning where collaborative learning events are designed around learners' real-world problems and scenarios
- experiential learning
- reflective conversations.

PROS AND CONS OF SOCIAL THEORIES OF LEARNING

Social theories of learning are more complex to act on than those that focus solely on the individual learner. It is easier for the trainer or developer to make adjustments to their own training methods or design, than it is to recognise that in many organisations what really needs to change if learning is to be enhanced is an organisational culture to better support interaction between employees.

A further implication of the significance of the socio-cultural environment learning conducted by Sarason (1990) is that the conditions for people to be lifelong learners cannot be created and sustained unless they also exist for the trainers or developers themselves.

In the social learning approach:

> learning is understood as something that is done; learning is practical and embodied, that is, it involves our emotions and our bodies as well as our brains. Moreover, learning is (in the main) done with others which means that it is 'a thoroughly social process' (Coffield 2008, p9).

However, as the illustration above suggests, a further implication of this socio-cultural approach, in drawing attention to the social, ethnic and gender positions of learners (as well as trainers), is to make the notion of universal best practice dubious (Coffield 2008).

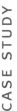

CASE STUDY

PRACTICAL IMPLICATIONS OF LEARNING THEORY APPLIED TO E-LEARNING

Behaviourism: Design of an e-learning course involves structured, step-by-step guidance. Content is broken up into small chunks and tests, such as multiple choice questions, are provided for learners to assess the knowledge they are building up. This is useful when the knowledge required is 'bite-sized'.

Cognitive: design includes methods intended to incite mental processes of organising and linking content to past knowledge. Examples include problem-solving and compare-and-contrast activities.

Constructivist: methods to facilitate sense-making and interpretation, for example, problems, cases or scenarios presented for learners to stimulate active creation of knowledge through exploration of concepts in practice.

Social constructionist: methods to facilitate sense-making and interpretation. For example, problems, cases or scenarios presented for learners to explore and resolve with peers, to stimulate active creation of knowledge through exploration of concepts in practice. Group discussion, team simulation activities and cognitive coaching are examples of such methods, the latter being a peer review approach, where participants comment on each other's online responses, with the aim of provoking deep learning.

ACTIVITY

Look up the website www.support4learning.org.uk/education/learning_styles.cfm.

Based on the information there and in this chapter, make notes on why you might expect simulation to result in a better-trained new pilot than simply asking her to read a manual.

THEORIES OF LEARNING – THE ROLE OF TRAINERS AND DEVELOPERS

The implication of the theories of learning explored above is that the role of trainers and developers will vary significantly depending on what kind of learning they want to stimulate, whether un-learning is required, who the learners are and what the organisation context is:

Sometimes trainers instruct or tell, serving as transmitters of information that learners have to acquire, memorise and be able to reproduce under test conditions as a measure of their learning. At other times developers show and demonstrate, acting as mentors and coaches rather than as instructors. Sometimes the developer/manager must discover what the employee already knows, which may include identifying their misunderstanding, and then find ways in which they can be helped to develop new and richer insights into problems and how they might be solved (adapted from DEMOS 2005, p7).

It is important for learning and talent development practitioners to develop their own sense of professional purpose and identity. One way of envisaging this, suggested by Coffield (2008), is to consider a choice between the metaphors of acquisition and participation because they imply different activities and ways of thinking about the role. The acquisition metaphor sees learning as the individual

> gaining possession of knowledge, skills and qualifications, just as people acquire cars, watches and houses (Coffield 2008, p8).

The participation metaphor, very differently,

> locates learning not in the heads of individuals, but in the simultaneous social processes of: learning to belong to different 'communities of practice' ... to recognise changes in our identity ... to create meaning out of our experiences; and learning what it means to know in practice (Coffield 2008, p8).

With the participation metaphor:

> learning is viewed as a process of participation in a variety of social worlds, and the learner is seen as someone being: transformed into a practitioner, a newcomer becoming an old-timer, whose changing knowledge, skills and discourse are part of a developing identity – in short, a member of a community of practice (Lave and Wenger 1991, p122, cited by Coffield 2008, p9).

The participation metaphor has great relevance for work-based learning and situations of apprenticeship or learning to become a professional, where learning is about joining a community of practice, learning how to be, acquiring status and identity, as well as developing skills and competence (Hargreaves 2004).

 ACTIVITY

Which of the metaphors 'acquisition' and 'participation' do you feel better describes the way you think about your own role as a provider or commissioner of learning and talent development? Reflecting on this in the light of this chapter, how well does this fit with the context and objectives of your work?

SUMMARY

This section has discussed perspectives on what learning can be understood to involve, as both process and outcomes, and has introduced four families or clusters of learning theories. Each has some strengths as well as limitations, and each has different implications for the position of the learner, the role of the trainer/developer and influence of the context. Each also gives us differing ideas for methods to use to achieve learning. Which to choose is strongly dependent on what kind of learning outcomes are wanted: procedures, routines, protocols, values, behaviours, attitudes, conceptual frameworks, competences, transformation – no single family of learning theories is best for each. Sometimes

Table 6.1 Implications of learning theory families for methods and design

Learning theory family	Behaviourism	Cognitive	Constructivist	Social constructionist
Assumptions about learners	Passive recipients of input	Cognitive information processors	Able to self-direct their learning Motivated	Learn through interaction Enabled or disabled by context
Assumptions about learning professionals	Expert deliverers In control	Expert deliverers Varying format to accommodate learning styles In control	Facilitators of meaning-making	Choreographed interactions
Methods	Bite-sized chunks of information Repeated instructions Repeated practice at tasks Role plays Instruction Reinforcement	Concept maps Varied presentation method and format A framework + sequenced learning steps Plan the KSA objectives Progress from simple to complex tasks	Action enquiry-based methods, such as action learning, appreciative enquiry Reflective journals Problem-based learning Coaching Mentoring Other learner-directed methods	Peer review, action learning, coaching, mentoring, buddying, appreciative enquiry Team working Cross-organisational project work Post-project reviews Reflective conversations
Applications	Learning outcomes that are behaviours – skills, competences, that can be clearly specified	Job roles and competences that can be clearly specified	Learning for complex roles, developing judgement, experienced learners	Joining communities of practice – professional groups, merged teams, apprenticeships, induction
Weaknesses	Limited for more complex learning outcomes, higher-level skills	More limited for complex learning outcomes Assessment of memory, not ability Inappropriate use of learning style models	Not necessary for simple learning outcomes	Not necessary for simple learning outcomes

they can be combined, as the case study of e-learning shows. This section concludes with Table 6.1 above, which summarises the principles of the four clusters and their implications for learning and talent development methods and design. The following section moves to look in more depth at the ideas and debates concerning learning styles.

LEARNING STYLES, THINKING STRATEGIES AND COGNITIVE STYLE – FAD OR SCIENCE?

Ideas of learning style have had considerable appeal to learning and talent development practitioners as well as to academics, for a number of years. In the field of learning and talent development in Britain the most familiar models are likely to be Kolb's learning cycle, Honey and Mumford's learning styles, VAKT[1] and Myers-Briggs type indicator (MBTI). Certainly the busy professional can expect to be bombarded with commercial offers of learning style courses and assessment questionnaires which make impressive claims for revolutionising learning. However, there is a growing recognition that the field is much more problematic and uncertain than can justify many such claims. In this section we will look at some of the ideas and claims for learning styles as well as the pitfalls cautioned.

TERMINOLOGY – WHAT IS MEANT BY 'LEARNING STYLE'

The first problem is that there is no common, agreed language among practitioners, academics or commercial protagonists of learning styles. Various terms are used, sometimes with different meanings and sometimes interchangeably. They include, but are not limited to, 'learning styles', 'thinking styles', 'cognitive styles', 'learning modalities' and learning strategies. The definitions in Figure 6.1 illustrate some of this confusion.

It should be clear from these definitions that, whilst all relate to some aspect of processing, organising, representing, retaining and retrieving information, they each mention differing combinations of only some of these. Not only is there no agreement on what aspects of learning, 'learning style' refers to, there is also variation in the extent to which this is seen as a fixed attribute of individual personality as compared to acquired habits and behaviours that are flexible and could change. There is also controversy over whether some of these ideas have any evidence to back them up at all.

The most recent systematic and critical review of learning style models was conducted by Coffield *et al* for the UK Learning and Skills Development Agency (Coffield *et al* 2004). They identified 71 different learning styles models and categorised them into five types on a spectrum from fixed genetic traits to flexible, habitual and changeable approaches:

1. genetic/constitutionally based
2. cognitive structure

Figure 6.1 Learning styles, strategies and modalities – some definitions

---

Learning style

A 'biologically and developmentally imposed set of characteristics that make the same teaching methods wonderful for some and terrible for others' (Dunn and Griggs 1998, p3) 'the way in which individuals begin to concentrate on, process, internalise and retain new and difficult information' (Dunn et al 1994, p2)	'distinctive behaviours which serve as indicators of how a person learns from and adapts to his environment' (Gregorc 1979, p234) 'structural properties of the cognitive system itself ' (Messick 1984, p60) 'a coherent whole of learning activities that students usually employ, their learning orientation and their mental model of learning' (Vermunt 1996, p29)

Cognitive style

'an individual's preferred and habitual approach to organising and representing information' (Riding and Rayner 1998, p8) 'are static and are relatively in-built features of the individual' (Riding and Cheema 1991, p196)	'the way people process information, for example how they perceive, remember and use information from their surrounding environment' (Graff 2006, p144)

Learning strategy

'those processes which are used by the learner to respond to the demands of a learning activity' (Riding and Rayner 1998, p8)	'conscious or unconscious choices made by teachers or students as to how to process given information and demands of a learning activity' (Bostrom and Lassen 2006, p179)

Learning modalities
Modality refers to the idea that our bodies have different primary ways of taking in and storing information. A commonly used model [though severely criticised; see below and Coffield 2008] is VAKT:

- Vistual: learning based on observation and seeing what is being learned
- Auditory: learning based on listening to instructions/information
- Kinaesthetic: learning based on hands-on work, movement and practical activity

(Barbe *et al* 1979)

---

3. stable personality
4. flexibly stable learning preferences
5. learning approaches and strategies.

For 13 of the most influential and widely used models, Coffield *et al* conducted a systematic critical assessment of their reliability and validity.

Figure 6.2 shows the five types and how these 13 models were categorised. Table 6.2 (p160) elaborates on the core principles of each of these.

Figure 6.2 Families of learning styles

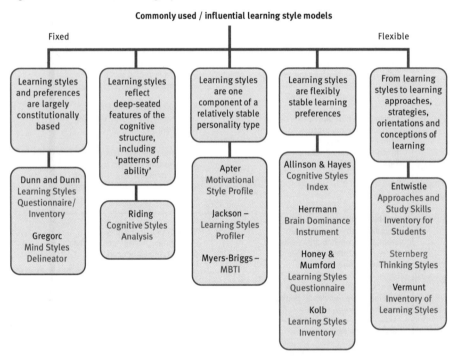

Source: Adapted from Coffield *et al* 2004

WHY THE APPEAL OF LEARNING STYLES?

There are several reasons suggested for the appeal of learning styles:

1. Intuitively and empirically many people have observed that individuals vary in the ways they appear to learn and to process information.

2. Learning professionals and development practitioners hope that if individuals' preferred styles are diagnosed, learning interventions can be designed to work with these strengths, with the result that such a match will lead to accelerated learning.

3. It is suggested that developers can build on knowledge of diversity of learning style to design interventions that consciously integrate and accommodate all approaches.

4. Those concerned to see learners maximise their development (and learners themselves) hope that learners' increased knowledge of their strengths and weaknesses could lead to more deliberate actions to strengthen their less-preferred approaches so to become more rounded.

5. Managers and policy-makers who are concerned to maximise learning from the resources they invest hope that if learners develop greater understanding of their own strengths, weaknesses and preferences they might better manage their own learning processes.

6. Some have observed that, from a managerialist perspective, if the lever for effectiveness in design of development interventions can be pinned on learning styles it provides a distraction from considering how learning and talent development improvements might actually need more resources, or changes to subject or contextual issues such as employment relations.

The implications for learning and talent development professionals is whether learning and development can be improved by matching to cognitive style or whether employees' learning could be enhanced by improving their self-insight on how to learn. For example, two of the more widely used dimensions of cognitive style are the verbal–imagery dimension and the wholist–analytic dimension. Verbalisers are said to represent information in the form of words and therefore to learn best through text or the spoken word; imagers are thought to think in terms of pictures and to therefore learn best from graphic representations of information. The wholist–analytical dimension is applied to the organisation of information. Wholists are said to take a holistic, interconnected overview of information and to prefer to learn through a breadth-first structure which gives an overall view of a topic before introducing detail; analytics are said to break information down into small, constituent parts and so to prefer to learn through a depth-first approach, where one topic is explored fully before moving on to the next.

This illustrates how and why learning styles might have had such appeal to learning and talent development practitioners, as well as to educationalists. However, in addition to the confusing and problematic terminology of the field, a second major weakness is its poor theoretical basis.

THEORETICAL BASIS FOR 'LEARNING STYLES'

The second problem with learning styles is the absence of consensus on underpinning theory of learning and the confusing assortment of models and assessment tools. The core knowledge underpinning different models named in Figure 6.2 have varying origins in psychology, psychotherapy, philosophy and neuroscience/neurobiology. For example, the MBTI (Myers-Briggs Type Indicator) is based on Jungian theory of personality, whilst the experiential learning theory underlying the model of Kolb is indebted to the educational theories of John Dewey, Kurt Lewin and Jean Piaget, among others. Multi-disciplinary roots are not necessarily a weakness and such diversity could be a rich source of ideas. However, in the field of learning styles, the multi-disciplinary roots seems to be producing silos of thought and practice that are not helpful either to practitioners or to advancing understanding of learning more generally. Coffield *et al* (2004, p135) concluded that the 'field of learning styles consists of a wide variety of approaches' involving numerous groups that rarely interact either with each other or with other fields that might be expected to be relevant, such as mainstream psychology or neuroscience. There is no agreed common language or conceptual framework, and different approaches derive from different perspectives with few similarities.

EVIDENCE-BASED PRACTICE? EASIER SAID THAN DONE

The third major problem with the learning styles field is a poor evidence base for many of the claims made, particularly for the legitimacy of the many learning styles questionnaires. Increasingly in management there is talk of evidence-based practice, but what evidence is sufficient and by what criteria do we judge? This is very important for learning and talent development practitioners, because they need to be able to be confident that, when they are designing development interventions or commissioning external delivery of training and development, the ideas about learning styles underpinning such development are valid. However, it is not easy at present to know what learning styles ideas and models are valid, even though they may be well known.

Whilst intuitively the idea that we each have a distinctive learning style might seem appealing, there is in fact little evidence to support the existence of fixed styles. Also, when research has been conducted into the impacts on learning of matching learning design to learning style, there are conflicting findings on whether such matching does produce better learning. Improving our knowledge in this area is not helped by the multitude of learning style instruments, each associated with a different learning style model, so measuring different aspects of learning. A learning style questionnaire or instrument can only be used with confidence if it meets the following conditions:

 ILLUSTRATION

Learning style instruments

- Do they measure what they intend to?
- Will the results be the same if the same person took the test again at another time?
- Do the results really predict how an individual will approach a future learning incident?
- Do the results really predict how successfully a person might learn when learning design is matched to their learning style?

In 1987 Curry judged that

> the poor general quality of available instruments makes it unwise to use any one instrument as a true indicator of learning styles ... using only one measure assumes that measure is more correct than the others. At this time (1987) the evidence cannot support that assumption (Curry 1987, p16, cited by Coffield *et al* 2004, p140).

In 2004 Coffield *et al* concluded much the same:

> None of the [learning styles] models we reviewed passed all of the 'good' test criteria of reliability and validity, with the result that one cannot use a learning styles instrument and be sure that all the items are measuring what they intend to measure [or] that the results will be the same if the test is taken again (Coffield *et al* 2004, p140).

AT WORST...

> the belief that styles are fixed has led to propositions that marriage partners should have compatible learning styles, that people from socially disadvantaged groups tend to have a particular style or, as Gregorc (1985) believes, that styles are God-given and that to work against one's personal style will lead to ill-health (Coffield *et al* 2004, p2).

Table 6.2 summarises the conclusions for each of 13 models and learning style instruments scrutinised in depth by the Coffield study, but these authors' concluding advice for practitioners is very cautionary:

> Some of the best known and widely used instruments have such serious weaknesses (eg low reliability, poor validity and negligible impact on pedagogy) that we recommend their use in research and in practice should be discontinued (Coffield *et al* 2004, p138).

More recently Coffield has reasserted the conclusion regarding the VAKT model of learning modality that:

> there is no scientific justification for teaching or learning strategies based on VAKT and tutors should stop using learning style instruments based on them (Coffield 2008, p32).

In reviewing these 13 models, independent evidence was looked for 'that the instrument could demonstrate both internal consistency and test–retest reliability and construct and predictive validity. These are the minimum standards for any instrument which is to be used to redesign pedagogy' (Coffield *et al* 2004, p141).

Several of these models are widely known and extensively used, but this review found that very many studies had been commissioned specifically to provide evidence in support of a particular model, and there were few independent or longitudinal studies. Their strong conclusions are:

> Only three of the 13 models – those of Allinson and Hayes, Apter and Vermunt – could be said to have come close to meeting these criteria. A further three – those of Entwistle, Herrmann and Myers-Briggs met two of the four criteria. The Jackson model is in a different category, being so new that no independent evaluations have been carried out so far. The remaining six models [Kolb, Honey and Mumford, Riding, Dunn and Dunn, Sternberg, Gregorc] despite in some cases having been revised and refined over 30 years, failed to meet the criteria and so, in our opinion, should not be used as the theoretical justification for changing practice (Coffield *et al* 2004, p141).

These hard-hitting conclusions have significant implications for learning and talent development where practitioners have been using some of these models for many years. It raises difficult questions for professionals as to what ideas and models they can draw on in confidence and how to differentiate between a sound evidence base and those advocated with commercial interests. Some have argued for more research that builds on practitioners' experiences. In the study

Table 6.2 Coffield study conclusions re common learning style models

Learning styles and preferences are largely constitutionally based	Reflect deep-seated features of the cognitive structure	One component of a relatively stable personality type	Flexibly stable learning preferences	Learning approaches, strategies, orientations and conceptions of learning
Dunn and Dunn (Dunn and Griggs 2003) **Learning Styles Questionnaire/ Inventory** Four styles: environmental, emotional, physical, sociological Includes VAKT* Widely used in USA and internationally. Aims to help teachers adapt individual instructional preferences and adapt the learning environment. *Limitations in many of the supporting studies and lack of independent research ... need to be addressed before further use is made in the UK (37)*	Riding & Rayner (1998) **Cognitive Styles Analysis** Two dimensions: wholist–analytic (ways of organising information), verbaliser–imager (ways of representing information) *The simplicity and potential value of Riding's model are not well served by an unreliable instrument, the CSA (44)*	Apter (2001) **Motivational Style Profile** Four motivational domains: means–ends, rules, transactions, relationships A systemic theory of personality that acknowledges interplay between emotion, cognition and volition *A theory which poses a threat to fixed-trait models of learning style and ... merits further research (55)*	Allinson & Hayes (1996) **Cognitive Styles Index** Measures a single dimension of cognitive style: intuition–analysis Designed for adults in organisation settings *the CSI has the best evidence for reliability and validity of the 13 models studied ... although the pedagogical implications ... have not been fully explore*	Entwistle (1997) **Approaches and Study Skills Inventory for Students** Three orientations/approaches to learning: deep (seeking meaning), surface (reproducing), strategic (reflective organising) Very influential in UK higher education *For adult learning: potentially useful model and instrument ... but significant development and testing will be needed*

Model	Description
Gregorc (1985) **Mind Styles Delineator**	Two dimensions: <u>concrete–abstract</u> and <u>sequential–random.</u> Individuals said to be strong on 1 or 2 categories. *Theoretically and psychometrically flawed. Not suitable for the assessment of individuals (21)*
Jackson (2002) **Learning Styles Profiler**	Four styles: initiator, reasoner, analyst, implementer; LSP. Relatively new instrument designed for use in business + education. *A sophisticated instrument, but has some relatively weak aspects (58)*
Myers-Briggs (Myers and McCaulley (1998)) **MBTI**	Widely used personality type measure, based on Jungian theory. *Despite the enormous commercial success of the MBTI the research evidence to support it ... is inconclusive, at best (51)*
Herrmann (1989) **Brain Dominance Instrument**	Four categories of learned patterns of behaviour: theorists, organisers, innovators, humanitarians. Inspired by brain research, and informed by ideas of socialisation. Less well known in UK. *pedagogical implications ... have not yet been fully explored and tested ... A model which ... offers considerable promise (84)*
Honey & Mumford (2000) **Learning Styles Questionnaire**	Four preferred ways of learning: activist, reflector, theorist, pragmatist. A popular UK self- and management development tool. Derived from Kolb cycle. *more evidence is needed before LSQ is acceptable (76)*
Sternberg (1999) **Thinking Styles**	13 thinking styles, based on a theory of mental self-government involving 3 functions, 4 forms, 2 levels, 2 scopes and 2 leanings of government. Learners have a profile of styles, not just one single style; these may vary with gender and cultural background. *There is a need for independent evaluation ... An unnecessary addition to the proliferation of learning styles models (117)*
Vermunt (1996) **Inventory of Learning Styles**	Four approaches to learning: meaning-directed, application-directed, reproduction-directed, undirected. Each style encompasses 5 dimensions: cognitive processing, learning orientation, affective processes (feelings about learning), mental model of learning, regulation (planning & monitoring). Emphasis on the wider teaching–learning environment. *A rich model, validated for use in UK HE context (109) ... not tested and may not be applicable to all types of lifelong learning*

Learning styles and preferences are largely constitutionally based	Reflect deep-seated features of the cognitive structure	One component of a relatively stable personality type	Flexibly stable learning preferences	Learning approaches, strategies, orientations and conceptions of learning
			Kolb (1999) **Learning Styles Inventory** Four preferred orientations for learning: diverging, assimilating, converging and accommodating Developed from Kolb's theory of experiential learning One of the most influential models for practitioners *dispute over reliability of LSI* *notion of a learning cycle may be seriously flawed* *Research findings of pedagogical impact are contradictory and inconclusive (70)*	

Source: Adapted from Coffield *et al* 2004, p138

Notes: Quotes from original report cited in italics. *VAKT: Auditory/Visual/Tactile/Kinaesthetic modalities by Coffield *et al*, the standards of scientific research are being used to assess the value of the models. Another influential report from DEMOS (2005) offers a somewhat different benchmark, advocating both practitioner and scientific evidence (see Illustration below). This report argued:

> Sometimes scientific evidence can be ahead of practice evidence, but it is possible for practice evidence to be ahead of scientific evidence. Where there is widespread practice evidence about an activity, the lack of a scientific basis for it does not prove it is worthless, but does suggest caution. In such cases we believe it is essential to follow practice evidence with scientific evidence. We are concerned that there is currently no procedure by which scientific evidence can be commissioned to confirm practice evidence, even when it seems very important that this be done (DEMOS 2005, p16).

This is certainly not a justification for learning and talent development practitioners to ignore the warnings of misguided use of learning styles models, rather to look for opportunities to participate in research that will help to build up our knowledge of learning styles and so to improve the evidence base for practice.

 ILLUSTRATION

Evidence about learning – a perspective

It is when the two kinds of evidence are mutually supportive that the evidence base for a practice is most powerful.

We suggest that it is helpful to distinguish two types of evidence about learning and learning to learn, which we call *scientific evidence* and *practice evidence*. By scientific evidence, we mean evidence that derives from formal research, such as experiments conducted according to scientific canons, or from a study of practice in schools/colleges and classrooms that also adopts recognised scientific methods. Scientific evidence is regarded by cognitive scientists as the primary and most trustworthy form of evidence. By practice evidence, we mean the experience, testimony and findings gathered by one or more practitioners to assess the impact of a practice on students and their learning. Practice evidence is regarded by teachers as the primary and most obvious source of evidence about the value and effectiveness of a practice. Both kinds of evidence involve research, enquiry and investigation and the collection, analysis and interpretation of data relevant to the practice. Both vary in the quality of the evidence. For example, it is sometimes argued that the highest level of scientific evidence is that based on multiple randomised controlled trials. At the other end of the scale might be a single study using a small, unrepresentative sample in unusual conditions. In the same way, practice evidence might involve the collation of high-quality evidence of different kinds by a range of teachers in multiple contexts over a sustained period. At the other extreme, it might be the claim by a single teacher that a new practice is working to good effect in her classroom. Sometimes there is practitioner evidence alone, since the practice has not been subjected to formal research and a scientific base is lacking. Sometimes there is scientific evidence alone, since the evidence that, say, a particular method of teaching is demonstrably effective in experimental conditions does not necessarily mean that the practice is adopted by teachers in schools and found to work in their experience. Ideally, in our view, the two kinds of evidence should be combined to provide warrant that the practice is indeed a good practice. It is when the two kinds of evidence are mutually supportive that the evidence base for a practice is most powerful (DEMOS 2005, pp10, 11).

ACTIVITY

Read the DEMOS extract, then consider where your own ideas about learning have come from. What personal experiences do you particularly draw on? When did you last look up any scientific evidence on learning (and what was it)?

THE FUTURE FOR 'LEARNING STYLES'

Whilst there is wide agreement that people do differ in ways they process information, use learning strategies, and prefer to be instructed, unlike measuring temperature or calculating weight, when talking of 'learning styles' there is no agreement on what to measure and no standard, reliable measuring scale.

Learning styles research and practice is probably at a cross-roads. It could continue to be driven by commercial and professional interests into further fragmentation and conceptual confusion to a tipping point where consumers become cynical, the whole field becomes tarnished as a fad and, as with other management fads, users begin to turn away. This would be a loss, in that the potential from understanding thinking and learning styles more robustly would also be threatened. The alternative route is perhaps that highlighted by the DEMOS report (2005) of collaboration between practitioners and research scientists to develop a common vocabulary and improve the quality and co-ordination of research so as to strengthen the evidence base for learning practices. This latter route recognises the current weaknesses in the field when judged against the scientific standards applied by Coffield *et al* (2004) but is also cognisant of the empirical value placed by many professional practitioners on ideas about approaches to learning.

> There is, in short, a substantial body of work, both academic and practical, for which there is a real need for a supportive and comprehensive combination of scientific and practice evidence (DEMOS 2005, p20).

This is echoed by Evans and Sadler-Smith, who argue that practitioners need to:

> cut through the swathe of terminology; hone in on those constructs and measures that are theoretically sound, reliable and valid; be critically aware of the benefits and limitations of the available models for their practice; use evidence-based practice which is scientifically robust; and work with researchers to be in a position to disseminate 'what works' effectively to a wider audience (Evans and Sadler-Smith 2006, p78).

A number of people in the broad learning style field have responded to recent critiques to begin to talk of 'personal learning styles pedagogy' (Evans and Cools 2009) and more integrated learning instruments to assess learning patterns (Vermunt 2007) or to advocate 'learning profiles' to represent an umbrella concept to include cognitive style, learning style, learning strategies, preferences, motivation and self-perception (Riding and Raynor 2000; Evans and Sadler-Smith 2006; Evans and Graff 2008).

The CIPD offer the following view:

ILLUSTRATION

CIPD (2008): At risk of over-simplifying a complex subject, learning styles might be said to consist of three interrelated elements:

- information processing – habitual modes of perceiving, storing and organising information (for example, pictorially or verbally)
- instructional preferences – predispositions towards learning in a certain way (for example, collaboratively or independently) or in a certain setting (for example, time of day, environment)
- learning strategies – adaptive responses to learning specific subject matter in a particular context.

Rather than representing a single concept, 'learning styles' is therefore an umbrella term covering a spectrum of modalities, preferences and strategies.

Source:www.cipd.co.uk/subjects/lrnanddev/general/lrngstyles.htm?IsSrchRes=1 January 2010, accessed 25 January 2010

ACTIVITY

What use, if any, is made of learning styles in your organisation? In the light of the debates discussed in this section, what are the strengths and weaknesses of your organisation's approach?

Compare with others in your group.

SUMMARY

This chapter has introduced a number of theories and models related to people's learning. It is clear that the term 'learning' encompasses a broad range of cognitive as well as affective processes, which arguably makes it impossible for a single perspective on learning to provide the answers for all contexts and all people. Four clusters or families of learning theory were explored: behaviourist, cognitivist, constructivist and social, and the potential contribution of each to designing learning and talent development programmes and interventions was examined. In particular, the chapter looked at the practical implications of learning theory for selecting methods and designing programmes for varying kinds and levels of learning outcomes at different levels. Each theoretical perspective has contrasting implications for learning and talent development professionals, and in particular practitioners were invited to consider their own approach through the metaphors of participation and acquisition.

A more detailed examination of the debates surrounding learning style was given. The idea that each individual has an individual inbuilt or preferred style has been popular in learning and talent development practice, and a thriving commercial industry has built on this popularity. However, exaggerated claims, lack of agreement on the many related terms describing learning/cognitive and thinking styles, and doubtful scientific evidence underpinning the validity and benefits of even some of the most popular models has led to calls for more caution in the use of learning styles and more collaborative research between practitioners and research scientists.

From reading this chapter, its extended case study and completing the activities, you should be able to:

- understand that the term 'learning' refers to a variety of mental and social processes
- differentiate between a range of learning theories and models
- identify how these can be applied to inform the design of learning and talent development programmes and interventions
- connect specific methods of learning and talent development to theories of learning
- critique the misapplication of learning theory
- make evidence-based choices in the design of programme and selection of methods appropriate to intended outcomes.

The following key terms have been scrutinised and explored and, whilst they do not have a single, commonly agreed definition, we hope the chapter has provoked further thought on their connection and contribution to understanding learning:

- learning
- learning style
- learning strategy
- information processing
- learning modality
- experiential learning
- action learning

- constructivist
- constructionist
- social learning
- behaviourist
- cognitive dissonance
- mental schema

 REVIEW ACTIVITIES

1. Summarise five key things you have learnt from this chapter.

   a. Write down two or three new questions the chapter has raised for you or things that you are unclear about.

   b. Select one of these questions that you will enquire into further.

   c. Write down what action you can take next in pursuit of your question. (For example, read one of the references in this chapter, talk to someone more experienced at work, look on CIPD website, take time to reflect on your own experience.)

2. Create a statement for each of the following terms that summarises your understanding of each in your own words:

   a. learning

   b. experiential learning

   c. behaviourism

   d. cognitive theories of learning

   e. constructivism

   f. social theories of learning

   g. learning style

   h. cognitive style

   i. learning strategy.

3. Discuss in groups of four some of your most significant learning experiences. This could be from any area of your life – work, college, school, leisure. Take an example each and think about how you learned, as well as what you learned. What could you say had changed about you as a result of your learning?

4. In your organisation what examples exist of training or talent development interventions that could be said to be informed by social learning theories?

5. Select and describe one major or significant learning/talent development initiative you are currently involved with or affected by.

   a. Map out the following:

     i.   Who is it for?

     ii. What are the intended learning outcomes?

     iii. What learning methods are used?

     iv. What assumptions are being made as to how the participants will learn?

     v. What is working well and what is not working so well?

     vi. How might any of the learning theories help explain this? (Behaviourist, cognitive, constructivist or social theories of learning.)

   b. In the light of the discussion in the chapter, identify any changes you would recommend.

   c. Share the results with colleagues and examine how they compare. Discuss whether any differences can be explained by the different kinds of organisations you work for.

EXTENDED CASE STUDY + DISCUSSION QUESTIONS

CASE STUDY

Learning IT systems[2]

There is a typical approach taken in most organisations to learning how to use a new IT system, the 'default position' as the CIPD termed it. When a system is introduced or a major update takes place, the first step typically involves an initial period of classroom training for those staff who are seen as important to the change process, the champions or implementation team. This is designed, and often delivered by the IT system suppliers and can cover both the following aspects, although often the second is neglected:

1. How to do the required task: What is the activity that the individual must perform?

2. What are the implications of the task? This is the wider contextualisation. 'Where does my piece of the world fit and impact on this?'

The second stage is the identification of users and an initial short period of off-the-job classroom instruction followed by self-directed learning with the facility to call on the services of expert co-workers. Often the follow up support is provided by members of the implementation team.

New joiners who arrive after a new system has been introduced rarely receive adequate training and are often neglected. Sometimes their training is dealt with at the workplace through on-the-job training, delivered by champions. On occasion they are overloaded at induction with training on everything including the IT system, but this rarely works effectively.

A CIPD study of staff in organisations asked how they prefer to learn new IT systems. Not once did anyone say they would have preferred more off-the-job training in the classroom. There was a distinct preference for learning through supported hands-on practice. There was an evident comfort with less formal learning delivered in the workplace by colleagues.

A common comment from the champions was that classroom training provided by the suppliers tended to be too generic; that you could role play their examples as much as you liked, but you needed scenarios exactly like those you faced in your own context, to really learn how to use a new system.

Discussion questions

Using what you learned in this chapter on theories of learning, consider the following questions:

1. Why do you think the survey found that people preferred to learn a new IT system through supported hands-on practice, with less formal learning delivered in the workplace by colleagues?

2. Why might induction be the wrong context in which to introduce how an IT system works?

3. The trainer's intention is that the classroom is the place to give people the first principles of a new IT system, which they then learn how to apply on the job.

   In what contexts might this approach work well and in what contexts might it be ineffective?

4. How do constructivist and social learning theories help make sense of the champions' comment about needing context-specific scenarios in their training?

EXPLORE FURTHER

Essential

Evans, C. and Cools, E. (2009) The use and understanding of style differences to enhance learning. *Reflecting Education*. Vol. 5, No. 2, May, pp1–18.

Wenger, E. (2002) *Communities of Practice: Learning, meaning, and identity.* Cambridge: Cambridge University Press.

Recommended

Bostrom, L. and Lassen, L. (2006) Unravelling learning, learning styles, learning strategies and meta-cognition. *Education + Training*. Vol. 46 No. 2/3 pp178–189.

Buzan, T. (2006) *Mind Mapping: Kickstart your creativity and transform your life.* London: BBC.

CIPD (2008) Learning styles revised, August 2008. www.cipd.co.uk/subjects/lrnanddev/general/lrngstyles.htm?IsSrchRes=1, accessed 25 January 2010.

Coffield, F. *et al.* (2004) *Learning Styles and Pedagogy in Post-16 Learning: A systematic and critical review.* London: Learning and Skills Research Centre. Available at: www.lsda.org.uk/files/PDF/1543.pdf.

Journals

Human Resource Development International

Journal of European Industrial Training

International Journal of Training and Development

Human Resource Development Quarterly

Advances in Human Resource Development

Human Resource Development Review

Useful websites

www.cipd.co.uk/helpingpeoplelearn/casestudies.htm, accessed 19 January 2010.

DEMOS Learning Working Group: www.demos.co.uk/learningworkinggroup/.

Campaign for Learning

The Campaign for Learning works to shape learning policy to create a society where individuals are able to learn to sustain them for life.

www.campaign-for-learning.org.uk/cfl/index.asp.

The Campaign for Learning's **National Workplace Learning Network** has been established to build on expertise in the workplace learning. It is open to interested parties to share good practice, keep up-to-date, network and discuss, and influence development and change with regard to all workplace learning issues.

www.campaign-for-learning.org.uk/workplacelearningnetwork/about/index.asp.

Encyclopedia of the Sciences of Learning.

A comprehensive reference work by Springer.

http://refworks.springer.com/mrw/index.php?id=2885.

Three linked sites exploring learning and teaching in college, adult and professional education.

www.learningandteaching.info.

Etienne Wenger's Communities of practice site.

www.ewenger.com/theory/.

CHAPTER 7

Establishing Needs and Solutions to Talent Development

OVERVIEW

The notion of development need can seem quite straightforward and indeed it can be treated in that way. We will adopt that position for most of this chapter. However, we should and will recognise and acknowledge that the position is open to question and challenge and that alternative views exist. These alternatives apply both to the idea of 'need' and to the meaning of 'talent' that is applied in establishing development needs. The chapter structure will focus first on ideas of development need and then move on to how those can be and are applied in talent development. We will then examine possible and common solutions to developing talent as they are applied to various and differing contexts or foci of talent development. The chapter will close with a brief critique of the approaches described based on alternative analyses.

LEARNING OUTCOMES

After reading this chapter and completing the activities, the intention is that you will be able to:

- evaluate and critique alternative conceptions of the notion of development need
- articulate a reasoned and justified understanding of the concept of development need
- describe, compare and evaluate a range of methods and techniques for establishing development needs
- design and apply approaches to establishing talent development needs in varying organisation contexts.

THE NOTION OF DEVELOPMENT NEED

ACTIVITY

Consider the two illustration case studies below and then complete the associated activity.

CASE STUDY

DEVELOPMENT NEED

Illustration one

Peter is a 23-year-old graduate trainee recently recruited into Oxyco, a very large multinational oil company based in the UK. Peter has just finished a meeting with his mentor where his short, six-week placements for the next six months have been discussed and agreed. The purpose as described by his mentor is to 'dry behind Peter's ears' in order to get him used to life in the real world in contrast to what he learned on his economics course at university. The placements will be part of the initial 12-month graduate development programme at Oxyco and will be interspersed with attendance at five intensive, three-day residential courses with others on the graduate development programme before each begins a longer six-month placement in one of the company's operating divisions or head office departments. Peter has a desire to work in economic analysis in the company's strategic development department, but his mentor's view is that it is too early to determine Peter's long-term future, and that both Oxyco and Peter need to know much more about his development needs before long-term decisions are made.

Illustration two

Julia is graduate talent manager for Oxyco. She led the design of the current graduate development programme three years ago and has managed it since implementation. A review of the programme is now underway and is due to be delivered to the Europe, Middle East and Africa (EMEA) Management Board in three months' time. The programme recruits at least 50 graduates each year from European universities, lasts two years and aims to provide a mix of common, collective and individual learning and development to meet the needs of the business and of each individual graduate. Julia is most concerned about the extent to which those two aims can be met in a single programme.

Discussion questions

What is the common understanding of development need shared by Julia and Peter's mentor? To what extent is Peter likely to share this understanding? Will his be different? Produce a personal answer to these questions and then discuss them with colleagues to determine an agreed response.

In professional terminology and common practice the idea of development need is directly linked with work organisations and their objectives. Thus, in theory different organisations with varying objectives will have different needs. Or, more accurately the particular needs will be different but the meaning attached to the concept will be the same (see Harrison 2009, Griggs *et al* 2010).

The focus on organisation objectives in relation to development needs arises from two main factors. First, organisations are composed of individuals, and it is the personal and collective work of those individuals that determine the achievement, or not, of organisation objectives. Thus, organisation objectives are commonly cascaded to inform construction of functional, department, team and individual objectives. In the case of individual employees this is commonly achieved through performance management systems (see Harrison 2009; Gold and Iles 2010). However, employees need development in order to perform to meet their personal objectives and so establishing and meeting individual needs is central to performance management. So, the existence of organisational objectives creates and to an extent also specifies individual development needs. The second main factor is current performance levels against stated and desired objectives. Failure to meet organisational objectives is likely to some extent to be associated with some individual employees not meeting their personal objectives. And, in some but not all cases, that failure to meet personal objectives can be because of a need for development. Thus, in professional practice the idea of development needs is directly associated with performance against stated and desired objectives of both individual employees and organisations.

What should be clear from these two factors is the idea of a development need being associated with a 'gap' (Buckley and Caple 2009; Griggs *et al* 2010). In this formulation and in simple terms, a development need exists when there is a gap between existing capabilities and the capabilities required to achieve performance objectives. There is an important distinction and clarification to be drawn here. A development gap is not the same as a performance gap. The latter can arise for a great variety of reasons at both individual and organisational levels, and at levels in between the two; team and departmental level, for example. A development need exists only when the reason or cause for a performance gap is a gap in the necessary abilities, normally expressed as a lack of required knowledge, skills or attitudes (Griggs *et al* 2010). As Harrison (2009) points out, there has been a great deal of research into reasons and causes of performance and much research on the connection between HR practices and both individual and organisation performance. The results of this research effort are contested and ambiguous, but one piece of research that seems to identify three main causes of individual performance is that by Purcell and his colleagues (Purcell *et al* 2003; Purcell and Hutchinson 2007). This work suggests a combination and interaction of ability, motivation and opportunity, mediated by the role adopted by first line managers, as being key causes of individual performance in work organisations. Each of these factors encompasses myriad subordinate and related factors and so proposed causal chains are complex and dense. The research does, though, confirm a clear message from previous research over many years that development needs are only one of many possible causes of underperformance and failure to achieve objectives on the part of both individual employees and organisations. The research by Purcell, though, also does helpfully seem to confirm a connection between those two; that is, the performance of individual employees is a contributory factor in organisation performance.

Return to the first activity of this chapter, above. To what extent does the idea of a gap represent the understanding of development need applied by Julia and Peter's mentor? How would you feel in Peter's position about that understanding being applied to you?

THE NOTION OF LEVELS OF DEVELOPMENT NEEDS

Boydell (1983) proposed a notion and framework of three levels at which development needs can exist. While it is now quite a while since that idea was proposed, it is still commonly advocated and applied in professional practice (Buckley and Caple 2009; Griggs *et al* 2010), largely because it is of practical value. The framework has been modified by some writers, eg Harrison (2009), but the essential idea remains the same. The framework suggests that development needs exist at three interrelated levels: at organisational level, at job or occupational level and at individual level. It is useful to aid understanding of this framework to begin with the middle level of job or occupation.

Job or occupational level

As we suggested earlier and as shown by the work of Purcell and his colleagues (Purcell *et al* 2003; Purcell and Hutchinson 2007), among others, performance in any particular job or occupation depends on a complex set of factors. Harrison (2009) points out that many of these are unique to each particular organisation and will include each unique organisational culture. However, it is reasonably well recognised that one set of factors is applying a given 'body of knowledge' and a range of skills associated with the job or occupation (Buckley and Caple 2009). This is true whether the job is assembling components on a production line, selling mobile phones in a high street store, managing a clinical directorate in an NHS trust hospital or working as a chief executive of multinational financial services company. In some and perhaps all cases, adoption of certain attitudes rather than others will also be important for successful performance. Thus, it is possible to specify what any individual needs to know and understand, and to be able to do in what kind of manner, if successful performance in the job or occupation is to be possible. Note that we say 'is to be possible' since factors other than applying the needed abilities affect performance. A specification of necessary abilities constitutes development needs at the level of job or occupation. The specification is independent of any particular individual, and it identifies what all individuals need to know and to be able to do if they wish to work successfully in the job or occupation.

Individual level

Identifying individual development needs first requires some specification at job or occupational level and follows from that level. Any individual, even if newly recruited, will possess knowledge, skills and attitudes, *some* of which will be relevant to performing in the job or occupation. However, it is unlikely that any newly recruited person will possess *all* the KSA specified as being required at the job/occupation level. Therefore, individual development needs exist to the extent that there is a gap between the KSA currently held by a particular individual and the KSA specified at the job/occupation level. Identifying individual development needs is, in this model, constituted by establishing the extent and content of that gap.

Organisation level

It is useful to think of learning and development needs at the organisation level as being of two types. The first type follows in part from establishing needs at the level of job/occupation and at the level of individual employees. When these steps have been taken, it is possible to arrive at a summation of the total development needs of the organisation. In simple terms, an organisation needs X number of individuals trained and developed in B and C, Y number in C and D, Z in E and F, and so on. The second type of organisation need is some KSA, which all members of the organisation, irrespective of their job or occupation, will be required to develop. The KSA in question will be related to some change in policy, strategy or objective, or perhaps to some generalised performance problem which affects the whole organisation or, finally, to an external factor such as new legislation. Examples might include entering new markets, or rising customer complaints, or new legislative requirements related to health and safety. At the very least, all members of the organisation need to *know* of these changes and developments and, therefore, an organisation training need is created.

ACTIVITY

Consider the following questions:

1. Produce a list of the second type of organisation training need experienced by your organisation over the last one to three years.

2. To what extent does your organisation attempt to establish training needs at each level? What methods are used?

3. Produce an analysis of the strengths and weaknesses, as you see them, of Boydell's three-level framework.

Discussion

It will be clear from this examination of the concept of development need as a gap that what might be termed conventional analyses adopt what is referred to in organisation theory as a realist position. Both organisations and individuals are treated as objective entities. The former are assumed to possess unproblematic objectives which guide and shape the actions, behaviour and performance of all members, and the latter are assumed to possess KSA which can be directly linked in causal relationships with performance in jobs and occupations. Thus, in conventional treatments, methods adopted to establish development needs are likely to focus on quantitative data and to see such data as 'facts'.

FOLLOW UP

See Chapter 12 for detailed discussion of research methods used in learning and talent development for more explanation of the term 'realist'. One application of these methods is to establish development needs.

Conceptualising organisations and individuals as unproblematic, objective entities is open to question and challenge (see, for example, the collection edited by Alvesson *et al* 2009). Also open to question and challenge, and for similar reasons, is treating individuals simply in terms of 'bundles' of KSA which they possess independently of those who surround them. It is unlikely that individuals are independent repositories of KSA which have meaning and application in any and all contexts and so probably limiting if not mistaken to treat them as such. This is clearly illustrated in the following quotations:

> The empirical self is always changing, and is never self-consistent. This means that the individual cannot be viewed as a basic unit … in terms of the systems of relationships investigated by sociology, the individual does not constitute a permanent uniformity (Park 1972, in May 1997, p135).

> Our unity as individuals is not something given. It is a continuing lifelong project, an effort constantly undertaken in the face of endless disintegrating forces (Midgley 1996, p88).

Arguments such as those illustrated in the quotes may be used to question the very idea and possibility of individual development needs as a gap. However, it is possible that we can take both and the first in particular as support for a view that development needs are socially determined and constructed. In other words, development needs identified at any and all of the three levels are not necessarily 'objective facts'. They are unlikely to have the same status as phenomena in the physical world. Instead, they are social and therefore phenomena subject to influences particular to specific social contexts. While it may be the case that a common influence across varying social contexts is to create the belief, and associated action, that development needs are indeed objective facts, it is advisable to bear in mind that such beliefs and actions are derived from sets of usually unstated assumptions. These common assumptions about organisations and individuals as they relate to processes of establishing development needs are usefully articulated by Boydell and Leary (1996). The point here is to recognise and accept the existence and potential value of a range of ways to conceptualise organisations and individuals in our examination of methods and techniques used in establishing training needs.

IDENTIFYING DEVELOPMENT NEEDS

We now turn our attention to examining how to establish development needs. We will continue to apply the three-level framework while recognising that the levels are interrelated and, therefore, that methods used at one level may well produce results of relevance to other levels. One issue that occurs at all levels is that of distinguishing what is a development need and what is not. Before examining methods of identifying development needs in any detail, we will take a brief look at this issue.

DEVELOPMENT AND NON-DEVELOPMENT PROBLEMS

We have already said that, in conventional terms at least, development needs are associated with performance levels of organisations and individuals. If performance requirements are not being achieved there can be a temptation to perceive this as indicating the existence of a development need. Current performance is defined as a problem, then associated with a learning need and therefore the problem becomes identified as a development problem. The temptation to follow this line of reasoning can be quite strong for line managers, for learning and development specialists and for other HR professionals. The political nature of organisations as discussed in Chapter 5, in part at least, accounts for this temptation. Managers and HR professionals can avoid any involvement in or contribution to being the cause of the problem and, related to that, avoid the risk of involvement in the solution. Learning and development professionals can be flattered by demands for their services and perceive potential opportunities for influence.

Labelling any or all performance problems as development problems can have drawbacks and negative consequences for all concerned. As we pointed out earlier in this chapter, factors other than lack of appropriate KSA can create or contribute to performance levels achieved by organisations and individuals. If other factors are significant, but a development solution is the only one adopted, then the following consequences are likely:

- The 'problem' remains unresolved.
- Resources allocated to development are wasted.
- Valued 'pay off' from investment in learning and talent development is not achieved.
- Opportunities to address substantive learning problems are missed.
- Belief in and support for learning and talent development is diminished.

These consequences can be argued to be negative and detrimental to all concerned, but especially to the long-term interests of learning and development practitioners. Therefore, it is important as a starting point to conduct some initial analysis to establish the extent to which any particular performance problem is a learning problem and therefore amenable to a development solution. Application of problem analysis can help with this, although to do so requires some understanding of the nature of problems, symptoms and causes.

A problem can be defined as the existence of a difference between 'actual' and 'desired'. In the context to which we are applying the concept, actual and desired will refer to performance. Thus, actual performance of X compared with desired performance of Y will be defined as a problem. Actual performance of X is not, of itself, the problem, or even *a* problem. It is the existence of a *difference* between actual X and desired Y that is the problem. An interesting feature of this way of specifying and analysing problems is the implication that the quickest and perhaps easiest way of solving problems is to modify *desired* to match *actual*. While this method of solving problems is unlikely to find much favour in work organisations, it does help to illustrate the view that problems are social and human creations. Performance problems in organisations do not have the status of objective fact. They are only problems because human beings, individually and collectively, define them as such because actuality does not meet their desires.

Symptoms are observable and/or measurable events or indicators which are used to identify and specify the existence and nature of a problem. So, in our context, symptoms are the full range of performance measures and indicators, or 'metrics' (Harrison 2009) used to monitor organisational, functional, departmental and individual performance. To use a medical analogy, performance measures are used to monitor and assess the 'health' of an organisation and to detect any areas of 'disease' or 'pathology'. This is one of the key purposes of management information systems. Recall that performance level X is not a problem. It is simply a symptom which, when compared with desired level Y, indicates the existence of a problem.

Causes are the explanation of the symptoms. In other words, they are the factors which produce the symptoms. In our context, causes are the reasons that the performance level is X rather than Y. To solve the problem therefore, we have to do something about the reasons that bring about performance level X so that we can change it to performance level Y. Thus, problems cannot be solved without tackling the causes, and causes cannot be established without examining and analysing symptoms.

This approach to problem specification and analysis is intended to form the basis of an initial analysis which is conducted as part of any attempt to establish development needs at individual and organisational levels. In this context then, the following six-step method can usefully be applied:

1. *Describe symptoms.* The critical point here is to focus on observable and measurable indicators, and not to confuse symptoms with the problem itself.

2. *Estimate importance.* Does the fact that performance is X rather than Y matter much to anyone? In other words, is it worth doing anything to attempt to make actual match desired? If not, amend desired to match actual as step six and miss out the other steps.

3. *Analyse cause.* Examine the symptoms in more detail and seek to establish the reasons for them. In doing so, decide whether the causes are related to learning and development; ie the cause is lack of required KSA; or are associated with other factors. In the case of non-development causes, go to step six.

4. *Generate solutions*. Decide possible learning and development solutions. This may include more investigation to establish development needs in more detail.

5. *Estimate cost/benefit*. Produce estimates of costs and benefits of each possible solution. Assess whether a worthwhile solution is available and feasible in cost/benefit terms.

6. *Recommend solution*. Report to decision-makers.

It can be quite difficult to distinguish between development and non-development causes in step three. The subjective rather than objective nature of problem specification in organisations, and the political pressures mentioned earlier, are two reasons why this is the case. Table 7.1 suggests some common development and non-development causes to help with this difficulty.

Table 7.1 Problem analysis

	Development causes	Non-development causes	
P E R F O R M A N C E	Inadequate development Inappropriate development Skill/knowledge gaps Inadequate recruitment and selection	Lack of feedback/motivation Job design faults Organisation culture R&S procedures Poor equipment/tools, etc.	P R O B L E M S

ORGANISATION LEVEL

The point was made earlier that organisation-level development needs can be of two types: a summation of needs at other levels, and what might be termed 'common needs' which exist across the organisation. The processes described here can be relevant to both types. They may highlight particular areas, functions or occupations which will require further analysis and, therefore, lead to establishing needs at the job/occupation level which, when completed, will feed back into the first type of organisation-level need. Similarly, the processes may identify a need for development which transcends occupational, departmental or hierarchical boundaries, and therefore contribute to the second type of organisation need.

The basic activity at this level is to conduct some form of organisation analysis. The depth and detail of the analysis will vary depending upon the timing and purpose of establishing organisation needs (Harrison 2009; Boydell and Leary 1996). For example, Reid *et al* (2004) suggest a number of possible reasons for carrying out an organisation-wide review, including establishing a Human Resource Development department, preparing a training budget and plan, or to meet the requirements of corporate planning. In all cases, there are likely to be two major focuses of analysis: current performance and future plans. The former will encompass the appropriate performance indicators and measures of efficiency and effectiveness, as well as health indicators such as labour turnover and absence levels, perhaps also including attitude surveys. The focus on future plans is concerned with significant changes in strategy, objectives, policies, technology and procedures. Such changes may be in response to dissatisfaction with current performance, external factors such as competitor activity or legislation, or the result of some perceived opportunity. In some ways, these two areas of focus are similar to the distinction between 'maintenance needs' (current performance) and 'development needs' (future plans) suggested by Truelove (1997) and can be considered congruent with the three-level categorisation of 'implementing', 'improving' (current performance) and 'innovating' (future plans) produced by Boydell and Leary (1996). The important point is that an organisation analysis identifies the development and talent required to enable the organisation to keep doing what it does to an acceptable performance standard, and the learning and development required to enable it to do new and better things (see Fredericks and Stewart 1996).

Conducting an organisation-level study requires the collection, analysis and interpretation of a significant amount of information (Harrison 2009). It is important to ensure that this information is relevant and appropriate. The information sought is likely to be of two types. The first type might be termed 'hard data'. This indicates data which is quantitative and, within the community which uses it, considered to be factual. Boydell and Leary (1996) refer to this as 'objective data'. Examples will include the kind of information produced by management information systems. We can label the second type 'soft data'. This indicates a mixture of individual and collective opinions, beliefs, judgements, predictions and aspirations. In general terms, hard data will be available in statistical reports such as analyses of productivity, market share or labour turnover, while soft data will need to be originated through methods such as interviews, focus groups and analyses of minutes of team meetings. While the distinction between hard and soft is useful, a word of caution is necessary. Apparently hard, or objective, data can be problematic. For example, attitude surveys produce statistical analyses of satisfaction ratings which are presented as objective facts. It is though arguable that the only fact in such reports is that x number or percentage of respondents ticked a particular box on a survey questionnaire.

Information, both hard and soft, will be needed from both internal and external sources. External information is required so that development needs arising from government policy and legislation, for example, can be established. It may also be required for purposes of benchmarking (Boydell and Leary 1996). Government departments, employer bodies such as the Confederation of British Industry (CBI), trade associations, research institutes, universities, trade unions, academic journals and professional/trade journals and magazines are all potential sources of relevant information on and about the external environment. Once collected, both internal and external information will require analysis and interpretation. Two broad methods are step analysis for external data and SWOT analysis for analysing internal data in a way which takes account of analyses of external data (Johnson et al 2006). (STEP analysis factors are social, technological, economic and political; SWOT analysis factors are strengths, weaknesses, opportunities and threats.) Other methods include trends analysis, flow charts, Pareto analysis and large system interventions (Boydell and Leary 1996).

ACTIVITY

1. Identify and list internal and external sources of hard data for your organisation.

2. Decide what methods and techniques of analysis would be suitable for the information each source would provide.

3. Categorise and prioritise sources of soft data within your organisation.

4. Decide what methods and techniques would be suitable for analysing the information each category of source would provide.

5. Discuss and compare your results with colleagues.

JOB/OCCUPATION LEVEL

Establishing development needs at the job/occupational level requires a detailed examination of the selected job or occupation. The purpose of the examination is to produce a 'job training specification' (Harrison 2009). This specification describes and details both the nature of the job, and the KSA necessary for the effective performance at the defined standard. The use of the terms 'effective' and 'defined standard' mean that prior to examining the job, or as part of that process, measures or criteria of performance have to be agreed. Once criteria are in place, standards of performance can be defined. Criteria or measures or indicators of performance are not the same as standards of performance. Sales achieved for example is a criterion or measure or indicator. A standard defines the required level of performance, eg how many sales per period. Determining measures/criteria and standards can be fairly straightforward for assembly operators and sales staff, for example. However, the issue can be much more complex even in a conventional approach in other cases; professional and managerial jobs, for example. There is, however, an assumption in establishing development needs at the job/occupation level that criteria and standards can be and are agreed and defined.

A job training specification is the purpose and the result of establishing development needs at this level. There are a number of approaches but generally the process of arriving at the specification is some form of 'job analysis' (Reid *et al* 2004). As we have seen, the outcome is a job training specification which details required KSA. It is useful, therefore, when conducting a job analysis to bear in mind the different forms KSA can take in relation to effective performance of jobs/occupations. These are commonly referred to as:

Knowledge

- *technical* – specific to the job, and without which the job could not be done
- *context* – relates to elements to do with employment, eg terms and conditions; elements to do with physical environment, eg hazards; and elements to do with role/purpose of job in function/department/organisation, eg contribution to final product or service
- *background* – relates to elements such as organisation history and relationship with stakeholders.

Skills

- *intellectual* – sometimes referred to as 'mental' skills, for example, judgement, decision-making and creativity
- *physical* – also known as 'manual', for example, sensory acuity, dexterity and co-ordination
- *interpersonal* – also known as 'social', for example, verbal communication, influencing and leadership.

Attitudes

The concept of attitudes is highly complex and controversial. However, in simple terms, and in the context of jobs, attitudes held by individuals can be good/bad or positive/negative or desirable/undesirable. The distinction will depend on the nature and requirements of the job.

This categorisation is useful when analysing jobs for development purposes. A useful device in applying the knowledge categorisation is to think of the distinctions as 'must know' (technical), 'should know' (context) and 'could know' (background). Any particular area of knowledge, for example, 'relationships with stakeholders', can fall into any category, depending on the nature of the job. It may form part of 'must know', for instance in the case of senior managers.

There is a wide range of methods and techniques available for conducting a job analysis. A useful categorisation of *approaches*, rather than methods and techniques, is that advocated by Harrison (2009). The following are the main approaches in her categorisation:

- *Comprehensive analysis.* As the name implies, this approach consists of a full and exhaustive analysis of all aspects of a job. It will produce a detailed specification of all tasks and associated performance requirements, together with KSA specifications for each task and activity.
- *Key task analysis.* Again, the nature of the approach is reflected in the name. The intention here is to first determine which tasks are *critical* to successful performance, and second to analyse only those and ignore others. This approach tends to be appropriate for more complex jobs with high degrees of discretion.
- *Problem-centred analysis.* A further descriptive title. The approach here is to

focus exclusively on particular and specific areas of the job which job-holders themselves and/or their managers find problematic. Thus, the analysis is limited and tightly focused, and is likely to involve job-holders themselves identifying and specifying problems.

Factors such as time, resources, urgency, degree of complexity and stability in the job, level of recruitment and associated levels of familiarity with the job on the part of job holders are argued to be relevant in deciding which approach to adopt. A final, and increasingly popular, approach is competency-based analysis (see Harrison 2009). Reid et al (2004) usefully distinguish between the 'input' and 'outcomes' versions of competence. The basic difference is that input models focus on *behaviours* displayed by individuals which result in competent performance, while outcome models focus on what is *achieved* by competent performance, ie the products. In the former, the focus is the person in that behaviour is associated with personal characteristics (including, but not restricted to, KSA), while in the latter the focus is the function or purpose of the job and its associated outcomes (see also Gold and Iles 2010).

INDIVIDUAL LEVEL

We saw earlier that establishing individual development needs requires some form of comparison and assessment of current KSA against that specified as being required for successful performance in the job. The results of job analysis in the form of job training specifications provide the benchmark against which individuals can be assessed. First, though, establishing individual needs assumes or requires that performance problems do, or will, exist. If that is the case, the question of whether development is an appropriate solution also needs to be addressed. As suggested earlier, there may be other causes of performance problems. Therefore, approaches to and methods of establishing individual development needs have to be capable of handling all these complex issues.

Perhaps the most common method of establishing individual needs is through some form of performance management system (Harrison 2009) and/or associated appraisal scheme. Certainly, in theory at least, performance appraisal has the potential for establishing the extent to which performance problems exist, and whether some form of development will help to overcome the problem. Depending on the design, performance appraisal systems may also enable the involvement of individuals in determining their learning requirements. One potential problem with appraisal is the focus on *performance* and, in some cases, allocation of reward, rather than learning and development. This can create tensions and conflicts (Harrison 2009; Boydell and Leary 1996). Therefore, use of staff development schemes, or 'development discussions' either in place of or complementary to appraisal schemes, can be useful to provide a specific and exclusive focus on establishing development needs.

More sophisticated approaches which apply similar principles are the use of 360° feedback and development centres. Development centres are the same in design and operation as assessment centres used in selection and promotion decisions, but are claimed to have a different focus and purpose (Gold and Iles 2010). The purpose is overtly to establish individual development needs. The experience of one of the authors working with three organisations directly on designing such centres, reinforced by informal discussions with students on professional and management programmes, leads us to be a little cynical about the true purpose of development centres in practice rather than intent. The use of 360° feedback involves individuals receiving information and data about themselves from a range of sources, usually including line managers, colleagues, their own staff and, perhaps, customers. Some form of rating scale, and self-assessment using the same instrument are additional features of 360° feedback. The process can also be used as part of, or as supplementary to, performance management or appraisal schemes. A feature commonly used within both development centres and 360° feedback is some form of competency framework as the benchmark for assessment (Harrison 2009; Gold and Iles 2010).

All the methods mentioned so far allow and enable some degree of self-assessment to establish individual development needs. Reid *et al* (2004) identify self-assessment as a discrete approach, with some support from Harrison (2009) and, especially, Boydell and Leary (1996). In some ways, 360º feedbacks can be considered a *method* of self-assessment although, in practice, it is likely to inform rather than constitute self-assessment. Methods such as self-and-peer assessment (Stewart 1996) are also relevant under this heading. Questionnaire surveys, conducted by HRD departments (Truelove 1997), can also be used as supporting mechanisms for self-assessment.

Provision for formal learning and development can also be used to establish individual needs. As Harrison (2009) points out, induction and basic training programmes can help both individual employees and learning and development practitioners establish further needs at the individual level. Finally, approaches and processes adopted at the organisation and job/occupation levels can and do contribute to establishing individual needs.

ACTIVITY

Consider current approaches to establishing job/occupation-level needs in your organisation and answer the following questions:

a. do they reflect the comprehensive, key task, problem-centred or competency approach? Or none of these?

b. what are the reasons for the approach adopted?

c. how do those reasons compare to those suggested earlier in the chapter?

d. how and why might current approaches be improved?

Compare and contrast your results with those of a colleague, and discuss how each might be revised and improved.

ESTABLISHING TALENT DEVELOPMENT NEEDS

The content so far in this chapter has general application within learning and development. To the extent of that general application it has relevance in talent development. There are, though, some specific considerations that arise when thinking about the notion of development need in the context of talent management and development.

We saw in Chapter 2 that the notions of 'talent' and 'talent management' have varying and contested meanings, and that definitions are contextual rather than universal. There are, however, some broad approaches which have generally accepted meanings and so some currency in professional practice as well as in academic research. These broad approaches enable us to identify the specific considerations of establishing development needs in the context of talent development. The first consideration is the range of meanings attached to the notion of 'talent'. There are a number of choices in defining talent, including whether it is applied to *positions* or is applied to *individuals* (Tansley *et al* 2007). As outlined in Chapter 2, the former case defines and identifies jobs/occupations/roles in the organisation as being critical to success and so those occupying them, irrespective of personal characteristics, as the target for talent management and so talent development. The latter case defines and identifies individual employees irrespective of position/job/role or occupation as the target for talent management and so for talent development. In this case current performance and/or future potential are the main criteria used to identify and specify talent. At a simple level, talent as *position* will emphasise job/occupational-level development needs, while talent as *individuals* will emphasise individual-level development needs. Talent as *position* will also emphasise organisational-level needs more than defining talent as *individuals* is likely to, although there will be connections.

Where talent is associated with *positions* then succession planning as a method of establishing organisational-level needs will be seen as important (see Iles and Preece 2010). The kinds of organisation that are more likely to emphasise positions as opposed to individuals are those that are referred to as 'knowledge intensive'. Included among these are professional service firms such as law and accountancy practices, professional and management consultancy firms, and what is referred to as the creative industries. There are examples of knowledge-intensive organisations in the public sector as well of course, eg in the justice system and in the NHS. The key point about such organisations is that they depend on specialist knowledge and skills in order to meet their objectives. These knowledge and skills are commonly scarce in the labour market and so securing and retaining people to occupy the positions is the critical contribution sought from talent management and development. Development needs are likely to be associated with professional and/or managerial and/or leadership roles and positions and so establishing needs at the job/occupational level is crucial.

The second key consideration in talent management and development indicated in Chapter 2 and that has implications for establishing development needs is whether *exclusive* or *inclusive* approaches are adopted (Tansley *et al* 2007; Iles and Preece 2010). In the former case talent management and so development is targeted at only some employees. In the latter case all employees are defined as either talent or potential talent. Some organisations do attempt to define all of their employees as talented and so talent management and development encompasses everyone (Tansley *et al* 2007). Other organisations have talent management and development programmes that are restricted in size and number but which all employees have equal but competitive access to through some sort of internal recruitment and selection process (Tansley *et al* 2007). Those organisations claim to have an inclusive rather than exclusive approach, although that is debatable. Exclusive approaches are likely to emphasise organisation and to an extent job/occupational-level development needs while inclusive approaches are likely to emphasise individual and to some extent organisational-level development needs.

The third consideration is the extent to which the first two considerations are combined. Defining talent in relation to positions is more likely to lead to exclusive approaches. Defining talent as individuals is more likely to lead to inclusive approaches. A common example of the former when applied to development needs is in relation to leadership and management. Many talent development programmes are targeted at future managers and in some cases entry can be open to all employees on a competitive basis while in other cases entry is restricted to specified individuals identified through processes that are closed and which may not be known even to those who are selected (Tansley *et al* 2007). A common process for identifying and targeting future managers is graduate recruitment and development. This process may be known to all employees but it does close off opportunities to existing employees.

A final point to make in this section is that establishing talent development needs provides a useful example of how the three levels described above, and methods within each, can and do combine. If we take the common focus for talent management of leadership, then how the levels combine becomes clear through the use of succession planning. This method will establish through analysis of labour turnover, age profiles and other data future requirements for replacements in senior and middle-level positions. The result will express the organisational-level need. There will need to be some specification of the managerial and leadership qualities, skills and abilities needed by those who occupy the senior and middle manager positions. So, job/occupational-level development needs will have to be established. Probably the most common method for doing that is some form of competence or competency analysis leading to a competence framework (Gold and Iles 2010); a name applied to what is essentially a job training specification. One output from that will be design of a management/leadership development programme intended to develop the required KSA of the role of manager/leader. Finally, individuals will be assessed against the framework, or specification. Probably the most commonly used method for that is an assessment centre; as we noted above, also sometimes called a development centre. An output of such centres will be that the personal development needs of the individuals who participate are established and an individual programme of development designed and agreed. Those individual and personal development plans commonly draw on and include some elements of the generic programme based on the competence framework. So, succession planning for ensuring a supply of future managers and leaders encompasses all three levels of development need.

DISCUSSION

Iles and Preece (2010) discuss a critique of dominant views on talent management and development based on the notion of 'social capital'. Dominant views emphasise individual levels, whether these are positions or employees. The underlying theory is that of 'human capital' whereby value is created by investing in the development of individuals. The notion of social capital in contrast emphasises the value gained by investing in collectives. These collectives can be teams, networks or cadres among other groupings. The example given by Iles and Preece is that of leadership. The human capital approach seeks to develop *individual leaders*, whereas the social capital approach seeks to develop *leadership* as a process and as a collective resource. Social capital is created through common ties, trust and firm bonds among members of networks and cadres. Establishing development needs with a view to developing social rather than human capital is likely to emphasise organisational-level needs rather than the other two levels. However, in our judgement it cannot be claimed that human and social capital are mutually exclusive or that they present an either/or choice. Both are probably needed. And, while it is the case that the notion of development need as a gap, and the three levels of development need, are premised on a human capital view of development, neither the notion of gap nor the three levels negates approaches to development that can and do build social capital.

SUMMARY

This chapter has examined the concept of development need and has shown it to be one which derives from human capital theory, at least from the perspective of conventional treatments. Accepting that as a starting point, the chapter has described processes involved in establishing development needs at the organisation, job/occupation and individual levels. How these processes are relevant to and are applied in talent management and development has also been described and discussed. Some specific methods that can be and are applied at the three levels and within talent development have also been briefly described. These methods include STEP and SWOT analysis at the organisation level; job analysis at the job/occupational level; and the use of performance management, appraisal and assessment centres at the individual level. The use of succession planning in talent management and development was used to illustrate how the three levels connect and combine in what can be a coherent approach to talent development. The next chapter will examine the stages that follow establishing development needs by focusing on common and practical strategies for talent development programmes.

REVIEW ACTIVITIES

1. Produce a list of approaches, methods and techniques discussed in this chapter which are commonly used in your organisation. Assess the strengths and weaknesses of each.

2. Discuss with colleagues the pros and cons of viewing development needs as a gap from the perspective of:

   a. an organisation chief executive

   b. a learning and talent development professional

   c. a line manager

   d. an individual employee.

3. Identify what you think are the relative strengths of the following methods used to establish needs at the job/occupational level:

   a. comprehensive analysis

   b. key task analysis

   c. problem-centred analysis

   d. competency analysis.

4. Discuss with colleagues the relative pros and cons of an exclusive and an inclusive approach to talent development.

5. Consider the approach to succession planning in your organisation and how it could be improved. Compare and discuss your results with colleagues.

EXTENDED CASE STUDY + DISCUSSION QUESTIONS

CASE STUDY

The 'Excalibur Scheme' is a new talent development initiative adopted by a large, government executive agency to encourage individual employees to take more responsibility for their own development. The agency espouses and seeks to achieve a truly inclusive approach to talent management and so Excalibur is available to all employees. A 360° feedback process lies at the heart of the scheme. This is intended to provide more rigorous information on the basis of which employees can formulate personal development plans. Such plans will in future, according to the rationale for the scheme, more accurately reflect actual learning and development needs,

rather than perceived or aspirational requirements.

The organisation enjoys greater freedom in determining its own policy and procedures in relation to human resourcing issues than in the past. Previously, as part of a government department, the organisation was tied to central civil service conditions of employment. The new freedom has allowed the agency to implement different arrangements in relation to recruitment, promotion and grading systems over the previous five years. The same time period has seen significant 'downsizing' from more than 50,000 employees to just below 30,000. As a national agency providing services to all citizens in the UK, most staff are employed in local offices in all parts of the country. The average size of a local office numbers between 50 and 75 employees who have direct contact with members of the public on a more or less demand basis. In providing the agency's services, employees are required to 'master' and apply complex technical rules and regulations governing implementation of government policy and various pieces of legislation. These change regularly and are usually amended and updated at least once a year. The agency nationally has agreed and contracted targets to meet its sponsoring government department and ministers. These relate to a range of performance indicators measuring services delivered and budget allocations. Regions, areas and individual offices are measured against similar indicators and devolved targets. Although the agency claims in various mission and policy statements to 'value employees' and qualities such as 'flexibility', 'autonomy' and 'initiative', many employees feel that senior managers have an overriding aim of meeting the national targets to the exclusion and detriment of any other considerations. This aim is reflected in the emphasis given to regional, area and office targets by managers at those levels.

Support functions for the office operations, such as HRM, IT, finance and 'technical support' (a function concerned with analysing, interpreting and providing guidance on the rules and regulations governing the agency's services) are located in a central head office and regional head offices. Ashok is employed as a talent management consultant in a learning and development unit which is part of the Personnel Division headed by the director of human resources, who is a member of the executive board of the agency and who reports directly to the chief executive. Ashok's unit, called the Development Unit, is one of four training and development units in national HR, which includes five other departments. Ashok has been tasked to investigate approaches to and systems

of 360° feedback and prepare a discussion paper for the HR division's management team on design principles.

Ashok has fully familiarised himself with the background of Excalibur. This scheme was initiated by the head of learning and development, Shirley Smith, as a contribution to a new HR strategy intended, overtly at least, to overcome declining morale and underperformance within the local offices. Evidence from annual staff attitude surveys has revealed increasing levels of dissatisfaction on the part of employees in relation to their work, their employment conditions and the way they are managed and developed. This evidence is supported by rising labour turnover and absence levels over the previous three years. The incidence of grievance and disciplinary hearings is also on the increase, and the executive board has concluded that these symptoms indicate low levels of staff morale and commitment as a major cause of failure to meet performance targets. Excalibur is one initiative among others within a new HR strategy designed to improve levels of staff commitment. While Ashok is unclear about the purpose or meaning of the label Excalibur, he understands that Shirley Smith considers it to be a critical initiative to demonstrate the contribution of the learning and development function.

Ashok will have to take into account two related and supporting pieces of work. The first is intended to devise a 'competency framework' for application within and by the field operations of the agency. The intended framework will focus on 'generic competencies' expected of all staff and at all levels in the operations division of the agency, and on 'role-specific' competencies which will vary according to the nature of particular jobs. Role-specific competencies will, where possible and appropriate, relate to existing occupational standards such as those for customer service, administration or management and will therefore enable employees to achieve NVQs. This project is being led by Ed Stevens from the NVQ unit of learning and development. Sheila Harrison, a HR Business Partner who works in the HR division but not in one of the training and development units, is leading a project to review the current performance appraisal system. Ashok will need to liaise with these projects in considering any principles he may recommend for design of a process of 360° feedback. He is clear that 360° feedback within the intentions of Excalibur will not form part of any changes to performance appraisal, will not directly relate to rewards or promotion and therefore will have an exclusively developmental purpose and focus. As Ashok sees and understands the nature of Excalibur, its major benefits will be in relation to accurate diagnosis of learning and development needs and so will make a direct contribution to talent development across the organisation.

Discussion questions

1. What evidence is there that the agency is experiencing a learning and development problem?

2. What potential advantages and disadvantages exist in using 360° feedback as a means of identifying learning and development needs in the context of an inclusive talent development strategy?

3. To what extent is the agency adopting a coherent inclusive talent development strategy? What are the reasons for your answer?

4. What principles would you advise Ashok to incorporate into his recommendations at this stage? What are your reasons for this advice?

5. How should Ashok proceed with his project? What actions should he take and how should he go about them?

EXPLORE FURTHER

Books
Essential

Boydell, T. and Leary, M. (1996) *Identifying Training Needs (Training Essentials)*. London: CIPD.

Gold, J. *et al* (eds). (2010) *HRD Theory and Practice*. Basingstoke: Palgrave.

Recommended

Bee, R. (2003) *Learning Needs Analysis and Evaluation*. London: CIPD.

Tansley, C. *et al* (2007) *Talent; strategy, management and measurement*. London: CIPD.

Journals

Human Resource Development International

Journal of European Industrial Training

International Journal of Training and Development

Human Resource Development Quarterly

Useful websites

www.cipd.co.uk

www.ufhrd.com

CHAPTER 8

Learning and Talent Development Practical Strategies

OVERVIEW

Previous chapters of the book have looked at the strategic and organisational context of learning and talent development, at the underlying theories of how people learn, as well as at the steps required to assess needs, identify solutions and evaluate learning and talent development interventions. The aim of this chapter is to present practical choices for intervention. It will describe and explore a range of common strategies and programmes. The use and role of external resources will be examined, as will management of third party suppliers such as educational partnerships and development centres. Strategies utilised for developing critical talent with key groups such as managers and leaders, professionals and knowledge workers will be explained and evaluated. Within a framework of learning through work, at work and away from work, discussion will include use of action learning, e-learning, coaching and mentoring, and international projects.

Core terms for this chapter include:

- action learning
- corporate university
- education partnership
- e-learning
- bite-sized learning
- coaching
- mentoring
- development centre.

LEARNING OUTCOMES

After reading this chapter and completing the activities, the intention is that you will be able to:

- differentiate between a range of approaches to delivering learning and talent development
- appraise the choice of approach for particular purposes
- recognise the opportunities for learning and talent development through work, at work and away from work
- identify options for learning and talent development interventions with key groups, such as managers and leaders, women and black and minority ethnic employees
- identify common uses of external resources for learning and talent development.

The chapter begins by discussing a range of practical approaches to learning and talent development in a variety of organisation contexts. This is followed by a look at common uses of external resources for learning and talent development, specifically development centres and external partnerships. The chapter ends by discussing ways in which learning and talent development interventions have been combined with key groups such as women and black and minority ethnic employees, and for specific occupational groups such as managers and leaders, and graduate trainees.

COMMON INTERVENTION METHODS

ACTION LEARNING

Action learning typically involves a small group of people meeting together at regular intervals to work on one or more issues that they can explore through questioning each other, and they can take action to experiment with potential resolutions. Groups (or learning sets) might vary in size from 4 to 14; duration of meeting can range from two to three months to two to three years, and occasionally longer; the issues addressed might be a single, corporate problem given by senior management or might be separate, individual questions brought by each group member.

Action learning is an approach to learning used in a variety of ways and for many individual, organisation and systemic development purposes (Rigg and Richards 2007). Despite the diversity, research shows there are core principles found within the practice of much action learning (Pedler *et al* 2005, p10), as summarised in Table 8.1 below.

Table 8.1 Core principles of action learning

Core principles of action learning	Assumptions about learning and talent development
1. The requirement for action as the basis for learning	Action learning is based on the assumption that adults learn from taking action and reflecting on real issues that are of direct concern to them, rather than from lectures or invented case studies that are not related to their experience.
2. Profound personal development resulting from reflection upon action	Action learning helps managers develop meta-skills such as self-insight, wider organisation–political understanding and influencing abilities.
3. Working with problems (that have no right answers), not puzzles (which are susceptible to expert knowledge)	Learning and development are greatest when issues are multi-faceted, with unclear boundaries and several stakeholders, rather than problems that have a simple technical right answer. Problems are ones on which the learners can take action, not merely offer diagnosis.
4. Problems are sponsored and aimed at organisational as well as personal development	Where action learners are drawn from across an organisation or network and focus on organisation or systemic problems, learning and development goes beyond the individuals involved to achieve wider change. Sponsorship by a senior manager is important to enable more junior staff to take action and influence change. Having said this, it is also not uncommon for action learning set members to choose their own tasks or problems, rather than have them given to them, and to work on them individually rather than collectively.
5. 'Comrades in adversity'* – action learners work in sets of peers (commonly of about 6) to support and challenge each other	Individuals working alone can limit their own learning by their mental models (Argyris and Schön) or unconscious patterns of behaviours (Schein). Based on assumptions of social learning (see Chapter 6), action learning creates a safe setting where peers can challenge and learn from one another, as 'critical friends'. 'Peers' are usually others with somewhat similar issues and in similar organisational hierarchy positions. This has to be balanced, in that too much homogeneity of experience and outlook can result in lack of challenge and greater learning also comes from diversity. Action learning sets meet regularly and allow adequate time for each member. Some sets meet fortnightly for two hours over three months until a task is complete. Some meet monthly for half a day, with a life of several months. Others have been known to exist over years, meeting three times a year for 24 hours.

Core principles of action learning	Assumptions about learning and talent development
6. The search for fresh questions and 'q' (questioning insight) takes primacy over access to expert knowledge or 'p'	Learning happens through asking questions, investigation, experimentation and reflection, rather than through reliance on external expertise. Set members are encouraged to ask each other questions, rather than rush to offer solutions. Members learn the value of a good question for opening up different perspectives. This enables opportunistic learning from action on the problem, to be brought into the action learning set for systematic reflection.
7. Use of facilitators	Facilitators or learning set advisers are commonly used (though not originally advocated by Revans). Their role is to model the peer challenge / critical friend behaviours, to help the group establish ground rules, to support the group in developing questioning, reflective and inclusive team behaviours. Good facilitators attend to the process of the group, rather than getting drawn into the content of discussions or becoming expert problem-solvers themselves. They have to be able to tolerate and interpret silence, ambiguity and conflict, as well as to be active listeners who can summarise back to set members. Facilitators are not always used, or sometimes are used just for early set meetings.

Note: *As Revans (1982) termed them

Reg Revans is generally described as the father of action learning, starting with his work in the 1940s in the UK coal industry and the Belgian Inter-University Programme (Revans 1982, 1983). When pit managers had problems, he encouraged them to meet together in small groups, on site, and ask one another questions about what they saw in order to find their own solutions, rather than bring in 'experts' to solve their problems for them. Revans' key idea was that 'there can be no learning without action and no (sober and deliberate) action without learning'. In other words, learning through work is essential.

In current times there are many and varied interpretations of action learning across the world. Raelin, in his introduction to the *Management Learning* special issue on 'The Action Dimension in Management' (1999, p115), draws from Brook and Watkins (1994) and categorises action learning as one of six forms of action-focused approaches to management and organisation development, along with action research, participatory research, action science, developmental action inquiry and co-operative inquiry.[1]

To this six could easily be added other action methods, such as appreciative inquiry (Cooperider 1995), and transformative action research (Bonnet *et al* 2000), as well as earlier experiential learning approaches such as Freire's advocacy of dialogue, praxis, working with others and conscientisation

(Freire and Shor 1987) and more recent ideas such as situated learning (Lave and Wenger 1991). Raelin (1999) argued that despite the variety the six action methods as he categorised them had in common two key features. One was that they tended to be longer term and with multiple aims linked to the development of useful new knowledge and learning in specific contextual situations. The second was an emphasis on relationships between action and concurrent feedback, for the purposes of both improving knowledge and developing more effective action.

Below we give two cases of its application, firstly within a programme for nurses and secondly to tackle intercultural miscommunication within a multinational company.

 ACTION LEARNING FOR NURSES

CASE STUDY

Hull and East Yorkshire NHS Trust and Hull University Business School have collaborated in a development intervention with nurses who have a specific responsibility for 'tissue viability' – prevention of pressure ulcers – with an action learning programme, entitled 'Leading Change in tissue viability'.

'Sets' of 14 nurses met for a total of six days over a five-month period, primarily using their experience to identify and analyse the current situation, to identify areas for improvement and to develop action plans for implementation. A minimal amount of time was spent on clinical input (half day) and facilitators introduced a small number of tools to assist thinking – most notably stakeholder analysis as a framework for the nurses to identify their relationships and influences with other stakeholders involved in tissue viability on the wards.

Participants had the option to present their analysis, action plan and a reflective paper for assessment towards academic credits from the university, and most took up this option. Outcomes from the programme include improved patient benefits such as fewer ulcers, reduced costs, in terms of expenditure on drugs and dressings,

and increased confidence and sense of empowerment within the nurses, including a number who have since put themselves forward for promotion. The combination of work on stakeholder relationships, combined with the peer work integral to action learning, was particularly helpful in enabling nurses to address their traditional sense of powerlessness within the medical hierarchy, and to develop their influencing skills within the spaces available to them. At the same time, where blocks to change were identified that resulted from hospital policy or structures, these were taken up either collectively by the nurses or through the facilitators.

As the NHS Trust Assistant Clinical Director said:

> We have paid for investment many times over in the savings we have seen and when I hear a nurse say, 'I was on the point of leaving nursing, but this programme has reminded me what the job is about', then I know it was all worthwhile.

Source: Kellie *et al* (2010) *Action Learning: Research and practice.*

CASE STUDY

USING ACTION LEARNING TO ADDRESS INTERCULTURAL MISCOMMUNICATION

Intercultural miscommunication was threatening productivity in the global team of a US multinational service provider after a series of mergers and acquisitions. A development intervention was designed to recognise the work pressure and time-zone challenges of the global team, using action learning to foster sustained, incremental learning in small, facilitated groups. The process of learning was evaluated in questionnaires, which tracked transference of learning into the workplace. There were adaptations such as the time frames of short meetings every two weeks, with ongoing charting of incidents.

The longitudinal study quantitatively demonstrated transfer of learning into the workplace. Specific business outcomes included company protocols for intercultural virtual communication. All skills were used regularly on evaluation nine months later.

The action learning approach offered a time-efficient, effective solution to prevent an imminent intercultural breakdown in communication and morale in a pressurised corporate environment, and can be applied to a range of diversity issues.

Traditional diversity and intercultural interventions are generally one-off, whereas action learning offered the opportunity over a longer time frame to tackle diversity issues, examine and act on cultural behaviours and breakdowns.

Source: Rosenberg, C. (2005) EMEA–US Culture Clash: Resolving diversity issues through reflective evaluated action learning. *Industrial and Commercial Training* Vol. 37, Issue: 6, accessed online 24 March 2010.

Action learning is commonly used in development programmes both within organisations and on a number of academic programmes, particularly postgraduate degrees. It is particularly applicable for professionals, practitioners and managers at all levels who have a level of discretion in their roles, even where, as with the nurses above, the space for professional autonomy within a hospital hierarchy is small. Evaluations of the benefits of action learning can be found in Pedler (1997), and many further applications can be found in the *Journal of Action Learning: Research and Practice*, published by Taylor and Francis. Theoretically the potential of action learning can be linked to social theories of learning and communities of practice (see Chapter 2), but newer work drawing from other areas or organisation theory such as actor–network (Burgoyne 2009) and discourse (Rigg 2008) offer further insights, which are beyond the scope of this book.

COACHING

Coaching is one of the most popular development methods, according to CIPD research, with almost 70 per cent of British organisations using it to support personal development (CIPD 2009a). However, this figure conceals the question of what kinds of coaching are being used, by whom and for what purposes.

Some definitions:

The CIPD define coaching as:

> developing a person's skills and knowledge so that their job performance
> improves, hopefully leading to the achievement of organisational objectives.
> It targets high-performance and improvement at work, although it may
> also have an impact on an individual's private life. It usually lasts for a short
> period and focuses on specific skills and goals (www.cipd.co.uk/subjects/
> lrnanddev/coachmntor/coaching.htm, accessed 17 March 2010).

Other definitions include:

> *coaching* relates primarily to performance improvement (often over the
> short term) in a specific skills area. The goals, or at least the intermediate
> or subgoals are set with or at the suggestion of the coach. While the learner
> has primary ownership of the goal, the coach has primary ownership of
> the process. In most cases, coaching involves direct extrinsic feedback
> (Clutterbuck and Megginson 2005, p4).

> Coaches help people perform tasks (Hackman and Wageman 2005, p269)

> a one-to-one process which, through skilful questioning, active listening
> and staying on the coachee's agenda, encourages commitment, enhances
> performance, promotes a climate of motivation and is the basis for mutual
> development learning (Customer Contact Association 2008).

> the facilitation of the performance, learning and development of another
> individual (Downey 2003).

> unlocking a person's potential to maximise their performance ... helping
> them to learn rather than teaching them (Whitmore 2009, pxx).

From these definitions it can be seen that coaching is generally seen as a
developmental relationship between a coach and one or more coaches, designed
to improve people's performance at work. However, the specific purpose can be
very varied, and coaching is regularly used with the following intentions:

- Career coaching – to help individuals clarify options and practicalities of career choices
- Remedial – developing job-specific skills, knowledge or behaviour of an individual; fixing problematic behaviour in a senior executive
- Leadership development – to support and stretch talented individuals (33 per cent) (CIPD 2009b)
- Employee engagement – 25 per cent of British organisations use coaching to promote employee engagement (CIPD 2009b)
- Team performance – not just reserved for sports teams. Using work projects to build strong team relations, and align performance with organisation goals
- Talent maximisation – develop high-potential performers.

Executive coaching 'provides one-to-one services to top-level leaders in an organisation on the principle that positive changes can be leveraged to filter down and enhance the entire organisation' (Peltier 2010, pxxiv). Forty-four per cent of British organisations use coaching for senior managers and directors (CIPD 2009b).

Who coaches?

A perennial question in organisations is: Who should be the coaches? In Britain at least, the most common situation is coaching is done by line managers, as one of many other ways of relating to staff, integral to a 'coaching culture' (Clutterbuck and Megginson 2005). External coaches are used in only 15 per cent of instances (CIPD 2009c). For some, this is a positive scenario as coaching is advocated as an addition to a manager's repertoire of behaviours, particularly suited to contexts of low hierarchy where the manager must lead rather than command, through setting standards, encouraging high-performance and stimulating individual talent development to maximise potential. Clutterbuck and Megginson, for example, describe a coaching culture as one where 'coaching is the predominant style of managing and working together and where commitment to improving the organisation is embedded in a parallel commitment to improving the people' (CIPD: Making coaching work). With this view of coaching, it is

> more than a skill or a technique for individual and team development. It is invaluable for task performance and delegation. Most importantly, it places people at the top of the agenda in action not just in word and is an essential management style of the high-performing company culture of the future (Whitmore 2010).

However, there are potential problems and ethical issues when coaching is undertaken by line managers. For example, if coaching is just part of a manager's repertoire, is its use integrated into a learning and talent development framework? There are other issues of the power relationship between a line manager and employees who report to them which can compromise the openness and confidentiality of a coaching relationship. There is the question of who owns the feedback, which ideally should be the coachee, but will inevitably become part of the line management relationship when the coach is also line manager.

In coaching the coach will meet the coachee at regular intervals over a period of time, usually focused on clear objectives. As illustrated in Figure 8.1, the purpose may be personal development (as with career coaching) or performance development (as with team performance or remedial coaching), and the benefit may be for the individual or the organisation, or both.

In practice it is not uncommon to find that even where the expressed aim is work performance, personal issues very often come onto the agenda. In coaching, feedback is generally owned by the coachee, unless the context is team coaching, or in the case of remedial coaching as part of a performance management system. Such confidentiality and the potential to be led by the coachee can make

Figure 8.1 Purpose of coaching

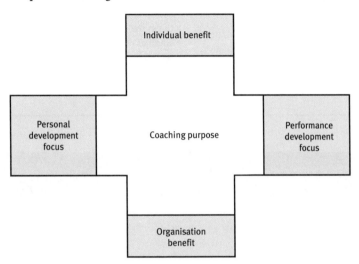

coaching particularly attractive to potential participants. However, acceptability with other senior organisation stakeholders may be compromised if the purpose is seen as too self-orientated without business benefits.

The case study below provides an illustration of executive coaching applied to stimulate a corporate coaching culture across a company.

 COACHING

CASE STUDY

Developing a performance-led coaching culture at VT Group plc

The VT Group is a leading defence and support services company which, in addition to its well-known ship-building business, operates across a wide range of markets providing engineering and other services to governments and large organisations throughout the world. VT's vision is to develop the organisation to build on its traditional engineering strengths to become the number one international government services group. In 2006 the top team recognised that achieving this vision would require a step-change in the development and leadership of people, so their Coaching for High Performance programme was initiated as part of the change process.

VT took a 'top–down' approach to the introduction of coaching within the organisation. Senior executives and managers have all undertaken training in coaching and as a result the approach has been embedded into the organisation. VT has taken a public approach to their commitment to it. Michael Staunton, Executive Development and Succession Planning Director, who has spearheaded coaching in the group, puts it like this:

> If you are joining the company there's a promise that you are going to be in a coaching environment and you are going to be coached rather than managed in a traditional top–down way. If you're working with us as a customer then you know that we've got that coaching mindset: you're

going to be treated fairly to achieve shared goals.

In the two years since the launch of the 'coaching for high-performance' initiative, VT has posted some impressive results. Both revenues and profits have increased and other 'softer' areas of business effectiveness have shown improvement. The coaching culture is helping the organisation to get the best out of people at all levels, whether they are experienced managers, technical experts, new graduates or apprentices.

 ACTIVITY

Find out how coaching is used in your own organisation – Who does it, who is coached, what are the intended outcomes? How does this compare with the list above? Exchange your findings with others in your group.

Models of coaching

There are various coaching models in use, all designed to provide some structure to the way coaching conversations start, proceed and end over time. Having said this, they are not generally intended as rigid stages, rather as guides that unfold from an initial assessment of the coachee's current status, and they may be cyclical rather than linear. A commonly known model is GROW (developed by Graham Alexander in 1970, and spread by John Whitmore), but there are many others, including Egan's Skilled Helper Model (Egan 1998) Lewin's field theory, Clutterbuck and Megginson's scaffolding (2005).

The role of the coach is to use skills of active listening, challenging questions and non-judgemental feedback to help the coachee set challenging goals, identify and deal with any blockages to achieving them and implement actions towards them.

 ILLUSTRATION

GROW model of coaching

Goals – Establish what the coachee wants to achieve from each session and the overall exercise.

Reality – Discuss what is really happening, check there are no false assumptions, gather information.

Options – What options are available, what can be done, what would the consequences be of doing nothing?

Wrap-up or will – Agree what actions the person will take towards their goal, identify potential obstacles and necessary resources and support.

ILLUSTRATION

Egan's Skilled Helper Model

What is going on?

What do I want instead?

How might I get what I want?

Outcomes of coaching

Evaluation by the CIPD (2009b) has shown that the development of coaching in organisations can deliver a range of benefits that include: enhanced individual performance; improved communication processes; higher productivity; greater clarity about goals and objectives; effective knowledge-sharing processes; increased creativity; enhanced staff engagement; and the development of an effective leadership style. Coaching empirically seems to be a suitable development tool for situations such as:

- helping individuals who are technically experts develop better interpersonal or managerial skills

- developing an individual's potential

- providing career support

- helping a person who has been promoted develop a more strategic perspective

- helping a person handle conflict situations more effectively.

Why does coaching work? – Theoretical underpinnings

Not unlike Chapter 6's evaluation of the evidence basis for learning styles, buyers of coaching are confronted with many commercial coaching models that are often not explicit about their theoretical underpinning or their research base. Coaching is an intervention or, some might say, an interference with people's minds. For this reason and because it is an expenditure of organisation resources, it is therefore important to consider what the evidence is for expecting coaching to work. Why might we be hopeful that setting goals with an external person will deliver performance benefits? In what contexts does it work well? Why does it work? What are the necessary ingredients for an effective coaching intervention? In what circumstances is coaching not suitable?

Fundamentally coaching makes assumptions about how people change and learn. Diverse psychological models have informed coaching practice such as solution-focused, psychodynamic and systems-psychodynamic, personal construct, cognitive and behavioural approaches (Palmer and Whybrow 2008). For every main psychological school, such as Gestalt, Jung or Freud, there is an approach evolved for coaching. McDowall and Mabey (2008) suggest there is a trend to increasing adoption of a positive psychological approach, influenced by the positive psychology movement which originated in the USA (Seligman and

Csikszentmihalyi 2000), which focuses on developing strengths and capability, rather than on ameliorating weakness. Somewhat worryingly, there is little research into the impacts of different coaching approaches and their applicability to different contexts and different kinds of people.

Peltier (2010) makes a recent contribution to explanation of psychological theory underpinning coaching, with a particular focus on executive coaching. An important reason for learning and talent development professionals to have an understanding of this is the finding that 'more than 75 per cent of coaches have assisted coachees with "personal issues"' (Coutu and Kauffman 2009, cited by Peltier 2010, pxxiii). McDowall and Mabey (2008) reviewed research literature on the long-term outcomes found by studies in the USA and UK. They suggest the question is still open as to what aspects of the coaching process are particularly effective. However, they cite research that found coaching following a 360° feedback process enhanced the value of the latter (London and Smither 1995) in that employees 'were more likely to adjust behaviours favourably and to set themselves more effective goals' (McDowall and Mabey 2008, p637).

Critical questions

Coaching has become widely popular in part because of its flexibility and relative cheapness. Yet there are still murky areas in our understanding of coaching. One issue is whether managers can coach their own staff, given the power relationship and the general requirement for some distance and impartiality in a coaching relationship. Perhaps it is more a question of identifying what kinds of goal are appropriate for coaching within a managerial relationship and what other kinds are not. Related to this, when coaches are internal is the question of who owns the feedback, who has access to it and for what ends (such as promotion, rewards or penalty). A further caution is that there are some individuals and some development issues that do not respond well to coaching. For example, coaching is not the appropriate intervention if an individual has psychological problems, or significantly lacks self-insight (Peltier 2000).

 EXECUTIVE COACHING

CASE STUDY

I was coaching the director of a government body. He was a senior figure who had recently been knighted, and was entering the final stage of his career as leader of this organisation. On the surface he was a confident, articulate, charming and powerful man, with considerable interpersonal skills; rather an archetypal, male leadership figure. I had worked with him over a number of years, and had always been rather in awe of him. I was eager for his approval and tried not to show it; I guess he attracted my paternal transference. I had previously worked fairly extensively with him and his various leadership teams, and this coaching assignment was a departure from the usual form of my relationship with him. He had asked for a year's coaching in order to help him change his leadership style. He knew people found him intimidating, and he wanted to grow his subordinates rather than scare them, and make a significant shift in the leadership culture of the organisation (Professor Bill Critchley, Relational Coaching, www.emccouncil. org/eu/public/international_journal_ of_mentoring_and_coaching/ volume_vii_issue_2_extract/ relational_coaching_extract/index. html, accessed 18 March 2010).

MENTORING

It may have occurred to you in the discussion above that it can be difficult to distinguish between coaching and mentoring, or even counselling. Indeed, in practice, 'mentoring' is not uncommonly used interchangeably with 'coaching'. Typically, however, mentoring describes a relationship in which a more experienced individual uses their learning or wisdom to support the development of a less experienced person, the mentee or protégé. In this section we discuss how mentoring is used as a learning and talent development intervention.

Some definitions

Mentoring

> relates primarily to the identification and nurturing of potential for the whole person. It can be a long-term relationship, where goals may change but are always set by the learner. The learner owns both the goals and the process (Clutterbuck and Megginson 2005, p4).

Feedback is intrinsic and the mentor helps the mentee develop self-awareness and insight.

Mentoring

> enables an individual to follow in the path of an older and wiser colleague who can pass on knowledge, experience and open doors to otherwise out-of-reach opportunities (www.coachingnetwork.org.uk/ResourceCentre/WhatAreCoachingAndMentoring.htm, accessed 18 March 2010).

> is a confidential one-to-one relationship in which a manager uses a more experienced, usually more senior, person as a sounding board and for guidance.

> is a protected, non-judgemental relationship which facilitates a wide range of learning, experimentation and development (Garavan et al 2009, p385).

> is the most intense and powerful one-to-one developmental relationship, entailing the most influence, identification and emotional involvement (Wanberg et al 2003, p41).

> is a protected relationship in which learning and experimentation can occur, potential skills can be developed, and in which results can be measured in terms of competence gained rather than curricular territory covered (Gibbons 2000, p18).

> [enables] individuals to acquire skills, open doors, increase confidence, widen perspectives, avoid many errors, and otherwise enhance their careers and lives (Phillips-Jones 1997, p9).

Uses of mentoring

From these definitions it is clear that mentoring focuses on more than short-term work performance. Mentors open doors to contacts and opportunities, enable access to the kinds of challenging work assignments that can be so developmental to mentees and facilitate visibility across a large organisation or social network. But mentors also commonly use their knowledge to counsel in the context of adversity, and as a sounding board, support growth in confidence. In terms of Figure 8.1, the purpose of mentoring within work organisations is some combination of individual–organisation benefit and personal-performance development. In other words, there are both career and psychosocial functions. This is not a straightforward balance and there is plenty of opportunity for points of tension in some mentoring relationships, particularly when the intervention is being funded by an employer. This puts pressure on the learning and talent development professional to be able to justify the longer-term benefits of mentoring.

ACTIVITY

Look at the definitions and cases of coaching and mentoring in this chapter. Draw up a list of what is common and what is different.

Theory and evidence

In addition to its sometime overlap with coaching, the term 'mentoring' captures a variety of practices and relationships, which makes it difficult to gather sound evidence to evaluate the impacts of mentoring across different applications. It is known that matching of mentor and mentee is important, because trust is central to an effective relationship. However, available evidence suggests the criteria for a suitable match vary between sectors. For example, Smith *et al* (2005) found that in the US military respectability and wisdom were highly ranked characteristics in mentors. For mentors for academic and business mentees sensitivity was more highly rated. New young professionals may value the experience and contacts of a mentor most, whilst managers moving into more pressured senior roles may value both the experience and personal support.

In-company mentoring, such as within graduate talent development programmes, requires particular thought. Matching works best when mentors are seen to have high status within the organisation (Arnold and Johnson 1997). Trust and openness tends to be compromised if mentors are also the mentee's line manager, so this is generally to be avoided. A further consideration is who owns the learning. Typically the content of mentoring discussions is kept within the mentor–mentee relationship; although, within some uses, such as graduate programmes, the mentor may have a role in feeding back comment on the graduate-mentee's developing potential.

Mentoring is a longer-term relationship, of anything from a few months to a number of years. Frequency, location and length of meetings are the kinds of parameters mentor and mentee tend to tailor to their own needs. Opinions differ as to whether a formal agreement or contract should be drawn up between mentor and mentee. Clutterbuck and Megginson (2005) place less value on a formal written agreement, but rather emphasise the importance of mentee and mentor talking explicitly about expectations and ways of working, as well as periodically reviewing the process and making changes if necessary.

 MENTORING

CASE STUDY

A public sector organisation of more than 500 employees provides mentoring as a workplace activity. There were many reasons for introducing this mentoring scheme, with one key rationale being to promote equal opportunities within the organisation.

The scheme aims to work with equal numbers of mentors and mentees, because the internal mentors take on the role in addition to their main job. Induction and follow-up training is provided to mentors by the internal scheme organiser, which is not an accredited academic programme. These are complemented by group meetings where the mentors get together and share experiences and by external sessions provided by external experts.

Mentors and mentees are advised that an ideal frequency of face-to-face meetings is monthly, with sessions lasting for between one and two hours for between 6 and 15 meetings. Some phone or email contact is used in addition. Mentees and mentors have a degree of choice over who they are matched with, and either party can withdraw from the relationship if it is not longer seen to be working.

The content of meetings and records of achievements are owned by the mentee and mentor, with no paper records being passed to the scheme organiser. Mentors can consult the organiser if they have questions or hit problems with their mentoring relationship, but this is not a formal reporting requirement.

Source: Adapted from data in Gibb and Telfer 2008.

Benefits of mentoring

Learning and talent development professionals will be concerned to evaluate the benefits of mentoring from the perspective of mentees, mentors and organisation-wide. However, evidence that systematically reviews the impact or effectiveness of mentoring is still fairly limited. Exceptions include Wanberg *et al*'s (2003) review of research. They report from 90 studies on the positive benefits for mentees in terms of career satisfaction, job satisfaction, higher expectations of advancement, career and organisation commitment. They also identified a small number of studies that report benefits for mentors, such as recognition and increased power base.

In terms of business benefits, one is the finding by Horvath *et al* (2008) that organisations increase their attractiveness to new recruits if they have mentorship programmes 'that are voluntary, that give protégé input into the choice of mentor, that link protégés with individuals who hold higher rank [that is, supervisors], and that offer both career and psychosocial support' (2008, p323).

A second organisation benefit from mentoring is the ability to retain talented staff. This follows from Wanberg *et al*'s finding above that mentoring increased mentees' commitment to their organisation. A third payback for organisations is the knowledge management implications that can result from internal mentorship relationships. Of course, in one sense knowledge transfer is explicitly recognised in the model of a relationship between the wise experienced mentor and the less experienced junior. However, some organisations have realised the contribution mentoring can make to retaining the tacit corporate knowledge from a mature member of staff near the end of their career.

A final organisation benefit is seen when mentoring is used to address inequality issues, thereby making full use of its talent potential.

FOLLOW UP

As explored later in the chapter, mentoring is one of the most frequently employed learning and talent development interventions to address imbalance in numbers of black and minority ethnic and women managers.

Critical questions

Clutterbuck suggests anyone can be a mentor if they have something to pass on and the skills, time and commitment to do it. However, there are more cautionary voices that suggest some additional principles to make the relationship work. In particular, if possible, mentors should not be a mentee's line manager and also, as with marriage, matching matters. Mentorship works best when both parties enter into the relationship voluntarily and can also withdraw. Effective mentors make themselves accessible, are empathetic and actively listen, but avoid controlling or directing the mentee. Effective mentees are proactive, are open to the mentor, but avoid becoming dependent on or dominated by them. An excellent senior manager cannot be assumed to make an excellent mentor without some training input.

MENTORING FOR WOMEN AND BLACK AND MINORITY ETHNIC STAFF

Formal mentoring programmes have been used as a positive action strategy to support the talent development of women and black and minority ethnic (BME) employees for many years. Often part of an equality and diversity strategy, such initiatives have been concerned to support the career progression of more women and BME staff into senior management and to avoid organisations wasting talent. The rationale has been that corporate leaders often attribute their success in part to having received mentoring, either formal or informal, coupled with the observations that women and black and minority ethnic employees disproportionately lack access to high-level informal mentors, at the same time as experiencing a glass ceiling effect (Ehrich 2008).

However, in a review of studies on mentoring for women managers, Ehrich (2008) cautions that research studies to date have mixed findings on how significant mentoring is for improving women's status in senior management and calls for more research, particularly longitudinal research. Avoiding a simplistic talent development intervention of 'just provide a mentor', she concludes:

> the advice of writers in the field (De Janasz and Sullivan 2002; Kram 1985; Kram and Isabella 1985; Long 1997; Riegle 2006) is very valuable. These writers argue that what is required is mentoring support that comes from many people and many directions since it is unlikely that one mentoring relationship is going to fulfil both psychosocial and career needs (Ehrich 2008, p479).

E-LEARNING

The jury is arguably still out as to how far the world of learning and talent development will be revolutionised by e-learning (electronic learning) technologies that enable learning content and process to be mediated through computers. Practitioners will have to judge in the coming years whether they offer unfulfilled promise or whether their potential has been over-hyped.

Terminology and technologies

The CIPD explains e-learning as 'learning that is delivered, enabled or mediated using electronic technology for the explicit purpose of training in organisations' (CIPD 2009a).

Early e-learning definitions referred to a somewhat passive view of learning that simply transmitted content: 'online delivery of instructional content as well as associated support services to learners'.

As technologies have developed, more recent definitions include:

> the use of online tools such as blogs, wikis or podcasts for learning and teaching. Learners can create their own content and exchange information in networks like the video platform YouTube (www.youtube.com) (Ehlers 2009, p296).

Other related terms include 'm-learning' (mobile learning), 'virtual ILT' (instructor-led training), 'edutainment', 'ubiquitous learning' and 'blended learning'. Kaplan-Leiserson (2005) defines *mobile learning* as 'the new possibilities that are available to people given the mass deployment of devices that everyone now has in their hands and the new connectivity that is coming'.

> *Mobile learning* (commonly referred to as *m-learning*) is the ability to learn independently of place and time, facilitated by a range of mobile devices, such as the iPod, mobile phone and MP3 player (anon).

Edutainment can be defined as 'the act of learning through a medium that both educates and entertains, or else, entertainment that is intended to be educational' (The Free Dictionary 2006a). Those that remember the John Cleese training videos for team management and other skills will say that edutainment has a long history, predating mobile devices. However, the potential to use the likes of mobile downloads and YouTube has injected new energy into this approach to learning.

Perhaps the most recent e-learning term to emerge associated with digital media is *ubiquitous learning*, which has a journal and conference associated with it: *Ubiquitous Learning: An International Journal* (http://ubi-learn.com/journal/ and http://ubi-learn.com/conference-2010/).

> *Ubiquitous Learning* is a counterpart to the concept 'ubiquitous computing', but one which seeks to put the needs and dynamics of learning ahead of the technologies that may support learning (http://ubi-learn.com/journal/, accessed 26 March 2010).

Early e-learning used web learning platforms. Newer technologies include mobile phones, MP3 players, PDAs, pocket PCs and BlackBerries, and Web 2.0 technologies. Web 2.0 technologies encompass several interactive innovations that encourage high levels of user participation. Examples include: blogs, peer-to-peer networking, podcasts, RSS feeds, social networking (for example Facebook), web services for online co-ordination, and wikis for collaborative publishing (CIPD 2008, p11). Implicit in Web 2.0 technologies is the notion of learning as an interlinked, social process in which the Internet is a learning resource for collaboration and communication.

 ACTIVITY

Look back at the Discussion section in Chapter 6 on how people learn. Consider what assumptions about how people learn underlie the enthusiasm for Web 2.0 technologies.

E-learning applications in practice

From the definitions and discussion above it is clear that e-learning enables the physical separation of learner from 'instructor' or 'facilitator' and provides the possibilities to radically change where, when, how and at what pace learning takes place, compared with both traditional face-to-face training and historical distance-learning methods.

Bite-sized learning

Mobile devices such as PDAs, MP3s and BlackBerries have spawned the notion of 'bite-sized' learning – chunks of information (such as online quizzes, assessments and skill audits), or access to online reference material.

CASE STUDY

BITE-SIZE TWO- TO TWO-AND-A-HALF-HOUR LEARNING SESSIONS

'A little bit of learning goes a long way'

Continuous professional development and investment in training can bring significant benefits to you and your organisation including cost savings as well as improved employee performance, motivation and retention. However, fitting training around increasing demands on time and budgets can be a challenge.

That's why CIPD Training have introduced bite-size learning sessions – a time efficient, cost effective and focused solution to your training needs.

Delivered by leading practitioners and facilitators, each two- to two-and-a-half-hour learning session focuses on a particular subject area and offers tangible take-aways that will make a difference to your performance straight away.

Bite-size learning sessions 2009

Bite-size learning sessions are designed to be topical as well as informative. Enhance your knowledge and keep ahead of the various challenges and opportunities affecting organisations today.

Source: www.cipd.co.uk/training/shortcourses/bitesize.htm?IsSrchRes=1, accessed 21 March 2010.

Simulations

Training pilots through simulators is a familiar approach, but new computer technologies are opening up simulations for training other professional groups. Business simulations provide realistic scenarios for developing managerial skills in strategy-making and operations management. New technologies such as haptics (the science of applying touch (tactile) sensation and control to interaction with computer applications) are opening up possibilities with three-dimensional virtual situations for training such as of medical staff in surgical procedures.

Blended learning

It is recognised that mobile learning technologies and devices will not, at least for the foreseeable future, be the main platform for learning. Blended learning refers to the approach where new media are combined with traditional face-to-face training as part of a 'blended approach'.

Benefits for learners

E-learning is frequently hailed as offering flexibility, autonomy and control for learners in that they can decide the time and place of study, and the sequencing and pace of their learning. Downloadable information can be a way of accessing information at the point of need – for example, just before a key meeting, an employee can review a client's share price, or remind themselves of the latest legislatory framework. It is seen as an effective way to provide both a personalised learning experience, while simultaneously offering opportunities for collaborative learning and support, though discussion forums and instant messaging technologies. Supporters claim that e-learning has the potential to help learners become more proactive citizens, with well-honed reflective practice skills.

Benefits for organisations

E-learning is claimed to offer cost-effectiveness benefits to organisations in a number of ways. E-learning can help companies address their time-pressures and minimise down times. Learning that can be undertaken in the employees' own time or in bite-sized chunks around work means less inconvenience for the employer and less cost to cover in terms of time away from work or covering shifts, as with traditional off-the-job training.

International businesses are able to translate a standardised product and roll out training across a business more rapidly and consistently compared with traditional training. Similarly organisations with split sites, even within a single country, can achieve a faster, more standardised delivery of training across its staff. Organisations are beginning to realise that the interactive possibilities of Web 2.0 media, the communication, feedback and exchange of information which contribute to a learning community, have benefits for knowledge management as well as for cultivating team-working and qualities of communities of practice.

However, despite this potential, a CIPD study in 2008 found most organisations had not fully embraced the opportunities afforded by Web 2.0 technologies.

Critical questions

Who drives the e-learning agenda? Is it the learners and their needs and preferences? Is it the IT specialists and the latest bells and whistles gadgets (Sloman 2008)? Are learners really empowered by having choice over where and when to study, or is the notion of a bite-sized mini-module fitted into the 10 minutes' gap between meetings, yet another claim on employees' time, and also yet another diversion from reflective time? Gold *et al* (2009) warn that the autonomy of learners is over-hyped, suggesting that the monitoring of use function built into e-learning platforms provides the potential to check and scrutinise learners' use in a way that could undermine trust.

 ACTIVITY

In groups of five, compare notes on the kinds of e-learning available in your organisations or others familiar to you. What technologies are used? What kinds of knowledge or skills are developed? What works well? What is frustrating? From your own experience of different e-learning and m-learning technologies, what has worked and why? What has not worked well and why?

E-LEARNING

CASE STUDY

B&Q were pioneers in the development of business-centred e-learning and branded their offering as 'B&Q University'. However, over an eight-year period they have moved from early adopters to becoming a mature user. The company began their e-learning project in August 2000. The first decision to be made concerned the choice of learning management system (LMS), as this was the heart of the e-learning infrastructure. It was recognised that there was a need for the systems to grow in line with the company: firm criteria were therefore established for the choice of the LMS; above all it should be straightforward and easy to use (user-centric). It also needed to have the ability to interface easily onto the other B&Q IT systems. Generally it was recognised that most LMSs will have more functionality than the organisation required. B&Q put considerable effort into their choice of the LMS, which would need the capacity to allow growth as e-learning became more accepted.

From the outset, B&Q recognised that the materials deployed would need to meet the needs of the store-based customer advisers and to be specific to the B&Q business as managers would not see the immediate relevance of generic materials. There were also questions on the scope of the content: Would customer advisers see basic IT skills, interpersonal modules and general management as important? In these early days B&Q made an explicit link with e-learning and their learning and development framework (LDF), which was launched in January 2003, in order to offer all staff a way to improve their capabilities and achieve greater job satisfaction. Initially the emphasis within the LDF was on customer advisors who could progress through five levels, which would result in enhanced remuneration if they were able to demonstrate relevant knowledge. Now the emphasis has shifted to supervision and expertise (for example,

plumbers, electricians, horticulturalists and joiners). For supervisors in particular there was greater emphasis on people skills – managing their staff. Progress on the implementation of the LDF was to be monitored using surveys and there was extensive reporting to stores on the use of e-learning.

Moving to maturity with e-learning

A number of other environmental factors have changed since the initial introduction of e-learning. PCs have improved and all e-learning material can be delivered via the intranet (in the early days distribution was achieved in part through CD-ROMs). Now almost all new joiners have PC skills and in 2005 the 'Introduction to e-learning' module was withdrawn. The main change, however, has been driven by the new demands for learning for performance. In the early 2000s, when B&Q was expanding rapidly, partly through acquisition of other stores and companies, there was a need to ensure that all customer assistants had the requisite product knowledge. With the growing emphasis on customer service a mixture of methods is appropriate. For example, a pilot initiative currently underway is called 'project confidence', where a group of customer advisors are taken away for two days to a local builders' centre and shown a small improvement job (for example, laying a laminated floor). This idea is not to make them experts in the job undertaken but to give them greater confidence when advising customers.

The title 'B&Q University' has now been withdrawn as it was seen as too closely identified with a taught top–down model, but e-learning remains a key component of the LDF. In the words of Barry Sampson, manager of the Learning Support Team, 'we now recognise that it doesn't matter how they learn so long as they do learn, and can turn that learning into performance'. There is therefore much more emphasis on making e-learning material available in the form of performance support where managers can direct the customer advisers as required or self-motivated customer advisers can access material themselves. Over this period the number of e-learning modules available has risen to 90. Importantly, all are prepared to B&Q specifications by a number of software houses with whom long-standing relationships have been established. Costs per hour delivered have dropped from £50,000 per hour delivered in the early 2000s to £10,000–15,000 per hour today. Some modules are compulsory for new joiners (for example, health and safety and diversity policies), but other topics may be delivered by a range of materials. An illustrative list of the modules is set out in the table below. Barry Sampson estimates that about 20 per cent of the LDF is delivered through e-learning.

Example modules:

Process modules	Management skills	Soft skills	Product knowledge
• Epos • Financial Services • Insurance Products • Health and Safety • Stock Management • Stock Loss	• Coaching • Mentoring • Effective Duty Manager • Planning and Prioritising	• Respect for People • Sustainability • Services In Store	• Decking • Garden Power Tools • Showroom Products • 50 × short (10 min) Product Knowledge modules

Source: www.cipd.co.uk/helpingpeoplelearn/_casestudies/_bq.htm, accessed 14 March 2010

OTHER DEVELOPMENT INTERVENTIONS

So far in this chapter we have looked at a number of core learning and talent development approaches in some depth – action learning, coaching, mentoring and e-learning. There are many others that organisations also use to develop skills, stimulate learning and develop employees' talent, which there is not space to cover in depth within this book. Table 8.2 summarises the most common of these.

Table 8.2 Other learning and talent development approaches in brief

Performance appraisals	Development appraisals involve systematic evaluation through face-to-face feedback against some pre-determined objectives or competency framework and identification of developmental goals.
Secondments	Secondments offer an employee the opportunity to expand work experience in a different organisation or branch for a temporary period, before returning to their original job.
External courses	Typically provided by a university or college, structured around specific learning outcomes, curriculum and assessment resulting in accredited certification.
International assignments	A specific time period or project undertaken in a different country. Typically of several months to 2–3 years' duration.
360° appraisal	A 360° tool gathers feedback against a set of behavioural characteristics from a number of people more senior, junior and at similar levels to an individual. Face-to-face feedback is designed to assist the individual to identify developmental priorities.
Reflective practice	Following introductory training or briefing, reflective practice involves the keeping of some kind of learning log, journal or diary to record critical incidents and systematic reflections to encourage double loop learning and critical reflection. Particularly useful for capturing informal and opportunistic learning.
Shadowing	A means of learning through which an employee spends time following another more experienced manager or practitioner for a small number of days and has opportunity to discuss the latter's practice.
Buddying	A means of learning through which an employee is paired with a slightly more experienced or established peer, who they can call on for advice on organisation routines. Particularly useful as part of an induction period and for transferring tacit organisation knowledge.

EXTERNAL RESOURCES FOR LEARNING AND TALENT DEVELOPMENT

So far this chapter has discussed common approaches to learning and talent development. In the next section we consider commonly used external resources, such as development centres and education partnerships.

DEVELOPMENT CENTRES

Increasing use has been made of development centres or developmental assessment centres. Originally developed for clear organisation purposes such as to assist recruitment and identify talent development potential, they traditionally included a suite of exercises designed to simulate the work environment so as to draw up a psychometric profile of participants. Typically lasting from half a day to three or more days, a combination of team exercises, role plays and other assessment methods like psychometric testing and interviews are used to assess particular competencies of individuals against a job-competency profile. The assumption is that the best way to predict future job performance is to have an individual carry out a set of tasks that mirror those required in the job and observe and measure their actual behaviours. Common behaviours include relating to people; resistance to stress; planning and organising; motivation; adaptability and flexibility; problem-solving; leadership; communication; decision-making and initiative. Key features include independent assessors, observation and multi-rater feedback.

Over the past 20 years centres have been used increasingly for development, sometimes in combination with assessment and selection, and often solely for development. When a systematic approach is applied underpinned by an organisation's competency framework, development centres can simulate situations with the aim of developing specific required competencies. It should be evident that the approach to learning assumed in this process is behavioural (see Chapter 6), in that the underlying theory is that people will change their behaviours as a result of feedback by following up on further training interventions to address the gap.

Critical questions

A major assumption is that behaviours under simulated conditions do accurately predict competency in a real work situation. There is a fundamental assumption that participation in development centres will increase individuals' motivation to develop their skills and engage in follow-up activities. This, according to Carrick and Williams (1998) has not been critically evaluated. A recent review of research by McDowall and Mabey (2008) also found limited evidence that development centres support transfer of learning back to the workplace. They also found development centres can have inconsistent results on participants, in that those receiving positive feedback can be elevated into a virtuous cycle of motivated performance, whilst those receiving negative feedback can be initiated into a downward cycle of under-performance. A key factor appears to be the ownership of results (Mumford and Gold 2004). Participants have greater trust in the process as a development intervention if they have control over what is done with the assessments. If they have little say over its sharing with line managers, they will tend to see the centre as more of an assessment intervention.

Some large organisations place high value on development centres, but they are expensive and time-consuming, and are not well tailored for small organisations.

CORPORATE UNIVERSITIES

A corporate university has loosely been defined as an education provider whose primary business is not post-school education (Carnegie Foundation for Advancement of Teaching 198). Allen (2002, p9) offers the definition:

> A corporate university is an educational entity that is a strategic tool designed to assist its parent organisation in achieving its mission by

conducting activities that cultivate individual and organisational learning, knowledge and wisdom.

He suggests there are four levels of corporate university defined by the scope of their activity (Allen 2002, p4):

1. training only

2. training plus managerial and/or executive development

3. courses offered for academic credit

4. courses leading to an academic degree.

Some so-called corporate universities are created and owned by a specific company and only provide job and company-specific training to that company's employees, what might be described as the corporate training department by any other name. As well as technical training, they might also deliver talent development programmes for graduates or existing managers.

For example, most of the global car companies have a corporate university, now typically online, as the case below illustrates:

CASE STUDY

Nissan University is a virtual campus servicing the learning needs of over 3,000 Nissan employees at dealerships across Canada. The Nissan University website has been created in order to support the need for accurate, up to the minute reports, resources and information on upcoming events (www.nissanuniversity.ca/, accessed 22 March 2010).

Courses offered for credit will be modules or short courses that include assessments, accredited by a university or other higher education provider (such as CIPD), that can enable credit accumulation within a vocational, undergraduate or postgraduate framework. The fourth category is a corporate university offering full degree (or other award) programmes. However, such an entity can only offer the awards of an accredited institution, and the power to award degrees is regulated by law, which can vary in different countries. In Britain, for example, only institutions authorised either by Royal Charter or Act of Parliament can legally award degrees. Perhaps it is this legal framework that has resulted in the evolution of provision of accredited awards through 'Education Partnerships'.

EDUCATION PARTNERSHIPS

Education partnerships have become a growing means for provision of workplace learning and talent development. The term 'education partnership' is used to refer to varying collaborative relationships for diverse partnerships:

- University/college–company partnership, for the purpose of customised corporate learning and talent development
- University/college–university/college partnership, for the purpose of knowledge sharing and new market entry
- Company–school partnership for the purpose of resourcing primary or secondary education.

In this chapter we will consider the first two only.

University/college–company partnership

The case below illustrates an example of a long-term, close working partnership between a particular organisation and an academic institution for the provision of accredited learning and talent development.

CASE STUDY

LIVERPOOL JOHN MOORES UNIVERSITY COLLABORATION WITH ISLE OF ANGLESEY COUNTY COUNCIL

In 2007 Liverpool John Moores University (LJMU) and the County Council were joint winners of the National Training Award for Wales, in recognition of the success and achievement of the collaborative management development programme developed over several years for council staff in partnership with LJMU. This is a bespoke, validated programme, leading to the award of MA Change Management. The partnership arose after LJMU successfully tendered for the authority's management programme. A prior relationship existed to some extent as a number of Isle of Anglesey County Council (IOACC) staff across the years had attended LJMU for certificated courses in a range of disciplines from accountancy, civil engineering and planning to personnel.

Carys Edwards of IOACC has said:

LJMU is unlike other providers in that it seeks to give the customer what the customer requires rather than what

LJMU has on offer. This is a rare trait in a provider and is greatly valued by those who procure services. LJMU is also very keen to continuously review and improve the programme for mutual benefit.

The major output from the programme is that the organisation gets improved management and leadership skills, individuals on the programme get a Masters qualification, which is excellent for career development, and the work that these managers are required to do on the programme leads to genuine organisational change. Participants are assessed by the university on projects identified by the senior managers at IOACC. The combined involvement of university and organisation in both the design and assessment of group projects has been a major factor in its success.

Source: www.ljmu.ac.uk, accessed 29 March 2010.

The case above describes one broad academic award strategically focused on the local authority's management and organisation development objectives. Other variations would find a university providing a range of accredited programmes, perhaps from Foundation degree through to Masters, or accrediting internally delivered programmes. It is common for university–corporate education partnerships to be formalised by contract (Ryan 2009) and to have an extended lifespan, rather than to exist just for one-off education programmes.

Ryan (2009) found that the primary reason that companies establish university–corporate education partnerships is to provide a recognised university award programme to complement an organisation's in-house education programmes (72 per cent). Ryan, echoing Prince and Stewart (2000), found 58 per cent of organisations valued what they saw as the credibility seen to accrue to their in-house corporate education programmes where they align with university programmes, because universities and colleges are known to have independently benchmarked quality assurance processes. A third rationale for organisations is that university partnerships enable them to access research expertise and to offer a wider curriculum to employees than they could internally provide.

According to Ryan's study, a further rationale for university collaboration (cited by 53 per cent of companies) is to deliberately expose the company to alternative thinking that might challenge 'the traditional self-validating thinking patterns of Executives' (2009, p1315). This is an interesting 'espoused theory' that HRD practitioners might need to be prepared for some contradiction with the 'theories in use' of some managers.

Key to the success of university–corporate education partnerships is senior management endorsement, to support the funds and time required for employees to participate, and alignment with strategic requirements and corporate goals. It is not uncommon for programmes to have a degree of joint delivery and for the chief executive or other senior executive to demonstrate their support through an opening address.

 PARTNERSHIPS FOR EDUCATION (PFG)

CASE STUDY

Partnerships for Education (PfE) is a joint initiative of UNESCO and the World Economic Forum, committed to enhancing understanding about the role of Multistakeholder Partnerships for Education and building global capacity for their effective implementation. Lifelong learning and employee development is one aspect of their focus.

Source: www.pfore.org/about, accessed 21 March 2010.

University/college–university/college partnership

Case study research by Walton and Guarisco (2007) into an international education–education partnership led to the conclusion that to work effectively there had to be three central nodes, with the occupants acting as relationship champions in sustaining ties:

a. an overall partnership coordinator to act as boundary spanner, oversee, and act as steward for, the relationship in their own locality and maintain regular ties with their counterpart;

b. an academic co-ordinator for each programme covered by the agreement with a structurally equivalent counterpart; and

c. administrative co-ordinators to support the above positions and who are themselves knowledgeable about and committed to the partnership and its objectives.

 FPL GROUP WITH CO-OP INTERNSHIP EDUCATION PROGRAM

CASE STUDY

FPL Group partnered with Co-op Internship Education Program (CEIA) to build an effective talent management strategy utilising a college and university co-op and intern programme. Increased cost-cutting measures in many companies have led to resource constraints, which have forced many to do more with less. FPL Group faced this challenge by working with CEIA, a non-profit agency, to hire interns and co-op students to fill the talent gap. This programme allows for the continuation of quality work while potentially recruiting a future qualified workforce. Colleges that participate in this programme include Texas A&M, Georgia Tech and Seton Hall. The results of this programme have enabled FPL to drastically reduce costs for on-boarding and recruiting, as well as see significant increases in the promotability and time to competence of employees.

Source: www.corpu.com, accessed 21 March 2010.

Partnering for lifelong learning

 INTERNATIONAL FEDERATION OF WORKERS' EDUCATION ASSOCIATIONS (IFWEA)

CASE STUDY

IFWEA is the international organisation responsible for the development of workers' education. It brings together national and international trade unions, workers' education associations, NGOs and foundations engaged in the provision of adult education opportunities for workers and the communities in which they live throughout the world.

IFWEA is part of the family of international democratic labour movement organisations. It has observer status with the ILO and UNESCO, maintains close relations with the International Trade Union Confederation and the Global Union Federations, and shares mutual membership with SOLIDAR in Brussels.

IFWEA's role

The core of IFWEA's activities are concerned with facilitating discussion, exchange and networks between member organisations on contemporary issues of workers' education, including educational method and technique, management, policy and practice. The central role of the Secretariat is to stimulate the development of a democratic workers' education movement, by providing contact between member organisations, assist with the development of partnerships and promote best practice in educational design and delivery, through the provision of newsletters, discussion bulletins, seminars and conferences.

Source: www.ifwea.org, accessed 21 March 2010.

TALENT DEVELOPMENT FOR SPECIFIC GROUPS

The case studies throughout this chapter illustrate ways in which different approaches to learning and talent development can be used alone or in combination, for the talent development of specific groups of employees. Groups that are often given specific strategic consideration are graduates, managers and future leaders, and those who are under-represented at senior levels, particularly women and black and minority ethnic employees. Some employers have focused initiatives on unqualified frontline staff, for example, to improve numeracy and literacy.

Talent development for specific groups does not generally call on radically different methods, rather for some combination of some of those discussed, and careful attention to matching mentors and trainers. So, for example, graduate training (as seen in Chapter 2, the Kerry Group case), often combines mentoring, an accredited university course and a series of work assignments which may, in international companies, include international assignments.

Interventions to promote black and minority ethnic leadership and women's leadership invariably include mentoring and/or coaching. Leadership development interventions generally also often include action learning, 360° feedback and some form of structured course, which may also be accredited through a university partnership. Larger companies may also use development centres.

DISCUSSION: LEARNING THROUGH/AT AND AWAY FROM WORK

Chapter 2 discussed how an 'intervention' can be defined as any event that is deliberately undertaken to support, provoke, stimulate or assist learning to take place, with individuals, groups or across organisations. In this chapter, we have looked in more detail at how the field of learning and talent development is made up of a wide variety of intervention activities, besides formal instruction and accredited courses, including mentoring, coaching, shadowing, e-learning, special work assignments, structured reflection to capture informal learning, action learning and 360° appraisal. We have also seen how provision can be internal or external, through third party suppliers such as consultants or colleges and universities.

In the past, learning and talent development was dominated by either an informal 'sit-by-Nellie' process, perhaps assuming nothing much was to be learned that couldn't be picked up from the older employees, or a formal attendance on training or education courses. The field of learning and talent development is now recognised as being much broader, offering the learning and talent development professional a much richer choice of interventions. There is also recognition that the workplace itself can play a very significant role in learning and development, often in combination with external suppliers.

From the discussion of learning and talent development approaches in this chapter, it should be clear that learning and talent development can be formal and away from work, for example attending a university programme, but is often achieved at the workplace or indeed can be facilitated through work. So bite-sized learning or buddying may well happen in the workplace, at work, whilst an international assignment is work and thus can be described as a deliberate intervention designed to develop talent and foster learning through work. Table 8.3 charts these possibilities. In practice, talent development strategies often combine a number of these interventions, as was illustrated in the examples of interventions for key groups above. In addition, university Masters programmes can be found that integrate learning away and learning through work, by inter-weaving action learning, academic content and work-based assignments, as the extended case study at the end of this chapter will illustrate.

Table 8.3 At, through and away from work

	Intervention method										
	Action learning	Coaching	Mentoring	International assignment	Shadowing	Secondment	Reflective practice	E-learning package	Buddying	Development centre	College/University course
Away from work								X		X	X
At work					X			X	X		
Through work	X	X	X	X		X	X				

SUMMARY

This chapter has described and explored a range of common strategies and programmes. Within a framework of learning through work, at work and away from work, insights have been offered into uses of action learning, e-learning, coaching and mentoring and international projects. The use and role of external resources such as educational partnerships and development centres (though larger organisations may provide these internally) has been examined and strategies utilised for developing critical talent with key groups, including managers and leaders, and we have looked at how intervention approaches can be combined for a strategy to develop the potential of groups who traditionally have hit a glass ceiling, such as black and minority ethnic employees and women.

The following key terms have been scrutinised and defined:

- action learning
- corporate university
- education partnership
- e-learning

- bite-sized learning
- coaching
- mentoring
- development centre.

Through reading this chapter and completing the assorted activities, you should be able to:

- differentiate between a range of approaches to delivering learning and talent development
- appraise the choice of approach for particular purposes
- recognise the opportunities for learning and talent development through work, at work and away from work
- identify options for learning and talent development interventions with key groups, such as managers and leaders, women and black and minority ethnic employees
- identify common uses of external resources for learning and talent development.

 REVIEW ACTIVITIES

1. Summarise five key things you have learnt from this chapter.

   a. Write down two or three new questions the chapter has raised for you or things that you are unclear about.

   b. Select one of these questions that you will enquire into further.

   c. Write down what action you can take next in pursuit of your question. (For example, read one of the references in this chapter, talk to someone more experienced at work, look on CIPD website, take time to reflect on your own experience.)

2. Select and describe one major or significant learning/talent development initiative you are currently involved with or affected by. Map out the following:

   a. What approaches to learning and talent development are used?

   b. To what extent is learning encouraged to happen away from work, at work or through work?

   c. In the light of the discussion in the chapter, identify any changes you would recommend.

   d. Share the results with colleagues and examine how they compare. Discuss whether any differences can be explained by the different kinds of organisations you work for.

3. The JISC e-learning programme enables the development and effective use of digital technologies to support learning and teaching in universities and colleges, so that staff benefit from e-learning and students enjoy a more flexible learning experience (www.jisc.ac.uk/).

   How does or could your company (or another with which you are familiar) make use of these resources?

4. Create a statement for each of the following terms that summarises your understanding of each in your own words:

- action learning
- corporate university
- education partnership
- e-learning
- bite-sized learning
- coaching
- mentoring
- development centre.

Appraise the strengths and limitations of each.

EXTENDED CASE STUDY + DISCUSSION QUESTIONS

CASE STUDY

THE INSTITUTE OF TECHNOLOGY TRALEE MBA (MASTER OF BUSINESS ADMINISTRATION), COUNTY KERRY, IRELAND

This two-year, part-time programme is designed to develop the managerial leadership of experienced managers, professionals, entrepreneurs and executives. Following a five-day Foundation Workshop and a 360° assessment activity, participants attend 12 workshops of two or three days' duration across 24 months plus a full-week international study trip in Year 2. Their learning is supported by action learning group meetings and independent study.

A range of teaching and learning approaches are employed, including:

- Coaching (participants learn to coach a less experienced member of staff)
- mentoring (all participants have a mentor, generally a highly experienced individual from outside their own organisation)
- lectures
- e-learning
- action learning

- work-based projects
- 360° appraisal
- video-conferencing
- interchange (similar to a short secondment, where participants spend a week in an organisation other than their own)
- consultancy projects
- shadowing (participants shadow a manager of their choice for two days)
- masterclasses (exposure to highly experienced practitioners and academics)
- international visit.

Aims

Strongly influenced by Mintzberg's critique of MBAs (Mintzberg 2002), the aim of this Masters degree programme is to enhance participants' practical capacity to manage; to develop perspectives and skills for dealing with the realities of organisations: analysis, judgement, ethics, people-handling, ability to act in contexts of uncertainty, capability to deal with complex and unpredictable issues. The underlying philosophy is that in a world of turbulence and increasing complexity, managers need to have advanced frameworks for making sense of their organisation environment to understand and deal with the scenarios they encounter. They also need a level of self-awareness and confidence to act competently in the face of challenges; as well as insights into their own as well as others' moral and emotional perspectives.

The teaching and learning model places experience at the heart of the programme, using live case scenarios as well as participants' own issues as a core source of learning. Through being challenged to look at familiar situations from new perspectives, exposure to diverse organisation models and practices, combined with emphasis on experimentation and action, the emphasis is on developing participants' practice as managers, enabling them to enhance their practical as well as theoretical capability for senior management and to develop transferable skills of learning from reflective practice.

Simultaneously the intention is that the MBA will deliver value to sponsoring employers through the many practical assignments participants undertake and also in encouraging intra and entrepreneurial skills that can contribute to future innovation.

Key features of the programme include:

Focus on developing leadership through:

- a 360° feedback tool to assess strengths in the current job role and identify development priorities
- mentoring, coaching, shadowing and interchange projects to develop leadership practice
- action learning to foster peer learning, fostering exchange of experiences, challenge and diversity of perspectives.

Live organisational projects provide a realism that develops participants' ability to act in a context characterised by complexity, continuous change and uncertainty.

International assignment through a study visit to venues such as India, China and Silicon Valley, because there is no substitute for experiential learning about cross-cultural working.

Interaction and exchange of experiences and diverse perspectives with experienced peers, from different organisations and a mixture of sectors, who challenge and motivate each other.

Staff whose role is to stimulate learning, facilitate, challenge and question as well as provide specialised knowledge.

A range of international academic specialists to lead sessions.

Exposure to corporate leaders and senior practitioners from Ireland and internationally.

Assessment

The programme leads to an MBA award through completion of assignments that combines written reports, selective use of examinations, computer simulations, presentations, consultancy assignments and reflective papers. Assessment methods include both the traditional and the innovative, but the emphasis is on practical assignments, based on live issues within the participant's own or other organisations.

Source: www.ITT.ie/mba.

Discussion questions

1. In what ways does this higher education programme manage to integrate learning through work?

2. A core feature of this programme is peer learning through exchange of experience between participants from different sectors and diverse organisations. If an employer were considering whether to finance managers on this programme or to enter into a university-partnership for

tailor-made programmes, how would you advise the employer on the strengths and weaknesses of this MBA approach compared with a university-partnership?

3. From the perspective of a learning and talent development practitioner, what questions would you ask about the combination of approaches employed in this programme?

EXPLORE FURTHER

Books

Essential

Pedler, M., Burgoyne, J. and Brook, C. (2005) What has action learning created to become? *Action Learning: Research and Practice*. Vol. 2, No. 1. pp49–68.

Chapters 8–11 on formal and informal development interventions in Garavan, T., Hogan, C. and Cahir-O'Donnell, A. (eds). (2009) *Developing Managers and Leaders*. Dublin: Gill & Macmillan.

Recommended

Anderson, V., Rayner, C. and Schyns, B. (2009) *Coaching at the Sharp End: The role of managers in coaching at work*. London: CIPD.

Clutterbuck. D. and Megginson, D. (2000) *Mentoring Executives and Directors*. Oxford: Elsevier Butterworth-Heinemann.

Clutterbuck, D. and Megginson, D. (2005) *Techniques for Coaching and Mentoring*. Oxford: Elsevier Butterworth-Heinemann.

Clutterbuck, D. and Megginson, D. 2009 *Further Techniques for Coaching and Mentoring*. Oxford: Elsevier Butterworth-Heinemann.

Rigg, C. and Richards, C. (2007) *Action Learning, Leadership and Organizational Development in Public Services*. London: Routledge.

Journals

Action Learning: Research and Practice

Human Resource Development International

Journal of European Industrial Training

International Journal of Training and Development

International Journal of Mentoring and Coaching

Human Resource Development Quarterly

Advances in Human Resource Development

Human Resource Development Review

Useful websites

www.cipd.co.uk/subjects/lrnanddev/general/lrndevoverview.htm

www.ufhrd.co.uk

www.ahrd.org

The Coaching and Mentoring Network, www.coachingnetwork.org.uk/Default.htm.

European Mentoring and Coaching Council, www.emccouncil.org/.

Social Media: Trends and implications for learning (Social Media) 2009, http://aace.org/globalu/seminars/socialmedia/.

Peer-reviewed and published articles and papers on educational technology and e-learning, http://0-www.editlib.org.acpmil13web.ancheim.ie/.

www.performanceconsultants.com/aboutus/sirjohnwhitmore.html

Podcasts

Download audio view presentation

Siemens, G. and Cormier, D. (2009). July 2009 – Social Media: Trends and Implications for Learning. In G. Siemens and D. Cormier (eds) *Proceedings of Social Corporate Universities*.

Tools

CIPD 2008 Developing coaching capability: how to design effective coaching systems in organisations:

Online tool designed to help HR professionals at all levels to assess the coaching capability within their organisation.

www.cipd.co.uk/subjects/lrnanddev/_dvchgcpbtl.htm.

CIPD (2009b) Coaching at the sharp end: developing and supporting the line manager as coach:

Online tool designed for HR professionals and their line management colleagues for improving their focus and co-ordinating their actions in developing and sustaining a coaching culture.

www.cipd.co.uk/subjects/lrnanddev/coachmntor/_coaching_sharp_end.htm.

CIPD (2009c) Coaching factsheet, www.cipd.co.uk/subjects/lrnanddev/coachmntor/coaching.htm.

CIPD (2010) Mentoring Factsheet, www.cipd.co.uk/subjects/lrnanddev/coachmntor/mentor.htm.

CIPD: Coaching and buying coaching services, www.cipd.co.uk/subjects/lrnanddev/coachmntor/coachbuyservs.htm.

A route map for coaching and mentoring, designed to help HR and others involved in the coaching relationship to manage coaching effectively and efficiently.

Part 3

CHAPTER 9

Designing and Evaluating Talent Development

OVERVIEW

The previous three chapters of Part Two of this book, which is concerned with the process of learning and talent development, have looked at the underlying theories of how people learn (Chapter 6), at assessment of need at individual and organisational levels (Chapter 7), and at practical strategies for learning and talent development (Chapter 8). Earlier chapters also illustrated how other contextual factors affect the design process. Chapter 2 demonstrated how the purpose of learning and talent development in work organisations is always related to achieving some combination of individual and organisational performance. It also illustrated how use of the term 'talent' can have quite different meanings, ranging from the totality of all organisation members to just certain individuals perceived as exceptional. Chapter 4 explored the contributions of learning and talent development programmes and processes to organisation strategy and culture. Drawing from all these, this chapter now turns to address the issues involved in design and evaluation of learning and talent development solutions.

Core terms for this chapter include:

- return on investment (ROI)
- return on expectation (ROE)
- alignment
- evaluation
- objective
- learning outcome
- business case
- value proposition.

LEARNING OUTCOMES

After reading this chapter and completing the activities, the intention is that you will be able to:

- make and justify choices of learning and talent development methods to meet various individual, team and organisational learning needs

- know how to argue the value or business case of a learning solution

- critically employ the use of objectives or learning outcomes to all levels of a programme

- distinguish between ROI and ROE and their application to evaluation

- understand the importance of stakeholder expectation in the design and evaluation of learning and talent development.

DESIGN – CREATING SOLUTIONS

A core function of the role of learning and talent development professional is, having conducted a needs analysis, and in the context of corporate strategy, to design and deliver solutions to address those needs. This is true whether the focus is an intervention to maximise the potential of a future CEO, a one-off conference, a repeated programme to induct new apprentices, or a multifaceted, long-term intervention designed to lead a corporate culture change. The challenge is to ensure solutions created deliver the maximum value for participants as well as for other intended stakeholders. This is easier said than done, and historically the field of learning and talent development is well sprinkled with stories of training mismatches, inability of participants to transfer learning to their workplace, non-learning and ill-conceived, expensive interventions.

 MISMATCHED OUTCOMES

CASE STUDY

In the early days of the European Social Fund (ESF – a source of funding used across poorer EU countries for training unemployed adults), applicants had to provide an estimate of the number of unemployed participants who would find jobs as a result of their participation in the ESF-funded course. After a few years an eagle-eyed administrator within the European Commission spotted that if all these estimated jobs across the EU had been achieved, unemployment would have been eradicated several times over. Either the outcome was never realistic or the training was not appropriate for the outcome.

ILLUSTRATION

Misaligned design

The first group a new lecturer was given to teach in her first university job was a group of part-time mature students studying a Diploma in Computing. Lacking concrete learning outcomes or any briefing from the course director and failing to ask questions about the participants' existing learning skills, their level and breadth of work experience or their expectations of and reasons for taking her Organisation Studies module, she thought, 'Ah-ha! Part-time, experienced learners taking a university diploma; that's half-way to a Masters degree. I'll design my module to suit – lectures, problem-based learning, experiential exercises for the students to carry out at work.'

In fact, this Diploma was a basic-level introduction to computers for junior administrative staff who had left school with few qualifications at 16, often many years ago. As with so many technical students, a generic module like Organisation Studies was seen as an unnecessary distraction from the interesting content – something they were compelled to complete.

The first evening was a disaster.

Great emphasis is put on the amount of time and money organisations are able and prepared to spend investing in their employees' training or structured learning. Benchmark comparisons are made with crude measures of the annual spend per head on training or the number of training days given per annum. However, it should be clear from other chapters in this book that these are very poor indicators of the real extent, quality and relevance of learning and talent development within any organisation. Arguably they are even less accurate as indicators of the quality and relevance of learning and talent development within small and medium companies and third sector bodies, which often lack a formal learning and talent development function or manager, but can nevertheless be highly effective at developing their employees.

 ACTIVITY

Brainstorm with colleagues to produce a list of reasons why measures such as the annual spend per head on training or the number of training days per employee per annum can be so inaccurate as a way of indicating the level and quality of learning and talent development activity in your own organisations (or others you are familiar with).

Funding and time are of course a necessary start, but the value of learning and talent development is only achieved if several other key factors are also appropriately addressed in the design and delivery of a solution, as illustrated in Figure 9.1 and elaborated in Table 9.1.

Simple structured training models are useful in guiding the learning and talent development practitioner to think through the steps in the design process required for planning, delivering and reviewing training. Such models include

Figure 9.1 Web of ten factors in the design of strong solutions

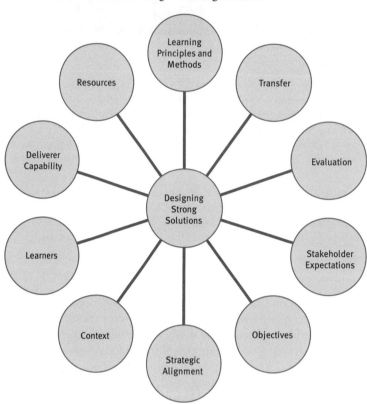

the ubiquitous four-step model and Harrison's six-stage training cycle (Harrison 2009, p184) (see Figure 9.2).

Figure 9.2 Structured training models

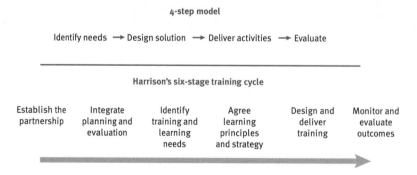

However, it should be clear from earlier chapters that successful design is dependent on a wider set of interconnecting factors, which we elaborate in Table 9.1.

Table 9.1 Essential questions in the web of ten factors in the design of strong solutions

Factors	Essential questions
i. Clear and appropriate objectives	What is the purpose of the intervention? What learning needs have been identified? What are its objectives and learning outcomes? Are there stated objectives for each stakeholder? Is there any risk of inappropriate objective-setting?
ii. Alignment with business strategy	How is the intervention to be aligned horizontally with other HR strategies and vertically with overall business strategy? How will the design align with specific organisation priorities? In the light of there being several key stakeholders, to what extent do they have differing priorities for the intervention?
iii. Stakeholder expectations	Who are the key stakeholders, both internal and external? What outcomes do they expect from the learning intervention? What concerns and needs does the line manager have? What opportunities can the line manager provide to support L&TD?
iv. Evaluation	Is evaluation built into the initial planning process? What performance indicators will enable review of the extent to which the intervention has achieved its intended purpose and delivered the expected learning outcomes for each key stakeholder? Are there external benchmarks that could be used?
v. Learners	Are they compelled or willing? What learning skills and experiences do they bring? What are their preferred ways of learning? Are they the right people? What are their expectations? Do these need challenging?
vi. Organisation context	Do the organisation culture and the management practices welcome and encourage learning, whether formal or informal? How is learning and talent development valued? Who leads on learning and talent development and what influence do they have?
vii. Resources	Who is paying? What time commitment is required from learners and others? What are the cost implications of this time? Which budget does cover come from? What facilities and equipment are required?
viii. Combination of learning methods and interventions	What are the options? How are learning methods combined?

Factors	Essential questions
ix. Transfer and application to work	How is application and transfer integrated into the learning methods? How are learners incentivised to transfer? Is there a system for encouraging learners to share and apply their learning? How is transfer followed up?
x. Deliverer capability – skilled learning architects and deliverers	Who is leading the design? How influential are they with key stakeholders? How skilled are they at design, project management, securing resources, managing conflict between stakeholders? Who will deliver and are they suitably skilled and experienced? Are they briefed on the organisation and learners' background?

PURPOSE – DESIGNING FOR ALIGNMENT

The starting point for any intervention is its purpose and the expectations key stakeholders have of it. Purpose needs to be defined both in strategic and local terms. As discussed in Chapter 4, linking a learning and talent development intervention to business strategy is described as *alignment*.

Alignment of learning and talent development has to happen in two ways:

Horizontal alignment of learning and talent development with other HR and talent management interventions. There is little point investing in specific learning interventions if their benefits are undermined by other contradictory practices such as reward or employee engagement, as illustrated in the case study below.

Vertical alignment of learning and talent development with overall business strategy, so the resultant skill and capability outcomes position the organisation with the competencies, behaviours and performance required for ongoing success.

CASE STUDY IN HORIZONTAL MISALIGNMENT

CASE STUDY

Market Redesign is a design and brand consultancy with a policy of paying 50 per cent fees for staff to attend postgraduate programmes, as well as providing flexibility to facilitate attendance and examinations. The company does not, however, have an appraisal system to help identify development needs, or any system for linking individual development to corporate strategic priorities. Also, inconsistently, there is a culture of disinterest from senior managers in the learning other staff acquire through such programmes and an absence of work practices that encourage informal and opportunistic learning, reflection or exchange.

To accomplish alignment of any specific learning and talent development intervention, it has to be clear how the intervention is intended to contribute to achievement of corporate strategic objectives. For learning and talent development professionals, or indeed individual learners themselves or line managers who want to secure resources for a course, conference, coaching programme or any other intervention, clarification of the purpose in strategic terms is the first step. In other words, they have to make the *business case* (see below) and communicate how the particular intervention contributes to achievement of their individual, team and/or strategic objectives. In many organisations the strategic objectives would be articulated in the organisation's strategic plan, team objectives in a departmental or divisional plan, and individual objectives in a performance review.

'Local purpose' is the objectives or learning outcomes intended for a particular intervention. These are the planned results that a specific programme or event is expected to deliver. See Figure 9.3 for examples.

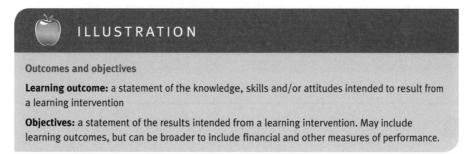

ILLUSTRATION

Outcomes and objectives

Learning outcome: a statement of the knowledge, skills and/or attitudes intended to result from a learning intervention

Objectives: a statement of the results intended from a learning intervention. May include learning outcomes, but can be broader to include financial and other measures of performance.

Figure 9.3 Examples of learning outcomes and objectives

Learning outcomes	Objectives
On completion of the three-day workshop participants will be able to design a simple website.	Attracts employees who have no post-school qualifications.
At the end of the online module trainees will be able to perform ratio analyses on a set of company accounts and interpret the results.	Results in a 30 per cent decline in customer complaints in the three months following training.
On completion of the 12-month programme, participants will demonstrate upper quadrant transformational leadership behaviours, as evidenced by 360° ratings.	Produces a 50 per cent increase in the number of black and ethnic minority applicants for senior management positions over the ensuing two years

Benefits of setting objectives

When designing a learning and talent development initiative, specifying objectives and learning outcomes communicates a golden thread between the wider strategic purpose, the learning needs analysis and the local purpose of an intervention. Objectives and outcomes help participants understand what they can expect from undertaking a course (or other intervention). They assist line managers to anticipate what performance changes they can expect from an employee. They also provide a basis for evaluation of an intervention, in the sense of giving targets that can be reviewed after the event. (See later in this chapter for further discussion on evaluation.) Clearly the more focused and specific the language used to write an objective, the easier it is to review its attainment. One approach is to write SMART objectives.

ILLUSTRATION

Writing SMART objectives

S – specific: The objective says clearly what results are wanted, for whom.

M – measurable: The objective refers to outcomes that could be measured, eg numbers, costs.

A – achievable: It is reasonable to expect this objective could be attained as a result of the intervention.

R – realistic: Achievement of the objective is realistic given the resources available.

T – time: The objective specifies the time within which it is intended to be achieved.

RUGBAÍ CHORCA DHUIBHNE (WEST KERRY RUGBY)

CASE STUDY

Rugbaí Chorca Dhuibhne is a Rugby Club based in the West Kerry Gaeltacht*, Ireland, with the objective of developing the extent of, and excellence in, the playing of rugby in the community, while simultaneously promoting the Irish language.

For under-age teams the Irish Rugby Federation's long-term player development strategy is followed, which has identified the need to develop capabilities in five areas:

i. technical

ii. tactical

iii. physical

iv. mental

v. lifestyle.

In practice the design of training developed to try and meet these needs includes:

- coach training

- skills training in schools

- collaborative training in generic skills in schools with other local sports clubs (Gaelic football, soccer, basketball)

- dedicated rugby club membership, fitness and skill training

- match experience.

*The Gaeltacht refers to statutory, geographical areas within Ireland where Irish Gaelic is considered the vernacular language and receives legal protection.

Source: Compiled with reference to: *Corca Dhuibhne Beo/West Kerry Live*, Issue 27, 15–28 July 2010, p14, www.IRFU.ie.

STAKEHOLDER EXPECTATIONS AND EVALUATION

The discussion so far in this chapter on specifying the strategic purpose and objectives of a learning intervention makes the pursuit of alignment sound straightforward. It might also suggest a unitary view of an organisation (see

Chapter 5), which neglects the reality that organisations tend to be composed of a range of stakeholders with diverse, not unitary, interests. Recent research by Anderson (2007, 2009) found that alignment can have quite diverse meanings for different stakeholders, because they have different strategic priorities. It can represent long-term or short-term capability. Alignment can mean direct integration of learning and talent development investment to measurable, bottom-line results. But for some stakeholders it implies contribution of learning and talent development activity to 'longer-term and less tangible organisational outcomes' (Anderson 2007, pix). Anderson (2007, p21) concludes that an organisation learning and talent development function has three opportunities for pursuing alignment, which, though interrelated, are distinct:

- involvement in business planning
- proactive articulation of a value or business case
- management of investment in learning and talent development infrastructure.

Alignment relates directly to the issue of the value placed on learning and talent development by organisation stakeholders and therefore to how such value is evaluated (e-valu(e)-ated), which we will examine further later in the chapter. There are two key implications for design of learning and talent development interventions that follow from recognising the existence of different stakeholders with potentially contrasting expectations of how such interventions will deliver strategic results. The first is that objective-setting may have to encompass expectations of not only the learners and learning and talent development professionals, but also the line managers and possibly others. This implies that objective-setting needs to be a collaborative process. The second, related, implication is that evaluation criteria and methods are best considered at the design and planning stage, so that they can generate feedback on what is of real value to the different stakeholders.

So far we have discussed the implications for design of strategic purpose, specific objectives and learning outcomes, stakeholder expectations and evaluation. Figure 9.1 and Table 9.1 also identified six other factors that require consideration in the planning and design stage, which we will now look at in more depth:

i.   learners

ii. organisation context

iii. resources

iv. combination of learning methods and interventions

v.   transfer and application to work

vi. deliverer capability.

FOLLOW UP

See Chapter 10 for more detailed discussion of stakeholders and stakeholder theory.

LEARNERS

A key question is whether learners have chosen to participate and come as willing learners or whether they have been compelled to attend. If the latter, very often their energy for learning is not high and the learning and talent development practitioner may have to overcome a degree of sceptical resistance. This can connect to how an intervention is presented to participants. If they are aware they have been categorised as 'talented' and see every course, conference or other intervention as part of a programme designed to nurture their potential to its highest level, they are likely to be highly intrinsically motivated. Similarly, if the learners are confident, with a happy past experience of learning and development, their motivation and optimism will be high. Design in this instance does not have to devote much time to 'selling' the benefits or helping the learners adjust. In contrast, if an individual has been instructed by their line manager to take a management development programme because their performance is considered problematic, the design is likely to need to include an early element that helps allay the individual's fears and anxieties and demonstrate how they can benefit. Similarly, if the group comprises individuals who have historically not been successful with formal learning and are short on social and cultural capital, that might not give them high expectations of learning and talent development.

As part of the design process it can be helpful to think about the learning intervention from a change perspective. This means giving consideration to what transition the learners are being asked to make in engaging in the intervention. What are they being asked to give up (for example, familiar skills, identity)? Are there costs to them individually of engaging with the new knowledge, skills or attitudes? Could there be pressures to 'willing ignorance' (Vince 2010)? If there are, then the design needs to build in some elements that helps, in change terms, both to unfreeze participants from their current state (Lewin 1943; Bridges 2009) and reconstruct or make the transition to new ways of being. Such elements could include one-to-one coaching or action learning, for example – look back at Chapter 8 for detailed discussion.

Besides experience of and confidence with learning, other learner-related factors that should be considered in the design process include the extent of their learning skills and their self-awareness of how they learn. (See Chapter 6 on our knowledge of how people learn and the implications for design.)

ACTIVITY

Look back at Chapter 6 to remind yourself of the ideas and debates that surround our understanding of how people learn and the implications this has for designing learning solutions.

Also review Table 9.2, Implications of learning theory families for methods and design.

Table 9.2 Implications of learning theory families for methods and design

Learning theory family	Behaviourism	Cognitive	Constructivist	Social constructionist
Assumptions about learners	Passive recipients of input	Cognitive information processors	Able to self-direct their learning Motivated	Learn through interaction Enabled or disabled by context
Assumptions about learning professionals	Expert deliverers In control	Expert deliverers Varying format to accommodate learning styles In control	Facilitators of meaning-making	Choreograph interactions
Methods	Bite-sized chunks of information Repeated instructions Repeated practice at tasks Role plays Instruction Reinforcement	Concept maps Varied presentation method and format A framework + sequenced learning steps Plan the KSA objectives Progress from simple to complex tasks	Action enquiry-based methods, such as action learning, appreciative enquiry Reflective journals Problem-based learning Coaching Mentoring Other learner-directed methods	Peer review, action learning, coaching, mentoring, buddying, appreciative enquiry Team working Cross-organisational project work Post-project reviews Reflective conversations
Applications	Learning outcomes that are behaviours – skills, competencies, which can be clearly specified	Job roles and competencies that can be clearly specified	Learning for complex roles, developing judgement, experienced learners	Joining communities of practice – professional groups, merged teams, apprenticeships, induction
Weaknesses	Limited for more complex learning outcomes, higher-level skills	More limited for complex learning outcomes Assessment of memory, not ability Inappropriate use of learning style models	Not necessary for simple learning outcomes	Not necessary for simple learning outcomes

ORGANISATION CONTEXT

Options for design of solutions will be shaped by the wider organisation context. For example, do the organisation culture and the management practices welcome and encourage learning, formal and informal? How is learning and talent development valued? Who leads on learning and talent development and what influence do they have? This is the issue addressed above of horizontal alignment or consistency between a specific learning intervention and wider HR, performance management and general management policies and practice.

RESOURCES

Availability of resources is obviously fundamental to design of learning and talent development solutions, because they determine how ambitious and comprehensive interventions can be, as Chapter 10 examines in further depth. There are crucial questions as to which budget funds an intervention and how decisions get made on its allocation. Anderson's study (2007) found that learning is often funded from a variety of budgets, held by different organisation stakeholders with differing strategic priorities. Timely involvement is important by learning and development professionals in the business planning cycle that secures investment in learning.

Availability and commitment of time is also significant, not only by learners themselves, but from line managers. This can be particularly difficult and costly for rostered staff – nurses, front-line retail staff, industry operatives, and others. Many organisations will integrate time into the roster to facilitate participation in formal learning events, but this presents the organisation with a double cost – funding the learner and paying for someone else to cover their roster. Other organisations minimise this double cost by using designs that prioritise learning-through-work and learning-at-work methods, including e-learning packages, buddying and reflective practice (see Table 9.3 below).

LEARNING PRINCIPLES AND METHODS

Learning principles refers to the overarching principles that are agreed as underpinning an intervention, for example:

- encourage independent learning
- integrate action and reflection
- challenge the individual
- be led by individuals' agendas
- balance benefit for the organisation and individual
- encourage experimentation
- be led by external expert.

Making these explicit provides some parameters for selecting a specific combination of methods. Chapter 8 describes a range of intervention methods, within a framework of learning through work, at work and away from work. These include:

- action learning
- coaching
- mentoring
- international assignment
- shadowing
- secondment

- reflective practice
- e-learning package
- buddying
- development centre
- college/university course

So-called *blended learning* combines e-learning with other methods. The choice of any particular method and combination will be guided partly by best fit, in other words, what will best stimulate the desired learning within available resources.

ACTIVITY

Review the sections in Chapter 8 on 'common intervention methods' and 'other development interventions' to appraise yourself of the key principles, strengths and limitations of each method.

TRANSFER AND APPLICATION TO WORK

As discussed in Chapter 8, experiential methods that promote learning through work can most seamlessly enable learners to apply learning to their work (see Table 9.3). Transfer from other methods is enabled when they include scenarios and problems that are close to the learners' actual challenges, are interesting, stretching (though not too far removed from the familiar), actively involve learners, provide reinforcement and positive feedback. Simulation activities and assessment through practical exercises also help to reinforce learning transfer (Bramley 2003).

Aspects of the organisation context also have an impact on learners' ability to transfer their learning to work, particularly the opportunity to use new knowledge and the support of line managers to do so.

Table 9.3 At, through and away from work

	Action learning	Coaching	Mentoring	International assignment	Shadowing	Secondment	Reflective practice	E-learning package	Buddying	Development centre	College/University course	Structured training
Intervention method												
Away from work										X	X	X
At work					X			X	X			X
Through work	X	X	X	X		X	X					

FROM BUSINESS STRATEGY TO TRAINING PLAN

CASE STUDY

Garvey Group is a family-owned retail and hotel company in Ireland, with 13 stores and hotels across the south of the country. A core belief is that investment in employee's learning and talent development produces results to the bottom line. A modified balanced scorecard (Kaplan and Norton 1996) is used to provide a framework for integrating learning and development into the overall business strategy.

A corporate training plan is prepared annually, costed and evaluated through measures such as sales and profitability. Linked to this an annual training plan is prepared for each branch. Employees' training needs are identified using the appraisal system, with the dual objectives of both providing opportunity for individuals to self-identify learning needs as well as informing a needs analysis conducted by HR for each job role.

The company uses a competence-based framework, with much emphasis put on behavioural competencies applicable to all jobs, such as customer care, working as a team and 'subtle selling'. For sales assistants in particular, great emphasis is placed on customer service training, acting as ambassadors for the company and subtle selling skills – telling customers about promotions in a way such that they might not even notice they are being encouraged to buy more. These skills are seen as essential for achieving business strategy, because sales, repeat business and reputation are so fundamental to corporate performance in this sector.

When sales training or training in particular foods are planned, objectives are set for metrics such as increase in sales and return on investment, balancing expenditure with increased sales of those foods.

MAKING THE BUSINESS CASE – ARTICULATING THE VALUE PROPOSITION

As we have discussed earlier in the chapter, alignment of learning and talent development in practice involves identifying and meeting different stakeholder expectations and these are not always consistent. Particularly when those stakeholders hold a budget that could usefully fund a learning intervention, practitioners have to become skilled in articulating the value proposition of the intervention and arguing the business case. This involves specifying the following for the proposed solution:

- rationale and purpose

- costs of direct training time

- other resources required in planning, delivery and evaluation

- costs and benefits

- objectives for measurable ROI metrics, eg savings, increased sales, reduced absenteeism

- objectives for intangible benefits, eg behavioural changes, cultural values, team synergy

- stakeholder expectations

- objectives for ROE

- risk assessment of contingencies

- communication strategy

- evaluation strategy.

 ILLUSTRATION

Definitions

Value proposition: *How does the intended learning/talent development intervention add value to the organisation? What value will be added?*

Business case: *What are the costs and benefits, both tangible and intangible?*

WHEN OBJECTIVES ARE NOT APPROPRIATE

It may seem unquestionable that objectives should always be set as part of the design of any learning and talent development intervention. However, there are some contradictory voices who caution that objective-setting can, in certain circumstances, stifle learning. For example, Kayes, speaking of management learning, asks:

> how can the possibility of insight, engagement or serendipity – just a few of the goals of experiential learning – be measured by such a narrowly defined outcome? (Kayes 2007, p421).

Hermina Ibarra, talking of career change, argues the impossibility of expecting this to be a planned journey down a linear path to a known destination:

> We like to think that the key to a successful career change is knowing what we want to do next and then using that knowledge to guide our action. But change usually happens the other way around: Doing comes first, knowing second. Why? Because changing careers means redefining our working identity – how we see ourselves in our professional roles, what we convey about ourselves to others, and ultimately, how we live our working lives (Ibarra 2003, p1).

The reasoning in both cases is that when the learning need is complex and may require a reconfiguration of assumptions, perhaps cognitive dissonance and a degree of transformational learning, the end destination cannot be tightly defined through objectives. In these scenarios, it is better to approach learning in an open spirit of enquiry, exploration and experimentation.

 ACTIVITY

Working in groups of four or five, can you think of any learning or talent development needs in your own experience where setting objectives may not have been appropriate? Why?

Compare notes with other groups in your class.

EVALUATION

To evaluate something is to assess its value or worth. In relation to learning and talent development, evaluation is concerned with the results and outcomes flowing from the intervention. This can be expressed in economic terms of the ROI or, increasingly, is expressed in relation to the extent to which stakeholder expectations were met (ROE).

Evaluation of organisational training has for many years been dominated by Kirkpatrick's model (Kirkpatrick 1975).

 ILLUSTRATION

Kirkpatrick Model of Training Evaluation

The Kirkpatrick model (Kirkpatrick 1975) proposes four levels to assess the effect of a learning intervention:

1. learners' reactions to the intervention

2. learners' learning achievements

3. changes in behaviour within the job role

4. organisational effects from the learning intervention.

Problems with this model

Most learning evaluation only touches on levels 1 and 2. Learning and talent development deliverers are concerned with being able to make direct correlations between a specific intervention and an impact. For example, to be able to say 'customer complaints went down 25 per cent in the two months after the team received customer care training' or '87 per cent of participants rated the e-learning platform highly'. They are generally incentivised by getting positive ratings by learners and positive statements from learners of what they believe they have learned.

It is more difficult, costly and less immediate to follow up 3 and 4, and many learning and talent development professionals do not do it. Looking for learner satisfaction ratings is also superficial because it puts learners in the role of consumers. But what commodity are they consuming exactly? Is it not more accurate to see learners as participants actively engaged in a learning process? This is certainly the case if we understand learning as a constructivist or social constructionist process. It also has to be recognised that at times learning will be uncomfortable, because it involves taking on something new and letting go of old ways. So there can sometimes be a tension between wanting this kind of disturbance and looking for high learner satisfaction.

Other models of evaluation give more weight to the contextual variables of particular learning and talent development activity. For example, Warr *et al*'s (1970) CIRO (Context, Inputs, Reactions, Outcomes) and Pawson and Tilley's (1997) realistic evaluation: CMO (Context, Methods, Outcomes) both attempt to examine the impact (outcomes) of a particular learning intervention (inputs/methods) within the particular organisational context. Warr makes a distinction between organisation outcomes and learner reactions, the latter being equivalent to Kirkpatrick's level I.

Kaplan and Norton's balanced scorecard (Kaplan and Norton 1996) has been developed for wider HR evaluation, but has useful application for learning and talent development evaluation with its guidance to consider impacts on four measures, including human capital, capacity to learn and finance.

Core decisions are when and how to evaluate. However, the starting questions of course have to be, why evaluate and value to whom? Anderson's recent studies (2007, 2009) found that organisations use four main approaches to judging the value of learning and talent development:

1. *Efficiency measures of the learning and talent development function*
   Learning and talent development professionals prioritised the cost, efficiency and effectiveness of learning/talent development interventions, as assessed by feedback from learners and comparison of pre-course and post-course data. They were interested in the extent to which their function was operationally efficient: how effectively the workforce capability profile was being developed, how well interventions were supporting corporate critical success factors and how all of these matched against other comparable organisations (Anderson 2007, p31).Commonly used efficiency indicators include number of training days per employee, proportion of salary bill spent on formal learning, organisational competency and qualifications profile, and benchmark comparisons of these (Anderson 2007, p51).

2. *Internal performance indicators and external benchmarks*
   In contrast Anderson's study found senior managers placed more value on
   the impact of learning interventions on internal targets and key performance
   indicators, such as service quality, productivity, management succession and
   employee retention. They are interested in how their organisation performs
   in comparison with other benchmark data, for example, revenue, profit and
   sales per employee. They also value data, such as appraisal review data and
   management feedback, that shows the extent to which employees are developing
   as expected with the organisation's strategic needs (Anderson 2007, p52).

3. *ROI measures*
   With the increasingly popularity of the idea that what gets measured gets
   managed, ROI has become popular with learning and talent development
   professionals as a way of trying to generate financial indicators of investment
   in learning and development. This is illustrated, for example, with the case
   study of Garvey's discussed earlier in the chapter, where investment in training
   of retail staff in soft selling or in particular food products, is evaluated in
   terms of increased sales of those food products, in the weeks following a
   course. Other economic benefits measured include, for example, the extent
   to which learning contributes to reducing costs incurred by absence or high
   turnover.

   Arguably, for discrete learning interventions, with clear objectives, well-defined
   costs and a short payback time, it is feasible to measure cause and effect – in
   other words, to be able to say that changes in sales figures or other costs are the
   direct cause of a particular course. However, often benefits take longer than a
   few weeks to show and it is also difficult to attribute changes in performance
   directly and unquestionably to a specific learning intervention. This becomes
   even more problematic the longer and more systemic a learning or talent
   development initiative is.

4. *ROE measures*
   Anderson (2007) found that, whilst ROI is popular with learning and talent
   development professionals, it carries little weight with senior managers, who
   place more value on such questions as the extent to which employees show
   'strategic readiness'; the delivery of performance improvements; the extent
   to which employees are showing anticipated new behaviours; the extent to
   which particular strategic people skills have been developed; the size of the
   talent pool and the successful management of succession. Anderson terms
   this ROE, which she suggests starts from the anticipated results looked for by
   various key stakeholders from a learning intervention. This is informed by
   their organisational position as well as the extent to which learning and talent
   development professionals have communicated and clarified expectations prior
   to designing an intervention.

ROE AND STAKEHOLDER EXPECTATIONS

As discussed earlier in the chapter, various organisation stakeholders can
have different expectations for what a learning intervention will deliver. For

example, participants in first line supervisor training might particularly value the qualification and might expect to see advancement in their careers soon afterwards. Their line managers might hope to see them expand in capability and confidence and hope to be able to delegate to them more. Senior management might expect the training to result in an increased pool of potential new team leaders, ready to be moved to wherever required. HR may share this expectation.

Participants in health and safety training might particularly value the qualification and might expect to be able to make immediate practical use of new knowledge. Their line managers might expect them to lead best practice in their sections. HR may place highest value on being compliant with the legal requirements for competency. Senior management might expect the training to show in the company's ability to avoid damage to its reputation from any breach of health and safety legislation.

 STAKEHOLDER EXPECTATIONS

CASE STUDY

One way of understanding the differing stakeholder expectations within organisations is through recognising that people can see any of 'four territories of experience' (Fisher et al 2000; Torbert 2004) as critical for effective action in the world: visioning, strategising, performing and assessing:

- Visioning is concerned with long-term intentions, purposes, and aims.

- Strategising is concerned with planning and implementing overall delivery.

- Performing is concerned with acting in pursuit of role-defined responsibilities.

- Assessing is concerned with observed behavioural consequences and the effects of action.

As a result of their work position and role, different stakeholder groups will inevitably vary in which of these four territories they occupy. This is illustrated below, with the example of the Public Services Leaders Scheme (PSLS) (Mead 2007), a development programme initiated by the British Cabinet Office, designed to strengthen leadership capability across public services by bringing together high-potential middle managers from across all services. Involving three cohorts of up to

100 participants each, the design comprised a three-year programme incorporating the following elements:

- 360° appraisal

- a personal coach

- a mentor

- action inquiry groups – action learning sets of 8–10 members from different parts of the public sector who met six times a year for a full day with a facilitator

- Three 'network learning events' annually – two- or three-day gatherings of all cohorts involving masterclasses, practical workshops and group meetings

- Interchange (three months spent working in a different public service sector).

Table 9.4 below illustrates how the 'territories of experience' model can help understand the contrasting expectations of each stakeholder. It attempts to show how these perspectives were, in effect, 'owned' by different stakeholders in the action inquiry group element of the PSLS and, consequentially, how tensions arose between them as each addressed different concerns. Each stakeholder had particular tensions.

Table 9.4 Stakeholder expectations of public service leaders scheme analysed through four territories of experience

Stakeholders	PSLS secretariat cabinet office	Director of action inquiry groups	Action inquiry group facilitators	Individual PSLS participants	Line manager of PSLS participant
Perspective + Expectation	Visioning Long-term impact of PSLS as a whole on public service leadership	Strategising Medium- to long-term impact and sustainability of action inquiry group process	Performing Medium- to short-term exercise of facilitator role to sustain life of the group	Assessing Short- to medium-term impact of learning in the group on work and life	Assessing Short-term impact of the programme on participant's work Performing Short-term impact of releasing participant for participation
Question	How do we know action inquiry groups are 'working well' and represent good value for money for sectoral sponsors?	How can I satisfy the client that we are doing good work whilst keeping the space open for very different needs of each group?	How can I meet the specific needs of my group which may not look much like the original plan whilst 'playing the game'?	How can this group meet my needs well enough to justify the time I have to take out of my busy life to be here?	How can this programme meet my service needs well enough to justify the time I have to release the team member for?
Pull towards	Control Tangible products that can be shown to others to prove value of PSLS	Co-ordinate Coherent stories of what groups are doing in relation to aims of PSLS	Facilitate Activities that promote reflection and improve practice of participants	Relate Friendships that help me cope with demands and pressures of life and work	Control Tangible outcomes that show me evidence of value
Tensions	Holding the space between the sectoral sponsors and the deliverers	Holding the space between the secretariat and action inquiry group facilitators	Holding the space between director of action inquiry and participants	Holding the space between 'system world' and 'life world'	Holding the space between short-term work demands and longer-term benefits of team member's development

Source: Adapted from Mead 2007

Perhaps the greatest implication of Anderson's study for learning and talent development professionals is the significance of trust from organisation stakeholders in the learning and talent development function. Where such stakeholders have high trust that learning and talent development will add value they are less concerned to micro-manage learning efficiency or to need ROI measures and are more concerned that evaluation gives data on ROE.

EVALUATION DATA

Data collection methods

Collection of data for evaluation can draw on a wide range of quantitative or qualitative research methods including:

- structured and semi-structured interviews
- focus group
- online questionnaire
- postal survey
- telephone survey
- observation of behaviour
- analysis of spoken or written language used
- analysis of financial figures
- document analysis

FOLLOW UP

See Chapter 12, Research.

Table 9.5 summarises the kinds of questions and data that could be expected to generate evidence for different evaluation measures.

Table 9.5 Evaluation measures, questions and sources of data

Measures	Typical questions	Sources of data
Learner reactions	Were your objectives met? How do you rate the programme/quality of materials/trainer/venue/catering?	End of course evaluation sheet
Learners' learning achievements	Has the learner achieved the intended learning outcomes?	Pre and post tests External assessment and certification
Changes in learners' behaviour within the job role	To what extent has the learner applied their learning in the workplace?	Line manager observation 360° appraisal Performance appraisal Critical incident review reports by learner
Efficiency measures of the learning and talent development function	What are the average no. of training days per employee? What is the proportion of payroll spent on L&TD? How does this compare with competitors? What proportion of the workforce are qualified to NVQ level 4?	Financial data External benchmarks Collation of performance reviews
Internal performance indicators and external benchmarks	To what extent are employees in a position of strategic readiness? How does the organisation compare with industry benchmarks on such figures as sales/revenue/profit per employee? To what extent are objectives within operational plans being met?	Collation of performance appraisal data Internal performance indicators compared with external benchmarks Internal performance indicators
ROI (return on investment) measures	What economic returns have resulted from L&TD expenditure? How has L&TD investment enabled achievement of strategic objectives? To what extent are employees achieving individual performance objectives?	Cost benefit analysis Management survey; internal performance indicators Pre and post performance appraisal reviews
ROE (return on expectation) measures	What are stakeholders' expectations prior to design? Are these expectations met following the L&TD intervention?	Management survey Workforce survey Focus group/interview Action research

SUMMARY

This chapter has reviewed issues and steps involved in the design and evaluation of learning and talent development solutions. It presents a web of ten factors that we suggest can be systematically worked through in the design process, to guide the selection and combination of learning methods:

1. clear and appropriate objectives
2. alignment with business strategy
3. stakeholder expectations
4. evaluation
5. learners
6. organisation context
7. resources
8. combination of learning methods and interventions
9. transfer and application to work
10. deliverer capability – skilled learning architects and deliverers.

The chapter has reiterated a theme that runs throughout the book, that learning and talent development interventions are strategic interventions, designed to add value by contributing to an organisation's social and human capital. Success and effectiveness of design comes more from the recognition and satisfaction of wider stakeholder expectations of learning and talent development than might traditionally have been acknowledged. This highlights once again the importance for learning and talent development professionals of interpersonal relationship-building and political competence. Achieving strategic alignment comes from ability to make a business case for learning and talent development interventions and to articulate the value proposition of any activity. A clear statement of objectives and learning outcomes is usually a pre-requisite for this, but we have also drawn attention to the fact that this is not always appropriate. In situations where learning might come in the form of insight, cognitive dissonance and transformational learning, tight objectives are unhelpful.

We have argued that evaluation has to be seen as a strategic activity, considered and planned for from the start of the design process. No single model or set of evaluation measures will suit all organisations, but evaluation that remains at Kirkpatrick's levels I and II is not sufficient. In designing evaluation, the learning and talent development professional needs to consider the following points:

- Is trust in the value of learning and talent development high, medium or low?
- Is alignment required for long-term strategic capability or short-term performance priorities?
- What are stakeholders' expectations of learning and talent development?
- What kinds of measures are required – efficiency measures, benchmarking, ROI or ROE?

This chapter has introduced the practical application of the following core terms as they relate to learning and talent development within work organisations:

- return on investment (ROI)
- return on expectation (ROE)
- alignment
- evaluation
- objective
- learning outcome
- business case
- value proposition

Having read this chapter and completed the activities throughout, you should be able to:

- design learning and talent solutions, with informed and justified choices of learning and talent development methods to meet various individual, team and organisational learning needs
- construct a value proposition or business case for a learning/talent development solution
- employ objectives and learning outcomes to all levels of a programme, but also know the kinds of scenarios where objective-setting can constrict learning
- distinguish between ROI and ROE and their application to evaluation
- apply the concept of stakeholder expectation in the design and evaluation of learning and talent development.

 REVIEW ACTIVITIES

1. Summarise five key things you have learnt from this chapter.

   - Write down two or three new questions the chapter has raised for you or things that you are unclear about.
   - Select one of these questions that you will enquire into further.
   - Write down what action you can take next in pursuit of your question. (For example, read one of the references in this chapter, talk to someone more experienced at work, look on CIPD website, take time to reflect on your own experience.)

2. List the benefits of making a statement of objectives and/or learning outcomes for a learning intervention. Give an example of a learning need where specifying SMART objectives may not be appropriate and explain why.

3. Conduct an interview with a senior manager and the head of learning and talent development in your organisation (or another you are familiar with), asking the following questions:

   - How does learning and talent development activity provide strategic value to the organisation?
   - How is the value contributed by learning and talent development activity measured?

   Compare the responses you get from each interview.

   To what extent do the two agree or differ with each other and with the content of this chapter?

4. Look back over the chapter and create a statement for each of the following terms that summarises your understanding of each in your own words:

- ROI
- ROE
- alignment
- evaluation

- objective
- learning outcome
- business case
- value proposition

5. Designing an intervention – problem scenarios.

Work in groups of three to five to look at the scenarios below and in each case design an appropriate learning/talent development intervention:

i.   Identify key stakeholders and what their expectations might be.

ii. Specify two or three learning outcomes and select a combination of one or more learning methods designed to achieve these. Specify any assumptions you make regarding the participants, context or resources.

iii. Explain what you would evaluate and how.

It was identified that black and minority ethnic entrepreneurs found it particularly difficult to break out of their own minority ethnic markets to enter the supply chain of large companies. Whilst their products and services were high-quality they had weak contacts within the large corporates and little understanding of their needs or procurement systems.

Cross-cultural training: A British company manufacturing car components has agreed a strategic alliance with an Indian partner and is negotiating another in Brazil. Whilst the British production and quality managers are generally accustomed to working across European boundaries, a training need has been identified for the development of their capability to work more internationally, to enable them to develop effective work relationships in India and Brazil.

Financial Services company: new tier of middle managers, rapidly promoted without the chance to gain experience on the job, cuts so minimal money for off-the-job training, early retirements meaning the majority of older experienced employees have gone.

Local authority: recognises that many of its employees on lowest scales, working as cleaners, porters for example, have greater potential and with training and more confidence, could be going for supervisor positions.

Medium-sized tourism company of 75 employees across three sites has recognised a training need for team development to strengthen the management team of six team section heads.

CASE STUDY OF NORTHERN COUNTY COUNCIL

Management development programme

Programme design

Northern County Council aspired to be an excellent local authority and recognised the significance of developing its managers if it was to achieve this strategic objective. A learning needs analysis was conducted with the following range of diagnostic information:

i. TLQ individual reports – Transformational Leadership Questionnaire (TLQ) is a 360° feedback instrument developed by Beverley Alimo-Metcalfe, which generates individual reports against a profile of leadership behaviours. This was conducted with 100 middle and senior managers.

ii. TLQ group report – Collating the 100 individual reports produced a group report highlighting the collective trends.

iii. Employee survey.

iv. Northern County Council strategic priorities – which included such objectives as developing transformational leadership (Alimo-Metcalfe 2002), integrating diversity across all activity, excellent customer service.

Following analysis of this diagnostic data the local authority tendered for suppliers to design and deliver a programme that would meet the identified needs and overarching objective of developing strategic and transformational leadership capability across the authority. The supplier selected was a local university. Price was a factor in the selection, but the other criteria for their choice were that they were international specialists in public sector policy and management, could draw on a network of high-level practitioners to contribute to delivery and, as a university, could offer Masters-level accreditation to any participants who wanted it.

The programme was designed to enable people to learn in a variety of ways both to suit preferred learning styles and to facilitate deep enduring learning. As such the design worked around cycles of action, reflection and conceptual input. The providers clearly differentiated the programme as a management development programme rather than simply a management education programme, meaning that it should deliver performance improvements for the organisation through the individuals' learning. Participants were told they could expect not simply to acquire new 'knowledge about' leadership and management, but also to enhance their 'know-how' and 'being able to' kinds of learning.

Running over two years, the programme involved a range of elements, including workshops, masterclasses and readings that explore different theoretical ideas. Core, however, were student-selected live organisational issues, presented within action learning sets that met periodically throughout the programme. Critical reflection was encouraged, particularly within the action learning sets, where each member was guided to work on an individual inquiry question (Torbert 1999; Mead 2006) making their own interpretation of the broad question 'How do I improve my managerial leadership?' So, for example, if one individual initially pursued the question, How do I improve my team meetings?, they would be facilitated to ask other questions, such as:

- Why am I using meetings in this format?

- How am I managing?
- What do I feel about what is going on?
- Where is the power in these meetings?
- What emotion is there?
- What are my choices?

All 100 managers (that is, all assistant directors and service heads, but not the senior management team of directors and chief executive) were invited to participate in the programme, whose design included the following range of elements:

- foundation event
- thematic modules
- half-day 'masterclasses' with keynote speeches from national leaders
- coaching groups
- action learning tasks
- partnership between tutors and learners
- Masters degree-level accreditation.

Thematic modules

Five 2-day thematic modules were designed to focus on the main content areas identified in the needs analysis. All participants would attend a Foundation event, but could select other thematic modules to attend depending on their individual development needs, as identified in the TLQ. Modules were repeated several times throughout the 18-month programme duration and, because of the interactive learning style of these workshops, a maximum of 24 participants could attend each time.

Module 1. Foundation event

Objectives

- to provide basic orientation to the programme
- to introduce concepts and models

to enhance capacity to think and act strategically

- to prompt reflection on their role as strategic leaders of the organisation
- to build on the individual TLQ feedback to further reflect on development needs and to clarify learning objectives
- to establish the programme's action learning approach
- to form the coaching groups and to establish the relationship with facilitators.

Module 2. Getting the best from staff

Objectives

- to strengthen capabilities to show genuine concern for others' well-being, including approaches to:
  - Communication and consultation
  - Maximising individual potential
  - Developing and stretching staff without imposing excessive stress
  - Promoting individual learning
- to develop abilities to empower and delegate without losing touch.

Module 3. High-performance team-working

Objectives

- to develop ability to inspire shared vision
- to strengthen ability to set clear corporate performance standards, to focus team effort and to clarify individual and team objectives, purpose and priorities
- to identify approaches for dealing with poor performance
- to enhance skills in facilitating team development, including handling disagreement
- to encourage questioning.

Module 4. Improvement and innovation

Objectives

- to support application of business planning

- to enhance abilities to turn plans into action

- to identify sources of innovation such as listening to customers

- to integrate environmental sustainability into the improvement cycle

- to support a developmental culture that encourages staff in learning from feedback, constructive criticism and reflection

- to strengthen creative and lateral thinking

- to develop abilities to encourage questioning and critical and strategic thinking.

Module 5. Collaborative working

Objectives

- to develop skills in networking and achieving

- to enhance ability to communicate with politicians and other partners

- to enhance ability to communicate with and genuinely listen to other partners

- to develop approaches and skills for inspiring internal stakeholders

- to develop approaches and skills for inspiring external stakeholders

- to strengthen capacity for inspiring a vision with multiple stakeholders

- to enhance political skills for balancing the needs of multiple stakeholders.

Coaching groups

At the Foundation event, so-called coaching groups of eight were formed with the intention they would meet at least three-monthly for half a day, over a period of 12 months. The group was intended to work as an action learning set, in which members act as critical friends to each other as they work on individual objectives under the umbrella question, 'How do I improve my leadership?' Each group had a nominated tutor as a coach/facilitator whose role was partly as personal coach to group members on a one-to-one basis, and also as action learning facilitator to the group at their meetings.

Masterclasses

During the life of the programme, a series of larger development events were to be staged to which all participants as well as the senior management team were invited. These were delivered by national high-level practitioners not necessarily from local government. The objective of these was partly to share important lessons from their own practice, and partly to offer role models for programme participants.

Accreditation routes

An option was made available to participants to gain credits for their work on this programme towards a university Masters degree, which a small minority took up. This required attendance of all five Northern County Council programme modules plus coaching group meetings, engagement in action learning tasks and submission of six pieces of assessed work. Successful completion would lead to the award of a postgraduate certificate, equivalent to 50 per cent credits required for a full MSc.

Stakeholders, expectations and evaluation

The key stakeholders were the:

i. sponsor (chief executive)

Ii. client (represented by the training manager who administered the programme)

Iii. university academic manager

iv. action-learning set facilitators

v. individual participants

vi. line managers of individual participant (who were either members of the senior management team or themselves were programme participants).

Commissioned by the chief executive for the purpose of raising the authority's overall capacity and performance, the programme was provided by a university, using a team of experienced facilitators with public policy backgrounds, from within and outside the university. The main point of contact with the client organisation and their project leader was the training manager, a representative from the local authority's human resources team. The client was very clear on the outcome wanted, namely: to increase across the organisation as a whole, the level of transformational leadership (as defined by Alimo-Metcalfe and Nyfield 2002). Alongside this fundamental objective was a secondary one expressed in the tender specification: '90 per cent sessions to be rated good or higher'. The latter was assessed through evaluation sheets completed at the end of each module. The change in transformational leadership was to be evaluated through a repeat of the TLQ exercise.

Discussion questions

1. Look at the objectives listed for each thematic module. Take any three of these objectives and consider (i) what data would enable you to evaluate how far they were achieved and (ii) what data collection method you would recommend.

2. The brief for the deliverer specified that participant satisfaction of all sessions should be rated good or higher by at least 90 per cent.

   What are the weaknesses of this as the main evaluation focus?

3. Use the 'four territories of experience' model introduced in the chapter to map the different expectations of the programme by the different main stakeholders in this case study (Fisher *et al* 2000; Torbert 2004).

4. The evaluation methods used were (i) feedback sheets at the end of modules and (ii) a repeat TLQ exercise to provide a comparison in the organisation's transformational leadership rating before and after the programme.

   Recognising the existence of the six stakeholders identified in the case study, with their varying expectations of this programme, apply the concept of ROE (return on expectation) to identify:

   i. What were the strengths and limitations of the evaluation undertaken?

   ii. Recommendations for a more comprehensive approach to evaluation.

EXPLORE FURTHER

Books
Essential

Anderson, V. (2007) *The Value of Learning: From return on investment to return on expectation*. London: CIPD.

Davins, D. and Smith, J. (2010) Evaluation of HRD. Chapter 8 in Gold, J., Holden, R., Iles, P., Stewart, J. and Beardwell, J. *Human Resource Development: theory and practice*. Basingstoke: Palgrave Macmillan.

Recommended

Anderson, V. (2009) Desperately seeking alignment. *Human Resource Development International*. Vol. 12, No. 3, pp263–278.

Ibarra, H. (2003) *Working Identity – Unconventional strategies for reinventing your career*. Boston, MA: Harvard Business School Press.

Kaplan, R.S. and Norton D. P. (1996) *The Balanced Scorecard: Translating strategy into action*. Boston, MA: Harvard University Press.

Pawson, R. and Tilley, N. (1997) *Realistic Evaluation*. London: Sage.

Reynolds, M. and Vince, R. (eds). (2007) *The Handbook of Experiential Learning and Management Education*. Oxford: OUP.

Warr, P.B., Bird, M.W. and Rackham, N. (1970) *Evaluation of Management Training*. Aldershot: Gower.

Websites and podcasts

European Evaluation Society, www.europeanevaluation.org, accessed 24 July 2010

A membership organisation that exists to promote theory, practice and utilisation of high-quality evaluation especially, but not exclusively, within the European countries. This goal is obtained by bringing together academics and practitioners from all over Europe and from any professional sector.

Participatory Action Research for evaluation, www.research-for-real.co.uk/, accessed 24 July 2010

UK Evaluation Society, www.evaluation.org.uk, accessed 24 July 2010

A professional membership organisation comprising evaluation professionals, practitioners and evaluation commissioners from national and local government, the research community, independent consultancies and the voluntary sector. It exists to promote and improve the theory, practice, understanding and utilisation of evaluation and its contribution to public knowledge.

CIPD podcast 29 August 2007 The Value of Learning www.cipd.co.uk/podcasts, accessed 24 July 2010

A roundtable discussion that considers what contribution learning makes to organisations, how to measure the effectiveness of learning and development activities, and quantify their value.

CIPD factsheet: Evaluating learning and development July 2009 www.cipd.co.uk/subjects/lrnanddev/evaluation/evatrain.htm, accessed 14 July 2010

CIPD Tool: Value of learning: assessing and reporting on the value of learning to your organisation www.cipd.co.uk/subjects/lrnanddev/evaluation/_vlulrngtl.htm, accessed 14 July 2010

A practical tool to help managers establish ways of assessing and reporting on the value of learning and training to the organisation. It includes instruments for: assessing the current alignment of learning and training activities with the organisation's strategic priorities; identifying a range of methods for assessing and evaluating the contribution of learning and training; establishing the most appropriate approach to assessing and reporting.

www.methodspace.com/

Methodspace is the home of the research methods community from across the world.

Journals

Practical Assessment, Research and Evaluation

http://pareonline.net/

Online journal of refereed articles that can have a positive impact on assessment, research, evaluation, and teaching practice.

Studies in Educational Evaluation

www.elsevier.com/wps/find/journaldescription.cws_home/497/description#description

Publishes reports of evaluation studies; focus is education, but includes some on vocational training.

Evaluation Review

Sage journal of applied social research – includes some vocational training programmes.

CHAPTER 10

Accessing and Managing Resources

OVERVIEW

It is now well recognised and accepted that learning and talent development can and perhaps should be seen as an investment rather than as a cost (Swart *et al* 2005; Tansley *et al* 2007). This can perhaps provide some confidence and reassurance to professional practitioners in that their work will come to be valued for its longer-term returns, rather than being viewed as a short-term expediency. The latter, certainly in the past and to some extent currently, leads to a situation where expenditure on development becomes an initial and prime candidate for reductions when costs are being cut to meet short-term contingencies (Buckley and Caple 2009).

In common with other functions, development of employees will require resources in order to operate successfully, and securing resources requires that a sound and convincing case is made in terms that make sense to, and which are valued by, key decision-makers (Harrison 2009; Swart *et al* 2005). Those terms are almost always likely to include financial and monetary considerations. Therefore, it remains important for practitioners to be able to apply concepts from the language of finance and accounting if they are to be effective in securing necessary resources, although as pointed out in Chapter 9 money and financial measures are not the only or even in some cases the most important considerations. It is also necessary to forge supportive relationships with key decision-makers and other functions. The notions of partnerships (Harrison 2009) and of politics examined in Chapter 5 are both important here. So too are those of strategic alliances and dominant coalitions from the business strategy literature (see for example Johnson *et al* 2008). A related term is 'stakeholders', and we will apply that term to examine how understanding that concept can support securing resources.

The primary focus of this chapter, then, is the nature of the resources required to provide effective learning and talent development services, and the financial arguments that can be used in securing allocation of those resources to that purpose.

This focus will require some examination of principles and concepts arising out of the disciplines of financial management and accounting. Our examination of these principles and concepts will be conventional. That is, we will treat the concepts as unproblematic. However, such a treatment relies heavily on a functionalist paradigm and an associated 'Tayloristic' (Puxty 1993) conception of organisation and management. As we keep mentioning, alternative and more critical treatments are possible (Alvesson *et al* 2009). In particular, the whole subject of financial management and accounting is being increasingly subject to analysis and critical appraisal from alternative perspectives (Barber 1997). So, we advise caution in accepting what is written in this chapter as the only perspective on accounting and financial management practice. Within that context, the chapter is intended to meet the following outcomes.

LEARNING OUTCOMES

After reading this chapter and completing the activities, the intention is that you will be able to:

- explain and apply critical concepts associated with the costing and budgeting of talent development

- evaluate and apply the notion of stakeholders to gaining support for talent development

- assess and evaluate the advantages and disadvantages of dedicated physical resources

- explain and critically assess the concept of 'learning resource centre' and its application in practical contexts

- articulate and apply key principles in the recruitment, selection and development of specialist talent development personnel

- produce costed and justified proposals for investment in talent development activities.

THE NOTION OF RESOURCES

The notion of resources is primarily associated with accounting and finance. While it is probably true that accounting practices in most if not all organisations follow the paradigm applied here, critically evaluating the results in the light of the existence of alternative paradigms can provide valuable insight. A particular example of this to bear in mind is that organisations can be viewed as political arenas consisting of competing interests, as we discussed in Chapter 5. The 'political game' or process in which these interests engage is, in part, played by the rules and through the language of accounting. Thus, accounting concepts, principles and procedures should not be seen as neutral, objective and value-free criteria by which rational decisions are reached. Rather, they can be viewed as a set of 'discursive activities' (Oswick *et al* 1997), which are used by both accountants and non-accountants to secure and maintain power in organisations (Barber 1997). Similar analyses are being applied to the total field of learning and talent development (Finch-Lees and Mabey 2007; Sambrook 2007) and this provides an additional reason for ensuring the critical faculties of readers are attuned to this chapter.

FOLLOW UP

See Chapter 5 for a full discussion of organisational politics and its role in learning and talent development.

A range of classifications of different types of resources required for learning and development is presented in the specialist literature (see Harrison 2009; Reid, Barrington and Brown 2004). We will be concerned here with three types: money, physical and human. The first of these will be dealt with through an examination of basic yet important concepts. Physical resources will focus on the use of buildings and equipment in the form of learning resource centres. Our concern with human resources will be focused on recruitment, selection and development of specialist staff. Some examples will be given to illustrate application of principles and concepts. Two caveats to this are important to state. First, actual accounting practices can and do vary from organisation to organisation and over time. These variations include differences in language and terminology. It will be necessary therefore for readers to produce their own translations. Second, we cannot predict how long this book will remain in print and therefore when it might be read. We can predict, though, that the price and cost of resources will be different (almost certainly greater) at the time of reading than at the time of writing. Therefore, readers will again bear the responsibility of updating any actual figures.

Some of these points will become clearer on completion of the activity below. It will also support the introduction of an additional key concept to be discussed in the next section.

 ACTIVITY

Nature of resources

Consider the two case studies below and then complete the following questions:

1. What kind of resources will both Jack and Sally need for their programmes?

2. What kind, if any will Jack need that Sally will not need? What kind, if any, will Sally need that Jack will not need?

3. Which other people in their respective organisations will Jack and Sally have to persuade to invest resources in their respective programmes?

4. Discuss your responses to these questions with other students or colleagues.

CASE STUDY

Case study one

Jack Bellamy is newly appointed talent development manager for Associated European Bank's personal banking division which operates across the globe from offices in most major cities. The bank has identified Personal Wealth Advisers as a critical role and key talent in the organisation and created Jack's position to create and manage a development programme for holders of that role as a means of identifying, developing and retaining the best current and future performers. As his first action Jack has to prepare a programme design and implementation plan with identified and justified resource requirements.

Case study two

Sally Carter is chief executive of a small law firm in a large city in the UK West Midlands. The firm consists of 10 partners, 30 Associates and 20 legal executives as well as 15 non-legal support staff. Because of her HR background Sally both wishes and is expected to do something about the high labour turnover of legal executives and non-legal support staff. Sally judges that lack of investment in their development is a contributory factor as the attractive development opportunities offered by the large legal firms in the City is often cited by those who leave for jobs with those firms. So, designing and implementing some form of development is high on her current agenda for discussion with the firm's managing partner.

THE NOTION OF STAKEHOLDERS

The activity above will have suggested that there are number of groups and individuals who have a 'stake' in the programmes being developed in each organisation. In each case we can identify the 'talent'; ie those who will be directly targeted for development; the managers of those employees; senior decision-makers and, perhaps only in the case of Jack, other talent management and HR staff. Those groups are fairly obvious. Perhaps less obvious are colleagues of those defined as talent and perhaps also their customers. So, even though the context of the two cases has many differences both individuals responsible for talent development have similar constituencies to at least take account of if not directly satisfy. The notion of stakeholders, examined and used in Chapter 9, is used to refer to these different constituencies. We will extend our examination of the notion here to look in more detail at the theoretical origins and perspectives.

THEORETICAL PERSPECTIVES

The word and concept of 'stakeholder' originated in the study and practice of business law and is now widely applied in management texts on strategic management and, especially, in business ethics and specifically corporate social responsibility. The concept is applied in debates about how organisations, and business corporations in particular, should be governed and whose interests should be served. These are mainly normative matters and so to do with how things should be rather than how things are. Such matters are generally much more difficult to settle and applying the notion of stakeholders is no exception. Stakeholders are generally defined as those who either affect or are affected by the decisions, activities and operations of an organisation (Stansfield and Stewart 2007). They are also generally held to be groups or categories of individuals and can be external and internal. Examples of the former include:

- governments
- trades unions
- pressure/interest groups
- international/national/local populations
- competitors
- suppliers
- customers
- professional bodies.

Examples of internal stakeholders include:

- all employees
- variable and varying employee groups, eg managers, professionals, operatives
- different levels of managers
- shareholders
- different kinds of owners, eg founders, institutional shareholders, individual shareholders.

Each of these groups has a stake, or interest, in the organisation and the outcomes of its activities. The stake or interest will vary in significance and importance to both the different groups and to the organisation. This leads to a further distinction, which carries a range of different labels, but which is encompassed by differentiating between primary and secondary stakeholders. One useful but not always accurate way of applying this is to think of those who have an interest in the outcomes, eg shareholders, managers and other employees, have a stake in the performance and continued existence of the organisation; and those who have an interest in the activities and operations, eg local populations and interest groups such as environmental campaigners. These examples suggest that the internal and external division is also useful in distinguishing between primary and secondary stakeholders and that can be the case. However, it is not so straightforward; eg suppliers may depend on a particular organisation for their business and customers of banks as opposed to supermarkets, as we have seen at the close of the first decade of the twenty-first century, depend on the outcomes as well as the operations of those organisations. So, which groups can be considered primary and which secondary has to be determined in each organisational case.

Stakeholder theory is applied in practice through techniques such as stakeholder analysis or stakeholder audits. These identify the varying stakeholder groups, the extent to which each is directly or indirectly affected by and also directly or indirectly affects the organisation, and their perspectives on and interests in organisation operations and outcomes. The implications and responses of these can then be formulated, agreed and adopted.

ACTIVITY

Using the list of potential stakeholders above as a guide, identify primary and secondary stakeholders for your organisation or one you are familiar with. Specify the stake or interest each has and the implications for decision-making in the organisation.

APPLYING THE THEORY TO TALENT DEVELOPMENT

The ideas around stakeholder theory have at least three implications for learning and talent development. First, they can usefully be applied in the overall process and each stage of talent management and talent development. This can be useful in identifying what and whose interests need to be served. The notions of commissioner, provider and consumer, for example, can be applied in identifying stakeholders in a talent development programme and their varying demands and expectations identified and taken into account in design and implementation (see Stansfield and Stewart 2007). Second, talent development programmes often utilise external providers acting as partners in learning and development of identified talent, and commonly in roles similar to those identified by Stansfield and Stewart. Such partners are by definition stakeholders in the talent development programme.

The third implication is related to the origins of stakeholder theory, which was debates about whether anyone other than those with a direct financial investment in an organisation had any rights in decision-making in and for the organisation. The debates focused on whether forms of investment other than financial should be recognised, for example, investment of 'cares and concerns' by employees (see Jennings and Happel 2003); and if so whether that recognition led to rights in the organisation. The traditional view held that those with a financial investment exercised property rights and also had exclusive rights based on their bearing financial risk. The alternative view expressed as stakeholder theory held that other forms of investment also conferred rights. That latter view is now much more prevalent than when the debates first occurred, but even so it is still the case that shareholders with a financial stake are afforded rights not available to other groups. And their financial interest, or stake, and expectation of a financial return, is one reason why the language of finance and accountancy is so significant in organisations. So we now turn our attention to that language.

COSTING AND BUDGETING TALENT DEVELOPMENT

A useful starting point is to consider other reasons why the situation implied by the last sentences of the previous section is the case. This question can be answered in part by examining the purpose or purposes of costing and budgeting per se in work organisations. In other words, why is it that all organisation activities are expressed in and represented by financial terms? There are at least three main possible answers to this question. The first is reasonably straightforward in that there are legal requirements placed on organisations which specify the form and content of the information they publish about their activities. This is related to the second purpose, which is to both *control* and *account* for scarce resources. Organisations would wish to control use of resources so as to ensure they are not wasted and that they produce some valued outcomes, or returns. Depending on the nature and legal status of their incorporation, organisations might also wish to account for their use of scarce resources to those who provide them. However, in most cases, though subject to the same provisos of nature and status, organisations are legally required to account for their use of resources. This is achieved through publication of annual reports. Such reports give an account of the use of resources in the given period, and those who made decisions on that use can, on the basis of the reports, be held to account for their use and control of resources.

The third main purpose of costing and budgeting is to assess the contribution of various activities to achieving organisation objectives. Decision-makers face choices about allocating resources in the future, and information on past results and performance can provide a valuable input in making those decisions. Costing and budgeting enables assessment of contribution and thus provides that information. In summary, costing and budgeting serves the following main purposes:

- to meet legal requirements:
- to control and account for scarce resources:
- to assess the varying contribution of varying activities to achievement of organisation objectives.

The final purpose is obviously related to allocation of resources. The assessment is focused on whether allocation of resources of a given amount to a particular activity, or set of activities, produced a worthwhile and valued return in terms of organisation objectives. Such assessments inform decisions on future allocations. In theory at least, it is possible for such a purpose to be achieved by means other than costing and budgeting, at least where objectives relate to non-financial criteria. This may also be true, again in theory, for other purposes, so long as legal requirements allow non-financial criteria. However, in practice, all organisations express some at least of their objectives in financial terms, even if the language used implies rather than directly states financial criteria, for example, concepts such as efficiency. This is one reason why financial criteria are used to achieve the three purposes. Other reasons include the following:

- *Measurement.* Using financial criteria creates a common and consistent yardstick against which resource allocation can be measured. In doing so, it facilitates comparison and assessment of the various activities undertaken.

- *Decision-making.* This reason relates to decisions on resource allocation. The common criterion provided by the language of finance and accounting enables and supports the negotiation and agreement of budgets, for example.

- *'Bottom line'.* We might refer to financial performance representing the 'bottom line' of organisation objectives. However, we can also argue that in the context of capitalist economies, the 'bottom line' is that organisations cannot operate without resources which are expressed in and accounted for in financial terms. That being the case, it makes sense to incorporate similar terms in managing organisation activities.

Given the purposes described so far, and the reasons for using financial criteria and concepts in meeting those purposes, it is perhaps understandable that decision-makers at all levels in organisations take a keen interest in money. 'How much will it cost?' or 'what will I get for my money?' are not uncommon questions to proposals submitted to decision-makers for approval. Answering these questions forms the basis of a 'business case' for organisation expenditure. Anticipating and providing answers to the questions within proposals is therefore advisable. However, the questions also illustrate the obsessive concern with matters of finance within organisations, and the associated need for all functions, including talent development, to be able to justify their existence and activities in financial terms. The process of costing that existence and those activities is the starting point in meeting that need.

 ## ACTIVITY

1. Imagine an organisation without an overt concern for financial criteria. What alternatives might be used to meet the purposes listed above?

2. Assess the extent to which decision-makers in your organisation or one you know well might be described as 'obsessed' with financial criteria. In doing so, answer the following questions:

    a. In what ways does a concern with finance express itself?

    b. What emphasis is placed on financial criteria in explicit organisation objectives?

    c. What implications can you identify for talent development arising from the level of interest in and attention to financial criteria?

3. Consider the current level of financial sophistication displayed within the talent development function in the same organisation. For example:

    a. Are all activities currently costed?

    b. Do all proposals for approval include anticipated results/benefits expressed in financial terms?

    c. Are alternative responses to talent development problems assessed/evaluated in financial terms before final decisions?

THE PROCESS OF COSTING LEARNING AND TALENT DEVELOPMENT ACTIVITIES

Costing any activity is a necessary precursor to formulation of budgets. In that sense, it can be seen as part of any budgeting process. Two stages are involved in costing. First, the items, or 'factors', that will attract costs need to be identified and specified. Second, the actual costs associated with each of the cost factors need to be established or estimated. Establishing or estimating costs depends on the extent to which actual costs are known at the time the costing exercise is undertaken. Some will be known and therefore can be established. Some will not be known and therefore will need to be estimated.

The fact that actual costs consist of some that are known and some that are unknown suggests that costs can be categorised into different types. A conventional categorisation uses three different types. The first is known as 'fixed costs'. Other terms used for this type include 'standing charges' and 'overheads'. The former is a term more often found in public sector organisations, while the latter is a little difficult since accounting practices allow variation in what is defined as an 'overhead'. Caution is therefore advised in translating these terms to particular contexts. The key principle to apply is that fixed costs will be incurred irrespective of the level of activity. In fact, fixed costs will need to be paid even if the level of activity is zero. This principle also distinguishes the second type of cost. This is 'direct costs'. Other terms for this include 'direct expenditure', 'variable costs' and 'marginal expenditure'. Strictly speaking, the last of these is a concept from economics which is misused/misapplied in this context. The key principle is that direct costs are those which vary according *to* the *level* of activity. In other words, the greater the level of activity, the greater the amount of direct costs incurred, and the lower the level of activity, the lower the amount of direct costs. Hence use of the term 'variable costs'.

The final cost type is more difficult to apply and more controversial in its use. It is known as 'indirect cost' or 'indirect expenditure'. An alternative term, 'hidden costs', perhaps suggests the nature of the difficulties and controversies. Two examples will illustrate the nature of this type of cost, and the associated controversies and difficulties. First, all organisations have certain costs which do not easily fall into mainstream activities. An example may be the remuneration of the board of directors, especially that of non-executive directors. Second, when employees are undertaking formal development activities, rather than doing their jobs, an 'opportunity cost' is incurred. For example, those employees are not directly contributing to producing a return for their salaries. Difficulties and controversies surround arriving at actual costs for these factors, defining them as either indirect or fixed and in allocating them to particular mainstream activities. To take the first example, should it be an overhead or part of indirect costs? To take the second example, should the cost, however specified and defined, be considered a learning and development cost or a cost incurred by the employing function, department, or division?

The questions raised by the notion of indirect costs have no simple or universal answers. Practices can and do vary across organisations. But the questions need to be answered in particular contexts in order that budgets can be formulated. Costing as a process can also serve additional purposes. It has obvious application in evaluation of talent development, especially where cost/benefit analysis is used in that process. Being able to cost development activities has potential value earlier in the process. First, the process of problem analysis intended to determine which are development and non-development problems, described in Chapter 7, is also intended to establish whether corrective action will be worthwhile. Applying the notion of investment appraisal, which seeks to answer that question in financial terms, requires that potential costs are known or can be realistically estimated. Second, the same process includes the stage of estimate costs/benefits. This activity is always relevant at the design stage of learning and talent development since an important factor to take into account in such decisions (for example, whether to design and provide an in-house course or to use an existing, external course) is the relative cost of available options. These two applications are illustrated with others in relation to the conventional learning and development cycle in Figure 10.1.

Figure 10.1 Financial techniques

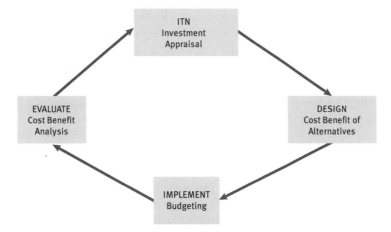

Source: Stewart 1999

 ACTIVITY

1. Identify and list the most significant cost factors involved in talent development.

2. Determine which type of cost each factor represents, and allocate each to one of three types.

3. Estimate realistic and current costs for each item. Remember that staff costs should be based on costs of employment rather than on salary (usually between 30 per cent and 50 per cent added to salary). Costs of consultants, external courses, facilities and equipment can be established to some extent through advertisements in professional journals.

FORMULATING A BUDGET

Once cost factors have been identified and actual costs determined, a budget can be formulated. Budgets serve two related purposes: to justify allocation and expenditure of resources, and to provide a management control tool to ensure available resources are not exceeded and are accounted for. Critical perspectives might emphasise the control function served by 'targets', whether budgetary or otherwise (see Fisher and Sempik 2009). The former purpose can be very useful in marketing learning and talent development. Budget proposals can highlight past successes, emphasising recent achievements in terms of valued outcomes. They can also focus on the returns, in the same terms, to be achieved by future investment to support a business case for the investment detailed in the budget. Both purposes can be applied to an annual budget for the whole function, or to a particular and specific activity. We will be primarily concerned with the former.

An annual budget should provide and account for the known fixed costs and the estimated expenditure of direct costs. In most organisations, projecting costs forward for 12 months will mean that the former are known and the latter can only be estimated. The relationship between annual budgets and indirect costs very much depends on accounting practices adopted in particular organisations. A useful process to follow in constructing a budget is as follows (Kenrick 1984):

- *Identify existing commitments.* The focus here is to establish the costs associated with running the learning and talent development function, ie fixed costs, and direct costs associated with continuing activities. An example of the latter might be fees for employees in a talent pipeline being sponsored on educational programmes such as an MBA. A significant consideration in each case is to allow for increases over the previous year in, for example, salary costs and college fees. Where these are not known, it is common practice to use an agreed percentage allowance for inflation.

- *Identify proposed actions/activities.* This stage follows from the process of establishing learning and talent development needs (see Chapter 7). The purpose is to identify and specify the cost factors associated with each new activity. This can be more difficult for some activities. It is, however, likely that most factors will be immediately obvious even if actual costs need to be estimated.

- *Cost-proposed activities.* There may be a need in a budget proposal to consider alternatives, with one option being identified as the preferred or recommended action. These options can be presented as part of this stage. However, whether options are presented or not, all proposed activities will be costed on the basis of a share of known, fixed costs and estimated direct costs.

- *Identify and specify income.* There can be sources of income for learning and talent development. External sources include funding from government agencies (see Chapter 3) or fees received through external sales of development products and services. The concepts of zero-budgets and service agreement contracts are being increasingly applied and therefore internal payments may be made to development function by client departments. Expected income from any source is normally included in budgets. Also of significance and importance is to identify the value added by the expenditure to support the business case (see Harrison 2009).

- *Summarise and present budget information.* The form that this final stage will take is too variable to attempt to specify here. Common practice, though, suggests that an overall total of learning and talent development costs will be broken down into specific budget headings. This can be by department, by category of employee, by type of development activity or any combination of these headings. Value added headings can also be used; eg projected and expected contribution to specified organisation objectives. This too helps to present and support a business case. One requirement that remains constant is to allocate fixed costs proportionally across budget headings on the basis of some agreed criteria or formula.

The above process applies to an annual budget, although the same principles can be applied to constructing a budget for a particular learning and talent development programme. Responsibility for learning and development is argued to be increasingly decentralised to line departments and managers (Harrison 2009) although talent development may be treated differently. This decentralisation may or may not include responsibility for learning and/or talent development budgets. In either case, decentralised responsibility will have implications for the construction and presentation of central budgets. A final feature of the budgeting process is to use the results in identifying trends and facilitating comparisons. These may focus on internal trends/comparisons through tracking changes in allocations and expenditure over time, and on external trends/comparisons through benchmarking. A useful device for producing such analyses is the notion of ratios. Moorby (1996) suggests the following five ratios as useful for such purposes:

- cost per day of training
- training cost as a percentage of payroll
- budget variance
- training days per trainer per annum
- average training days provided per employee.

The arithmetic involved in calculating these ratios is straightforward, though defining some of the terms may not be, eg 'day of training'. Access to external comparative data can be through trade associations, government reports/ statistics, professional journals and informal networks. The following activity closes our discussion of costing and budgeting.

 ACTIVITY

Imagine you are a talent development specialist who has agreed with a senior manager a priority need for developing the leadership skills of 20 supervisors in an operations department. You have also agreed that a formal programme of no more than five days would be appropriate, with no more than ten supervisors away at one time. A well-respected provider, with facilities just over 50 miles from the location of your organisation, provides a suitable, 'open' course with the range of participant numbers limited to a minimum of 18 and a maximum of 25. The provider also offers an in-house course specifically tailored to organisation requirements. However, they insist on five days' consultancy in addition to the direct training time to identify specific needs, design/amend the course and prepare original materials. Consider and respond to the following questions:

a. what options are available to you in this scenario?

b. which cost factors will be associated with each option?

c. what is your estimate of the actual cost of each factor in each option?

d. what other factors will you take into account, other than costs, in reaching a decision or recommendation?

e. how will you proceed to arrive at a final decision?

Discuss your responses to this activity with student or work colleagues and compare and contrast your results.

PHYSICAL RESOURCES

Physical resources can, generally, be regarded as falling into two types: buildings and equipment. The latter will consist of items such as furniture, electronic projectors and screens, smart boards, flipchart stands and electronic equipment such as PCs and DVD players. Buildings will include office space for staff employed in the learning and talent development function, as well as space dedicated for and to development purposes and activities. These can include residential leadership and management development centres and learning workshops. All these resources will normally form part of the fixed costs of the learning and talent development function. However, some items, for example, DVD players and projectors, can be hired for use as and when necessary. The same is true of physical space, for example, using the facilities of hotels or specialist conference centres. In these circumstances, the costs become direct rather than fixed, since expenditure will vary according to the amount of development undertaken. One set of costs which are normally always direct costs are the materials used by and with items of equipment. The actual cost of equipment and 'consumable materials' at any particular time are easily determined through advertisements in the professional and trade press, and through contact with established suppliers.

Establishing the fixed costs of dedicated physical space, for example, offices for staff, will depend on varying practices adopted by particular organisations. Common practice would suggest some formula based on £X per square metre per annum, where X takes account of expenditure on rent, rates, heating, lighting, etc. The same type of formula can be used where the learning and development function shares space with other functions and departments and, depending on the particular arrangements for shared space, can be used to calculate either fixed or direct costs associated with physical space.

This brief overview provides an illustration of the kinds of issues and principles involved in considering physical resources from a costing and budgeting perspective. The rest of this section will be concerned with the particular resource of a learning and development centre. There is a particular form of that generally referred to as a learning or learning resource centre (LRC). We will initially be concerned with some general principles which can be applied to both but will not discuss the LRC form in any detail. Both types of learning and development centre are commonly part of and associated with what are also commonly called corporate universities or corporate academies (see Chapter 8, Stewart and Shaw 2005 for full discussion of these terms).

An important point to state first is that physical space tends to be expensive, and therefore dedicating space for the exclusive purpose of learning and talent development will, in most cases, represent a significant investment. The decision on whether or not to have such space will therefore require careful deliberation. An important factor to bear in mind in making this decision is the notion of opportunity cost. What this means is that any expenditure on a learning and development centre, of whatever form, cannot be used to fund alternative development activities. So, the case for such facilities in the sense of expected benefits needs to be carefully examined and thought through, especially in terms of comparing the benefits with those that might be expected from expenditure on alternative activities. A key factor, as always with such decisions, will be the level of support from top managers and the relationship between expected benefits and their valued outcomes. For example, leading edge or state of the art centres may be associated with corporate image and prestige. The development case for and against use of dedicated space may be secondary to the 'corporate image' case. And this could well be associated with employer branding as a means of attracting and retaining key talent (see Tansley *et al* 2007 on employer branding). Criteria outside a strict interpretation of advantages/disadvantages from a development perspective may therefore need to be considered.

A number of other issues need to be taken into account. First, the categories of staff and the nature of the development the physical space is intended to support. An example of each will illustrate the point. It is unlikely that a physical resource intended to support leadership and management development will be quite the same as one intended to support craft or professional employees. Similarly, a resource capable of supporting development of social skills will probably require different facilities from one dealing with technical knowledge and skills. The second issue is, in part, related to the first since it concerns volume of use. The expected use of the facilities will depend on the size of the intended population and the need/demand for replacement, refresher and updating development. This will in part be related to the general approach to talent management, for example, where an exclusive approach is prevalent then usage is likely to be less than where an inclusive approach is adopted. This also of course depends on organisation size. Expected volume, though, is a critical criterion in its own right. A third issue is that of privacy. This is also related to the intended audience, for example, in the case of sales training or senior management workshops where confidential or sensitive information may need to be disseminated or discussed. The criterion of privacy can be very significant in talent development for a variety of reasons, for example, strategically valuable information is disclosed and discussed. The fourth issue is the amount of flexibility that needs to be planned into the resource. For example, it may be necessary to be able to respond at short notice to the requirements of new initiatives. Finally, there is the issue of costs. An important factor here is to consider both the start-up costs, ie the investment required to establish the resource, and the operating costs, ie those arising on a continuing basis from the resource providing its intended services.

All these issues need to be considered whether the resource is a traditional learning and development centre or a learning resource centre (LRC). Some additional issues arise more or less specifically with each of these. We will now look at some of those more likely (although not necessarily exclusively) to arise when considering a traditional learning and development centre.

LEARNING AND DEVELOPMENT CENTRES

A critical and early issue to consider is whether the centre will provide residential accommodation. Many large organisations, such as Lloyds TSB and National Westminster Bank in financial services and the John Lewis Partnership in retail, own and operate centres with extensive and high-standard accommodation. These facilities are not essential, however, especially if arrangements can be made with local hotels for staff travelling from a distance and so centres do not have to be residential. A related decision, assuming a centre does provide accommodation, is whether to directly operate this service, including employing the necessary staff, or whether to contract out management of these services and facilities to specialist organisations, for example, hotel or catering companies. As with any outsourcing decision, there are arguments for and against and no simple or definitive answer.

The issue of residential accommodation is related to two further questions. The first is that of location. Obviously, a centre needs to be accessible and to have good transport links, especially if the organisation operates nationally or internationally. Other considerations might include local facilities for recreation to provide breaks from the centre, and the closeness or otherwise to the normal place of work and/or a main or head office of the organisation. Giving colleagues and/or managers easy access to learners at the centre may be disruptive. However, given the abilities of modern communications technology, physical access can be the least significant form of disruption. The second issue is that of learning accommodation. As a general principle, the aim is normally to minimise a classroom or school atmosphere and to create a relaxing and supportive climate. The quality of learning accommodation, for example, the standards of decoration and furnishing, can also signal the value attached to learning and talent development.

Whether or not a centre is residential, and irrespective of the intended users, a range of domestic services needs to be considered. These include reception, catering and cleaning. In the case of a non-residential centre located on the same site as a main or head office operation, the latter two can share in or be part of more general provision. However, reception services are always likely to have to be provided by the learning and development function. Similar considerations apply to maintenance. Physical space and equipment need to be refurbished, replaced, maintained and repaired. These services can be provided directly by the function, or through a contract agreement with a supplier or through the general services of the organisation. These factors raise the related issue of centre staff. This is obviously a critical question in terms of the number and nature of staff who will be dedicated to the centre. Whatever arrangements are arrived at in relation to all these issues, the costs associated with the arrangements need to be allocated to the operating costs of the centre, and therefore to form part of the learning and talent development budget (see Moorby 1996).

A final consideration is that of potential income. A number of sources are possible. Residential accommodation not being used for particular periods can be 'sold' to external users. The same is true of learning accommodation, which can be sold independently or in combination with residential accommodation. Lloyds TSB, for example, makes its facilities available in all three ways during slack times. The service of centres, including training and development courses, can be sold on the open market. Finally, the services of the centre can be charged to user departments on the basis of either full or subsidised costs (see Moorby 1996). All such income will be credited to the learning and development budget as a contribution towards the costs of the centre. The difficulty of some of these practices, however, is balancing the priorities of the organisation's own development activities against the opportunities for income generation.

ACTIVITY

1. Assuming a medium-sized organisation, what would you consider to be the minimum requirements in terms of physical resources?

2. Using your knowledge of current, actual costs, produce an estimated annual costing for these resources.

3. Consider and produce a list of advantages and disadvantages associated with ownership and operation of an 'own-use' centre.

4. Using the results of 1 to 3, assess the provision of physical resources in your organisation or one you know well and decide whether you believe more or less investment is needed.

5. Discuss the results of 4 with colleagues.

6. Based on the results of 5 revise, if necessary, your response to 4.

SPECIALIST LEARNING AND DEVELOPMENT STAFF

Recruiting, selecting and developing specialist learning and development staff is of critical importance in ensuring the function achieves and maintains the necessary credibility and status to provide a positive contribution to organisation success. For this reason, specialist staff can be argued to be the most important resource (Harrison 2009). However, simple rules cannot be stated. An important variable affecting recruitment, selection and development will be the intended role or roles of specialist staff. Reid and Barrington (1997) list more than 25 potential job titles, each of which implies variation in the intended role. Such variation will have impact on decisions such as where to place recruitment adverts, the content of person specifications and programmes of development for new recruits. It is increasingly common for roles to specialise in talent development, or at least to appear to do so from job titles such as Talent Development Manager. However, there are in our view no specialist activities or competences associated with such roles or titles; it is simply a matter of applying learning and development activities and competencies to the development of those identified as talent. That is no different from doing so for any other employees. And in any case this book is about learning and talent development and not about just talent development. So, we examine only general principles here, and in our view variations to those are more likely with roles with a stronger case for specialist skills such as those concerned with e-learning (see Stewart 2010).

It is also true that recruitment and selection of learning and development staff does not need to differ significantly from any other category of staff. Therefore, general principles which apply to recruitment and selection more widely can and should be used in the particular case of learning and development staff. So, the purpose and focus of this section is merely to highlight particular features of specific relevance to specialist development staff.

A widely advocated technique in planning recruitment and selection is that of job analysis. The technique can be useful in drawing up job descriptions or role definitions, from which person specifications can be derived. Three sources of information can be useful in carrying out job analysis for learning and development staff. The first is the occupational standards for learning and development (see www.ento.co.uk/). The standards can provide specifications of competence relevant to a wide range of specialist roles. A second source is the Professional Map of the Chartered Institute of Personnel and Development (CIPD) which can fulfil a similar purpose. These two sources can be seen as competing or complementary. Taken together, they are likely to encompass any and every generalist or specialist role within the learning and development function, and thereby provide a valuable starting point in producing job descriptions and person specifications. The final source is, as might be expected, the particular organisation context and a specific analysis of an intended role, especially as it will relate to achieving the intended contributions of learning and talent development.

The outcomes, or products, of job analysis will be critical in recruitment and selection. It is important, therefore, that professional and experienced individuals, as well as professional processes, are used in the selection of learning and development staff. The former means individuals who are experienced in and knowledgeable about development, as well as in selection processes. The latter means processes which are capable of assessing expertise in development in general and the particular abilities required in the specific organisational role. As Harrison (2009) argues, this needs to focus on the expectations of a particular organisation culture as well as the demands of a particular professional role.

Development of specialist staff needs to focus on short-, medium- and long-term time horizons. Reid *et al* (2004) persuasively argue the need for induction and initial training and development which focuses on facilitating entry into the particular organisation context, and on the requirements of the intended professional role. The application of probationary employment periods, supported by regular appraisals, as part of induction and initial training and development, is also widely used.

Turning to the medium term, two broad choices are available, although they are not necessarily exclusive. These are acquisition of NVQs in learning and development or acquiring qualifications of the CIPD. As Harrison (2009) recognises, there are some who see the CIPD qualifications as being more relevant to generalist HR staff than to learning and development specialists. Those qualifications and the Professional Map they are based on, though, are relatively recent and are different to the qualifications available at the time of Harrison's book. We have written this book to support the new qualifications in learning and talent development. The answer seems to be seeing how the new qualifications are received by and play out in the L&D profession.

The learning and development occupational standards and associated NVQ units provide for vocational qualifications which do not meet the requirement of a full NVQ. This allows accreditation for very tightly focused and specific roles. Perhaps the best example of this is the range of assessor and verifier awards for people, especially managers and supervisors, involved in assessing staff for NVQs in other occupations. The new CIPD professional qualifications will also allow individuals to receive development relevant to their role through awards for individual units at various levels. However, such arrangements and possibilities are perhaps of more value in considering the long-term development of specialist staff. Selecting NVQ or CIPD units can be an approach to supporting continuous professional development. The range, in both quantity and quality, of short courses and conferences promoted in professional journals provides another way of keeping up to date and extending and developing professional expertise. Gold and Smith (2010) emphasise the importance of self-development and varied work experience as additional approaches to achieving continuous professional development. There are increasing numbers of masters degrees in HRD and related subjects provided by universities which offer a further means of CPD. The important point here is that learning and development staff need to practise what they preach in terms of actively engaging in continuous learning and development.

Two final points can be made to close this section. First, responsibility for managing learning in organisations is, as already argued, becoming more decentralised (Harrison 2009). Indeed, it is argued that such a role is central to the management task (eg Salaman 1995). Therefore, approaches to recruitment, selection and, especially, development of specialist development staff may have a wider relevance and application. An immediately obvious application is in terms of line and operational managers who may be increasingly involved in managing the development of their staff. Perhaps less obvious is the notion of 'non-employee development' (Walton 1996). With ED being increasingly outsourced, potentially at least (Harrison 2009), the principles discussed here may be increasingly applied to temporary staff, consultants and sub-contractors. They may also be relevant to wider networks of non-employees. The final point is that the training cycle is a useful starting point in considering specialist roles within the learning and development function. Individual staff members may be required to specialise in, for example, design or delivery/implementation in their particular role, especially perhaps in large organisations. Matching the relevant stage or stages of the training cycle to specification such as the occupational standards, or the CIPD Professional Map, can be a useful starting point in such cases.

 ACTIVITY

1. Select one of the following job titles and produce a job description which you judge would be associated with the implied role:

   a. learning and development officer

   b. management development adviser

   c. talent development manager

   d. open learning co-ordinator.

2. Now produce a person specification based on the job description.

3. Consider the arguments for and against using NVQs and CIPD qualifications in developing specialist learning and development staff. Produce a statement of your own view, with a reasoned justification.

4. Assess the extent to which, in your judgement, line/operational managers should be involved in managing the development of their staff in your organisation or one you know well. Produce some proposals on appropriate development to support them in meeting the demands of their involvement.

LEARNING AND TALENT DEVELOPMENT POLICY

All of the processes and elements of resourcing and budgeting learning and talent development will take place in the context of an organisation's policies. There are many policies that will potentially affect and influence the overall process as well as specific elements, for example, financial policies governing expenditure on external suppliers and policies on recruitment and selection of staff which will be applied when recruiting specialist professionals. We close this chapter therefore with a discussion of learning and talent development policy with an aim of also illustrating some general principles.

THE NATURE OF POLICY

Organisation policies are part of the governance structure. In that sense, they are similar to laws in societies. Indeed, some policies are required by law and have a direct connection to legal statutes; eg on health and safety. The Greek etymology of the word is also instructive here. The same root produces 'police' as both verb and collective noun. So, it is reasonable to say the connection between laws and policies is legitimate. There will be policies in most organisations specifically related to governance and these will specify stakeholders and the relationship between them and the organisation, although they may not use the word stakeholder. And these policies will also to an extent reflect legal obligations required by statute. The points made so far suggest a number of things we can say about the meaning of the concept (Stewart *et al* 2010):

- Policies are distinct and separate from practice.
- Policies specify principles to guide and inform practice.
- Policies identify what can and cannot and what must and must not be done.
- Policies provide the framework within which decisions are made.

There is an assumption that organisation policies are written documents. There are good reasons to ensure they are written down, but there at least two senses in which they may not be. First, in small and especially micro organisations it might be a literal sense since such organisations may not have written statements. However, such organisations also illustrate the second sense. Even where there are no written statements there are still policies; everyone knows what is and what is not desired and valued behaviour based on precedent and established norms, and also knows what the organisation wishes to achieve. This also applies even when there is a written statement. Consider, for example, how many employees of a large multinational corporation have read every single policy statement. Or even how many have read the written learning and development policy. So, employees can and do know policies without necessarily having written documents to read, or having read them where they exist. And it is always the behaviour of organisation members which is the best indicator of policy in practice rather than written statements.

Formulating a written and formal learning and talent development policy can be a linear and planned process or it can be emergent and iterative. In either case it is important to realise that the principles which govern learning and talent development practice are not universal givens; they are a matter of human choice (Stewart *et al* 2010). The process and the outcome will be influenced by a range of factors and stakeholders. These will include (Ibid):

External factors

- government policies and programmes
- competitor and stakeholder actions
- technological developments
- social conditions and trends.

Internal factors

- organisation structure and culture

- history and tradition
- levels of management support
- current and expected future performance
- other and especially HR policies.

These factors do not operate independently and so they are mutually interactive and interdependent. For example, senior management support will depend to some extent on current and future performance, which in turn will depend on competitor actions and social conditions and trends. Senior management support will also depend on their view of the ability of learning and talent development to make a contribution to future performance, and that in turn will depend on the strength and persuasiveness of the business case made in a budget proposal. And that illustrates the connection between resources and policies.

Stewart *et al* (2010) suggest a number of headings which will structure the content of a learning and talent development policy statement; these are the items which are generally found to be in policy statements. They are as follows:

- purpose and objectives
- current priorities
- roles and responsibilities; eg of senior managers, of line managers, of learning and talent development professionals and of individual employees
- cost allocation policy and process
- application of policy to various categories of employees
- application of policy to various categories of learning and talent development methods; eg qualification programmes, other external courses, internal provision, use of external resources
- place of and access to learning and talent development records.

Some of these items illustrate the need for policy statements to be regularly reviewed and changed, for example, priorities change and sometimes over short time periods, and often in relation to different categories of staff. This is especially the case in relation to talent development where new or different jobs and roles may become critical to organisation success. The items also illustrate one of the benefits of a written statement: it can be used to settle disputes over for example sponsorship for a qualification programme. From a professional practice perspective a written statement can also be very useful in presenting a business case for resource allocation. So, in leading the process of developing and/or reviewing and revising learning and talent development policy statements practitioners need to be aware of the role of policy as an argument in potential support of securing resources.

ACTIVITY

1. Consider the factors listed above. Produce an analysis of how each of them might impact on learning and talent development policy.

2. Now reverse your focus. Consider how L&D policy might impact on each of the factors.

3. Discuss your responses with a colleague.

4. Access an organisation's written statement of learning and talent development policy. Identify which of the factors have influenced the content of the policy, and in what ways.

5. Now reverse your focus again. Consider the implications/influences of the organisation's learning and talent development policy may have for and on each of the factors.

6. Discuss your responses with a colleague. Attempt to identify any necessary or desired changes to either the current learning and talent development policy or to other existing policies.

SUMMARY

Learning and talent development professionals compete with other professionals and functions for resources and so have to be able to engage in that 'competition' by using the common organisation language of finance. This in turn means understanding and applying the rules of costing and budgeting which help to build a business case for expenditure on and investment in LT&D. Success in constructing a business case will help to secure the material and human resources needed to deliver effective learning and talent development programmes and activities. The value placed on financial arguments as well as the particular meanings and terms used will vary from organisation to organisation; accounting practices are not the same in all contexts. But, all organisations utilise financial metrics and accounting principles in decision-making to some extent and so familiarity with those metrics and principles is essential for professional practitioners.

Organisations also commonly adopt policies on a wide range of matters to inform and guide decision-making. Learning and talent development is commonly one of those matters. A written policy statement is not a requirement as custom and practice both illustrates and determines policy. Written statements, though, are advisable and serve to specify options and preferences, which help to settle disputes and to provide definitive guidance in the event of ambiguity and varying interpretations. Policy can also be helpful in constructing business cases since they can indicate declared priorities and so can indicate support for investment in learning and talent development. It is therefore usually in the interests of professionals to have a written policy statement.

As we saw in Chapter 5, organisations are political entities and arenas. It is therefore unrealistic to expect purely rational decision-making, not least because of the notion of 'local rationality', which suggests that what is rational depends on particular perspectives and interests. So, it is important that learning and talent development professionals can utilise the power of financial arguments and that derived from policy statements to serve the interests of their function and secure necessary resources.

REVIEW ACTIVITIES

1   Summarise five key things you have learnt from this chapter.

   a. Write down two or three new questions the chapter has raised for you or things that you are unclear about.

   b. Select one of these questions that you will enquire into further.

   c. Write down what action you can take next in pursuit of your question. (For example, read one of the references in this chapter, talk to someone more experienced at work, look on CIPD website, take time to reflect on your own experience.)

2. Explore the accounting practices in an organisation you know. Establish what approach is taken to dealing with indirect costs. Discuss with colleagues the possible advantages and disadvantages of the approach from a learning and talent development perspective.

3. Identify a minimum of three providers of leadership development programmes an organisation you know could use as part of their talent development. Produce an assessment of the relative value of the costs of each provider.

4. Access three job adverts for learning and talent development staff and secure the details of the appointments; eg job descriptions and person specifications. Assess the similarities and differences in role and attempt to identify the reasons for them from the point of view of resourcing the learning and talent development function in the organisations concerned.

5. Access learning and talent development policy statements from three different organisations. Identify similarities and differences and possible reasons for those differences based on organisation differences; eg size, age, history, economic and industry sector, current performance, nature of products/services, nature of roles/jobs/tasks.

6. Select one of the accessed policy statements. Evaluate how it could be used to help make a business case for expenditure on learning and talent development and how changes in the policy could enhance that purpose.

EXTENDED CASE STUDY + DISCUSSION QUESTIONS

CASE STUDY

Better Cover (BC) is a medium-sized insurance and pensions company. Like many others in the financial services industry, it has experienced performance problems in the last five years resulting in a reduction of employees from 4000 to 2800. However, both performance and staff numbers have recently stabilised. The organisation is subject to legal regulation which among other things requires formal assessment and certification of the competence of some staff groups. Scrutiny by regulators has intensified since the financial crisis. The majority of BC's staff are employed in administrative and clerical roles related to information processing and management. More specialist and professional roles are focused on product development and marketing. These roles demand high levels of technical knowledge and professional skill.

BC is mainly located in a large UK city, with staff spread across three office locations in the city centre. The HRD department, headed by Nakita Robinson as learning and talent development manager, has operated a learning resource centre (LRC) for over 15 years. The LRC is located in the main building of the three sites in the suite of offices and rooms allocated to the HRD department. The centre consists of a large room decorated in light, pastel shades which create an impression of open space. The room holds ten workstations, each of which provides comfortable seating, a spacious desk and hardware capable of running programmes on DVDs. The PCs are networked and allow access to the Internet as well as online learning resources available on the company intranet. Workstations are discreetly and effectively screened from each other, and from an informal coffee area with room for about 12 people to sit around low tables. As well as the technology-based development programmes, the centre provides a text-based library of books and journals. The range of courses available covers all the operations and functions of BC and includes subjects such as banking, finance, sales and marketing, PC skills, product knowledge and personal/interpersonal skills.

The LRC is open five days a week between 7.30am and 8.30pm. A member of LRC staff is available whenever the centre is open to provide whatever support and help users may require. Centre staff consist of Paul Jones, the centre manager, and Julie and James, two part-time open learning co-ordinators. A booking system is in operation. Any member of staff can book space in the centre outside or during working hours. However, bookings within working time have to be approved by an employee's line manager. Booking can be made by telephone, in person or through BC's intranet. The intranet is also used to advertise and promote the LRC's services, as are staff notice boards, the employee handbook and a regular six-monthly newsletter sent to all employees.

Use of the centre is monitored and reported by Paul on a monthly basis to Nakita.

They use these figures to analyse and plan development and purchase of new programmes. Nakita also uses them to target managers of particular departments who use the facility less than they could or should, and to justify continuing investment in the centre. In addition, all direct users of the centre are required to complete evaluation forms when they have completed a programme of study. Many of the technology-based programmes provide information on completion and duration rates, and this data is also used in monitoring and assessing the value of the centre. The twice-yearly newsletter always contains a feedback questionnaire to be completed and returned by previous, existing and potential users, and the annual survey of learning needs conducted by Nakita collects information on actual and potential use of the LRC. All of this information is used to attempt to ensure the LRC and its services remain relevant to and valued by the organisation.

At the moment, use of the LRC is very high, as are levels of satisfaction among employees and managers within BC. There is, therefore, no immediate cause for concern about the centre's short- to medium-term viability. However, its very success is beginning to create problems for the centre since waiting lists are being created for the most popular programmes. Nakita is aware that some of these at least are not directly related to individual or organisational development needs, and that some individuals wish to undertake the programmes for personal reasons. While she would wish to encourage this, Nakita is concerned that provision of the centre can be justified in relation to organisational needs as well as individual demand. To that end, she is considering proposing to the Board a system of charges for the LRC, which would have to be funded by the budgets of operational managers rather than, as now, the full costs of the LRC being allocated to the central HR budget. Charging would apply only where staff were undertaking programmes in work time authorised by their managers.

Nakita believes introducing a charging system would reduce or even eliminate waiting lists, would ensure that relevant training needs gained priority and would lead to all employees of BC placing a higher value on the LRC. Before proceeding any further, though, Nakita has asked Paul to prepare a report examining the implications of such a move.

Discussion questions

Imagine you are Paul Jones, and produce responses to the following questions:

1. What cost factors would be involved in producing a charge for using the centre?

2. Based on realistic estimates, what would each of these factors cost at today's prices?

3. How should the costs be aggregated to form a reasonable basis for charging, eg by day, by employee, by programme?

4. What other factors should Nakita consider in making her decisions? How will each of these support a decision to institute a charging system or not?

5. As manager of the LRC, what are your views on Nakita's idea?

EXPLORE FURTHER

Essential

Davies, D. (2005) *Managing Financial Information*. (2nd ed). London: CIPD.

Recommended

Puxty, A.G. (1993) *The Social and Organizational Context of Management Accounting*. London: Academic Press.

Journals

Human Resource Development International

Human Resource Management

Websites

http://businesslink.gov.uk/bdotg/action/layer?topicId=1074416511

CHAPTER 11

Ethics and Professionalism in Learning and Talent Development

OVERVIEW

The rise of corporate social responsibility (CSR) associated with publicised scandals such as the well-known Enron case has increased interest in and attention to the concept of ethics in business and management research and practice. The worldwide economic recession and financial crisis experienced at the end of the first decade of the twentieth century has served to emphasise this trend. While the focus on Enron and similar scandals, and the financial crisis, has been primarily to do with accounting practices, and banking and financial management and so with those professions, 'the management' of the organisations involved are held by most observers to be collectively responsible. So, those with responsibility for human resource management and development are no exception. There is a view argued by Torrington and Hall (1998) and by Connock and Johns (1995), among others, that the HR function and so HR professionals have a traditional and particular role in and responsibility for the ethical conduct of originations; in simple terms, to act as the 'conscience' of organisations. Such a role implies and to an extent presupposes that the HR profession itself can and does act ethically. According to Legge (1998), whether that is possible is dependent upon whether the capitalist economic system itself is capable of producing, or at least allowing and tolerating, ethical behaviour. Leaving that rather large question aside for the moment, what seems clear is that the practice of HR in employing organisations has at least some ethical implications and so there is a need for HR professionals to have some concern for ethics.

The last point is recognised and acknowledged by the CIPD (Chartered Institute of Personnel Development). In common with other professional bodies, the CIPD adopts and operates a Code of Professional Conduct. While there is no direct reference to or use of the word 'ethics' in the content of the CIPD example, such codes are in effect a statement of what the body concerned considers to be ethical behaviour. They are also associated with aspirations to become and to operate as a profession (Fisher and Lovell 2009). So there is a direct link between ethics and professionalism. Hence this chapter will explore the meaning of the two concepts and how they connect and relate in relation to professional practice. Our focus will be the practice of learning and talent development as an area of HR practice, but that focus needs to be set in the context of wider organisational, management and HR practice. That needs to be borne in mind as the chapter proceeds.

LEARNING OUTCOMES

After reading this chapter and completing the activities, the intention is that you will be able to:

- explain and define the concepts of ethics and professionalism
- critically evaluate a range of perspectives on their meaning and application
- identify, examine and evaluate implications for practice in learning and talent development
- recognise and analyse contexts, situations and decision choices from an ethical perspective
- produce reasoned and justified choices on ethical and professional dilemmas.

THE NATURE AND MEANING OF BUSINESS ETHICS

The application of the study of ethics to business, and indeed to organisation and management theory, is relatively recent. Torrington and Hall (1998) suggest that the concept can be, for many people, 'incongruous' in the context of business organisations. This implies a view that business organisations and their managers and other employees are somehow removed from ethical considerations, and that therefore the study of ethics has no relevance or application in organisation and management theory. However, such a view represents an ethical position in itself. In other words, an argument against the relevance of ethical considerations in business management has to be justified on some grounds or other and those grounds will necessarily have to draw on debates and arguments within the study of ethics. Therefore, any argument against the relevance of ethical considerations will itself represent an ethical position.

We can perhaps illustrate this point by considering the analysis of policy in the previous chapter. It was argued there that conventional treatments and analyses of policy formulation and implementation adopt a functionalist paradigm of organisations. There are, though, as we have seen in previous chapters, alternative paradigms. Each of these different paradigms suggests, more or less explicitly, varying perspectives on what constitutes an organisation, and these varying perspectives contain varying implications for how organisations should be managed. The phrase 'should be managed' provides an ethical dimension. First, it is normative in that 'should' suggests some imperatives about what is right and wrong or best and worst. Second, the word 'managed' refers to decisions, actions and behaviour of managers, both individually and collectively. Thus, each paradigm implies a different view of right and wrong managerial behaviour. The functionalist paradigm associates right behaviour with serving organisation objectives to ensure continued survival. Policy formulation and implementation therefore should, within the functionalist paradigm, serve that purpose and the behaviour of managers should follow that imperative. Given the existence of alternative imperatives on what is right and wrong, the functionalist view of policy formulation and implementation represents an ethical position since it assumes its own imperatives to be right and alternatives to be wrong. Justifying such an assumption will need to draw on and apply concepts and arguments from ethical theory since, in simple terms, ethics is concerned with establishing criteria to determine what is right and wrong (Fisher and Lovell 2009).

 ACTIVITY

We have yet to formally define 'ethics'. However, the opening paragraphs have provided a sense of its meaning, and you no doubt have your own understanding of the concept. It will therefore be possible to carry out the following activity which will also be useful as you go through the rest of this chapter.

1. Produce a definition of ethics in your own words, taking no more than two sentences.

2. Discuss your definition with a colleague and compare and contrast any similarities and differences. Attempt to produce an agreed definition and shared understanding.

3. Apply your agreed definition to the practice of learning and talent development. What are the main implications?

DEFINITIONS AND MEANINGS

As Fisher and Lovell (2009) point out, it is the case that, while applying the notion of ethics to organisations, business and otherwise is relatively recent, the notion has been the focus of human enquiry for centuries. Despite that long-standing effort, or perhaps because of it, there is relatively little agreement or certainty and there are many different perspectives on meanings and positions. This is in part because there are few, if any, facts in the study of ethics, which is in the main to do with beliefs and arguments built on theoretical positions (Fisher and Lovell 2009). Therefore, it is not possible to give a full account of all of the positions and associated arguments and theories in a single chapter. A further consequence is that ethics cannot be 'taught'; it is incumbent on individuals to work out ethical positions for themselves. What can be 'taught' is a range of ideas and tools that can help with that working out. A fundamental question to address in that task is 'What does ethics mean?' According to Bowie and Duska (1990, p3), the word 'ethics' can refer to many different things. Torrington and Hall (1998) suggest an important distinction between the singular and plural forms of the word. For them, the singular refers to 'moral value' and the 'principles that ought to govern … conduct', while the plural describes 'codes of behaviour considered to be correct, especially that of a particular group or profession' (Torrington and Hall 1998, p682). Connock and Johns (1995, p2) assert that ethics is about fairness and deciding what is 'right or wrong'. They also refer to 'practices and rules' which determine responsible conduct.

We can see similarities in these two formulations. The reference to fairness and right or wrong by Connock and Johns could be said to express the sentiments of Torrington and Hall on 'moral value' and 'principles' in a different way. The 'codes of behaviour' of Torrington and Hall is perhaps an alternative way of expressing 'practices and rules' in Connock and Johns's formulation. There seems to be agreement here that ethics is concerned with establishing what is right or moral and with translating what is established as right or moral into a system of codes or rules which govern behaviour. The two formulations discussed accord with the analysis and arguments of Bowie and Duska (1990). Here, ethics is defined as being concerned with 'a code of rules' or 'a set of principles' or 'the study of what is right and wrong' (Bowie and Duska 1990, p3). However, the formulation of Bowie and Duska suggests a separation which is less explicit in the other two formulations discussed so far. Thus, referring to ethics as a code of conduct or set of rules is not the same as referring to ethics as the *study* of what is right or wrong. We can perhaps argue that a code of conduct provides a system of ethics to govern behaviour, which in turn is based on a set of ethical principles which themselves are derived from a study of what is right and wrong. In more simple terms, 'ethics' refers to *the **study** of right and wrong* as well as to *a **specification** of what is right and what is wrong*. It is important to be clear about which meaning is being applied.

In terms of ethics as the study of what is right and wrong, Bowie and Duska (1990) argue that such study is concerned with providing guidance on the question 'What should one do?'. In other words, the focus of ethics is on human actions or behaviour. However, they go on to elaborate that the focus is not concerned with any or all human behaviour. According to them ethics is concerned only with actions and behaviour which are the result of free will and deliberate choice, and which have 'serious' consequences or effects for the individual concerned and/or others. To illustrate the latter condition, they give the examples of 'slurping soup' or 'not putting oil in my car' as resulting from free will but lacking serious consequences (Bowie and Duska 1990, p3). However, drawing a distinction between matters that are the concern of ethics and matters that are not is, arguably, a fundamental mistake (Stewart 2007). That argument will be examined and illustrated later in the chapter. For now, we will explore other arguments.

ACTIVITY

1. Search for some codes of practice from professional bodies.

2. Compare and contrast the content. Are there any similarities in subjects/topics covered?

3. Are there any significant or interesting differences?

4. What commonalities can you identify in standards of behaviour specified as required and as unacceptable?

ETHICAL ARGUMENTS

The discussion so far would suggest that most human behaviour or action, in theory at least, can be *claimed* to be ethical in the sense of conforming to a given set of rules or conforming to a certain code of conduct. This is particularly the case if we accept Torrington and Hall's (1998) assertion that codes of behaviour can be 'considered to be correct' by a 'particular group or profession'. This argument raises the possibility that different groups or professions can and will consider different, perhaps even conflicting or contradictory, actions and behaviour to be 'correct'. The consequence of this will be that contradictory actions and behaviour will be considered ethical in terms of the codes of behaviour of the different groups or professions. Therefore, this position adopts a view that what is considered ethical, in the sense of right or wrong, can and does vary according to the rules and standards of different groups.

Such a view is consistent with moral, or ethical, 'relativism' (Fisher and Lovell 2009). In this view, there are no absolute or universal answers to the question 'What should one do?' Instead, answers to the question will depend on the rules and norms of behaviour determined by particular groups at particular points in time. Individuals can answer the question for themselves, and behave 'ethically', by reference to and conformance with those rules and norms. Such a position would support an analysis and argument that, in an organisation context, the question of ethical behaviour can be associated with the concept of organisation culture (see Connock and Johns 1995). If we take the definition of organisation culture offered by Watson (1994, p21) as

> the system of meanings which are shared by members of a human grouping and which define what is *good and bad, right and wrong* and what are the *appropriate ways* for members of that group to *think and behave* [our emphasis],

we can see the connection. As Watson goes on to say, 'culture is, in part, a moral system' (Watson 1994, p21).

It is important to understand that ethical relativism is just one possible position in ethical theory, and one which is subject to debate and challenge. In a much-quoted article, Albert Carr (1968) uses the existence of different groups, each with their own codes of behaviour, to defend the fact that business standards and practices may not accord with what might be considered ethical, or right, or good, in other contexts or professions. In this sense then, Carr adopts a relativist position in relation to ethics. However, as Bowie and Duska (1990) demonstrate, there are conceptual problems with this position. These include defining the boundaries of a particular group, determining who speaks for the group and how they decide codes of behaviour, and finally the fact that all individuals belong at any one time to more than one group and that any sizeable social system, eg a nation or society, is composed of many groups. The latter condition creates the probability of conflict between different, and perhaps competing, codes of behaviour, and ethical relativism provides little or no help in resolving those conflicts.

There are, within the study of ethics, alternatives to ethical relativism. We might call these, collectively, universal systems of ethics (see Ferrell and Fraedrich 1997; Fisher and Lovell 2009). However, these alternatives raise additional arguments and debates. There are, broadly, two competing formulations of what constitutes right or good in universal systems. The first is referred to as 'teleological' (Fisher and Lovell 2009). This position follows the philosophy of Aristotle and Plato in applying the principle of determining whether an action or behaviour is right or good on the basis of whether it fulfils its function or purpose. Ferrell and Fraedrich (1997) explain this principle as one which considers an act morally right if it produces some desired result. This principle then provides a universal criterion which can be used to judge and evaluate the ethicality of any given action or behaviour. An alternative principle, derived from the second formulation, provides different criteria. This second formulation is known as 'deontological'. Here, the argument is that the *intentions*, rather than the consequences of actions and behaviour, are important in determining right and wrong, and that intentions have to be judged against the *potential* effects on individual rights (Ferrell and Fraedrich 1997). Actual effects, by definition, will provide an opportunity for *post hoc* assessment. However, the ethical standard is *intentions* in relation to individual rights. This formulation therefore has to also determine what those rights might or should be.

It will be clear that there are at least two significant differences between teleological and deontological ethics. First, one focuses on consequences or results, and the other focuses on intentions. Second, a deontological position focuses on individuals and individual rights, while a teleological position, in some versions at least (see below), focuses on collectivities such as society. It will also be apparent that adoption of a teleological position will produce different rules of conduct than will a deontological position and vice versa. The following activity will help you explore what these might be before we move on to examine the implications of ethical arguments for organisation and management theory.

ACTIVITY

1. Review your definition from the first activity in the light of these ethical arguments. Consider whether your definition reflects a relativist, teleological or deontological position, and whether you wish to revise/amend it to reflect an alternative position.

2. Review your response to question 3 in the first activity. Decide whether the ethical position you described for each implication reflects a relativist, teleological or deontological position.

3. Discuss with a colleague what ethical position is explicitly or implicitly adopted in the policies, practices and behaviour of your organisation or one you know.

4. Again with your colleague, determine what significant changes in policies, practices and behaviour would follow in that organisation from explicitly adopting an alternative ethical position.

ETHICS AND ORGANISATION AND MANAGEMENT THEORY

A teleological position can take two broad forms. The first is referred to as 'psychological egoism' (Bowie and Duska 1990), which more recently is associated with the work of Rand (2007). In this view, actions and behaviour can be justified on ethical grounds if the results achieved are in line with the rational desires and actions of an individual. There is therefore the teleological focus on consequences and functionality. The main criterion of 'function', though, is achievement of the purpose of a particular or given individual. Thus, in answering the question 'What should one do?', this perspective would suggest whatever achieves your purpose as an ethical response. There is an implicit assumption in this argument that satisfaction of individual desires will be enlightened, and part of this enlightenment will be an understanding that immediate and selfish gratification will not be in any individual's long-term self-interest. Thus, the ethical principle is not 'act selfishly', but rather 'act in your own long-term self-interest'.

This principle is central to the ethical justification of a free market system for the conduct of business and the management of organisations (Bowie and Duska 1990), although whether it can ever be actually fully applied is debatable (Donaldson 1989, 1992). An alternative principle which is applied to support what might be termed conventional business practices is that of utilitarianism. Here, the focus remains on consequences and functionality, but the principle is one of achieving the greatest good for the greatest number of people (Fisher and Lovell 2009). According to Bowie and Duska (1990), both of these principles, ie egoism and utilitarianism, were adopted by Adam Smith and other theorists to justify classical economics, and an associated capitalist and free market system in which business organisations were acting ethically if they pursued actions which maximised their profits. But, this is also the basis of Legge's questioning of the inevitability if not possibility of ethical behaviour in a capitalist economic system referred to earlier.

In a widely quoted analysis (Fisher and Lovell 2009; Torrington and Hall 1998; Connock and Johns 1995; Bowie and Duska 1990), Milton Friedman (1963,

1970) argues from, in part, a utilitarian position that it is ethical for business organisations to pursue the maximisation of profits. The argument is slightly modified by recognition that business organisations should operate within the 'rules of the game' and therefore, within a free market context, conduct their affairs legally and honestly. Friedman also draws on a relativist position in that he recognises that the rules of the game will reflect both the laws and 'ethical customs' prevailing in society, which can change from place to place and over time. The issue of non-profit-making organisations is accommodated in this analysis through what Friedman (1970) refers to as 'eleemosynary purposes'. This means that in non-profit-making organisations, it is ethical to pursue the stated purposes or objectives through whatever means are allowable by the rules of the game. A final feature of Friedman's analysis is worth highlighting. In examining the role of managers, a distinction is drawn between that of 'principal' and 'agent'. As individuals and citizens, people are principals who are free to adopt their own system of ethics. However, as managers, individuals are employees and therefore agents of the organisation, and thus have a duty to act in accordance with the desires and interests of those who own or establish the organisation.

We can summarise so far by saying that, according to a utilitarian position, managers of work organisations act in an ethical manner if their actions and behaviour are directed at achieving organisation purposes and objectives. However, a deontological position applies different criteria. Such a position follows the work of the philosopher Immanuel Kant (1724–1804), who argued that moral behaviour can be secured only if it is built on principles which are common; in other words, universal principles that can be applied in any and all places and which endure over time. In working out such a morality, Kant formulated what he referred to as 'the categorical imperative' which encompasses the two following formulations (Fisher and Lovell 2009):

● act only according to that maxim by which you can, at the same time, will that it should become a universal law.

● act so as never to treat another human being merely as a means to an end.

As Bowie and Duska (1990) point out, the first formulation is a version of what is known as the Golden Rule, ie do unto others as you would have them do unto you, and its parallel formulation, ie do not do unto others what you would not have them do unto you. Bowie and Duska also argue that the first principle can be described as a *principle of consistency of action*. In other words, we should not treat others in a manner different to that which we treat ourselves or wish to be treated by them. The second principle can be restated as *the principle of respect for persons* (Bowie and Duska 1990, p50). This principle provides an obvious focus on the human rights of individuals. In application to organisation and management theory, there is an immediate and obvious conflict with the teleological position. Individual human beings in a free market and capitalist economy are defined as a 'factor of production' and therefore as a means to an end. This violates both Kantian principles, but the second one in particular. However, as Bowie and Duska (1990) argue, the inclusion of the qualifier 'merely' allows some room for interpretation. The injunction means that individuals as employees, within a deontological position, cannot be defined and treated *exactly* the same as other, inanimate factors of production. Following this argument, the principle has clear implications for how employees are organised and managed.

The deontological system of ethics tends to support a focus on morality being concerned with human relationships. This perspective in turn supports the notion of organisations establishing and maintaining sets of social relationships with various groups who are often referred to as stakeholders (see Chapter 10). These relationships imply responsibilities, hence the notion of 'social responsibility' as part of business ethics (Fisher and Lovell 2009). From an ethical perspective Bowie and Duska (1990) suggest these stakeholders who are owed social responsibility can include shareholders, employees, customers, government, other businesses or organisations, and the communities in which an organisation operates. It is the latter that is usually referenced in support of responsibility to 'the environment' since communities are affected by the physical space in which they live. Stakeholder theory has wider application than the study of ethics, and it has also been criticised as a focus for ethical analysis (see Connock and Johns 1995). However, it does have value in pointing to issues in organising and managing that have a clear ethical dimension (Fisher and Lovell 2009). Some of these issues are listed below.

- *employees*
  - hiring and firing
  - right to liberty, eg freedom of speech
  - right to privacy
  - right to fair wages
  - quality of working life
  - information/confidentiality.
- *customers*
  - product quality and safety
  - pricing policies
  - advertising.
- *communities*
  - pollution
  - physical environment
  - closure of operations.
- *government*
  - compliance with legislation
  - implementation of regulations
  - tax returns.
- *shareholders*
  - honesty
  - providing a return.
- *other organisations*
  - act honestly and fairly
  - honour contracts.

These issues are by no means exhaustive. Some have obvious overlap; for instance, employees are members of communities and also citizens whose interests are represented by governments. The issue of safety is another example because it also concerns employees and communities. Each of the issues raises 'ethical dilemmas' (Fisher and Lovell 2009) for managers of work organisations. The overriding dilemma is in answering the question 'What should one do?' (Bowie and Duska 1990). However, the question can have a sharper focus when alternative courses of action conflict on ethical grounds. Perhaps the best example of this is what is referred to as 'whistleblowing' (Fisher and Lovell 2009; Connock and Johns 1995). Here, the dilemma is presented when individual employees become aware of, or perhaps are required to participate in, organisation actions and behaviour which they and others consider unethical. There is an obvious ethical dilemma in the latter case since there is a conflict between personal and organisational beliefs about what is right and wrong. However, one course of action open in both cases is to report and publicise the unethical behaviour, in other words, 'blow the whistle' on the organisation.

It is increasingly common practice for organisations to develop ethical statements, appoint senior managers to oversee social responsibility, train employees and to provide confidential telephone hotlines to help managers and other employees to deal with and resolve ethical dilemmas. However, such measures, while potentially helpful, are unlikely to eradicate the existence and occurrence of individuals having to confront such dilemmas. We might argue from this that individuals as well as organisations will benefit from thinking through and working out their own ethical position to inform and guide their actions and behaviour in carrying out their role and fulfilling their duties as employees. They will then be in a more informed and enlightened position to answer the question 'What should one do?' when faced with an ethical dilemma.

 ACTIVITY

1. Think of an example of an ethical dilemma that might be faced by a learning and development practitioner in relation to one of the issues listed against 'employees' above. Write a description of the scenario.

2. Produce a response to the question of what the person should do from each of the following ethical positions, providing a reasoned argument in each case:

   a. relativist

   b. utilitarian

   c. deontological.

3. Discuss and debate your response with a colleague who has also completed questions 1 and 2.

4. Consider each of the responses and determine which most closely reflects your own ethical position *and* that of your organisation. Examine any differences and the reasons for them, and consider the implications for your role.

ETHICS AND POLICY

The study of ethics has direct connections with and implications for policy formulation and implementation discussed in the last chapter. In broad terms, we can argue that a utilitarian position would support a view that senior managers are exclusively responsible for deciding policy since they are directly accountable to the 'owners' of the organisation. The same position would also lead to the policy emphasising, perhaps exclusively, learning and talent development that supports achievement of organisation objectives. In contrast, a deontological position might arguably support a consultative approach to policy formulation. It might also produce a policy which pays more attention to individual rights and aspirations in its content.

We can frame these connections in another way. A policy statement sets out intentions as a guide to actions and behaviour. In a very real sense, therefore, a learning and development policy is a statement of ethics. It is premised on beliefs about what is right and wrong and, in broad terms at least, it represents a code of conduct or behaviour. Policy statements are therefore capable of being subject to ethical analysis and criticism. We can develop this further with a specific example. It was argued in the previous chapter that policy statements should define and specify roles and responsibilities in relation to learning and talent development, including those of professional practitioners. As noted earlier in this chapter, the CIPD adopts a Code of Professional Conduct which sets out expected standards of professional behaviour. According to the definitions discussed earlier, such a code represents a system of ethics. Any member of the CIPD freely agrees, by virtue of seeking and accepting membership, to comply with the code. Therefore, in providing advice on the content of policy statements, a member of the CIPD should ensure that the role and responsibilities of professional practitioners specified in the policy are compatible with the CIPD Code. If any contradiction or conflict occurs, then practitioners working in the organisation who are also members of the CIPD will be faced with an ethical dilemma. So, we cannot consider learning and development policy in isolation from ethical arguments.

A final connection between ethics and policy comes from the association of organisation policy with societal or national law: both proscribe and prescribe behaviour. Specifying and pursuing what is defined to be 'justice' is one focus of ethics as an attempt to answer the question of what one should do. Justice is one leading perspective of ethics (Fisher and Lovell 2009). That perspective can then be a natural lens through which the ethicality of organisational policies can be assessed.

ETHICS AND LEARNING AND TALENT DEVELOPMENT

Formulating and implementing a policy on learning and development provides one example of a direct connection between learning and talent development professional practice, but there are others. Stewart (2007) has argued that HRD, and so learning and talent development which is arguably part of HRD, is in and of itself an ethical endeavour. An early argument to support that claim is the inevitable subjectivity of assessment (Stewart 1998). The argument is based on a premise of assessment always happening in the head of those doing the assessing. Despite the use of what is claimed to be criterion-based assessment in contexts such as selection and promotion through use of devices such as person specifications and competence frameworks, subjective judgements are always required since the judgements are made by human beings.

Consider the use of panel interviews in selection decisions. The rationale and justification for those is to remove or at least ameliorate the subjectivity and so potential bias of an individual interviewer. It is worth noting that the rationale and justification does accept and reinforce the basic premise of human subjectivity. However, the logic of that premise is then abandoned in the belief that more than one person will somehow remove human subjectivity and a panel will be objective as opposed to a single person interviewing alone. The reality is that the logic of the premise means that a panel simply adds a number of new and different subjectivities to the decision process.

We can argue from this that all contexts of assessments will be subjective. There are many such examples in learning and talent development: selection from either or both of internal and external candidates for talent development programmes; use of assessment and development centres; appraisal and performance management processes to assess potential and methods to assess and identify learning needs are the most obvious and common examples but they are not exclusive. So, given the subjectivity of decisions and choices being made in learning and talent development, it is inevitable that ethics is at play since that subjectivity is influenced by individual and personal beliefs and values; ie by a personal ethical code that may or may not be 'worked out'. Learning and talent development is also one clear example of where individual and corporate perspectives come together (see Fisher and Lovell 2009). There are additional examples of the relationship between learning and talent development and ethics in the literature and in particular in relation to critical HRD (see, for example, the collections edited by Elliott and Turnbull 2005, and by Rigg *et al* 2007). According to some critical analyses, learning and development, and therefore learning and talent development, can be emancipating and liberating, and therefore supportive of promoting human and individual potential. The professional practice of HRD can, however, serve the opposite purpose in promoting standardisation and conformity (see Fredericks and Stewart 1996), which is related to a conception of development as 'performative' (Rigg *et al* 2007). To some extent this dichotomy mirrors the reality experienced by most if not all practitioners: Do we promote individual or organisation development? There is, we suggest, a choice to be made and that choice is an ethical one.

A final area of interest is the connection between learning and talent development and managing diversity. These are in both academic study and in professional practice commonly separated and the focus of work of different individuals, for example, academic researchers and writers and professional practitioners tend to specialise in one or the other (Stewart and Harte 2010). Some recent research has suggested a potential ethical dilemma with similar characteristics in both talent management and in diversity management (Stewart and Harte 2010). As we have seen in previous chapters, in the former a basic choice is between inclusive or exclusive approaches. In simple terms, are all potential and current employees defined as talented or only some? That question is not simply a matter of empirical fact; it is an ethical dilemma. Attempts to manage diversity face the question of treating all potential and current employees the same or differently. The question is how do we achieve equality and fairness? The two possible answers are by treating everyone the same or by treating everyone differently. Legislation in the UK and elsewhere illustrates that both answers are possible in that some laws specify treating everyone the same, for example, in proscribing different treatment in selection processes; while other laws prescribe treating different categories of people differently, for example, men and women in granting of parental leave. Within the constraints of the law organisations and so HR professionals face the ethical choice and dilemma of treating people the same or differently. But the matter becomes more complicated when examining talent management and managing diversity together. As Stewart and Harte (2010) have found in their research, organisations can and do face conflicting choices in their talent and diversity management policies and programmes. The nature of these potential conflicts and of the separate but related and connected ethical dilemmas are illustrated in Figure 11.1.

Figure 11.1 Talent and diversity management

Managing diversity/talent management	The same	Differently
Inclusive	???????????	???????????
Exclusive	???????????	???????????

Figure 11.1 shows that HR professionals need to make decisions and broad choices on policies and programmes in relation to both talent management and managing diversity. The results of those decisions and choices will populate some of the four boxes; which boxes will depend on the choices made. It is certainly possible and perhaps likely that many or most organisations have adopted policies and implemented programmes without making a conscious and deliberate decision and choice between the alternatives suggested in Figure 11.1. This is more likely to be the case in relation to considering the connections and implications of the separate foci of talent management and diversity management (Stewart and Harte 2010). We suggest and argue here that decisions on approaches to both talent management and diversity represent ethical choices, and so further suggest and argue that decisions are being made without full ethical consideration. Our own ethical position argues that situation needs to change and that professionals working in talent and in diversity management 'should' be aware of and consider ethical implications of their decisions and their advice to other decision-makers.

Another perspective which informs some of the ethical considerations and implications is that of professionalism and we now move on to examine that concept.

ACTIVITY

1. Access details of a learning and talent development programme from your organisation or one you know. Analyse the detail to determine which quadrant in Figure 11.1 you would place the programme.

2. What ethical position do you think best represents the programme?

3. Access and analyse the diversity policy from the same organisation. Determine the quadrant in Figure 11.1 where you would place the policy.

4. Are there any actual or potential ethical conflicts between learning and talent development and managing diversity revealed from your analysis?

THE NATURE AND MEANING OF PROFESSIONALISM

We stated earlier in the chapter that codes of practice and conduct are associated with 'professions' and constructing such codes are in part support for becoming recognised as a profession. As we noted in Chapter 5, becoming a profession can be seen as either and both good and bad. But, in any case and as Harrison (2009) notes, individuals cannot avoid responsibility for working through and out their own ethical position by relying on a code from a professional body. One simple reason for this is that often such codes are lengthy and detailed and so very difficult to commit to memory to draw on in the day-to-day activities of doing a job. The idea of professionalism and of acting and behaving professionally can, though, be helpful in working out a personal ethical position. Harrison (2009) provides some useful guidance on that which we draw on for this section. But first, what is generally meant by 'professionalism'?

Professionalism can be associated with being a professional, using that latter word as a noun. In that case professionalism is an adjective describing a characteristic of a professional, that is, a member of a profession; and in that sense goes back to the work of the early sociologist Emile Durkheim (1893/1997), who emphasised the moral nature of the term. This was further emphasised by R.H. Tawney (1931/1964), who saw professionalism as a way of constraining individualism in favour of community interests. So, we can say as a basic definition that professionalism characterises behaviour that observes a set of moral, or ethical, principles that promote collective rather than individual good. Note, however, the potential and actual critiques of this statement discussed in Chapter 5. Related to this, a key distinction between professionalism and being a professional is that the former relies on individual self-discipline and control in meeting personal as well as collective ethical standards rather than on external or imposed codes of practice associated with the latter.

From what we have said so far, adopting professionalism as a principle in learning and talent development practice supports our previous arguments that individuals need to examine their own values and work out a personal ethical position, an argument supported by Harrison (2009). But what should form the main focus of the examination and the resulting position? Harrison (2009) suggests a number of specific and important examples, which include the following:

- a comparison of personal and organisational ethical positions
- how to promote common ethical values within the organisation
- how to promote equality and genuine valuing of diversity
- how to respond to the vast array of difference and diversity not subject to legislation.

A particular example of the last point can have direct application in talent development. The notion of 'reluctant talent' is used to describe individuals who have been identified and selected through an organisation process for inclusion in talent development but who do not wish to participate. There can be a variety of reasons for that wish, but a common example is unwillingness to engage in geographic moves for work-based development. In some cases this unwillingness may be because of care responsibilities. The ethical dilemma for the learning and talent development professional is how to respond to reluctant talent.

CONTINUING PROFESSIONAL DEVELOPMENT

One specific area of professionalism is engaging in what is referred to as CPD. This is of course often a feature of a profession and a requirement of professional bodies; that is true of the CIPD. Being professional and displaying professionalism then includes engaging in CPD.

Megginson and Whitaker (2007) define CPD as:

> a process by which individuals take control of their own learning and development, by engaging in an on-going process of reflection and action. This process is empowering and exciting and can stimulate people to achieve their aspirations and move towards their dreams (p3).

They go on to describe what they label core concepts of CPD:

- The learner is in control – CPD starts from the learner's dream.
- CPD is a holistic process and can address all aspects of life and the balance between them.
- Regularly looking forward to how we want to be, reflecting on how we are, and working from our present position towards the future direction, helps in achieving CPD's purposes and adds zest and direction to work and learning.
- CPD works if you have the support and financial backing of your employer, and it also works even if the employer is indifferent or hostile (Megginson and Whitaker 2007, p3).

It is clear from the above that CPD is self-managed learning and development (see Stewart 1996 for a full discussion of this). This is also evident in the principles added by Megginson and Whitaker for managing and implementing

CPD. What is also evident from the principles is that CPD applies the well-established processes of learning and development discussed in previous chapters. That being the case, then most if not all methods described in previous chapters are relevant to and can be applied in CPD. The principles are given below:

- Professional development is a continuous process that applies throughout a practitioner's working life.
- Individuals are responsible for controlling and managing their own development.
- Individuals should decide for themselves their learning needs and how to fulfil them.
- Learning targets should be clearly articulated and should reflect the needs of employers and clients as well as the practitioner's individual goals.
- Learning is most effective when it is acknowledged as an integral part of all work activity rather than an additional burden (Megginson and Whitaker 2007 p.3).

A final point is that it would indeed be strange of a practitioner to value the learning and development of others without valuing their own. So, adopting professionalism as a guiding principle does require a commitment to CPD.

 ACTIVITY

1. What does the term 'professionalism' mean for you? How can it be demonstrated in practice?
2. What are the advantages of engaging in CPD? Are there are any potential or actual disadvantages?
3. How can and does engaging in CPD support ethical practice?

SUMMARY

This chapter has considered the two concepts of ethics and professionalism. It has also demonstrated direct and inevitable connections and relationships between ethics and policy as well as identifying implications for learning and talent development practice. While it is the case that all aspects of HRD practice will have ethical dimensions, the argument here has been that ethical considerations become clearest when formulating policy and when designing and implementing learning and talent development programmes. Ethical considerations have been highlighted as of particular importance. For that reason, this chapter has provided a brief summary of ethical theory and debates. This has shown how varying ethical positions, especially those associated with utilitarian and deontological philosophies, will lead to different actions and behaviour on the part of organisations and individuals. Competing views on what is right and wrong can and will lead to individuals facing ethical dilemmas in carrying out their professional and organisational roles. This has been highlighted as particularly the case when considering learning and talent development in the context of managing diversity. Adopting professionalism was suggested as a possible approach to working through and out an ethical position to help deal with ethical dilemmas.

Two significant and important conclusions are possible. First, learning and talent development practice is always informed by a system of ethics which may or may not be consciously and deliberately applied. Second, the decisions and choices of learning and talent development specialists will occur in the context of a professional body plus an organisational system of ethics. For both these reasons, it is important that practitioners think through and work out their own, individual ethical position.

REVIEW ACTIVITIES

Using what you learned in this chapter on theories of ethics, consider the following questions:

1. What are the key differences between relativist and universal ethical theories?

2. What are the significant implications of adopting a teleological ethical position for the practice of learning and talent development?

3. What are the significant implications for learning and talent development practice of adopting a deontological ethical position?

4. What are the strengths and weaknesses for an individual professional of professional bodies having a code of professional practice?

5. Which specific methods of learning and development will be most appropriate and effective for use in CPD?

EXTENDED CASE STUDY + DISCUSSION QUESTIONS

CASE STUDY

Susan Sparrow has recently been promoted to Group Learning and Talent Development Adviser in the Teesdale Group of companies. The group consists primarily of engineering companies, one of which Susan previously worked at for five years as learning and development manager. Currently, Susan is responsible for reviewing and producing recommendations on the potential of talent management and development across the group, especially in relation to non-managerial and professional employees. However, as the Group Adviser, part of Susan's role is to provide advice and support to individual companies. She is therefore also currently active in advising Grahame Evans, chief executive of Pennycook Engineering Limited (PEL), a company within the Teesdale group.

PEL is engaged in the design and manufacture of high-precision engineering components which it supplies mainly to customers in the automotive and electronic industries. As a subsidiary of the Teesdale Group, PEL is subject to financial targets which are expected to improve year on year. Results over the past five years have been more than satisfactory and PEL has experienced consistent growth. The last full year's performance showed profits in excess of £50 million on sales close to £500 million. These figures reflect PEL's history as a successful and highly regarded company. The employees of PEL, numbering just over 1000, take this success for granted and have come to expect PEL to take the lead in technical advancements and to enjoy a reputation for high-quality products.

Grahame Evans, who has been in his post for just over 12 months, interprets the employees' view as complacency. He understands very clearly the demands of the Board of Teesdale Group for continuing success, and is fully aware of PEL's industrial customers' continuing demands for improvements in quality, cost and delivery. Grahame is under no illusions that he will have to prove his worth in the Teesdale Group by increasing profits at PEL, and that this will require improvements across the company, but especially in manufacturing which employs 70 per cent of the workforce. Grahame understands, too, that this will not be an easy task. Over a decade of success has been built on an authoritarian style of management where only managers take decisions and other employees do what they are told. The manufacturing manager, Richard Slater, is used to wielding the 'big stick' and, understandably, this style is adopted by the majority of production managers and supervisors. There is therefore clear evidence of a 'them and us' atmosphere in the company and a culture of sticking rigidly to the specified requirements of the job and little or no willingness to demonstrate flexibility.

Learning and development in PEL is part of the role of one of three HR officers who report to a HR manager. The HR manager, Ron Edwards, considers it his role to control employee behaviour on behalf of management. HR services are advisory and supportive to line managers in areas such as procedural advice, recruitment and selection and technical training. Ron Edwards is proud of the fact that PEL remains non-unionised and considers it a key part of his job to maintain that situation. The success of PEL and its ability to offer high wages are important in achieving that objective. However, Grahame

Evans believes the current approach to management, and especially to personnel and development, is old-fashioned and outdated, hence his decision to call on the services of Susan Sparrow.

Susan has been fully briefed by Grahame Evans on his view of the future for PEL. He believes it is essential to introduce significant changes based on more 'modern' management techniques. In particular, the chief executive is committed to continuous improvement through cellular manufacturing and the process known as 'kaizen'. The former will require greater levels of autonomy on the part of shop-floor employees, while the latter demands a greater degree of involvement in and responsibility for decisions among all staff. These are very different approaches to the established autocratic management style at PEL. Grahame Evans is certain, however, that they are required to ensure continuation of PEL's success in a changing marketplace.

In her investigations to assess current practices in PEL, Susan interviewed Richard Slater. He told her that when things go wrong in PEL, managers merely 'go around the factory with a bigger piece of wood and hit them a bit harder. It usually works.' Given this attitude, Susan is unsure that Grahame Evans fully realises the size and nature of the task facing him. At the moment, Susan is working on a draft policy statement for learning and talent development to discuss with Grahame Evans. Her immediate concern is how far it can go in the direction desired by the chief executive while still recognising and being relevant to the current situation in PEL. Susan has persuaded Grahame of the value of a written statement, but is unsure of his support for any content that does not fit in with his vision. The time for Susan's quarterly report to her boss, the Group HR director, is also fast approaching. Susan will have to report on her work and progress at PEL. The content of that report is also taxing Susan. The demands of Grahame Evans have resulted in some slowing of progress on Susan's work on talent across the group, and she is concerned that this will not be well received by her boss. Life seemed a lot simpler as learning and development manager in a factory.

Discussion questions

1. Identify at least two decisions facing Susan that could be said to present her with an ethical dilemma.

2. How would an understanding of ethics help Susan resolve these dilemmas?

3. What are the ethical considerations of Grahame Evans's proposed changes in PEL?

4. How, if at all, can professionalism inform and help Susan in her new role?

5. How would you recommend Susan and Grahame set about writing, implementing and communicating a new L&D policy for PEL?

EXPLORE FURTHER

Books
Essential

Fisher, C. and Lovell, A. (2009) *Business Ethics and Values*. (3rd ed). Harlow: FT Prentice Hall.

Harrison, R. (2009) *Learning and Development*. (5th ed). London: CIPD.

Recommended

Bowie, N.E. and Duska, R.F. (1990) *Business Ethics*. (2nd ed). Upper Saddle River, NJ: Prentice-Hall.

Connock, S. and Johns, T. (1995) *Ethical Leadership*. London: IPD.

Journals

Human Resource Development International

Human Resource Management Journal

Journal of Global Ethics

Journal of Business Ethics

Business Ethics Quarterly

Websites

www.ibe.org.uk/

www.business-ethics.org/primer.asp

www.ebenuk.org/

www.csrinternational.org/index.php

www.ecgi.org/

http://ecseonline.com

CHAPTER 12

Doing a Student Research Project

By Victoria Harte

OVERVIEW

This chapter covers the main aspects of the process of doing a research project in HRD. As a single chapter and not a whole book, there are necessarily elements that are not covered in full detail. The main thrust of this chapter is on understanding your own take on the nature of the world and applying this to the research process. This take on the world is about the philosophy of research and in particular of ontology and epistemology: concepts and words which can be challenging but which will be explained and discussed at length throughout this chapter. In addition, I recommend further reading to supplement the sections of the chapter where less attention is given. The two main recommended texts are *Research Methods in Human Resource Management*, by V. Anderson (2009) and *Business Research Projects* (4th ed), by A. Jankowicz (2007). These two texts are both excellent and will both support and complement what I have written here.

Embarking on a research project can be a daunting prospect, particularly if doing one for the first time. The process can be frustrating when juggling with other modules as part of your course. This chapter is intended to help take away some of the many pressures, frustrations and stresses of the research project and assist you in looking at it differently and in a positive way.

LEARNING OUTCOMES

After reading this chapter you will be able to:

- articulate and justify a philosophical position for a student research project
- formulate appropriate and realistic research questions

- produce a justified research design appropriate to formulated research questions

- search, select and review literature and other sources

- select, design and apply relevant research methods and techniques.

ONTOLOGY AND EPISTEMOLOGY

The terms 'ontology' and 'epistemology' are branches of philosophy, but they are not to be feared. Dealing with them will enable you to understand the research process and the reasons for research with much deeper clarity, and help give context to your own ideas for a research project.

Ontology relates to the study of the nature of reality and existence, ie why and how we came to be here; and epistemology relates to the study of the nature of knowledge, ie how we know what we know.

As individuals, we each have our own assumptions related to ontology and epistemology, but we do not refer to them using these terms and don't necessarily understand them as these terms (unless you have studied a philosophy degree!). For example, think about a general everyday conversation you might have that relates to freedom, God or human rights. You can have a conversation with someone in accordance to how you feel and think about these issues, but consider if you asked yourself why do you feel the way you do, where does your knowledge come from that builds up your opinions, feelings and answers to the questions that are raised about these issues? What would you say? Would you say you have made your own mind up from listening to lots of different people speak about such issues? Were your parents involved in shaping your thinking? Do you change your mind in response to the more conversations you have about such issues? On a basic level this is our own knowledge and are our own beliefs and assumptions. However, it is this basic level that helps us to make sense of the terms 'ontology' and 'epistemology'. We also need these basics to help us understand why these branches of philosophy are applied to the research process.

In order to think about the research process and why ontology and epistemology are important, it helps to ask ourselves a simple question: What is research? Research is concerned with knowledge and doing research produces knowledge, contributes to existing bodies of knowledge and also creates new bodies of knowledge. As a student doing your research project you will be contributing to an existing body of knowledge and in some circumstances may even be creating a new body of knowledge, depending upon your area of research and inquiry. Every postgraduate student participating in higher education can consider themselves a researcher and part of the academic community, because we are all researchers, academics staff and students alike. Research tends to be defined by the notion of being an academic or someone that is researching all the time for a living. This is not the case, and the skills you develop through doing your research project will prove to be valuable life skills not just in the workplace, but also in your personal lives.

A key question that now arises is: What constitutes knowledge? A simple way to break this down is by using the terms 'belief', 'justified belief' and 'knowledge'. Do our beliefs constitute knowledge? If we can justify our beliefs, does that constitute knowledge? Hence, the key question is what constitutes knowledge? I shan't digress too much on this because it becomes more important later on. So, to return to 'your' knowledge and where it will be placed in the whole scheme of knowledge, this is easy to do when we think about the types of knowledge that we become aware of on a daily basis. Examples of this include details of research we hear about on the news that has been undertaken on behalf of the government on issues such as social problems like anti-social behaviour or increases in drinking, or research done by the Health Service that relates to factors that cause certain types of cancer. These seem to be very high-level types of scientific research and are generally carried out by specialist researchers often working for research institutions retained by the Government or the Health Service to specifically carry out such high-level research. This doesn't make research undertaken by you, a student, any less important because the research undertaken by you is important for your studies, your career and advancement and development of your own knowledge. What is important here is that as a student you must give due consideration to your contribution to knowledge just like the high-level researchers do, and ensure it takes its place within the knowledge domain within which you are studying.

Ontology and epistemology are important because each forms part of our philosophical view of the world which is applied to the research process. This in turn helps us to determine our approach to how we research and what knowledge we are producing and creating. The type of knowledge creation here is important. To clarify, I am discussing social science research and not research done in the natural and physical sciences. For further clarification, the natural and physical sciences consist of disciplines such as, biology, chemistry, physics and astronomy. The social sciences consist of the study of societies, organisations, cultures and people.

REAL WORLD VIEWS OF ONTOLOGY AND EPISTEMOLOGY

There are two paradigms that are generally argued to encompass the two different views on ontology and epistemology, and these are widely known as the objectivist approach and the constructionist approach. In brief, for the moment, the objectivist approach suggests that the nature of existence and knowledge is separate and independent of individuals and groups. The constructionist approach suggests that the nature of existence and knowledge is not separate and independent from a person. An explanation of the 'constructionist' approach is needed here. Constructionist, or rather 'constructionism' in the action sense, refers to a concept known as social constructionism, which deals with human constructs within social contexts. These human constructs are formed by *collectives*: groups of people within society and not individuals. The concept of *individuals* forming human constructs is known as 'constructivism'. The two are the similar in that they deal with human constructs in society, but constructionism deals with collective human constructs and constructivism deals with individual human constructs. This chapter refers to constructionism for the main part, but I highlight, where appropriate, when I refer to constructivism.

Each of these two paradigms will be discussed in more detail in the following section. We will take each one in turn and look at how the philosophical stances sit with the paradigms.

INDIVIDUAL VIEWS OF ONTOLOGY

Thinking about the nature of existence, think about you as an individual existing within the world. What are your ontological beliefs and assumptions? Do you already have very knowledgeable viewpoints about this or have you not really thought about it very much? As a child you probably spent time thinking about where you came from and why you exist. In childhood it is common for answers to sometimes be provided by religion. But, as you grew older you may have taken on another viewpoint, such as Darwin's theory of natural selection. This is part of the ontological argument that asks the question where do we come from, why do we exist, but this is something that can never be 'truly' answered. However, as an individual you will come to a point in life where you are satisfied with what knowledge is available about the nature of existence and adopt a personal philosophy. But you will still engage in and enjoy discussions and debates about the nature of existence.

INDIVIDUAL VIEWS OF EPISTEMOLOGY

What about your knowledge: Where did it and does it come from? How do you take on your own knowledge and form your own opinion? I touched on this above about how our parents might have influenced us, but as we grow do we change the knowledge that our parents told us? Do you believe things to be true based on what you know? How do you know things are true? A key element of our epistemological beliefs and assumptions is being able to decide what is truth and what is not. Ask yourself this question: is there really truth out there? Can we know it? How can we come to know it? How do we know that the knowledge we have is knowledge and is even true?

NATURAL VERSUS SOCIAL SCIENCES

Answers to questions on reality and truth are what separate the social sciences from the natural and physical sciences. Jankowicz (2007) explains this eloquently, suggesting that objectivist (later referred to as 'positivist') research has been highly successful because most people base their understanding of research on the natural and physical sciences model. However, he believes that the kinds of issues which are important to research in the social sciences, eg organisational contexts and phenomena, are different to those in the natural and physical sciences because different ontological and epistemological assumptions apply. I have to agree. He further explains that

> the positivist approach works in the physical sciences because the phenomena it investigates can be understood and predicted accurately enough by believing that there are events out there, that the status of the data is unarguable, that truth exists independently of the people who seek it, and that the researcher can in principle remain separate from, and uninvolved in, the phenomena being investigated. Unfortunately, this doesn't work well with organisational phenomena (Jankowicz 2007, p115).

This raises the question of people who seek to investigate organisational phenomena whilst applying the positivist paradigm. Can they do this independently and remain separate and uninvolved from the phenomena being investigated?

There are arguably some elements of the natural and physical sciences that cannot be answered through investigation. For example, scientists cannot determine whether the universe is the shape of a doughnut and goes round and comes back on itself, whether it is infinite or whether there are other universes. There are some things that we just cannot know, which support the view that there is and can never be any true objectivity. For me, objectivity applies to phenomena that we know of the world but we cannot change; for example, we know the sun will rise and can say what time it will rise and that the tide goes in and out and what times this will happen.

Just thinking about what was discussed in the sections above and thinking about philosophy in relation to life, now have a think about how you feel about God. I am not going to try to provide an example here because this is not possible as everyone's position of this subject is very different and personal. However, as you have been reading about the nature of existence and the nature of knowledge, think about how you feel in relation to how you come to exist and how you come to know about God. Irrespective of your responses to this subject, the more you consider these the more you will come to understand the relationship of ontology and epistemology to the research process, which we discuss next.

ONTOLOGY AND EPISTEMOLOGY AND THE RESEARCH PROCESS

You are probably wondering what all of this has to do with the research process. This section will develop the abstract meanings of ontology and epistemology into something more practical. We will look at each of the branches of philosophy in turn and illustrate how we make sense of each for the research process and the purposes of producing knowledge in the social sciences. I will make reference to two of the most common terms that are central to business and management research within the social sciences – these are 'organisation' and 'culture'. However, an important observation needs to be made here about the two paradigms mentioned above. The objectivist and constructionist paradigms are purely viewpoints held by individuals relating to organisation and culture. Objectivists view existence and knowledge as objects, something external to individuals which they participate in, and constructionists view existence and knowledge as something that individuals participate in but also construct through meanings and beliefs to create social phenomena. The two views are polarised, but you have to remember that these are views and may not necessarily be your view. You need to decide for yourself how you see organisation and culture, how they come to exist, how they are formed and how knowledge is created, whether this be through human interaction and construction or otherwise.

SOCIAL ONTOLOGY AND SOCIAL ENTITIES

Let's begin with ontology – the nature of existence. The viewpoints here can be 'objectivist ontology' or 'constructionist ontology' and the themes we will look at are:

- objectivist ontology – organisations
- constructionist ontology – organisations
- objectivist ontology – cultures
- constructionist ontology – cultures.

Bryman and Bell's (2007, p22) explanation of objectivism is succinct and describes the position perfectly. They state that

> objectivism is an ontological position that asserts that social phenomena and their meanings have an existence that is independent of social actors. It implies that social phenomena and the categories that we use in everyday discourse have an existence that is independent or separate from actors.

OBJECTIVIST ONTOLOGY – ORGANISATIONS

In terms of 'organisation' the objectivist view is that an object reality (the organisation) is separate and independent from people (eg its employees). This view suggests that we participate in an organisation willingly, but our daily work routines and patterns and so on are internalised within us without us realising it. We have no influence over these functions becoming internalised; it just happens without our knowing.

Figure 12.1 illustrates the separateness of the social entity and the social phenomena and how each of these operates independently of the social actors. The social entity (the organisation) sits within the external reality (the box in black outline) and its existence is independent of the social actors (the employees, outside the box). The social phenomena and meanings (the organisation structure, hierarchy, rules and regulations that make up the social entity) are not independent or separate from the social entity but are separate from the social actors and also have independent existence from them. This diagram illustrates a two-way relationship between the social entity and the phenomena as these two are dependent as the phenomena go back and forth; the phenomena then become a social order, which is where the employees learn how to act and behave, and this is a constraining force on the employees as they are there to do their job.

This constraining force is depicted by the three arrows suggesting that constraining force as pressure. The social actors are outside and external to the social entity and its goings on. The two arrows from the social actors suggest that they are participating in the organisation, but fail to have an influence on the social phenomena and meanings, hence the arrows do not quite break through the external reality.

Figure 12.1 Objectivist ontology in organisation

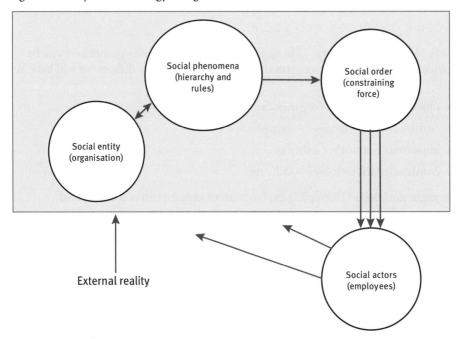

The organisation displays characteristics of an object having an external (object) reality. The social phenomena of the social entity such as the hierarchy, the standardising procedures, division of labour and the mission statement appear beyond reach and influence of the social actors. Such viewpoints create prescribed social orders that pressurise the social actors to conform to the social entity's requirements.

In essence, this means that the organisation, its structure and hierarchy, operates without any influence from its employees. This is quite a difficult concept to grasp, not least because it raises questions like 'how did the organisations come to exist', 'who developed it', 'who made up the rules, the regulations', 'what if the rules and regulations change', 'do the rules and regulations change automatically without any social intervention', 'what if an employee or group of employees suggest a change to the regulations that will improve the organisation', is this social actor intervention? It is difficult to see how all these questions can be part of an organisation and that it operates independently of its social actors and without their influence. However, there are scholars and researchers who hold this viewpoint and suggest that their research produces the evidence and knowledge to suggest that organisations operate independently.

In relation to the research process, how do we contextualise objectivist ontology to the real world? The example below will help to do this.

 THE POLICE FORCE

CASE STUDY

The Police Force is an organisation that upholds the law and does this by employing law enforcement officers (police officers). The issue of the law and organisation pre-existed the particular police officers that currently uphold the law. Therefore, the objectivist view is that the existence of the organisation is an external reality for the police officers: they participate in it, but it operates without their influence.

Issues to consider are:

- They just do their job as an unconscious action, it's their job.

- They follow the law prescribed by the law makers.

- The law cannot be interpreted.

- However, they are allowed to make discretionary judgements on matters

such as 'on the spot penalty notices', only because the organisation allows this.

If you were a HR professional working in the police force, where there was a problem with absenteeism and a high proportion of sick leave, how might you view this as a research question if your philosophy was objectivist ontology? What part of the relationship between the organisation, the employees and reasons for absenteeism might be apparent? If this view is that the employees are independent of the organisation your research into absenteeism would have to suggest that the reasons for absenteeism were caused by the organisation and not by the individual.

The activity below will help to contextualise at a deeper level the participation of employees in the organisation from an objectivist position.

 ACTIVITY

Have you ever worked in an organisation where as an employee you were asked to be part of a change management consultation process? This would consist of the directors and senior managers communicating to the workforce (employees) that there was to be change and the opinions and ideas of the employees were valued. An example of this might have been to review and rewrite the organisation's mission statement. If yes, did you participate and offer your views, opinions and ideas? What happened? Was there evidence to suggest that yours or another member of staff's ideas were taken on board? Did you submit an idea as an individual employee or as a group of employees such as a work team?

Think about your participation within the consultation process and within the organisation. Did you influence the redesign of the mission statement? Could you influence the redesign of the mission statement? Is the nature of the organisation something that is external to its employees that can't be influenced?

Think about this activity and the questions in relation to the discussion above and try to deepen your understanding about employees' participation in an organisation where change is happening.

CONSTRUCTIONIST ONTOLOGY – ORGANISATIONS

Constructionist ontology has the reverse view in that the existence of the organisation is influenced by its social actors and that social phenomena and meanings are not independent but are developed and evolved through the ongoing influence of the social actors. This is a viewpoint that you might find yourself much more at ease with and initially understand particularly if you work within an organisation. This paradigm is known as social constructionism, as discussed in the first section.

In relation to the research process, how do we contextualise constructionist ontology to the real world? The example below will help to do this.

 ILLUSTRATION

Equality and diversity policy

You are a HR professional and your HR department is implementing a new equality and diversity policy along with delivering diversity training through HRD for all employees to attend. While there is a large part of the new policy that has to be based on government policy and employment law, you and your HR colleagues acknowledge that, as HR professionals, a level of experience and human perspective is required. You and your colleagues work in your teams to brainstorm some particular aspects to humanise your new policy and diversity training. A key aim is to humanise the new policy for the employees and acknowledge differences in your workforce rather than a 'one size fits all' approach.

Aspects you explore are:

- What does equality mean and how does it differ from diversity?

- What does diversity mean?

- How to deal with the 'sameness' and 'difference' agenda.

Your new policy is approved and is based in part on the discussions that took place between the teams.

If you were to research this issue you could do it using an action research methodology on the question 'can active participation from HR professionals successfully develop a new equality and diversity policy?' An action research methodology enables you to research in action, collect data as you go along and actively participate in constructing meaning and phenomena within the organisation.

The activity below will help to contextualise at a deeper level the participation of employees in the organisation from a constructionist position.

 ACTIVITY

The 'organistic organisation'

Some organisations purport to operate differently from what is termed the mechanistic organisation, eg no hierarchy, no bureaucracy, no procedures and so on. In these types of organisations employees can actively participate in the organisation freely, they share out workloads, do not adhere to any prescribed standardised procedures or sit within a hierarchy and are not constrained by certain regulations.

They are perceived to be doing more than just participating in the organisation and are involved in constructing meaning and sharing beliefs, but also set their own procedures to work by.

How does this differ from the suggested constraining forces of the objectivist viewpoint? Are the employees participating? Are they participating in groups or as individuals? What influence do they have over their organisation by not being bound by constraining forces?

Think about this activity and the questions in relation to the discussion above and try to deepen your understanding about employees' participation in an organisation like this one.

Whatever are your own ontological beliefs and assumptions about existence and knowledge in life, it generally follows that your viewpoint in the research process will be the same. The question of social ontology cannot be separated from issues concerning research conducted within the business and management discipline. Ontological assumptions and beliefs will play a part in the formulation of your research question and how your research is carried out. Look at the examples below illustrating ontology and epistemology.

 ILLUSTRATION

With an objectivistic world view, a *mountain* is a mountain for everyone, a *product* is a product for everyone, and a *work process* is a work process for everyone. The meaning of a phenomenon is inherent to the phenomenon and can be experienced by interacting with it.

Let's look at this example of pain. An objectivist view suggests that pain pre-exists you and I and that it is the result of external forces acting on your body like a knife cutting you, being thumped or falling down. This produces physiological actions and sends messages to the brain. This suggests that it has nothing to do with the physical you, ie your body, but that it is in your mind.

 ILLUSTRATION

With a constructionist world view the mountain may not look the same to you as to me, the product may serve a different reason and purpose for you than me, and your approach to work may be drastically different to that of mine again in reason and purpose.

Again, using pain as an example: A constructionist view is that pain is experienced by people and that they can differentiate between feelings, ie this feeling is pain, but this is not. People experience pain in different ways and have different pain thresholds, from a person feeling a lot of pain in pricking their finger with a needle to another person not being bothered by it at all. Take childbirth as an example. Some women insist on having pain relief because they don't want to feel or experience the pain, because they know it will be too painful; whereas other women insist on not having pain relief for a variety of reasons, one being that they believe they have a high pain threshold. Another example is muscular and joint conditions such as rheumatism and arthritis. Many sufferers whole lives are centred on the pain, discomfort and suffering they experience as a consequence of these conditions. This suggests that pain is not external and independent of individuals.

OBJECTIVIST ONTOLOGY – CULTURES

We will now look at the second theme central to business and management research within the social sciences, culture. As with the theme of the objectivist organisation, objectivist culture is dealt with in the same way. This paradigm suggests that culture is also not influenced by social actors, ie that individuals or groups in societies and civilisations have no part in the creation or development of culture. The development of cultures within organisations is also included in this as organisations are, as was discussed above, independent social entities. Culture as an external reality may seem an odd proposition, but, as mentioned earlier, it is one that is accepted by many individuals. This is explained more through the following discussion and Figure 12.2 below.

Figure 12.2 Objectivist ontology culture

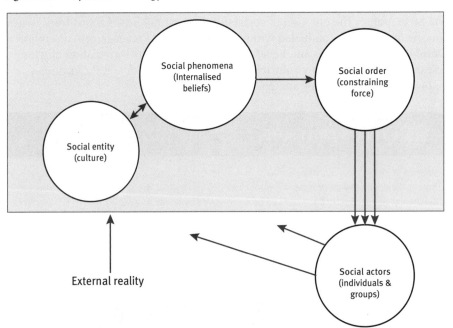

As above, like 'organisation', 'culture' is an external (object) reality and is separate and independent from people. This view suggests that we participate in culture willingly, but our beliefs of culture, like monogamy, marriage and having children, are internalised within us without us realising it, and we have no influence over these beliefs becoming internalised, that it just happens without our knowing.

Figure 12.2 illustrates culture as social entity with the social phenomena having a two-way relationship, like organisation. What happens between the social entity and phenomena becomes the constraining force on individuals and groups, suggesting that they participate in culture, are independent of it and it is an external reality. Once again, the two arrows from the social actors outside the box are suggesting that participation is happening but, in terms of influence on the external reality, the connection is not being made.

In relation to the research process, how do we contextualise objectivist culture to the real world? The example below will help to do this.

ILLUSTRATION

Employer brand

The idea of employer brand has grown in popularity in recent years. One function of an employer brand is to represent an organisation's culture. This is done through cultural artefacts such as logos, straplines, corporate identity and corporate wear. Some of these such as corporate wear have physical properties while others such as corporate identity have symbolic rather than physical properties. However, both sets of properties can be viewed to have independent existence.

HR professionals now have an interest in brand and branding. While there are links with brand as a marketing concept the HR interest is the use of brand to promote an organisation as an employer of choice in order to attract and retain key talent. So, HR professionals will want to be able to influence the nature of and perceptions of the employer brand.

If you were a HR professional wishing to improve perceptions of your organisation's employer brand, how might you view this as a research question if your philosophy was objectivist ontology? What part of the relationship between the brand, current and potential employees might be of interest? If this view is that the brand has independent existence your research will probably examine factors which form and build up the brand, eg HR policies and employment conditions.

The activity below will help to contextualise at a deeper level the participation of individuals in culture from an objectivist position.

ACTIVITY

In many cultures, but not all, it is usual to grow up thinking you will get married and have children. This happened to me in my culture but mine is very different from the next person. For instance, a girl in India might know she is to get married and know who to from a young age, whereas a Pakistani girl might also know she is to get married but does not know to who until she gets older. Also, when I grew up my parents did not choose my suitor, but suitors are more likely to have been chosen for the Indian and Pakistani girl.

Do you remember ever saying to yourself as a child when you were maybe 9 or 10, 'When I grow up I'm going to get married and buy a house?' As a culture within society this is what we do – we get married. Also, think about monogamy, The fact that you wanted to get married might suggest that you are to an extent monogamous – or will be when you get married. However, in other cultures men have more than one wife and can have children with these wives. This is known as polygamy and is an important part of those cultures, for example the Mormons.

Ask yourself where these cultural beliefs come from. Why do we grow up with the belief that we will get married? Why does a woman grow up knowing that potentially she will share a man with many other women and that he will also bear children with those other women? Why do people accept these beliefs, where do they originate from and can we change these beliefs?

In this activity objectivism is the view that such cultural and societal norms and values become part of us without us knowing. Hence culture is an external reality.

CONSTRUCTIONIST ONTOLOGY – CULTURES

In contrast to the objectivist paradigm, culture is viewed in the constructionist paradigm as being constructed by individuals and groups in societies within organisations. Organisations are social entities and social institutions and to suggest that culture is an external reality without social interaction does seem a little strange.

Figure 12.3 Constructionist ontology culture

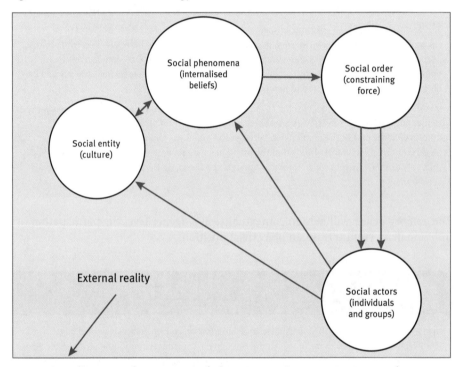

Figure 12.3 illustrates the opposite of objectivism. Constructionist ontology suggests individuals do more than just participate in culture; they actually construct it via meanings and beliefs to form social phenomena.

In Figure 12.3 we still have the social entity and phenomena and the social order which is the constraining force, as discussed above. However, in this diagram, though the constraining force is still there, it is less of a pressure, as it is depicted by two arrows and not three as in objectivist ontology. This is because we have become aware of it as a constraining force and our internalised beliefs are being challenged. The social actors have influenced these two variables and the culture is no longer independent of their thinking or influence. Thus, reality is no longer external to the social actors; they are not only participating in it but are creating and affecting meaning and beliefs and so on.

In relation to the research process, how do we contextualise constructionist culture to the real world? The example below will help to do this.

EMBRACING DIVERSITY IN THE WORKPLACE

CASE STUDY

An example of internalised cultural beliefs being challenged is the campaigning of the Lesbian, Gay, Bisexual and Transsexual (LGBT) societal group in today's Western society.

As a collective they are showing society that they are different, are challenging their own internalised beliefs and attempting to change those of others.

This is an example of how groups might develop societal constructs to change the mindsets of individuals now and in the future to accept that gay people are a part of today's society. Some people have begun to accept these individuals because the LGBT group have campaigned tirelessly for equal human rights for their members. As a consequence it is now against the law to discriminate against same-sex couples adopting children, they are allowed to unite in a civil partnership and from a welfare point of view they are allowed to register as same-sex relationships and obtain the same benefits that a heterosexual couple are entitled to. So, in relation to social constructionism, we have a collective, ie a group in society that have formed together to change the mindsets of not only individuals but also the law about sexual orientation, human rights and adopting children.

From a research perspective, how might you consider this as a research question for embracing diversity? As a HR professional and in relation to your own organisation, how would you see this law as being incorporated into the fabric of the organisation? The potential topic area is 'Ensuring the rights of the LGBT employees are fully included and stated within the maternity and paternity rights and benefits policy to oppose discrimination', and the constructionist view is that the employees would participate and be involved in its development within the organisation. What questions might you ask as with a constructionist viewpoint?

With regard to the example above this view is also applied to the black and minority ethnics group, disabled people and females.

You may well view either paradigm of objectivist and constructionist as not being possible or too prescriptive, and this view is certainly becoming the norm within social science research, where individuals are acknowledging that it is not either/ or but that the paradigms can merge and not compete. Figure 12.4 illustrates the merging of the objectivist and constructionist ontology to form an 'emergent reality' about how we form cultures.

This figure depicts development from the beginning of something; here, civilisation. However, it does beg the question about the creation of something, right from the very beginning. How does an organisation form its culture? Does it happen on its own? Do the people at the top of the organisation prescribe a way that the employees should follow to create the culture? Can the people at the top of the organisation prescribe a way that the employees should follow to create the culture? Do the employees all follow this prescribed way to form a prescribed culture? Is culture mechanistic or organic? How is culture formed?

Figure 12.4 An emergent reality

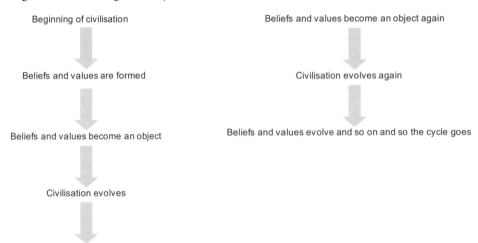

It is interesting to look at examples of culture and social norms and one that illustrates both sides of the paradigm – objectivist and constructivist – let's think about monogamy and marriage in more detail.

 ILLUSTRATION

Through a widely shared bank of values and customs within our culture are we so socialised into believing that we have to have one life partner and get married to function as good citizens?

Is monogamy a social construct? In many cultures, the cultural norm of monogamy is internalised within many of us all our lives but is said to be at its most prominent in our lives when we learn the fundamentals between the ages of 7 and 11 years old.

Is marriage a social construct? In many cultures, the cultural norm of marriage is also internalised within many of us all our lives. In fact, if individuals decide not to get married out of choice they may generally be faced with people who are clearly confused that as an individual they have not bought into the institution of marriage. Below are both the objectivist and constructionist viewpoints on the subject of marriage.

Objectivists understand marriage as a given; it is normal and natural to marry and personal choice is not an option because of our internalised beliefs. Marriage is a social institution that shapes our lives without our active participation in the creation of the institution but we participate in the continuation of the institution by getting married.

Constructionists, on the other hand, view all social institutions as 'person made' and their continuing operation as dependent on the participation of social actors in the continuous co-creation and recreation of the institutions. So, given that marriage is person made, and depends on active participation for survival, individuals do have a personal choice and the more individuals choose not to participate in recreating the institution the more likely it is to wither. Another example that marriage is person made is the ability to marry in a variety of locations by a law allowing the undertaking of civil ceremonies in licensed buildings and other settings, eg football pitches.

EPISTEMOLOGY

I now deal with epistemology – the study of the nature of knowledge. Once again, the viewpoints here can be 'objectivist epistemology' or 'constructionist epistemology' and still remain within the central themes that have been discussed above.

OBJECTIVIST EPISTEMOLOGY

Objectivist epistemology can also be described as empiricist epistemology. Empiricism is the foundation of positivism and views reality as universal, objective and quantifiable, and is also a dominant discourse of science. From this viewpoint it is argued that 'reality' (the external object) is the same for you as it is for me and through the application of science we can identify and 'see' that shared reality (Darlaston-Jones 2007). This is in relation to natural and physical sciences. It could be argued that by adopting the positivist viewpoint, research in the social sciences reduces the individual to the condition of a 'passive receptacle'. This suggests that there is little notion of the person as the *perceiver* of his or her world, and even less thought appears to be afforded to the possibility of the person as a *conceiver* or *constructor* of his or her world (Ashworth 2003).

Darlaston-Jones (2007) argues that the belief that a single universal reality exists for us all, and that this reality can be discovered and so known via systematically controlled investigations, fails to recognise the ability of the human person to interpret and make sense of his or her world. This 'single universal view' informs the generalisations that are borne out of positivist research within which controlled, objective, value free (or value neutral) findings and knowledge are able to be generalised to a broader population.

On a basic level, an example of this single universal view is the proposition that 'every human being has 2 eyes, 10 fingers, 10 toes, 2 arms and 2 legs'. This is a clear generalisation about the population which we know is not the case and know it not to be true. If we did all think the same then we would all consider this statement to be true.

 ACTIVITY

The Police Force

Go back to the example of the police force in the objectivist ontology section. Think about the kinds of questions that can be asked which will provide us with knowledge about absenteeism. For example, within objectivist epistemology knowledge about reasons and causes of absenteeism which will apply to all employees is thought to be possible.

What research questions do you think might lead to this kind of knowledge?

CONSTRUCTIONIST EPISTEMOLOGY

The basic assertion of the constructionist argument is that the reality of knowledge is socially constructed by and between the persons who experience it (Gergen 1999). The action that occurs and creates the constructionist reality is as a consequence of context and is shaped by cultural, historical, political and social norms and conditioning. Thus reality is different for each of us based on our unique understandings of the world and our experience of it (Berger and Luckmann 1966).

Reality in this perspective is completely subjective; that is, need not be something that is shared by anyone else but at the same time is independent of the person living it (Darlaston-Jones 2007).

Social constructionism provides a distinct viewpoint to enable a view of the world which allows the unique differences of individuals to come into focus, as a collective, while at the same time allowing the essential *sameness* that unites human beings to be identified (Ashworth 2003). This does not mean that we must share the views of others but at the same time we cannot change or alter *our* reality simply because we might wish to. In this manner each individual reality is true for the person because he or she experiences it but it is independent of that person due to his or her inability to alter it (Darlaston-Jones; 2007; 20: Gergen 1999).

Below is an example of a PhD study that illustrates how the two world views of objectivism and constructionism differ. This is an interesting case illustration because it will not only enable you to get a grasp of the paradigms of epistemology but also to embrace that higher education is also a form of HRD intervention and not just a practice found in organisations or workplaces.

 The issue of retention in students in higher education

CASE STUDY

Dawn was a PhD student who was interested in the topic of student retention, mainly due to her own circumstances and regular thoughts on leaving university. Her main question was: 'Why do some students complete their degree and others do not?' Most of the literature in this area talked of the role of the student in terms of motivation, commitment and ability, as if they were isolated constructs that occur independently of the person or the context in which the person exists.

Imagine two students that come to university each from very different backgrounds. The first is from a privileged background; both her parents are university graduates, and she attended a well-resourced high school that facilitated her social and academic ability. She was encouraged by her teachers and family to explore her potential in every area and university was regarded as the natural progression in her post-secondary development.

In contrast the second student is the first in her family to attend university; her family and teachers are equally supportive and encouraging of her achieving her potential but the nature of her experience is fundamentally different from the socially advantaged student.

The first student regards her university experience as 'more of the same' in that she is continuing a family tradition almost. The second student, though, is experiencing university as a life-changing challenge. She sees university not simply as a natural progression but as an opportunity for her to help her family and to become a role model for others in her neighbourhood.

These two students share the same experience at a surface level in that they both attended university from high school, they are the same age and gender, and both are committed to completing their degree. Therefore as far as the student attrition literature is concerned both have the same opportunity to succeed, ie in relation to motivation, commitment and ability. Or do they?

This position of 'opportunity to succeed' is supported by a plethora of eminent researchers in the area all of whom employed quantitative techniques to examine completion and non-completion among undergraduate students. The approach adopted by these studies was to assume that students enter university on an equal level and to track them over the course of their degree (or more commonly for the first semester or first year).

A range of demographic quantitative data (age, ethnicity, gender, financial resources and so on) is gathered on these students and then, depending on their status at the end of the study (still enrolled, graduated or withdrawn), various conclusions are drawn to 'explain' non-completion. However, the realities are in fact vastly different for each student, as a result of their prior experiences, the socialisation process they were subject to and the cultural differences resulting from their different economic and social positions.

In the examples presented, neither student can change her view of what university represents to her or her family, nor is she in a position to immediately see the world of the other. Each of them has a separate and unique reality and each is independent of her interpretation of that reality. Simply sitting in the same classroom for the same lessons does not make their experience of university identical. Consequently, trying to know and explain their experience of university and the fact that one of them might withdraw by looking solely at demographic data cannot hope to succeed in capturing the unique reality of the individual, and as a researcher one is poorly placed to claim any degree of 'understanding' of her experience. One has to look at the question differently and employ a different approach to the research process for any real understanding to emerge.

 ACTIVITY

Answer the following questions in relation to the case above. Discuss your response with colleagues.

- Is this case in favour of the objectivist or constructionist view? Why? Write down your answers for both to determine the research paradigm.

- What are the 'realities' of the students? How do these differ in the two students?

- How would you approach answering this question? Revisit this once you have read the section on methods.

- Would you change the research process described in the case? If yes, what would you change?

A final word and example on the philosophies here illustrates that we won't necessarily follow one viewpoint and be either/or objectivist or constructionist. We could have objectivist ontology and a constructionist epistemology. The example and activity below explain this point.

ACTIVITY

Imagine you are researching the issue of whether trust was a key factor in contributing to distributed leadership (DL) in teams within an organisation. The things you were looking to find out are: is there a relationship between DL teams?; what are the factors that affect this relationship?; how do these factors impact on practices for teams?; how important is trust in this relationship?

Following your understanding of the philosophies and paradigms, let's say your view of ontology in relation to teams was objectivist and your rationale for this is that the concept of 'teams' and 'distributed leadership' within teams pre-existed the team members. Therefore, implying that the team is an external reality that exists independently of its social actors. With regard to epistemology let's say your view is constructionist and your rationale for this is because you believe that individuals and collectives construct their own meanings of a given social phenomena within that external reality of the team – truth and meaning do not exist in some external world but are created by a person's interaction with the world.

- What do you think are the strengths and advantages of mixing objectivist ontology with a constructionist epistemology?

- What are the weaknesses and disadvantages of mixing objectivist ontology with a constructionist epistemology?

RESEARCH PARADIGMS

WHAT ARE RESEARCH PARADIGMS AND THEIR RELATION TO ONTOLOGY AND EPISTEMOLOGY?

Research paradigms are clusters of beliefs which dictate in particular disciplines, for instance the natural and physical sciences, what should be studied, how research should be done and how results should be analysed (Jankowicz 2007). However, in the social sciences the paradigms can compete somewhat, dependent upon your view of them, as we saw in the exercise above.

As a general rule the paradigms sit at each end of a continuum and deal with the objectivist (positivist) views and the subjectivist (constructionist) views, which are also referred to as positivist and non- or anti-positivist, respectively.

Traditionally, the natural and physical sciences is positivist by nature, as discussed earlier, because research in these domains is only generally carried out by laboratory experiments or observations. The results of such research generalises about these sciences because they will generally all do the same thing and produce the same results. An example is mixing chemical A with chemical B, which turns yellow. Then, if the test is repeated the same will happen again.

However, the positivist paradigm has been applied to the social sciences to investigate 'social reality'. This social reality is what was mentioned above relating to social entities, social phenomena and social actors. To experiment with and observe a social reality, in the positivist way, made up of people, meanings, languages, cultures and behaviours as opposed to chemicals, rocks, blood and physiological actions by experimentation and observation alone presents the positivist researcher with a significant challenge (Cohen et al 2005).

This brings us back to our objectivist ontology (above) of organisations and culture, ie social reality. Can we research social reality by observing social phenomena and social actors and generalise about the populations we are observing? Can we conduct non-laboratory-based experiments in social settings with social actors and again generalise about the populations we are using to experiment on? Think about the above example of the two chemicals. If we observe one human being, will they do exactly the same as the human being prior to them? What about if we ask a human being a question, will the human being that follows them give the same answer? Maybe yes, but what if they don't? Are humans the same and can we successfully generalise about populations using the positivist approach?

 ACTIVITY

What if you were to observe a group of humans at work as a non-participant observer while they operated machinery? Imagine you are in a car factory watching a production line. You do not interact with them in a vocal sense, you just watch them.

What might these results produce? With regard to the research process, does this suggest that we have objectivity in social reality?

POSITIVISM IN THE SOCIAL SCIENCES

We can apply positivism in the social sciences but it is not without its problems. Kurt Lewin was one of the first to undertake positivist research using observations, experiments and qualitative research methods among a population of a group of mothers experiencing rationing during World War II. He proposed that with the advancement in research methods and techniques such as observations, experiments and interviews in the social sciences, and with due consideration given to all factors pertaining to individuals and groups, research could be undertaken with the outcome being applicable to any individual or groups in society in order to change social phenomena. The factors he includes are the personality of the individual members, the group structure, ideology and cultural values and economic factors (Lewin 1947). In this case, the social phenomena were groups of women dealing with the difficult problem of rationing. He proposed that to vary social phenomena experimentally the experimenter has to take hold of all essential factors and this will lead to a natural integration of the social sciences. In essence what he was saying was that, his research on groups of women could be used to change group life in society. Figure 12.5 below depicts the structure of the research process and the paths we are *directed* to follow in relation to the subjectivist and objectivist continuum. I agree with the school of thought that suggests you can undertake positivist research in the social sciences although my preference is for non-positivist approaches.

RESEARCH METHODS ARE METHODOLOGICALLY NEUTRAL

Figure 12.6 illustrates how the research process is structured and the choices we make once we have determined our ontological and epistemological stances. The main thrust of the diagram is that of the choices that follow the main sections such as philosophy, paradigms and methodology and so on, we are free to select those appropriate to our research question, ie that research methods are methodologically neutral. I am proposing that the choice of methods which we choose to undertake our research is not confined to a particular paradigm. We can look at this neutrality of methodology by thinking about the advent of science and the use of science to make discoveries and know about objects in the material world such as rocks, stars, chemicals and blood and so on. Physical laws such as gravity preceded humans, but science did not. Science had to be created to discover physical laws, such as gravity, and it was humans that created science and made those discoveries. Or, another way to look at it is in relation to medicine. For example, in the seventeenth century many conditions were unknown to doctors, and patients were misdiagnosed, which led to the death of many individuals because conditions and treatments were unknown. It has only been with the advent of science, the study of the human body and experimentation with plants and chemicals and more recently advances in technology, that doctors have come to be able to correctly diagnose conditions and treat them with the correct medicines.

Figure 12.5 The neutral research structure

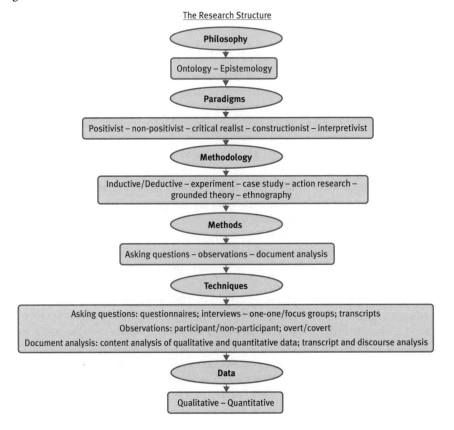

If we were to follow a conventional and traditional explanation of the way things should be in relation to positivist and non-positivist research and their use of methods and so on, then we would subscribe to the information in Figure 12.6. However, this is not as straightforward as it seems due to the techniques and data types we obtain, as will be discussed next.

Another misconception about positivist research is that the techniques used generally only obtain quantitative data, to reflect the scientific approach, but this is not necessarily the case. In the subjectivist domain a multi- or mixed-methods approach has become increasingly common in recent years (Bryman 2006), with a typical example being the use of a questionnaire along with a series of interviews, as can be seen in Figure 12.6. However, it is apparently more accepted to combine the use of qualitative and quantitative techniques in the subjectivist/ constructionist paradigms, whereas it is often seen as more difficult to justify and accept positivist research with methods such as interview and participant observations, opposing the constructionist paradigm. Questionnaires are typically placed within the objectivist domain and are viewed as scientific, but as we will see later in the research methods section questionnaires are not as objectivist as we first think and are open to scrutiny.

Figure 12.6 Conventional research structure: the prescribed and widely accepted view of the subjectivist–objectivist continuum

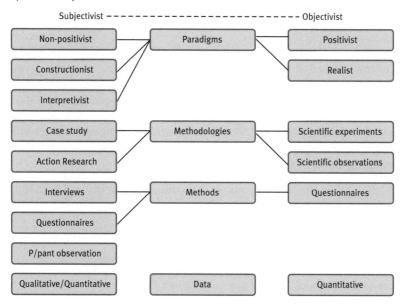

Note: P/pant, participant

CLAIMS TO TRUTH

Finally, a key point that has high relevance to this is 'truth' or claims to truth. The notion of something being more credible in the quest for truth generally lies in the natural and physical sciences because of the scientific and laboratorial underpinning to these domains. For example, truth can be claimed about objects in the material world, eg this is a piece of limestone rock and I know it is because it is an external object and I can prove it via scientific methods of analysis. Whereas, the quest for truth in the social sciences is apparently less credible due to the nature of the way truth is constructed through social entities, social phenomena and social actors, for example, people, cultures and language. This brings us back to knowledge and what constitutes knowledge. Can we claim that research obtained from an individual or collectives in the constructionist ontology and epistemology be considered merely a belief or truth? If we test a bug in the lab and grow it and it meets a scientific formula as a well-known 'cold virus', is this a belief or truth?

SHAPING HOW WE RESEARCH

Now I have gone through the basics of ontology and epistemology this should go some way to assisting you in determining your own philosophical stance and paradigm for your research project. The one caveat about determining philosophical stances, though, is that as a researcher or someone that does research for a living it is sometimes the case for philosophical stances and paradigms to alter slightly, but not drastically. This will be dependent upon the type of research that is to be undertaken and the question that needs to be answered. The way you shape your question has a lot to do with the way you want to do research and your philosophical stance. In most cases researchers do have the luxury of shaping the way the research is done, which will be like your own circumstance, but in other cases some research organisations set how a particular piece of research is done and they fit the most appropriately trained people to those research projects. For instance, someone who is a skilled qualitative researcher will not be assigned to a project where a mass questionnaire is required to be distributed and analysed using statistical analysis, unless of course they are also skilled in that area. But the same will be said of the quantitative researcher, it is unlikely that they will be assigned to a piece of research that is reliant heavily upon qualitatively skilled researchers.

This leads us on to developing your research question, but before I turn to that a short discussion on methodology is necessary.

METHODOLOGY

Methodology is a body of practices within a discipline that refer to the theoretical analysis of the methods that are appropriate to a field of study or to the body of methods and principles particular to a branch of knowledge. The body of practices that I refer to are detailed in the research structure diagram above and are part of the philosophical framework within which your research will be guided. So once we have determined our philosophical take on the real world, applied this to the research process and determined our ontological beliefs and assumptions for both our life and our research, we are then able to determine our paradigm, ie positivist or constructionist. Once we are at this point we can then determine our methodology. Methodologies are approaches to research

ILLUSTRATION

If a social scientist has a non-positivist ontology and epistemology and wanted to undertake comparative research with a case study design, then they would probably be more inclined to design research methods that fitted with their non-positivist epistemology. These might be a series of interviews either face-to-face, using technology or both with maybe a series of participant observations.

However, a caveat here is that the comparative research component might suggest a more positivist outlook because of the objectivist view that comparisons are best reached through analysing numerical data. This, though, is not necessarily the case as this can also be done through interviews with participants as long as interview questions remain the same and participants of equivalent job roles are interviewed in the comparative organisations, eg two finance directors, two HR directors and two shopfloor supervisors. This is an argument that would need to be considered and thought through if an objectivist were to challenge a non-positivist approach to comparative research.

and are sometimes referred to using different terms such as research strategies, research design or research approach. Typical methodologies are case studies, cross-sectional research, comparative research, action research, experiments and inductive/deductive reasoning.

INDUCTIVE/DEDUCTIVE REASONING

A key point to bring up here is an explanation of the inductive/deductive reasoning methodology. There are generally two ways to the development of a theory – theory generation and theory testing. Inductive reasoning is the generation of a new theory and deductive reasoning is the testing of an existing theory. However, the deductive approach is not just about testing a theory but also about refining an existing theory either by changing it or improving it through your own research. I raise this here because when you embark upon your own research this is a methodological choice that may be considered and will have an impact upon how you research. For instance, using the inductive methodology any prior assumptions are put to one side, no initial literature searching is done at the beginning to formulate the research question and the main literature review is done after all the data sets have been collected and analysed.

Detailed below are points summarising both approaches. I have taken these directly from Anderson (2009, p147), with a few annotations of my own.

Induction [theory building]:

- Induction involves observation and investigation into the relationship between *meaning* and *actions* of human subjects.
- Data is collected without prior assumptions about categorisation and measurement.
- The context of the situation [i.e. observation of meanings and actions] is incorporated into the analysis process as the research seeks to understand the internal logic and purposive nature of human actions.

- The analysis process is extended via an appropriate literature review, if necessary, to further understand the data collected with prior research and theories.

- The outcome of the enquiry is to suggest/build a credible explanation of behaviours that have been observed, ie generate a theory.

- There is less concern with the need to generalise although further avenues for research may be identified.

- In essence, induction is undertaking research without any prior assumptions.

Deduction [theory testing]:

- Deduction can involve the formulation of *hypotheses* [statements which the existing theory suggests would be true].

- Hypotheses are then *operationalised,* ie researched such that the variables involved can be identified and measured. This measurement can be undertaken for this enquiry, but also the same approach could be repeated in a different situation.

- Data is gathered and the information is used to test whether the hypotheses can be confirmed.

- The outcome of the enquiry, as shown against the original hypotheses, is either to modify or to confirm the theory from which the hypotheses were derived.

Figure 12.7 also supports descriptions above.

Figure 12.7 Inductive and deductive reasoning

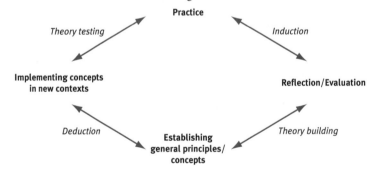

The inductive/deductive approach is discussed in slightly more detail in the literature review section below.

DEVELOPING YOUR RESEARCH QUESTION

Despite the research paradigm section coming before this section, consideration of the research question and the paradigm can be 'chicken and egg' – What to decide first? Your philosophical stance will give you the foundation for that and you might have an idea about your methodology, but your research question will no doubt play a considerable part in deciding how you want to do your research.

That said, acknowledging your philosophy first is the most important component (Bryman and Bell 2007; Jankowicz 2007; Anderson 2009).

Developing your research question is probably one of the most important components of the research process. Getting the question right will enable the successful answering of it and underpin your research with reliability and validity and ensure the research findings are significant. Again, as mentioned in the paragraph above, your philosophical stance will play a big part in determining the appropriate paradigm and the way you research. The discussion above on ontology and epistemology will help you to determine how you want to research.

The case example below details a conversation with a social science researcher when asked about their philosophical stance. It will give you an insight into how determining your own take on the world helps you determine the right paradigmatic and methodological path for your project.

 ILLUSTRATION

After years of research my thoughts on research philosophy have changed somewhat because, in reality, getting to grips with all this ontological and epistemological stuff does not happen overnight. It has taken a while to shape my thinking and just as soon as I think I am there it changes again because I read something new or my views on something philosophical evolves. However, that said, I am in the main a critical realist with more of a leaning to post-positivism (constructionism). What I mean by this is that this is how I feel from a philosophical point of view. My mind is not so closed off to other ideas that I only truly believe that I exist because God made me and the world around me; I am open to new forms of research and science that discuss the issues of the nature of existence; I can't subscribe to the objectivist view that individuals don't influence life, cultures, organisations, systems and societies; I have also come to realise that the quest for truth in research is very difficult and that there are varying degrees of the quality of knowledge, and some knowledge that claims to be knowledge in fact isn't. With this mindset I know that I am a post-positivist and that wherever possible I will seek to undertake post-positivist research that is realistic. I will probably never embark upon the positivist paradigm of research for two simple reasons: firstly, my philosophy does not lend itself to the positivist approach, particularly when researching human beings, and secondly I don't feel confident enough to be able to remove myself from a positivist research question, ie to be objective, to be able to produce a piece of positivist research. My thoughts on philosophy are so strong in the realist field that I don't accept that positivist research can be meaningful.

To start work on the research question you obviously need to have an area of interest that can be researched. Your knowledge within the HRD discipline will help with the initial development of the research question. The best approach to start is to think about your area of interest as this will naturally start to turn itself into a question, think about your epistemological beliefs and assumptions of the area and carry out a small-scale literature search and review. This initial literature search will also open up ideas for questions if you are finding it difficult to work one up for yourself. The literature will have gaps in the research or authors sometimes highlight areas for further research that they have been unable to fulfil. It will, therefore, aid the development of your basic idea into the desired research question.

ACTIVITY

To begin the development of your research question think about the key words from your area of interest that are beginning to form the question and use these as search terms to search for the appropriate literature.

Alternatively, use the topic in the illustration below to try to determine some search terms.

Once you have determined your data set from the preliminary literature sources, ie journals, books, published and unpublished reports, and websites and so on, it is important to read the literature to increase your knowledge of the subject to develop the question. The activity below will give you an insight into developing search terms. This is a useful exercise to do, because in some areas there will be thousands of returns, whether you search within the relevant journals or just do a simple search using Google, and it is very common to get high-volume returns in the HRD discipline. You will also need to undertake this practice for your comprehensive literature review.

ILLUSTRATION

An example topic for possible research project:

I am interested in evaluating the coaching and mentoring scheme in my organisation with a view to improving the training and development opportunities for the coaches and mentors, which will subsequently benefit the recipients of the scheme.

This is a topic that will typically return a high volume of potential pieces of literature and the skill is in narrowing it down without excluding the most relevant documents.

An example search

Here I describe a search that I undertook on this topic using Google Scholar. I started off by putting the phrase 'coaching and mentoring' into Google Scholar, which returned 42,000 hits. I changed this to 'evaluating coaching and mentoring' and it was reduced to 26,000. This is where the 'sifting' starts and where you get to grips with what you want to search for. For my search on the first Google page, displaying 1–10 results, there is already a vast difference emerging in the topic of coaching and mentoring. Some results refer to new graduates; some to leadership; some to business coaching using external providers, and some to evaluating SME retailers. Defining search factors such as organisations only and the size of the organisations as well as the type of coaching and mentoring in relation to in-house or external business coaching all play a big part in defining the search terms. If the search term is changed to 'evaluating coaching and mentoring in organisations' this is reduced to 9830 results, but that does not mean that the quality of the results are any better or are more related to your specific topic. Only by reading through ones that look relevant will you start to find your literature. However, another route is to go direct to the relevant journals via your university's library and journals databases and search directly within the appropriate discipline and sub-discipline areas. It is useful to seek advice from the lecturer or allocated supervisor, who should be able to quote the titles of appropriate journals and publications.

Alternatively you can start with what I call 'Google triangulation'. This is an easy way of identifying appropriate journals and publications using Google Scholar just by doing the simple search that was described above. In the latter search where I added the word organisations, five academic journals appeared on the first page displaying 1–10 results. What this does is highlight the names of the journals for you so you can then go back to your university's library and journal database and, with the exact names of the journals, search directly within them to source the articles that were highlighted on the Google Scholar search and also search for other relevant material at the same time.

The last tip for searching for material to aid your literature search is to scan the bibliographies or references lists at the back of the articles you have sourced. This will reduce some of the workload in the search process, will give you the exact publication details, and if you source a particularly recent article then you can also use that bibliography to source relevant material going back over a specific time period. This is what I refer to as the 'golden thread'. The golden thread is a virtual piece of thread that runs throughout your research project and remains intact all the way through. Sourcing and using literature in a sequential and chronological manner will further underpin your research with the historical data available and provide a good basis for discussion with your results.

Starting to work with ideas for your question and even writing it out in a number of different ways will help. The way you word your research question will give an indication of your philosophical and paradigmatic stance. The exercise below will help to illustrate how we develop the research question. Though I mentioned above that you need to use your own assumptions about the subject to develop the question, once you have begun to develop a number of potential questions, those assumptions need to be removed, as illustrated in the exercise.

 ACTIVITY

Look at the research question below and try to identify the assumptions contained within it:

'How will continuous investment in employees' training and development aid financial services organisations' survival in an economic crisis?'

Answers to activity

Some of the assumptions in this question are:

- *Will* continuous investment in training and development aid economic survival? The question assumes it will.

- *How* do we determine investment? The question assumes this is not a problem.

- Define economic crisis.
- The question assumes that you can measure employee training and that it can be measured and attributed to investment in training and development.

A reworking of the question is detailed below:

'An investigation into whether continuous investment in employee training and development can aid survival in an economic crisis in financial service organisations.'

Do you agree or disagree with these assumptions and can you add your own? Also, think about how you might rework the question.

COMPREHENSIVE LITERATURE SEARCH

THE INDUCTIVE APPROACH

As discussed earlier, literature searches are not conducted until the end in the inductive approach, if conducted at all. Because the inductive approach is theory generation, the use of existing theories in literature will bias and taint any inductive inquiry. Literature searches are generally undertaken following data collection and analysis but some may not be, dependent upon the quality of data collected and results of analysis.

THE DEDUCTIVE APPROACH

For a deductive approach, the small-scale literature search and review discussed earlier is necessary to confirm how much is known already about a topic or subject you are considering researching, as well as helping to confirm its viability. However, once you have got passed the development of the research question and have an initial idea of your research methods, you need to expand the literature search. So, applying what was discussed above will enable you to expand your search for relevant literature and build up a resource to underpin your research.

Expansion of the literature search to a comprehensive review is essential to be able to underpin your research with a theoretical and conceptual framework. The theoretical and conceptual frameworks that you will find in the literature are necessary for you to be able to discuss your research and findings in the context of previous research. Remember, you are adding to a body of knowledge and to not acknowledge the research that has gone before and to exclude reputed and tested theories is not acceptable when applying the deductive methodology.

WHAT WILL THE LITERATURE SEARCH DO?

A second key component to the literature review is the introduction to previous studies of similar research questions within your discipline so you can assess the methods, techniques and literature that they used. Also, a third component is it will enable you to develop lines of questioning for your chosen techniques in the research methods. Thinking about the questions to ask and the way they should be worded, whether for an interview schedule or a questionnaire, is quite a difficult process and not as easy as one would initially think. Reading literature that reports research which is similar to your own will increase your knowledge of the subject and give you an advantage over choosing the most appropriate research methods and techniques. It will also give you an insight into any difficulties the authors encountered and so illustrating what 'not to do' with your study if you replicate the methods and so on.

CHOOSING YOUR RESEARCH METHODS

The literature review will introduce you to research in your area of interest and the methods used by those authors. This is a good way to determine whether you will replicate the research, slightly amend the research or decide not to do the same as an author has done previously and so do yours completely differently. Whatever you decide, the literature will give you the initial foundation that you need to make those decisions.

Data collection

There are two types of data that are collected within the research process: primary and secondary. Primary data is the data that you collect yourself through the design of your own methods, whether this be to generate qualitative, quantitative or a combination of the two. Secondary data is the data that you collect through a literature review and other sources, as discussed above. Secondary data is data that has been originally collected by another person.

There is often a misconception that the methods we choose are either quantitative methods or qualitative methods. This is not the case, certainly if you follow the research structure above (Figure 12.6) which methods are methodologically neutral. The research methods are the ways in which we obtain the data and the techniques are what give us our different types of data, ie qualitative and quantitative.

So for instance, an interview schedule developed to ask questions for a face-to-face, one-to-one semi-structured interview will give us qualitative data. If we were to record the interview and transcribe it, this would give us a qualitative data transcript.

If we developed a series of questions and designed a questionnaire with forced choice possible answers, eg closed-ended questions for distribution among a sample that self-administered the questionnaire then this would produce a quantitative data set. However, not all questionnaires return numerical data. A questionnaire can have predominantly numerical responses but with areas for open-ended questions so the respondents can provide free responses. The open-ended boxes can be woven into the main questionnaire at different points or can be left until the end.

Research methods to generate qualitative data

The main methods to generate qualitative data are:

- Interviews for asking questions, and these can be a series of one-to-ones, focus groups, diaries, use of online social media such as blogs or other similar technology to generate a qualitative data set.

- Participant and non-participant observations. This method will generate qualitative data generally through both the observer methods because as the researcher is participating in, let's say, the organisation as an employee they will have the opportunity to observe what is said, any physical behaviour and body language. It is more likely, though, that the participant observer will make notes of what other employees have said in addition to behaviours. However, the non-participant observer will also generate qualitative data in the same way but may do less so due to their obvious non-participation. The nature of the non-participant observer may mean that they are somewhat removed from the organisation's activities than the participant observer and in this case may potentially restrict access to what individuals are saying, possibly only resulting in data that records behaviour and body language.

- Document analysis is also another way to generate qualitative data for your research. This is somewhat different from the literature search and review. Document analysis for qualitative data can be used to complement your own primary qualitative data. An example of document analysis might be 10 years of annual reports for a single or number of organisations that relate to your research. Annual reports might also be used for quantitative data, eg financial performance figures; but they also provide interesting narratives, eg the report of the chief executive and reports on corporate governance and/or corporate social responsibility. This type of data, though, is classified as secondary data and not primary, because you will not have originally collected the data yourself. Another example is analysing transcripts from interviews done in a previous study by another author that also relates to your research.

Designing your own techniques to generate qualitative data will involve your own knowledge, that of others' research and generally reading around the subject of research methods.

Analysing qualitative data

There are numerous methods to analyse qualitative data, but predominantly analysis is of the words in terms of the language, terminology and meaning from the spoken words. Other aspects that can be analysed are non-spoken behavioural signifiers such as the rolling of the eyes, raising of the eyebrows or a grimacing frown. All of these are reactions by respondents to questions either by a researcher conducting an interview or undertaking an observation. Lastly, audible sounds not classified as the spoken word can also be analysed, such as grunts, moans or sounds of excitement like laughing or sounds of exasperation like sighing. These latter two techniques of analysing behaviour and audible sounds are generally analysed by linguists or psychologists as further meaning is taken from such signifiers. However, that is not to say that you are not entitled to consider these if you aren't a linguist or a psychologist. This will depend upon your research question, to an extent.

The way to analyse data can differ also depending on your research question and philosophy and your background, eg HR manager or psychologist. However, a key underpinning to analysis relates back to the questions you devised to generate the data. For example, if you undertake a series of face-to-face interviews then the questions would normally have been devised on the basis of your own knowledge and that which you gained from the literature review. These become your guide for starting the analysis. The analysis is generated by developing a series of codes or labels (can be known as either), which are underpinned by the literature review and your questions but are drawn from the actual data. The coding or labelling is generally undertaken twice at a first and second level, then the third level starts to develop overarching themes. Use this resource to visually understand qualitative analysis using coding http://www.sciencelive.org/component/option,com_mediadb/task,play/idstr,Open-feeds_dse212_exploring_psychology_dse212interviews4_4m4v/vv,-2/Itemid,97.This is an OpenU video on analysing interview transcripts. Note down the procedures for analysing interview transcripts and watch it a few times to deepen your understanding. Once you have developed your themes you then begin to analyse the data by reading it and pulling out elements of the spoken word and placing these under the themes. Figure 12.8, taken directly from Anderson (2009), illustrates an indicative overview of the steps in the process of qualitative data analysis.

Figure 12.8 Overview of the process of qualitative data analysis

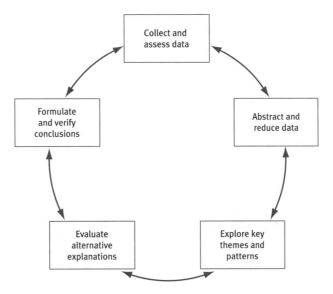

However, if you are undertaking a piece of inductive research then this generally would not be the case. Data collected would not have been underpinned by prior knowledge gained. The process of analysis would be inverted and you would take meaning from the data to generate themes and not from other secondary sources. Analysis is initially based purely on your primary data collected. Refer back to the section on inductive and deductive reasoning as a reminder.

Owing to space limitations with this chapter a full account of qualitative data analysis cannot be given here. However, Anderson (2009) provides an excellent chapter on analysing qualitative data in her book (pp208–240).

Research methods to generate quantitative data

Designing techniques to generate quantitative data requires obtaining a fair amount of knowledge, particularly about survey and questionnaire design.

Questionnaires can also be designed to capture qualitative data or a combination of the two: quantitative and qualitative. This is why I suggest you undertake some further reading (see the References). All I can do in this section is give you some insights into the realities of using such techniques and where they are placed in the philosophies and paradigms, with some supporting resource on designs and other considerations. However, this section will concentrate on the use of the questionnaire to capture quantitative data.

There are a number of misconceptions about questionnaires. The first is that they are positivist and scientific in nature. This is not necessarily the case. They are usually more positivist, but to say they are scientific is to imply other techniques are not scientific, which is not the case. Some positivists, though, may argue this point. The main reason for this is because questionnaires are viewed as being objectivist, as opposed to subjectivist, and are supposed to remove any biases on the part of the researcher, who designed the questionnaire, and on the part of the respondents. However, dependent upon what philosophical stance you subscribe to, and I am arguing the point here of the subjectivist, questionnaires can never be truly positivist. This is because there are factors at play that indirectly hinder the design of questionnaires. In order to believe in this objective practice the positivists would have to prove that these factors – their inherent historical, cultural, social and political conditioning – had no effect on their positivist stance and the subsequent design of questionnaires.

Methods to generate quantitative data go beyond the misconception that questionnaires are the only means to generate and provide such data. There are a number of techniques that we can use to generate quantitative data, as indicated in the illustration.

 ILLUSTRATION

Participant and non-participant observations

This method will generate quantitative data through both the participant observer methods through the use of activity sampling.

Activity sampling is a statistical technique that can be used as a means for collecting data. It is defined by BS 3138:41008 as:

A technique in which a large number of observations are made over a period of time of one group of machines, processes or workers. Each observation records what is happening at that instant and the percentage of observations recorded for a particular activity or delay is a measure of the percentage of time during which that activity or delay occurs.

It is normally used for collecting information on the percentages of time spent on activities, without the need to devote the time that would otherwise be required for any continuous observation.

One of the great advantages of this technique is that it enables lengthy activities or groups of activities to be studied economically and in a way that produces statistically accurate data. (http://managers-net.org/activity_sampling.html, accessed 14 September 2010).

There are some key points you need to be aware of on the numerous ways to ask questions to obtain quantitative data. Some of these are:

- Asking questions:
  - Purposeful – ie questions that are logically related to the research questions and objectives.
  - Concrete – ie questions that are precise and unambiguous.
  - One-dimensional questions – ie a single question in a sentence. For instance, don't use 'How many times have you attended the training and did you enjoy it?' – this is a two-dimensional question. It should read, 'How many times have you attended the training?' and 'Did you enjoy it?'
- Types of questions – here are some examples of the types of questions to use on a questionnaire:
  - open-ended questions
  - closed/closed-ended questions
  - yes/no questions
  - ordinal
  - tick all that apply
  - Likert scale
  - semantic differentials
  - rank order
  - non-linear – for qualitative responses.

Bias, misrepresentation and interpretation

There are two forms of bias with questionnaire design; bias on the part of the respondents in response to the question and in selecting samples from populations. I will deal with population biases first.

Population bias

In order to select the correct sample from a population for distributing your questionnaire, you first need to get to know and understand the context of your population. Below are some key pointers to take into consideration:

- Populations – the population is the universe to be sampled, ie a country, residents of a housing estate, a category of employee or a group of university students.

- Samples – a sample is a portion or subset of the population. A good sample is a miniature version of the population.
- Types of samples – there are numerous types
  - Cluster; convenience; multistage; non-probability; probability; quota; random; representative; snowball; stratified; systematic.
- Good representative samples – if the population is 1000 (45 per cent women and 55 per cent men) then a good sample size would be 500 (45 per cent women and 55 per cent men).
- Preventing bias – in representation of population, ie not enough women, or all men. This would depend on your research question. If you were researching men's health then you will not need a female sample. However, certain categories pertaining to a male sample might become important such as age, lifestyle, occupation, fitness levels, prior illnesses and so on.
- Sample size – how much is enough depends on the type of sample, but a general rule is no less than 33 per cent (a third).
- Caveat – over-sampling should always be considered to overcome sampling error.

Respondent bias

The removal of biases on the part of the respondents always needs to be considered and is not easy, as individuals interpret statements and questions into their own meanings. For instance, if there are a series of closed-ended questions with responses required on a scale of 'strongly disagree' to 'strongly agree', measured by numbers one to seven, then one respondent's response of 'one' might be another respondent's response of 'three'. Thus, interpretation on the part of the respondent affects the responses, and the mere fact that we are human beings means that we have to accept that we cannot achieve objectivity. A tip for reducing bias and interpretation is to keep the scales as close as possible, so instead of a seven-point scale use only five points. An example is given below. Also, a point to remember is that a person's feelings, emotions, and opinions are translated into numbers when you ask them to complete such a questionnaire, and these can and do vary and change over time

It is only the vastly experienced social science quantitative researchers that can design perfect questionnaires, but we all have to start somewhere.

Lastly, when you design a questionnaire make sure you do well in advance of the first distribution date because it is very unwise to distribute it without having piloted it and revised it at least a couple of times.

Examples of questionnaire scales and types of questions

Table 12.1 Example of a 7-point scale questionnaire

Strongly disagree	Somewhat disagree	Disagree	Neither	Agree	Somewhat agree	Strongly agree
1	2	3	4	5	6	7

This example illustrates the Likert scale. It leaves more room for interpretation from the respondents by adding extra measurements and you should be looking to reduce interpretation.

Table 12.2 Example of a 5-point scale questionnaire

Strongly disagree	Disagree	Neither	Agree	Strongly agree
1	2	3	4	5

This example also illustrates the Likert scale, but leaves less room for interpretation from the respondents by keeping the number of measurements to a minimum.

Table 12.3 illustrates a closed-ended question – with four answers:

Table 12.3 'How often during the past month have you accessed Internet sites related to your job?'

Not often	1
About 10 per cent of the time	2
Much less often than the month before	3
Never	4

These questions are ambiguous because 10 per cent of the time for one respondent could also mean 'not often' to another respondent. The example below also illustrates a closed-ended question – with five answers:

Table 12.4 'How often during the past month have you accessed Internet sites related to your job?'

Less than 5 times	1
6–10 times	2
11–15 times	3
16–20 times	4
More than 21 times	5
Never	6

This question example is much clearer and provides clarity for measurement and analysis and reduced interpretation.

Table 12.5 illustrates some of the strengths and weaknesses of questionnaire design.

Table 12.5 Questionnaire design

Strengths	Weaknesses
Data is easier to manage than qualitative	But limitations in richness of data, no 'respondent's social world' responses
Results are neat and data is descriptive	But allows for generalisations only to be made about your area of research Your research evidence will be a series of statements, such as: 25 per cent of the sample agreed with… 75 per cent of the sample ranked questions…
Analysis and results are computed	The need to learn specialist software packages
Can be administered online – reduces inputting costs	Ability to use web design software necessary
Face-to-face/self-administered reduces attrition and postage costs	Postal surveys are time-consuming and costly including follow-up reminders/attrition/non-response
Telephone interviews save time	Affect the quality of response from the respondent – limits the response
Easy to design a questionnaire	Even easier to design a bad questionnaire
	Turn-around time can impact on research
	Access and ethics, ie distribution
	Questionnaires must be pilot tested to test for flow, routing errors, grammatical mistakes and so on

Questionnaire distribution

Your decision to use a questionnaire for your data collection will generally be determined in relation to how confident you are with statistical analysis and the various levels there are to this. You may even need to learn specialist software in order to understand the analysis of quantitative data. Should you need to do this, I recommend Andy Field's book on using SPSS (2009). However, there are a number of relevant points you need to consider when designing and using questionnaires.

- If you use paper copies, you need to build in time for distribution and return and costs of distribution and costs of return postage.
- If using paper copies, you will also need to build in time for following up your sample and possibly even sending out a second or third copy of your questionnaire, increasing printing and postage costs further.
- Manually inputting responses from paper copies into Excel or SPSS is time-consuming and the margin for error is much higher.

- Use of e-mail to circulate copies of questionnaires in Word documents may also pose constraints of inputting but will significantly reduce printing and postage costs and alleviate pressures on timescales.

- Access to your sample: can you be sure that you can get access to your proposed sample and that the organisation will grant you access? Not all questionnaire responses are obtained from random samples in the street, so if you are looking to use an organisation or company in your research then you must seek permission to access it or them prior to making any firm decisions on using a questionnaire.

Analysis of quantitative research

Analysing quantitative data can be simple or very difficult. Keeping your questionnaire design standardised by applying a consistent approach such as the 5-point Likert scale will keep things simple and easy for analysis and producing graphs or pie charts. You will no doubt need to explore with a few versions before getting it right, but remember to pilot it first too.

Analysing responses can also be simple or difficult. A list of methods is explained in the table below.

Table 12.6 Analysis of quantitative research

Type	Distribution mode	Input	Specialist analysis	Generalist analysis
Paper copy: in the street or by post	Person-to-person completion or self-administered by respondent	Manual input of responses into specific software	SPSS	Excel
E-mail	Respondent completes in a Word document and e-mails back or prints off and completes paper copy	Manual input of responses into specific software	SPSS	Excel
Virtual	Online	Survey Monkey or equivalent	Survey Monkey or SPSS (choices can be made as to whether Survey Monkey provides questionnaire service only or additional analysis too)	Excel

As can be seen from Table 12.6, distribution and inputting of the respondents' responses is necessary, but can also be a labour-intensive job with a wide margin for inputting errors, especially with a large sample. However, with modern technology there are now facilities such as Survey Monkey (www.surveymonkey.com) and other equivalents. These online services provide the ability to be able to design the questionnaire and distribute online so the respondents are actually self-inputting whilst responding. Once the respondent's data is collected it is stored in a database for you to access and analyse. They can also offer an extended service where they do all the analysis for you and present you with the raw data and a series of charts or graphs, in whichever format you prefer.

There are obvious advantages to such a service, but with some disadvantages. Cost is a key factor as this service has to be purchased. In addition and most importantly, you are removing yourself from a key part of the analysis, which is the construction of it, and will no doubt leave you without an understanding of how the results were constructed. This may make the discussion of the results a little more difficult purely because of your limited relationship with the data. However, whichever approach you adopt I would suggest sourcing a recommended textbook on quantitative analysis as this will help you from the start in designing a questionnaire also.

Given the limitations with this chapter a full account of quantitative data analysis cannot be given here. However, Field (2009), *Discovering Statistics Using SPSS* is an excellent new edition, Anderson (2009) provides an excellent chapter on analysing quantitative data in her book (pages 241–315) and encompasses both the construction and analysis of quantitative data.

SUMMARY

This chapter has considered many concepts in relation to the research process and applying this to undertake a research project. However, the key component of this chapter has been to provide an in-depth discussion and practical element to the philosophy of science and to enable a deeper student and practitioner understanding of the philosophies of research. Such subjects are often only touched upon in research methods books, and it is my belief that a much clearer understanding through discussion, examples and activities is what is needed to enable this understanding. In addition, it is also my belief that students undertaking research should understand and embrace that research is knowledge, how it comes to exist and how we come to know about knowledge. This in turn enables the students to assess and learn about their own philosophical viewpoints and the articulation of this within their own research. It is important that students and practitioners think through and work out their own philosophical position.

A second aspect to this chapter has been to articulate and pass on to learners many of the nuances in the form of 'tips' that are found in tutorials and seminars and generally not articulated in textbooks. It is these nuances that help to connect the parts of the research process and form the underpinning between such components like the formulating of the research question and what is the most important element of the literature review through to misconceptions about methods and techniques to generate data.

CHAPTER 13

Conclusion

OVERVIEW

This closing chapter has three purposes. First, we will attempt to identify some significant themes that emerge from the main content of the book. Second, an attempt will be made to predict how these themes may develop in the future and to anticipate some consequences and implications for the professional practice of learning and talent development. These first two purposes therefore have direct connections. The third and final purpose is to provide some advice and guidance to those readers preparing themselves for formal examinations as part of a course of study. Given the speculative nature of the first two purposes, and the unpredictable nature of examination success, we have not formulated or stated specific objectives for the chapter. We have also not included any reader activities. However, we hope readers will join in our speculations and that those provided here will inform and stimulate both thought and debate. In addition, we hope the advice provided on preparing for examinations will prove useful and valuable.

SOME SIGNIFICANT THEMES

The book has covered a lot of ground and drawn on writing and research from a wide range of disciplines and perspectives. This makes drawing out significant themes both a difficult and an arbitrary task. We are aware therefore that any themes identified are likely to be different to those identified by others. However, in writing the book we have intended to produce messages on three related themes. We consider each in turn, and in doing so will signal possible connections and implications each may have for the others.

UNDERSTANDING ORGANISATIONS

There are two major points to make about our understanding of organisations. The first is to do with the context in which they operate. This book makes the claim that learning and talent development and HRD are contested terms with no settled or agreed meaning and so professional practice is perhaps always in flux. This claim is based on a belief that the same is true of work organisations. The established certainties, if ever they really were certainties, concerning the purpose of work organisations and how best to manage them seem to us to no longer hold true. Two examples will illustrate this argument. First, the processes of globalisation call into question the relevance and appropriateness of established approaches to managing organisations. Whether these processes spread and intensify 'Taylorist' forms of organising and managing, or demand and produce new and innovative solutions to the inherent contradictions of capitalist and market economies illustrated by the financial crisis of 2008/2009, is a question beyond the scope of this book. We can say, though, that the crisis and related economic recession experienced in so many parts of the world add support to the globalisation thesis. We can also say that experience suggests a degree of fluidity associated with globalisation which enables and perhaps even demands new organisation forms.

The second example is to do with the possibilities created by advances in information and communication technologies. We are now beyond the paperless office and into the realm of the office-less organisation. The term 'virtual organisation' is now established as having some concrete meaning rather than being a rhetorical flourish, as are terms such as network and third level organisation. The development of Web 2.0 technology which has made social networking and social marketing part of the everyday experience of most people in the developed world continues to have impact on how people are employed and how work is done. The point is that contextual factors such as globalisation and technological advance create a state of flux, which in turn allows and enables new organisation forms to both emerge and be deliberately pursued. We therefore have different choices available to us about the nature, purpose and form of work organisations and how to go about managing them.

The second point concerns how we go about analysing and theorising the phenomenon of organisation. It would be a mistake to characterise alternative approaches to analysing organisations as advances since most of those included in this book have been available as long as the dominant functionalist paradigm. However, what is an advance is the strength of the challenge to functionalist analyses arising from application of alternative paradigms. There is something of a paradox here. In the case of critical theory, at least, the theoretical and conceptual tools used to understand social experience have their roots in Marxist analyses of society. At a time when the results produced by such tools lose favour at that level, the results produced at the level of organisation analysis are becoming increasingly significant and valued. In any case, what is most important and significant is that analyses produced by paradigms and perspectives other than functionalism allow and support a questioning of the purpose of work organisations. This provides a useful and valuable challenge to the received or conventional wisdom that work organisations exist to serve exclusively economic ends. Such a challenge also raises important questions about the form of organisations and how they are managed. Questioning ends calls into question means. Therefore, the growing influence of alternative paradigms is likely to reinforce the attempts to find new and innovative organisation forms and approaches to management associated with a changing context.

The conclusion here seems to be that organisation forms and approaches to managing will continue to change in response to changing conditions and different ways of understanding social experience. The professional practice of HRD can expect many opportunities from this situation. A broad possibility is that serving emancipatory purposes through processes of organising becomes more and more legitimate. Development is central to emancipation and therefore the professional practice of learning and talent will be central to serving and achieving such purposes.

UNDERSTANDING LEARNING PROCESSES

The second significant theme is that of developments in understanding learning processes. There are two related themes here. The first is advances in understanding individual learning. The second is advances in understanding the notion of organisation learning, and how this relates to individual learning. Both of these will be important if HRD as an area of academic enquiry and a field of professional practice is to be able to respond to the opportunities suggested in the previous paragraphs. A more effective contribution to achievement of individual and collective emancipation will be possible if greater understanding of individual and collective learning is achieved.

Over a decade ago, in a paper presented at a British Psychological Society conference, Professor John Burgoyne examined the case for attempting to create an overarching or 'meta' theory of learning (Burgoyne 1997). We have yet to see any progress in that endeavour. One interpretation of Burgoyne's arguments suggests such a theory would produce a synthesis of current understandings of individual and organisational learning. In the sense of improved understanding of 'institutions of learning' and 'institutionalised learning' (Burgoyne 1997), such a theory would go further in terms of informing concepts such as lifelong learning and the learning society. While Burgoyne remains uncommitted either way in his paper on the desirability or possibility of such a theory, our view is that an overarching theory is both necessary and feasible. We find the existence of learning theories applicable to different types of learning, for example, child and adult learning or formal and informal learning, deeply unsatisfactory. Some writers seem to be of the view that experiential learning theory applies to learning by and through 'experience' and therefore is inapplicable to formal settings such as study in a university. A similar example is a separation of work-based learning from academic courses. The logical implication of this is that study at university is neither experience nor work. While we resist both intellectually and emotionally the reductionism of behaviourist learning theory, for example, we hold the view that learning is learning wherever and to whomever it occurs. One aspect of a meta theory which is largely ignored in research and writing on the topic based in the social sciences is the role of biological imperatives and limitations in learning processes. While we do not lend credence to much of the work within evolutionary psychology and sociobiology, which represent mainstream attempts to combine the perspectives of the natural and social sciences to the study of human behaviour, we do believe that biology – for example, in the emerging study of neuro-education – cannot be discounted in coming to a full understanding of human learning and so will need to be accommodated in any meta theory (see Stewart 2007).

Our prediction is that the work suggested and begun by Burgoyne's paper will continue until it bears fruit in a unified theory of learning. In addition, this will create important and significant implications for the practice of HRD. We do not suggest that our understanding of learning will ever be such that professional practitioners will be totally confident of guaranteeing learning outcomes from their work. However, we do suggest that the increased understanding provided by a unified theory will provide greater confidence in the design and delivery of development interventions in individual and organisational learning. This confidence will in turn provide greater insight into the form and nature of interventions of relevance to supporting the creation and development of new organisation forms discussed in the previous section.

UNDERSTANDING THE PRACTICE OF LEARNING AND TALENT DEVELOPMENT

The previous sentence leads us into discussing the final significant theme. We have argued throughout the book that understanding learning lies at the heart of professional practice. Any advances in that understanding will therefore lead to advances in professional practice. Advances in practice will occur for additional reasons, including the emergence of new organisational forms. In particular, the effects of different paradigms being applied to organisational analysis will lead to a greater emphasis in professional practice on facilitating agreement of objectives rather than their achievement. This is likely to be emphasised as a result of changing beliefs about attitudes towards and trust in organisations as a result of the financial crisis already mentioned. Such a shift will mean that learning and talent development as an organisation function will become less of a management tool adopted to ensure compliance with and pursuit of objectives which serve the interests of exclusive elites, and more of a collective resource which is used to facilitate articulation and synthesis of the objectives of a variety of stakeholders.

The argument expressed in the previous sentence may be both radical and idealistic. However, there are sound reasons for holding such a view. The idea of what we might call pathways of developments in the practice of learning and talent development, described in earlier chapters, suggests continuing threads in practice. These threads seem to include a focus on reconciling individual and organisational objectives and a concern with realisation of individual and collective potential. These threads seem to be apparent, for example, in work on the concept of the learning organisation. There also seems to be a shift over time in the stages of the development pathway from an emphasis on the demands of organisations to the demands of individuals. This might be characterised by a shift in talent development from being concerned to 'fit' the individual to the organisation to a concern to 'fit' the organisation to the individual. If current trends continue, it therefore seems reasonable to argue that the shift in focus from organisation to individual will bring about a related shift in focus from means to ends.

This argument can be further supported by a greater concern with spirituality and ethics, and a wider constituency of stakeholders clearly evident in research and writing on organising and managing. The messages of this book both reflect and support these concerns. It also seems to be the case that the factors support a greater concern with the objectives pursued by organisations rather than a concern with the technical means of their achievement. We do not mean to suggest by this argument that talent development will have no concern with means. Different organisation forms and approaches to management are concerned with means, and talent development practice, informed by greater understanding of learning processes, will have a significant contribution to developing new forms and approaches. It is therefore a matter of balance and emphasis. What we are suggesting is a shift in emphasis from means to ends, rather than an exclusive focus on one or the other.

A FINAL THOUGHT

Organisations pursue economic and financial ends such as return on investment. The HR profession has long focused on justifying itself by demonstrating a contribution to those ends. That in itself is a dilemma for the profession and professional practitioners: what means can be supported and legitimated to meet the financial ends? Labour cost reduction is easily achievable through the use of slave or child labour but we doubt any HR and so L&TD professional would advocate either of those means. But, the profession and you as a practitioner do have to make professional judgements on what means, as well as what ends, are ethically supportable. But, the distinction between means and ends is not as simple as it may seem. Those who seek to justify the pursuit of profit as an ethical endeavour do so by shifting that pursuit from ends to means. Their argument is that profit maximisation is the means to the end of a more affluent society, which is to the benefit of all citizens; a more affluent society becomes the end with profits the means. Our view on this can be put very simply. As a practising or aspiring professional you have to grapple with and resolve the complexity.

SUMMARY

To summarise, we have argued in this section particular views related to the themes of understanding organisations, learning processes and the practice of talent development. These themes in turn suggest related trends which seem to point in the direction of greater autonomy and control on the part of individuals in their experience of work organisations, and a significant contribution from learning and talent development practitioners in supporting and facilitating movement in that direction. However, the arguments have the status of mere speculation and may prove to be wildly inaccurate. We will now move on to more certain ground to provide advice and guidance on sitting formal examinations. This short section is written by Jim Stewart who has provided the advice to his students for many years but with no real clue as to either its application or success. The recommendation is based on the approach working for him in his student days, which were of course a long time ago!

SUCCESS IN EXAMINATIONS

My advice in this section is based on what I term the 'managerial approach to examinations'. I use this term because the advice is derived from applying a formal strategic planning process to the task of achieving success in a formal examination. The discussion of such processes in this and other books suggests that they involve thorough analysis before action is taken. The nature and number of steps involved in the analysis vary from model to model. For the purposes of the task in question I have applied a six-step process of analysis, which I commend to you before you take the action of putting pen to paper in the examination room. The first step is that of determining your mission.

MISSION STATEMENT

I cannot write a mission statement for this task because there will be many different reasons for studying and sitting examinations. I can, however, suggest two examples:

- Help achieve CIPD membership
- Secure high-level/well-paid employment.

According to the theory of strategic planning, the value of mission statements lies in providing a clear and desired focus. I once heard Alan Sugar, chairman of Amstrad, speaking on the radio and declaring that the mission of his company was captured in the phrase 'we want your money!' This seems to capture the essence of clarity and desirability recommended by the theory. I suggest you use the two examples given above, plus the one from Alan Sugar, to formulate your own statement.

SET OBJECTIVES

Once a mission statement is written it is easier to set out some objectives. These need to be specific and measurable. Such characteristics will facilitate the steps that follow. One objective related to success in examinations, irrespective of your mission, will be:

- to achieve a minimum grade of 50 per cent (could be 40 per cent).

You will need to add any other objectives of your own related to achievement of your personal mission.

DEVISE STRATEGY

Strategy in this model is concerned with the means by which the objectives will be achieved. Strategies can be and often are composed of a number of elements. In the case of the objective given above, there are two elements:

- score points
- score enough points.

These elements and the use of the words 'points' may seem a little cynical. My argument would be that managing, whether it is seen as science or art is above all else pragmatic. Being pragmatic means recognising that examinations are conducted by certain rules and success requires performing well in the context of those rules. Like other activities governed by rules, examinations are a form of game and, as in other forms of games, scoring points is required for success. We will return to the detail of the strategy when we examine tactics.

ASSESS RESOURCES

Before tactics can be planned, resources need to be identified and assessed. The resources available to a candidate in an examination are:

- time
- questions on the examination paper
- knowledge
- experience
- intelligence
- self-belief
- composure.

These are the resources available to implement the strategy. Each of them is finite at the point of their use and therefore they need to be used to maximum effect. The first two are common and equal, that is, they are the same for all candidates. Time will generally be either two or three hours. It is important to emphasise that the questions are a valuable resource. They are a friend to and ally of each candidate. Without the questions, the strategy cannot be implemented and the objective cannot be achieved. They should therefore be anticipated in a positive frame of mind because, in simple terms, the questions enable candidates to exercise their intelligence to demonstrate their knowledge and experience in the time available, and thereby score enough points to achieve the objective. The final five resources will vary from candidate to candidate and therefore each individual needs to produce their own assessment. It is imperative that this is done well before the examination since the assessment will inform and influence application of the tactics.

PLAN TACTICS

Tactics are concerned with plans for implementing the strategy, based on an assessment of resources. Each element of a strategy requires a set of tactics which will make most effective use of available resources. Those suggested for the proposed strategy are:

- Score points.

Points will not be scored if the wrong questions are attempted. There are two definitions of 'wrong'. First, answering a question which the candidate either thinks or wishes is being asked, rather than the question actually asked. Second, answering a question which does not allow a candidate to demonstrate knowledge and ability. In other words, attempting questions on what are for a particular candidate weak subjects or topics. This illustrates the importance of assessing personal resources. On the positive side, points will be scored for demonstrated knowledge and understanding, for demonstrated ability to apply this in practice, for independent thought and for originality. These are cumulative, ie for each additional feature demonstrated additional points will be scored. Answers to questions are much more likely to demonstrate these features if they are thought through and planned before being written. The tactics for this element of the strategy can be summarised as follows:

a. analyse and understand the questions

b. select 'strong' subjects in relation to knowledge and experience

c. demonstrate knowledge and understanding

d. illustrate application in practice

e. show independent thought, critical analysis and, if possible, originality

f. plan answers, perhaps with notes, before writing them.

- Score enough points.

While the above tactics will score points, it is equally important to score enough points to achieve the objective. This requires two tactics. First, answering enough questions, which means the required and specified number, and second, providing consistently good answers. This is a matter of quality and quantity. One excellent and two or three poor answers will not score enough points. It is much more effective to have, say, four answers of more or less equal length and quality than four of variable length and standard. The final point here is that an answer is more likely to be good rather than poor if it is complete, ie it works towards and arrives at a logical conclusion. In summary, the tactics for the element of this strategy are:

a. attempt/answer the required number of questions

b. aim for consistency in length and quality

c. structure each answer to a logical conclusion.

FORMULATE ACTION PLAN

The final step in this model is to formulate an action plan. This identifies the activities that have to be undertaken to implement the strategy, and sets timescales for completion for each activity. It would not be useful for me to set out an action plan since the requirements of examinations vary. I can, however, identify the activities and suggest proportional time allocations for each within the exam. This results in the following:

Activities	Time allocation
reading	1/6
thinking	1/6
writing	2/3

Some words of explanation are necessary. The time allocation for thinking means time for doing nothing other than thinking. It may be difficult to sit in an examination room without reading or writing, especially when others around you are doing either one or both. However, I strongly recommend that you do so since it will pay off in the quality of your answers. The focus of thinking time is analysing and selecting questions and planning answers. Reading time is allocated to reading the question paper and reading your answers when they are complete. The former is in addition to any officially allocated reading time, and the latter is to ensure your hand has not lagged too far behind your brain and left incomplete sentences, or to fill the gaps if they have occurred. My final suggestion is that the time allocations and activities are translated into a specific action plan which meets the requirements of any particular examination.

DISCUSSION

The advice and guidance provided in this section so far has general application and is not therefore specific to CIPD-associated examinations. The principles do apply to the specific case of CIPD-associated examinations, however. In addition, I recommend candidates to bear in mind two points. First, the syllabuses of the CIPD modules are too large to be fully represented on a single examination paper. It is therefore useful to categorise the syllabus of any module into subject headings such as those used to structure this book, and to expect questions derived from each of the subjects. The whole syllabus may not be represented on a paper, but each part or subject/topic can be included.

Second, the guiding principle informing the CIPD scheme, and therefore all stages in the examination process, is that successful candidates have demonstrated their ability to perform successfully in professional personnel and development roles in work organisations. The purpose of examinations therefore is to assess and enable demonstration of this ability. I can confirm from personal experience of the process that those involved work very hard to ensure consistency and fairness in the process and start from the point of wanting to enable candidates to demonstrate their ability, rather than from the point of seeking to impose hurdles. There is no hidden agenda or any trick questions in examination papers. However, the implication of the guiding principle is that, to be successful, candidates need to demonstrate more than knowledge of relevant theories or research. Likewise success requires more than mere description of organisation activities. This is undoubtedly important. Success requires candidates to demonstrate understanding of organisation contexts and possession of the professional judgement and skills necessary for application of theory and research in practical contexts. My final piece of advice, therefore, is to ensure your preparation for examinations enables you to demonstrate that judgement and those skills.

SUMMARY AND CONCLUSION

That final advice brings the book to a close. We hope and intend that the content of the book will have made a useful contribution to preparing those readers studying formal programmes for their assessment by developing their professional judgement and skills. We hope, too, that other readers have found value in the book. Learning and talent development is an important field of professional practice, too important to be left to chance or circumstance. Serious study of relevant concepts and theories is necessary to inform practice. This book represents one contribution to that study. We invite readers to assess the value of the contribution by reviewing the extent to which the book has achieved its aims and objectives detailed in Chapter 1, and the extent to which their personal objectives in reading the book have been met. Reviewing aims and objectives, and their achievement or otherwise, reflects currently defined 'best practice' in HRD. It also provides a basis for planning future learning objectives and a future learning cycle. Inviting and encouraging such a review therefore seems an appropriate way of ending the book.

Notes

CHAPTER 5

1 We are aware that there is some critique that the extent of Inuit words for snow might be something of an urban myth, but we still think the example is useful to illustrate the connection of language and thought.

2 For further background on the earlier history of the CIPD, see Factsheet History of the CIPD: http://www.cipd.co.uk/about/howcipdrun/history. htm?IsSrchRes=1.

CHAPTER 6

1 Learning modalities of visual, auditory, kinaesthetic and tactile – see later in chapter for further explanation

2 Based on research presented in CIPD discussion paper 'How do people learn IT systems?': http://www.cipd.co.uk/helpingpeoplelearn/_hdpl.htm, accessed 19 January 2010.

CHAPTER 8

1 *action research*, a process wherein researchers participate in studies both as participants and observers with the explicit intention of addressing deep-rooted organisational issues through recurring cycles of action and reflection.

participatory research, is research in which ordinary people play a key role in undertaking research, for the purpose of knowledge creation, and with a wider social change agenda.

action science is an approach, using reflection-in-action, that is based on the principle that people can improve their interpersonal and organisational effectiveness by exploring the beliefs that underlie their actions.

developmental action inquiry, described by Torbert (1999), interweaves first-person inquiry, second-person inquiry, and third-person inquiry so as to become aware of transformations between intuition, thinking, communicative practices, and effects on others.

co-operative inquiry is a radically participative form of inquiry in which all those involved are both co-researchers and co-subjects, participating in the context that is being researched.

References

Alimo-Metcalfe, B. and Nyfield, G. (2002) Leadership and organizational effectiveness. In Robertson, I. *et al. The Role of Individual Performance in Organizational Effectiveness.* London: Wiley.

Allen, M. (2002) *The Corporate University Handbook: Designing, managing and growing a successful program.* New York: Amacom.

Allison, C. W. and Hayes, J. (1996) The Cognitive Style Index. *Journal of Management Studies.* Vol. 33. pp119–135.

Alvesson, M., Bridgman, T. and Willmott, H. (2009) *The Oxford Handbook of Critical Management Studies.* Oxford: Oxford University Press.

Anderson, V. (2007) *The Value of Learning: From return on investment to return on expectation.* London: CIPD.

Anderson, V. (2009a) Desperately seeking alignment: reflections of senior line managers and HRD executives. *Human Resource Development International,* Vol. 12, No. 3, pp263–278.

Anderson, V. (2009b) Research methods. In *Human Resource Management.* (2nd ed). London: CIPD.

Apter, M.J. (2001) *Motivational Styles in Everyday Life: A guide to reversal theory.* Washington, DC: American Psychological Association

Argyris, C. and Schön, D. (1996) *Organizational Learning II: Theory, method and practice.* Wokingham: Addison-Wesley.

Arnold, J, Johnson, K. (1997) Mentoring in early career. *Human Resource Management Journal.* Vol. 7, No. 4. p61.

Ashworth, P. (2003) The origins of qualitative psychology. In Smith J. (ed.) *Qualitative Psychology: A practical guide to research methods.* Thousand Oaks, CA: Sage.

Badrach, E. (1998) *Getting Agencies To Work Together: The practice and theory of managerial craftsmanship.* Washington, DC: Brookings Institution Press.

Barbe, W.B. and Swassing, R.H., with Milone, M.N. (1979). *Teaching through Modality Strengths: Concepts and practices.* Columbus, OH: Zaner-Bloser

Barber, P. (1997) Money talks: the influence of the accountant on organisational discourse. *Journal of Applied Management Studies.* Vol. 6, No. 1.

Bateson, G. (1973) *Steps Towards an Ecology of the Mind.* London: Paladin.

Beckett, D.D. and P. Hager (2002) *Life, Work and Learning: Practice in postmodernity.* New York: Routledge Kegan Paul.

Belenky, M.F., Clinchy, B.M., Golderger, N.R. and Tarube, J.M. (1986) *Women's Ways of Knowing: The development of self, voice and mind*. New York: Basic Books.

Benington, J. (2007) in Moore and Benington, In search of public value. *Administration Review*. May/June. Vol. 60. No. 3.

Berger, P. and Luckman, T. (1966) *The Social Construction of Reality*. Harmondsworth: Penguin Books.

Bloom, B.S. (1956) *Taxonomy of Educational Objectives*. Boston, MA: Allyn and Bacon.

Bonnet, M., Harris, M., Huxham, C. and Loveridge, R. (2001) Mapping action research practices. Paper for EGOS 2001, Lyon.

Boström, L. and Lassen, L.M. (2006) Unraveling learning, learning styles, learning strategies and meta-cognition. *Education + Training*. Vol. 48, No. 2. pp.178–189.

Boud, D., Cohen, R. and Walker, D. (1993) *Using Experience for Learning*. Buckingham: Open University Press.

Bourdieu, P. *et al.* (1993/1998) *The Poverty of Society: A study in social suffering*. Cambridge: Polity Press.

Bowie, N.E. and Duska, R.F. (1990) *Business Ethics*. (2nd ed). Upper Saddle River, NJ: Prentice-Hall.

Boydell, T. and Leary, M. (1996) *Identifying Training Needs*. London: CIPD.

Boydell, T.H. (1983) *A Guide to the Identification of Training Needs*. London: British Association for Commercial and Industrial Education.

Bramley, P. (2003) *Evaluating Training*. London: CIPD.

Bridges, W. (2009) *Managing Transitions*. Reading, MA: The Perseus Books Group.

Brittain, S. (2007) How to manage key talent. *People Management*. Vol. 13, No. 12, 14 June.

Brooks, A. and Watkins, K.E. (1994). A new era for action technologies: A look at the issues. In Brooks, A. and Watkins, K.E. (eds). *The Emerging Power of Action Inquiry Technologies: New directions for adult and continuing education*. San Francisco, CA: Jossey-Bass.

Bruner, J. (1996) *The Culture of Education*. Cambridge, MA: Harvard University Press.

Bryman, A. and Bell, E. (2007) *Business Research Methods*. (2nd ed). New York: Oxford University Press.

Buckley, R. and Caple, J. (2009) *The Theory and Practice of Training*. (6th ed.) London: Kogan Page.

Burgoyne, J. (1997) 'Learning: conceptual, practical and theoretical issues', British Psychological Society Annual Conference, Heriot-Watt University, Edinburgh. April 1997.

Burgoyne, J. (2009) Issues in action learning: A critical realist interpretation. *Action Learning: Research and Practice.* Vol. 6, No. 2. pp149–161.

Burns, T. (1955) The reference of conduct in small groups: cliques and cabals in occupational milieux. *Human Relations.* Vol. 8. pp467–486.

Burns, T. and Stalker, G.M. (1994) *The Management of Innovation.* Oxford: Oxford University Press.

Buzan, T. (2006) *Mind Mapping: Kickstart your creativity and transform your life.* London: BBC.

Carr, A. (1968) Is business bluffing ethical? *Harvard Business Review.* January/ February.

Carrick, P., Chance, C. and Williams, W. (1999). Development centres – a review of assumptions. *Human Resource Management Journal.* Vol. 9, No. 2. pp. 77–92.

Casey, D. (1983) Where action learning fits in. In Pedler M., *Action Learning in Practice.* London: Gower.

Child, J., Faulkner, D. and Tallman, S. (2005) *Cooperative Strategy – Managing alliances, networks and joint ventures.* Oxford: Oxford University Press.

CIPD (2002) *Training in the Knowledge Economy.* London: CIPD.

CIPD (2008) Learning styles revised, August 2008. www.cipd.co.uk/subjects/ lrnanddev/general/lrngstyles.htm?IsSrchRes=1, accessed 25 January 2010.

CIPD (2009a) *Learning and Development Annual Survey.* London: CIPD. www. cipd.co.uk/surveys/.

CIPD (2009b) Coaching at the sharp end: developing and supporting the line manager as coach. www.cipd.co.uk/subjects/lrnanddev/coachmntor/_coaching_ sharp_end.htm.

CIPD (2009c) Coaching factsheet. www.cipd.co.uk/subjects/lrnanddev/ coachmntor/coaching.htm.

CIPD (2009d) Taking the temperature of coaching. http://www.cipd.co.uk/ subjects/lrnanddev/coachmntor/_taking_temperature_coaching.htm

Clark, H., Chandler, J. and Barry, J. (1994) *Organisations and Identities.* London: Chapman & Hall.

Clutterbuck, D. and Megginson,. (2005) *Techniques for Coaching and Mentoring.* Oxford: Elsevier Butterworth-Heinemann.

Clutterbuck, D. and Megginson, D. (2009) *Further Techniques for Coaching and Mentoring.* Oxford: Elsevier Butterworth-Heinemann.

Coffield, F. (2008) *Just Suppose Teaching and Learning Became the First Priority*. London: Learning and Skills Network.

Coffield, F. *et al.* (2004) *Learning Styles and Pedagogy in Post-16 Learning: A systematic and critical review*. London: Learning and Skills Research Centre. Available at: www.lsda.org.uk/files/PDF/1543.pdf.

Cohen, L., Manion, L. and Morrison, K. (2005) *Research Methods in Education*. (5th ed). New York: Routledge Falmer.

Collins, R. (1981) On the microfoundations of macrosociology. *American Journal of Sociology*. Vol. 86. pp984–1014.

Conklin, J. (2005) *Dialogue Mapping: Building shared understanding of wicked problems*. New York: Wiley.

Connock, S. and Johns, T. (1995) *Ethical Leadership*. London: Institute of Personnel and Development.

Cooperrider, D.L. (1995) Introduction to Appreciative Inquiry. In French, W. and Bell, C. (eds). *Organisation Development* (5th ed). New York: Prentice Hall.

Crawford, K. and Smith, D. (2005) The we and the us: Mentoring African American women. *Journal of Black Studies*. Vol. 36. pp52–67.

Customer Contact Association. http://www.cca-global.com, accessed 18 March 2010.

Darlaston-Jones, D. (2007) Making connections: the relationship between epistemology and research methods. *The Australian Community Psychologist*. Vol. 19, No. 1.

De Geus, A. (1988) Planning as learning. *Harvard Business Review*. Mar./Apr. pp51–59.

De Janasz, S.C. and Sullivan, S.E. (2002) Multiple mentoring in academe: developing the professorial network. *Journal of Vocational Behavior*. Vol. 64, No. 2. pp263–283.

DEMOS (2005) Learning working group. www.demos.co.uk/learningworkinggroup/.

Department for Business Innovation and Skills (2009) Small and medium enterprise statistics for the UK and regions 2008. http://stats.berr.gov.uk/ed/sme/smestats2008-ukspr.pdf, accessed 28 November 2009.

Dewey, J. (1938) *Experience and Education*. New York: Collier Books.

Dicken, P. (2004) *Global Shift: Reshaping the global economic map in the* 21st *century*. London: Sage Publications.

Donaldson, J. (1989) *Key Issues in Business Ethics*. London: Academic Press.

Donaldson, J. (1992) *Business Ethics: A European casebook*. London: Academic Press.

Downey, M. (2003) *Effective Coaching*. London: Texere.

Dunn, R. and Griggs, S. (2003) The Dunn and Dunn learning-style model and its theoretical cornerstone. In Dunn, R. and Griggs, S. (eds). *Synthesis of the Dunn and Dunn Learning-style Model Rresearch: Who, what, when, where and so what?* New York: St John's University.

Dunn, R., Dunn, K. and Perrin, J. (1994) *Teaching Young Children through Their Individual Learning Style*. Boston, MA: Allyn & Bacon.

Durkheim, E. (1997) *The Division of Labour in Society*. London: The Free Press.

Egan, G. (1998) *The Skilled Helper: Model, skills, and methods for effective helping*. (6th ed). Pacific Grove, CA: Brooks/Cole Publishing.

Ehlers, U.D. (2009) Web 2.0 – e-learning 2.0 – quality 2.0? Quality for new learning cultures. *Quality Assurance in Education*. Vol. 17, No. 3. p20.

Ehrich, L.C. (2008) Mentoring and women managers: another look at the field. *Gender in Management: An International Journal*. Vol. 23, No. 7.

Elliott, C. and Turnbull, S. (eds). (2005) *Critical Thinking in Human Resource Development*. London: Routledge.

Entwistle, N.J. (1997) *The Approaches and Study Skills Inventory for Students (ASSIST)*. University of Edinburgh: Centre for Research on Learning and Instruction.

Eurich, N.P. (1985) *Corporate Classrooms: The learning business*. Princeton, NJ: The Carnegie Foundation for the Advancement of Teaching.

European Commission (2005) SME definition: user guide and model declaration. http://ec.europa.eu/enterprise/enterprise_policy/sme_definition/sme_user_guide.pdf, accessed 28 November 2009.

Evans, C. and Cools, E. (2009) The use and understanding of style differences to enhance learning. *Reflecting Education*. Vol. 5, No. 2, May. pp1–18.

Evans, C. and Graff, M. (2008) Guest editorial. *Education + Training*. Vol. 50, No. 2.

Evans, C. and Sadler-Smith, E. (2006) Learning styles in education and training: Problems, politicisation and potential. *Education + Training*. Vol. 48, No. 2/3. pp77–83.

Ferrell, O.C. and Fraedrich, J. (1997) *Business Ethics: Ethical decision making and cases*. Boston, MA: Houghton Mifflin.

Field, A. (2009) *Discovering Statistics Using SPSS*. (3rd ed). London: Sage.

Finch-Lees, T. and Mabey, C. (2007) Management development: a critical discursive approach. In Stewart, J. and Hill, R. (eds). *Management Development: Perspectives from research and practice.* London: Routledge.

Fisher, C. and Lovell, A. (2009) *Business Ethics and Values.* (3rd ed). Harlow: FT Prentice Hall.

Fisher, C. and Sempik, A. (2009) Performance management and performing management. In Leopold, J. and Harris, L. *The Strategic Managing of Human Resources.* (2nd ed). Harlow: FT Prentice Hall.

Fisher, D., Rooke, D. and Torbert, W.R. (2000) *Personal and Organizational Transformations through Action Inquiry.* Boston, MA: EdgeWork.

Foucault, M. (1969) *The Archeology of Knowledge.* Paris: Gallimard.

Fredericks, J. and Stewart, J. (1996)) The strategy – HRD connection. In Stewart, J. and McGoldrick, J. (eds). *Human Resource Development: Perspectives, strategies and practice.* London: Financial Times Pitman Publishing .

Fredericks, J. and Stewart, J. (1996) The strategy–HRD connection. In Stewart, J. and McGoldrick, J. (eds). *Human Resource Development: Perspectives, strategies and practice.* London: Financial Times Pitman Publishing.

Free Dictionary (2006) Edutainment, available at: http://encyclopedia. thefreedictionary.com/Edutainment.

Freire, P. (1972) *Pedagogy of the Oppressed.* Harmondsworth: Penguin.

Freire, P. and Shor, I. (1987) *A Pedagogy for Liberation: Dialogues on transforming education.* London: Macmillan.

Friedman, M. (1963) *Capitalism and Freedom.* Chicago: University of Chicago Press.

Friedman, M. (1970) The social responsibility of business is to increase its profits. *New York Times Magazine.* 13 September.

Garavan, T., Hogan, C. and Cahir-O'Donnell, A. (2009) *Developing Managers and Leaders: Perspectives, debates and practices in Ireland.* Dublin: Gill and Macmillan.

Gergen, K. (1999) *An Invitation to Social Construction.* London: Sage.

Gibb, S. and Telfer, S. (2008) Strategic concerns in mentoring schemes. *The International Journal of Mentoring and Coaching.* Vol. VI, Issue 1. 02/2008 on-line, accessed 18 March 2010.

Gibbons, A. (2000) Getting the most from mentoring: Recent developments and learning. *Training Journal.* March. pp18–20.

Giddens, A. (1989) *Sociology.* Cambridge: Polity Press.

Goffee, R. and Jones, G. (2009) *Clever: Leading your smartest, most creative people.* Boston, MA: Harvard Business Press.

Gold, J. and Iles, P. (2010) Measuring and assessing managers and leaders for development. In Gold, J., Thorpe, R. and Mumford, A. (eds). *Gower Handbook of Leadership and Management Development*. 5th ed. Farnham: Gower Publishing.

Gold, J. and Smith, J. (2010) Continuing professional development and lifelong learning. In Gold, J. *et al*. (eds). *Human Resource Development: Theory and practice*. Basingstoke: Palgrave Macmillan.

Graff, M. (2006) Constructing and maintaining an effective hypertext-based learning environment: Web-based learning and cognitive style. *Education + Training*. Vol. 48, No. 2/3. pp143–155.

Gregorc, A.F. (1979) Learning/teaching styles: Potent forces behind them. *Educational Leadership*. Vol. 36. pp234–237.

Gregorc, A.F. (1985) Style Delineator: A self-assessment instrument for adults. Columbia, CT: Gregorc Associates Inc.

Griffin, V. (1987) Naming the processes. In Boud D. and Griffin V., *Appreciating Adults Learning: From the learners' perspective*. London: Kogan Page.

Griggs, V., McCaulley, Glaister, C., Holder, R. and Sold, J. (2010) The identification of training needs. In Gold, J. *et al*. (eds). *Human Resource Development: Theory and practice*. Basingstoke: Palgrave Macmillan.

Hackman, J.R. and Wageman, R. (2005) A theory of team coaching. *Academy of Management Review*. Vol. 30. pp269–287.

Hamel, G. and Prahalad, C.K. (1994) *Competing for the Future*. Boston, MA: Harvard Business School Press.

Hardy, C., Lawrence, T.B. and Phillips, N. (1998) Talk and action: Conversations and narrative in interorganizational collaboration. In Grant, D., Keenoy, T. and Oswick, C. (eds). *Discourse and Organization*. London: Sage. pp65–83.

Hargreaves, D. (2005) About Learning: Report of the Learning Working Group. London: Demos: http://www.demos.co.uk/publications/aboutlearning

Harri-Augsten, S. and Thomas, L.(1991) *Learning Conversations*. London: Routledge.

Harrison, R. (2009) *Learning and Development*. 5th ed. London: CIPD.

Hay, D.B. and Kinchin, I.M. (2006) Using concept maps to reveal conceptual typologies. *Education +Training*. Vol. 48, No. 2/3. pp127–142.

Herrmann, N. (1989) *The Creative Brain*. Lake Lure, NC: Brain Books/Ned Hermann Group.

Hofstede, G. (1991) *Cultures and Organisations*. London: HarperCollins.

Honey, P. and Mumford, A. (2000) *The Learning Styles Helper's Guide*. Maidenhead: Peter Honey Publications.

Horvath, M., Wasko, L.E. and Bradley J.L. (2008) The effect of formal mentoring program characteristics on organizational attraction. *Human Resource Development Quarterly*. Vol. 19, No. 4. pp323–349.

Huxham, C. (1996) *Creating Collaborative Advantage*. London: Sage.

Ibarra, H. (2003) *Working Identity – Unconventional strategies for reinventing your career*. Boston, MA: Harvard Business School Press.

Iles, P. and Preece, D. (2010) Talent management and career development. In Gold, J., Thorpe, R. and Mumford, A. (eds). *Gower Handbook of Leadership and Management Development*. 5th ed. Farnham: Gower Publishing.

Illich, I. (1977) *Disabling Professions*. Reproduced in Clark, H., Chandler, J. and Barry, J. (1994) *Organisations and Identities*. London: Chapman Hall. pp207–208.

Jackson, C. (2002) *Manual of the Learning Styles Profiler*. http://www.psi-press.co.uk/

James, D. and Biesta, G. (2007) *Improving Learning Cultures in Further Education*. London: Routledge.

Jankowicz, A.D. (2007) *Business Research Projects*. (4th ed). Andover: South-Western CENGAGE Learning.

Jennings, M.M. and Happel, S. (2003) The post-Enron era for stakeholder theory: A new look at corporate governance and the Coase Theorem. *Mercer Law Review*. Vol. 54, No. 1. pp873–938.

Johnson, G., Scholes, K. and Whttington, R. (2006) *Exploring Corporate Strategy*. (7th ed). Hemel Hempstead: Prentice-Hall.

Kaplan-Leiserson, E. (2005) Mobile reality: A tale of two experts. *Learning Circuits*. American Society for Training Development (ASTD), online publication: http://www.astd.org/LC/2005/0405_kaplan.htm, accessed 20 March 2010.

Kaplan, R.S. and Norton, D.P. (1996) *The Balanced Scorecard: Translating strategy into action*. Boston, MA: Harvard University Press.

Kay, J. (1993) *Foundations of Corporate Success*. Oxford: Oxford University Press.

Kayes, D. Christopher (2007)) Institutional barriers to experiential learning revisited, Conclusion. In Reynolds, M. and Vince, Russ (eds). *The Handbook of Experiential Learning and Management Education*. Oxford: OUP

Kellie, J., Henderson, E. and Milsom, B. (2010) Leading change in tissue viability best practice: a development programme for link nurse managers. *Action Learning: research and practice*. Vol. 7, No. 2. pp213–219.

Kelly, G.A. (1955) *The Psychology of Personal Constructs*. New York: Norton.

Kenrick, P. (1984) *Costing, Budgeting and Evaluating Training*. Luton: Local Government Training Board.

Kerr, C. (1983) *The Future of Industrial Societies: Convergence or Continuing diversity?* Cambridge, MA: Harvard University Press.

Kirkpatrick, D.L., (1975) *Evaluating Training Programs.* Alexandria, UA: American Society for Training and Development.

Kolb, D.A. (1984) *Experiential Learning: Experience as the source of learning and development.* Englewood Cliffs, NJ: Prentice-Hall.

Kolb, D.A. (1999) *The Kolb Learning Style Inventory, Version 3.* Boston. MA: Hay Group.

Kram, K.E. (1985) *Mentoring at Work: Developmental relationships in organizational life.* Glenview, IL: Scott Foresman.

Lave, J. and Wenger, E. (1991) *Situated Learning: Legitimate peripheral participation.* Cambridge: Cambridge University Press.

Legge, K. (1995) *Human Resource Management: Rhetorics and realities.* Basingstoke: Macmillan.

Lewin, K. (1943) Defining the field at a given time. *Psychological Review.* 50. p292–310. Republished in *Resolving Social Conflicts and Field Theory in Social Science,* Washington, DC: American Psychological Association (1997).

Lewin, K. (1951) *Field Theory in Social Science: Selected theoretical papers,* ed. D. New York: Harper & Row.

Lewin, K. (1958) *Group Decision and Social Change.* New York: Holt, Rinehart and Winston.

May, T. (1997) *Social Research: Issues, methods and process.* 2nd ed. Buckingham: Open University Press.

McDowall, A. and Mabey, C. (2008) What are the hallmarks of effective development activities? *Personnel Review.* Vol. 376. pp629–646.

McLagan, P. (1989) Systems model 2000: Matching systems theory to future HRD issues. In Gradous D.B. (ed). *Systems Theory Applied to Human Resource Development.* Alexandria, VA: ASTD.

Mead, G. (2007) Developing public service leaders through action inquiry. In Rigg. C. and Richards, S. (eds). *Action Learning: Leadership and organizational development in public services.* London: Routledge, pp145–163.

Megginson, D. and Whitaker, V. (2007) *Continuing Professional Development.* London: CIPD.

Messick, S. (1984) The nature of cognitive styles: Problems and promise in educational practice. *Educational Psychologist.* Vol. 192. pp59–74.

Michaels, E., Handfield-Jones, H. and Axelrod, B. 2001. *The War for Talent.* Boston, MA: Harvard Business Review Press.

Midgley, M. (1996) *The Ethical Primate: Humans, freedom and morality*. London: Routledge.

Mintzberg, H. (2004) *Managers Not MBAs: A hard look at the soft practice of managing and management development*. San Francisco: Berrett-Koehler.

Mintzberg, H., Lampel, J., Quinn J.B. and Ghoshal, S. (2003) *The Strategy Process: Concepts, contexts, cases*. (4th ed). Upper Saddle Rover, NJ: Pearson Prentice Hall.

Moorby, E. (1996) *How to Succeed in Employee Development*. (2nd ed). Maidenhead: McGraw-Hill.

Myers, I.B. and McCaulley, M.H. (1998) *Manual: A guide to the development and use of the Myers-Briggs Type Indicator*. Palo Alto, CA: Consulting Psychologists Press.

Ni Mhaolrúnaigh, S. (2009) Ag foghlaim le chéile chun dul i mbun oibre le chéile: 'learning together to work together'. *Journal of Interprofessional Care*. Vol. 23, No. 5. pp526–527.

O'Donnell, D., Gubbins, C., McGuire, D., Jorgensen, K.M., Henriksen, L. Bo and Garavan, T.N. (2007) Social capital and HRD: Provocative insights from critical management studies. *Advances in Developing Human Resources*. Vol. 9, No. 3, 1 August. pp413–435.

Palmer, S. and A. Whybrow (eds) (2007) *Handbook of Coaching Psychology: A guide for practitioners*. London: Routledge.

Pavlov, I.P. (1927) *Conditioned Reflexes: An investigation of the physiological activity of the cerebral cortex*, translated and edited by G.V. Anrep. Oxford: Oxford University Press.

Pawson, R. and Tilley, N. (1997) *Realistic Evaluation*. London: Sage.

Pedler, M., Burgoyne, J. and Boydell, T. (2004) *A Manager's Guide to Leadership*. London: McGraw-Hill.

Pedler, M., Burgoyne, J. and Brook, C. (2005) What has action learning become? *Action Learning: Research and Practice*. Vol. 2. No. 1. pp.49–68.

Peltier, B. (2010) *The Psychology of Executive Coaching*. New York: Routledge.

Penrose, E. (1959 *The Theory of the Growth of the Firm*. Oxford: Blackwell.

Perkin, H. (1989) *The Rise of Professional Society: England since 1880*. London: Routledge. Reproduced in Clark, H., Chandler, J. and Barry, J. (1994) *Organisations and Identities*. London: Chapman Hall. pp204–206.

Phillips-Jones, L. (2001) *New Mentors and Proteges: How to succeed with the new mentoring partnerships*. Grass Valley, CA: Coalition of Counseling Centers.

Piaget, J. (1971) *Psychology and Epistemology: Towards a theory of knowledge*, trans. A. Rosin. New York: Grossman Publishers.

Prahalad, C.K. and Hamel, G. (1990) The core competence of the corporation. *Harvard Business Review*. Vol. 68, No. 3. pp79–91.

Prince, C. and Stewart, J. (2000) The dynamics of the corporate education market and the role of business schools. *Journal of Management Development*. Vol. 183. pp207–219.

Purcell, J. (2003) *Understanding the People and Performance Link: Unlocking the black box*. London: CIPD.

Purcell, J. and Hutchinson, S. (2007) *Line Managers in Reward, Learning and Development*. London: CIPD.

Puxty, A.G. (1993) *The Social and Organizational Context of Management Accounting*. London: Academic Press.

Raelin, J.A. (1999) The action dimension in management: Different approaches to research, teaching, and development. Editorial in special issue of *Management Learning*. Vol. 30, No. 2. pp115–125.

Rand, A. (2007) *The Fountainhead*. London: Penguin.

Redford, K. (2005) Shedding light on talent tactics. *Personnel Today*. 26 September. p22.

Reid, M. and Barrington, H. (1997) *Training Interventions*. (5th ed). London: IPD.

Reid, M., Barrington, H. and Brown, M. (2004) *Human Resource Development: Beyond Training Interventions*. (7th ed). London: CIPD.

Revans, R. (1982) *The Origins and Growth of Action Learning*. London: Chartwell-Bratt.

Revans, R. (1983). *ABC of Action Learning*. London: Chartwell-Bratt.

Revans, Reg W. (1980) *Action Learning: New techniques for management*. London: Blond & Briggs.

Reynolds, M. and Trehan, K. (2001) Classroom as real world: propositions for a pedagogy of difference. *Gender and Education*. Vol. 13. No. 4. pp357–372.

Riding, R. and Cheema, I. (1991) Cognitive styles – an overview and integration. *Educational Psychology*. Vol. 11. pp193–216.

Riding, R.J. and Rayner, S. (2000) *Cognitive Styles and Learning Strategies*. London: David Fulton.

Rigg, C. (2008) Action learning for organizational and systemic development: towards a 'both-and' understanding of 'I' and 'we'. *Action Learning: Research and Practice*. Vol. 5, No. 2. pp105–116.

Rigg, C. and Richards, C. (2007) *Action Learning, Leadership and Organizational Development in Public Services*. London: Routledge.

Rigg, C. and Trehan, K. (2004) Reflections on working with critical action learning. *Action Learning – Research and Practice* Vol. 1, No. 2. pp149–166.

Rigg, C. and Trehan, K. (2008) Critical reflection in the workplace – Is it just too difficult?' *Journal of European Industrial Training.* Vol. 31. No. 2. pp.219–237.

Rigg, C., Stewart, J. and Trehan, K. (eds). (2007) *Critical Human Resource Development: Beyond orthodoxy.* Harlow: FT Prentice Hall.

Ritzer, G. (2004) *The MacDonaldisation of Society.* London: Sage Publications.

Robertson, R. (1992) *Globalisation.* London: Sage Publications.

Rogers, C. (1983) *Freedom to Learn.* Columbus, OH: Charles E. Merrill Publishing.

Rothwell, W.J. (1994) *Effective Succession Planning: Ensuring leadership continuity and building talent from within.* New York: AMACOM.

Rourke, S. (2007) Collaboration and inter-organisation work within the disability sector: opportunities and challenges. Presentation, Disability Federation of Ireland Conference. 22 November.

Ryan, L. (2009) Exploring the growing phenomenon of university–corporate education partnerships. *Management Decision.* Vol. 47, No. 8.

Salaman, G. (1995) *Managing.* Buckingham: Open University Press.

Sambrook, S. (2007) Discourses of HRD in the NHS. In Sambrook, S. and Stewart, J. (eds). *Human Resource Development in the Public Sector: The case of health and social care.* London: Routledge.

Seligman, M. and Csikszentmihalyi, M. (2000) Positive psychology: An introduction. *American Psychologist.* Vol. 55, pp.5–14.

Skinner, B.F. (1953) *Science and Human Behavior.* New York: Macmillan.

Sloman, M. (2009) Learning and technology – what have we learned? *Impact: Journal of Applied Research in Workplace E-learning.* Vol. 11. pp12–26.

Smith, W.J., Howard, J.T. and Harrington, K.V. (2005) Essential formal mentor characteristics and functions in governmental and non-governmental organizations from the program administrator's and the mentor's perspective. *Public Personnel Management.* pp31–58. Online at http://www.ipma-hr.org/sites/default/files/pdf/ppm/ppmspring05.pdf, accessed 18 March 2010.

Stansfield, L.M. and Stewart, J. (2007) A stakeholder approach to the study of management education. In Stewart, J. and Hill, R. (eds). *Management Development: Perspectives from research and practice.* London: Routledge.

Sternberg, R.J. (1999) *Thinking Styles.* Cambridge: Cambridge University Press.

Stewart, J. (1996) *Managing Change Through Training and Development.* (2nd ed). London: Kogan Page.

Stewart, J. (1998) Intervention and assessment: the ethics of HRD. *Human Resource Development International*. Vol. 1, No. 1.

Stewart, J. (1999) *Employee Development Practice*. London: FT Pitman Publishing.

Stewart, J. (2007) The ethics of HRD. In Rigg, C., Stewart, J. and Trehan, K. (eds). *Critical Human Resource Development: Beyond orthodoxy*. Harlow: FT Prentice Hall.

Stewart, J. (2010) E-learning. In Gold, J. *et al.* (eds). *Human Resource Development: Theory and practice*. Basingstoke: Palgrave Macmillan.

Stewart, J. and Harte, V. (2010) The implications of talent management for diversity training: an exploratory study. *Journal of European Industrial Training*. Vol. 34, No. 6. pp.506–518.

Stewart, J. and Shaw, S. (eds). (2005) The corporate university. *Journal of European Industrial Training*. Special Issue. Vol. 29. p1.

Stewart, J. *et al.* (2010) Strategic HRD and the learning and development function. In Gold, J. *et al.* (eds). *Human Resource Development: Theory and practice*. Basingstoke: Palgrave Macmillan.

Sullivan, H. and Skelcher C. (2002) *Working Across Boundaries: Collaboration in public services*. New York: Palgrave Macmillan.

Swanson, R.A. and Elwood, E.F.H., III (2009) *Foundations of Human Resource Development*. San Francisco: Berrett-Koehler.

Swanson, R.A. and Toracco, R.J. (1995) The strategic roles of human resource development. *Human Resource Planning*. Vol. 18. pp10–21.

Swart, J. *et al.* (2005) *Human Resource Development: Strategy and tactics*. Oxford: Elsevier Butterworth-Heinemann.

Tansley, C. *et al.* (2007) *Talent: Strategy, management and measurement*. London: CIPD.

Tawney, R.H. (1964) *Equality*. London: Allen & Unwin.

Torbert, B. (2004) *Action Inquiry: The secret of timely and transforming leadership*. San Francisco: Berrett-Koehler.

Torbert, W.R. (1999) The distinctive questions developmental action inquiry asks. *Management Learning*. Vol. 30. pp189–206.

Torrington, D. and Hall, L. (1998) *Human Resource Management*. (4th ed). Hemel Hempstead: Prentice-Hall Europe.

Truelove, S. (1997) *Training in Practice*. Oxford: Blackwell Business.

Ulrich, D. (1997) *Human Resource Champions: The next agenda for adding value and delivery results*. Boston, MA: Harvard Business School Press.

Vermunt, J.D. (1996) Metacognitive, cognitive and affective aspects of learning styles and strategies: A phenomenographic analysis. *Higher Education*. Vol. 31. pp25–50.

Vermunt, J.D. (2007) Student learning and teacher learning. Keynote address at The European Learning Styles Information Network, 12th Annual Conference: Exploring Style: Enhancing the Capacity to Learn. Trinity College, Dublin, 12–14 June 2007.

Vince, R. (2001) The impact of emotion on organizational learning. *Human Resource Development International*. Vol. 5, No. 1. pp73–85.

Vince, R. (2002) Organizing reflection. *Management Learning*. Vol. 33, No. 1. pp63–78.

Vince, R. (2010) *Rethinking Strategic Learning*. London: Routledge.

Vygotsky, L.S. (1978) *Mind in Society*. Cambridge, MA: Harvard University Press.

Wacquant, (2006) Pierre Bourdieu. In Stones, R. (ed). *Key Contemporary Thinkers*. London and New York: Macmillan.

Walton, J. (1999) *Strategic Human Resource Development*. Harlow: FT Prentice Hall.

Walton, J.S. and Guarisco, G. (2007) Structural issues and knowledge management in transnational education partnerships. *Journal of European Industrial Training*. Vol. 31, No. 5. pp358–376.

Wanberg, C.R., Welsh, E.T. and Hezlett, S.A. (2003) Mentoring research: A review and dynamic process model. *Research in Personnel and Human Resources Management*. Vol. 22. pp39–124.

Warr, P.B., Bird, M.W. and Rackham, N. (1970) *Evaluation of Management Training*. Aldershot: Gower.

Warren, S. and Webb, S. (2007) Challenging lifelong learning policy discourse: Where is structure in agency in narrative-based research?, *Studies in the Education of Adults*. Vol. 39, No. 1. pp5–21.

Watkins, K.E. and Marsick V.J. (1992) Towards a theory of informal and incidental learning in organizations. *International Journal of Lifelong Education*. Vol. 11, No. 4. pp. 287–300.

Watson, T. (2006) Managing to manage, power, decision making, ethics and the struggle to cope. In Watson, T. *Organising and Managing Work*. Chapter 6. London: FT Prentice Hall.

Watson, T.J. (1994) *In Search of Management*. London: Routledge.

Weber, M. (1978) *Economy and Society*. Berkeley, CA: University of California Press.

Whitmore, J. (2009) *Coaching for Performance: Growing people, performance and purpose*. London: Nicholas Brealey.

Whitmore, J. (2010) www.performanceconsultants.com/aboutus/ sirjohnwhitmore.html, accessed 17 March 2010.

Williams, P. (2002) The competent boundary spanner *Public Administration*. Vol. 80, No. 1. pp103–124.

YEP (2009) www.youngentrepreneur.ie, accessed 15 November 2009.

Zeus, P. and Skiffington, S. (2005) *The Coaching at Work Toolkit: A complete guide to techniques and practices*. Sydney: McGraw-Hill.

Index